a consumer's dictionary of cosmetic ingredients

Also by the author

Poisons in Your Food
Beware of the Food You Eat
How to Reduce Your Medical Bills
A Consumer's Dictionary of Food Additives
Ageless Aging

a consumer's dictionary of cosmetic ingredients

New, Revised, and Expanded Edition

RUTH WINTER

Crown Publishers, Inc., New York

Printed in the United States of America
Published simultaneously in Canada by General Publishing Company Limited

Library of Congress Cataloging in Publication Data

Winter, Ruth, 1930-
    A consumer's dictionary of cosmetic ingredients.

    1. Cosmetics-Dictionaries.   I.   Title.
TP983.W54   1976   668'.55'03   76-17846
ISBN 0-517-527367 (cloth)
        0-517-527375 (paper)

10 9 8 7

Introduction

To the consumer—male and female—cosmetics are a means for becoming more attractive and desirable. Their use can be fun; frequently they are necessary to our mental well-being, and often they take more of our dollars than do medicines, educational materials, and self-defense.

But to the United States Food and Drug Administration, they are: "(1) Articles intended to be rubbed, poured, sprinkled or sprayed on, introduced into, or otherwise applied to the human body or any part thereof for cleansing, beautifying, promoting attractiveness, or altering the appearance and (2) Articles intended for use as a component of any such articles, except that such terms shall not include soap."

To the United States government, a cosmetic improves appearance, while a drug diagnoses, relieves, or cures a disease.

It is not quite that simple, and therefore the reason for this dictionary. Its purpose is to allow the consumer, for the first time, to look up specific cosmetic ingredients and to determine their origins, functions, and safety. To understand why this is a unique text, it is necessary to describe the long and frequently stormy history of cosmetics.

In the beginning of recorded history, powders, perfumes, and paints were employed in religious rites. It was the Egyptians who really developed cosmetics as beautifiers. The Persians improved upon their techniques, but of all the pre-Christian users, none was more famous than Cleopatra, Queen of Egypt. Although through the years many claimed to have reproduced her cosmetics, no such products have been authenticated.

However, the first modern cosmetic compound—still in use today—was developed by a Greek physician, Galen, around A.D. 200. We call it cold cream.

Cosmetics were to remain a part of the practice of medicine until the thirteenth century when a Norman, Henri de Mondeville, wrote a medical text differentiating between skin treatments and beautifiers.

Whether or not Cleopatra or any other early users of cosmetics had serious side effects from ingredients is unknown, but the first significant observation of potential dangers from beauty products occurred in the seventeenth century when there was an epidemic of poisonings in Europe due to a beauty wash containing arsenic. This led to the forerunner of modern cosmetic laws when Italy, in 1633, required the registration of poisons.

1

During the seventeenth and eighteenth centuries most cosmetic products were made in the home, but a few shops began to sell commercial packages. The market has been growing ever since. By 1952, in the United States alone, commercial cosmetic sales reached the billion dollar mark. Today, sales exceed $6 billion.

But as more and more people began to buy cosmetics, side effects from ingredients increased. The first United States regulation concerning cosmetic sales was passed as part of the Federal Food, Drug, and Cosmetic Act in 1938. It provided for the seizure of adulterated products, prosecution in court of those responsible for putting them on the market, and an injunction, if need be, to prevent distribution. But the penalties were light—a maximum of a $1,000 fine or one year in jail for a first offense and three years or a $10,000 fine for a repeated offense. Furthermore, the question of when a product is adulterated was controversial. How many adverse reactions must a product cause before it is considered adulterated remains a problem since there is no cosmetic that does not cause an ill effect in someone.

Nor did the cosmetic law provide for registration of cosmetic companies. Anyone could go into the business no matter how dirty or strange the ingredients used. The law also did not require pretesting of cosmetics or reporting of adverse effects.

Cosmetics received and still receive the lowest priority in the offices of the Food and Drug Administration. The agency spends less than 1 percent of its budget on cosmetic safety surveillance. In its cosmetics division in Washington there are only 17 chemists to check the safety of an estimated 15,000 to 20,000 cosmetic formulations.

Cosmetics have received little attention because it has been wrongly assumed that such products do not really affect our health and safety. The skin was believed to be a nearly perfect barrier that prevented chemicals applied to it from penetrating into the body. This belief went unchallenged until the 1960s when the much heralded—but unmarketed—miracle drug DSMO proved its ability to carry substances with it through the skin and into the body's tissues and bloodstream. Until it was shown that rabbits' eyes were adversely affected by the drug, DSMO was being promoted as a through-the-skin carrier of all sorts of medications.

Then, in 1968, two researchers explained how, when they applied radioactive "labels" to drugs and cosmetics applied to the skin of human volunteers, they could measure the appearance of these tagged chemicals in body waste products.

Penetration varied according to the area of the body. For example, the ratio was 42 to 1 between the scrotum and the forearm for a topically applied salve containing hydrocortisone. The forehead, scalp, and angle of the jaw, compared to the forearm, had up to 13 times as much absorption.

It is now accepted that all chemicals penetrate to some extent and many do in significant amounts. The recent removal of hexachlorophene and mercury from American cosmetics is confirmation. These two germ-fighting preservatives were found to accumulate in the body and to have serious systemic effects.

Because of this new understanding, as well as pressure from consumer advocates, the FDA, in 1973, instituted tighter controls on the manufacture of cosmetics.

Registration of cosmetic companies was begun so that, for the first time, the FDA would know who was in the business.

Since November 30, 1976, all cosmetics on the market must list ingredients. Only fragrances and certain "trade secrets" are exempted.

New labeling regulations require that ingredients be listed prominently, in their decreasing order of prevalence, on the label of a cosmetic product. If the label is not of sufficient size, then a tag containing the ingredients must be attached. Furthermore, with the exception of fragrances, flavors, and colors, all ingredients have to be listed by standardized names. This dictionary contains not only those standardized names but also the specific flavors, colors, fragrances, and any chemicals used in the manufacturing process of cosmetics that may not be listed by their exact names on the labels.

The FDA has also set up a procedure for voluntary twice-a-year reporting of consumer complaints resulting from cosmetic use. The information will be used by the FDA to pinpoint those ingredients that may be causing allergic reactions or injuries and that might call for product reformulation or regulatory action.

The cosmetic industry fought with vigor such tightening of the regulations, proclaiming dire consequences for the multibillion dollar industry. And yet, even our new regulations are much more lenient, perhaps unwisely so, than other countries.

Japan, whose Shiseido is one of the largest cosmetic companies in the world, in the early 1960s passed laws that distinguish between three categories of products. One is cosmetics, the second is quasi-drugs, and the third is drugs. The distinction between quasi-drugs and drugs is that the former are products for the prevention of disease—such as sunscreen products—while drugs are products for the treatment of disease. Cosmetic manufacturers, as well as manufacturers of quasi-drugs, must be licensed by the government. In order to get that license, the appropriate cosmetic executives must have minimum educational qualifications. In addition, the Japanese require that labels not only include the ingredients but the amounts of those ingredients, and fanciful names and claims are prohibited.

The Japanese also prohibit a number of ingredients, including mercury and its compounds, bithionol, dichlorophene, hydroquinone, and pilocarpine. For about 200 other listed ingredients, the chemicals must conform to government standards and specifications, and there are restrictions on the amount of such substances that can be used.

In Australia any poisonous compound in a cosmetic must be so designated on the product label. For instance, sunburn creams containing benzocaine must be labeled as containing a poison. The label must describe the amount of benzocaine in the product and how the product should be used. Furthermore, any cosmetic containing a poisonous substance, including sunburn creams, must be sold by pharmacies or registered sellers of poisons rather than ordinary shops. Phenylenediamine hair dyes are included under this regulation.

Chile requires that label claims and television ads be approved. In the United States, on the other hand, if a false claim is made on the label, it is within the jurisdiction of the FDA, and if it is made in an advertisement it falls within the province of the Federal Trade Commission unless it is a mail-order claim. In that case it is under the jurisdiction of postal officials. All three agencies dread following through on false claims made by cosmetic companies because it takes years to bring the offender to court, plus thousands of dollars, and the penalty is usually no more than a slap on the wrist. Furthermore, after conviction, many such offenders merely change the name of their companies and start all over again.

The United States government allows claims for vitamins and hormones in cosmetic products but the Chilean government does not allow these substances.

In Spain there is mandatory registration and licensing of manufacturers and products, and the manufacturers must have control laboratories. In the United States registration and pretesting are still voluntary.

Since 1971, Sweden has had an ombudsman who handles complaints concerning the efficacy of cosmetics; he has the power to summon a manufacturer to a hearing where the matter may be threshed out.

In Switzerland, since 1967, baby cosmetics and feminine intimate products are regulated as drugs and not as cosmetics. Complaints concerning these products are markedly down. Switzerland also prohibits a number of ingredients in cosmetics, including arsenic, antimony, barium, lead, cadmium, mercury, selenium, thallium and their compounds; also anilines, nitrophenols, and nitroanilines, beta-naphthol, benzopyrene, and related carcinogens. Swiss hair dyes, unlike American products, may not contain paraphenylenediamine or paraformaldehyde or pilocarpine. Also, preparations for the skin, hair, nails, mouth, and teeth may not contain acetone, formaldehyde, methanol, nitrobenzene, or thioglycerin. Permanent wave preparations are restricted to small amounts of thioglycolic acid. Advertising claims are strictly controlled.

The Netherlands, since 1970, has required that cosmetics shall neither be injurious if used as directed nor be *possibly* injurious. The Dutch prohibit the inclusion of silver, strontium, barium, beryllium, cadmium, mercury, thallium, zirconium, lead, antimony, chromium, arsenic, uranium, selenium, or their compounds. Cosmetics may not contain methanol (except as a denaturant), benzene, anilines, para-phenylenediamines, benzocaine, resorcinol, tricresyl phosphate, pilocarpine, Vitamins A and D, certain steroids and sex hormones, and antibiotics.

In France (one of the leaders of the cosmetic industry) advertisers are not allowed to use medical terms such as "allergy," "acne," or "dandruff." Fragrances must be categorized, such as "eau de Cologne" or "Perfume." If the name of a natural oil is used in a fragrance, such as oil of lavender, it must contain no less than the legally specified minimum.

A major influence in European cosmetic laws has been the European Economic Commission, which has been working in the area since 1964. It was originally composed of France, Italy, Germany, the Netherlands, Belgium, and Luxembourg, but other countries have now joined. As with all industries involved in the European alliance, technical representatives of cosmetic manufacturers from each country joined to eliminate barriers to free trade and to achieve uniformity in regulatory legislation. There is already a list of 442 compounds that cannot be used in cosmetics of member countries. There is also another list of provisionally permitted substances that, at the end of three years, will be prohibited unless proven safe. Included in this category are chloroform in dentifrices and xylocaine in after-shave lotions.

As will be seen in the text of this book, a large percentage of the ingredients banned by other nations are permitted in American cosmetics.

The more chemicals permitted, of course, the greater the chance of adverse affects, particularly allergic responses. Allergies to cosmetics on the skin, hair, nails, and around the eyes are very common. They may cause skin eruptions, brittle hair, discolored nails, and tearing eyes.

Allergies derive from a sensitivity certain people develop to normally harmless substances. A susceptible person—one out of ten Americans—when exposed to an allergen has symptoms of disorder in the respiratory tract, the digestive organs, or the skin.

An increasing problem is cross-sensitivity, as we use ever more chemicals on our skin, as well as in our foods and in our drugs. For instance, men and women who are allergic to the paraphenylenediamine dyes used in permanent black and brown hair dyes quite frequently will be allergic to azo dyes used in nonpermanent hair tints. Many persons allergic to aspirin will also be allergic to FD & C Yellow No. 5 used in cosmetics, foods, and drugs.

Ever responsive to public demand, the cosmetic manufacturers have proclaimed many of their products as "hypoallergenic." But just because a manufacturer says a product is hypoallergenic, the government maintains, it is not necessarily so.

A nonallergenic product is an impossibility. There is always someone who will be allergic to something. However, there are sixty known ingredients in past or present cosmetics that cause an allergic reaction in a significant percentage of those exposed. Included in this list are such common substances as acacia, benzaldehyde, corn starch, gum arabic, oil of spearmint, and wheat starch. By leaving the sixty offenders out of cosmetics or by reducing the number of ingredients altogether, particularly perfumes, manufacturers then proclaim their product "hypoallergenic."

The FDA wrestled for years with the idea of setting standards for hypoallergenic cosmetics. The problem was that to set standards, it was necessary to prescribe specific testing methods and then demand conformity with that standard. Since it seemed impossible to get any agreement on which testing methods should be used and how many allergic reactions should be allowed before a product could not be considered hypoallergenic, the FDA made the following ruling: two and a half years after a company claims a product is hypoallergenic, it must come up with evidence substantiating the claim.

FDA experts have expressed the opinion that any product calling itself hypoallergenic should, to a statistically significant degree, cause fewer reactions than a reference product. That reference product— as yet unchosen—would be a widely used proven hypoallergenic cosmetic.

As the mandate now reads, it is up to the manufacturer to decide the testing method used to determine the safety of his product. However, the FDA believes that a manufacturer who wants to promote a product as hypoallergenic "should do more than the minimal testing."

Another area, not as sticky as the hypoallergenic one, concerns organic cosmetics. Attempting to cash in on the back-to-nature fad, cosmetic manufacturers and other entrepreneurs are promoting "natural," or "organic," cosmetics made from plants and animal materials. The truth is that many things in nature have always been used in cosmetics, as can be determined from this book. One will be able to see how many products from the kitchen can be substituted for those natural cosmetics that have been widely advertised. For instance, salad oil or butter serve the same purpose as many of the more expensive "moisturizers." But whether they are as much fun to use is up to the individual. Fancy bottles and chemicals with awesome-sounding names do not a better cosmetic make. Neither does a completely natural product necessarily offer a better result than an all synthetic one.

Another questionable area concerns children's kits containing cosmetic jars and plastic bottles that imitate mothers'. Aside from the psychological factor of encouraging youngsters to use cosmetics, these add an unnecessary risk. Among problems reported to the FDA concerning the toy cosmetic kits are skin rash, face irritation, and swelling.

So you can see there are thousands of chemicals used and that many have unwanted side effects. There are many false claims made and insufficient protection offered for the consumer.

Are you getting your money's worth from the cosmetics you use? If you consider only the basic ingredients, probably not. Few consumers know, for instance, that private contractors often prepare nail polish, lipstick, and other products for many popular cosmetic manufacturers who then sell the product under their own names.

One well-known giant cosmetic firm's cold cream costs a penny and a half and its container seven and a half cents. It is sold for $1.50 under one name and $5.00 under another.

Sometimes, when a product does not sell well, retailers will mark up the price of the cosmetic and then put it on sale. They do this because they realize fully well that many of us believe that the more a cosmetic costs, the better its ability to improve our looks.

However, as you will read in this book, price is not a guide to the worth of a product.

For most cosmetics, there is a 500 to 1,000 percent spread between costs and sales price. This margin is needed, according to manufacturers, to meet heavy promotional costs. The industry is the biggest advertiser on TV and in magazines.

The vast difference between cost and price is due, in large part, to the low cost of raw materials, which often are other industries' throwaway products. Wonder ingredients such as turtle oil, pearl essence, and royal jelly are examples.

Adding to the price of cosmetics is where they are sold. In a self-service operation, cosmetics are cheaper than if they are purchased in a store with a trained well-made-up salesgirl picking out the proper shades. But the product's ingredients whether at a variety store or a boutique may be exactly the same.

However, the container may be more elegant in the more expensive store. This is nowhere more apparent than with lipsticks. All lipsticks are basically the same but this cosmetic is often applied in public and many women feel an elevation in status if they present an elaborate lipstick container to the world. Manufacturers are well aware that a valuable ingredient in any cosmetic product is the customer's belief in it. A cosmetic that makes you feel better inside as well as look better outside could be worth the freight.

The purpose of this dictionary is to enable you to look up any cosmetic ingredient under its alphabetical listing to determine if a product is safe or not. Thereby you can choose between products on the basis of what is in them, whether or not they do what the advertising claims they do, and at the same time avoid any unnecessary injury to your health. The dictionary includes most of the cosmetic ingredients in common use, a large percentage of which have been kept secret. For the sake of clarity and ease of use, their many functions are grouped under the following broad categories:

Preservatives

A preservative used in cosmetics is required to offer protection against infection under conditions of use and prevent the decomposition of the product due to microbial multiplication. For example, many kinds of yeast, fungi, and bacteria have been identified in cosmetics. Just the presence of water and various organic components, such as lanolin or cocoa butter, provides an excellent environment for the growth of germs. Furthermore, as consumers, we are constantly introducing new germs into open jars, bottles, and boxes. In many instances a product may show no evidence of contamination and yet contain germs that, when in contact with the skin or eyes, may cause infection.

A cosmetic preservative should be active at low concentration, against a wide range of microorganisms, and over a wide acidity/alkalinity range. According to cosmetic chemists, it must also be compatible with other ingredients of the formulation, be nontoxic, nonirritating, and nonsensitizing. It should also be colorless, odorless, and stable, as well as economically feasible and easily incorporated into the product.

Quaternary ammonium compounds, such as benzalkonium chloride, are widely used today as preservatives. So are the various alcohols such as ethyl and isopropyl. Aldehydes, particularly formaldehyde and benzaldehyde, are common preservatives as well as phenolic compounds, such as phenol and p-chloro-m-cresol. Essential oils, such as citrus and menthol, have been used for hundreds of years as preservatives.

An additional use for preservatives is for fatty products in cosmetic creams and lotions. Such substances are called antioxidants. They prevent the production of off-colors and off-odors. Examples are benzoic acid and BHA.

Acids, Alkalies, Buffers, and Neutralizers

The degree of acidity or alkalinity (known as the pH) of a product is important in cosmetics because too little or too much of either may irritate the skin. Furthermore, the formulation of a product is dependent upon properly maintaining the intended pH. Citric acid, widely used as the acid, and ammonium carbonate, an alkali, are frequently found in cosmetic formulations. Buffers and neutralizing agents are chemicals added to cosmetic formulas to control acidity or alkalinity in the same way that acids and alkalies might be added directly. Some common chemicals in this class are ammonium bicarbonate, calcium carbonate, and tartaric acid.

Moisture Content Controls

Humectants are necessary to keep many cosmetics from drying out. An open jar of cream, for instance, may stiffen and crumble without a humectant to keep it soft and pliable. Substances used for this purpose include glycerin and propylene glycol, which keep cleansing lotions and moisturizing creams smooth and spreadable. On the other hand, chemicals may be necessary to keep cosmetics from absorbing moisture from the air and becoming sticky or caky. Calcium silicate, for instance, is used in powders to prevent moisture absorption.

Coloring Agents

These ingredients, of course, are extremely important in cosmetics. Without pleasing hues, lipsticks, rouges, and eye makeup would remain on store shelves. Colors of both natural and synthetic origin are extensively employed in cosmetics. However, the indiscriminate use of color can cause adverse reactions when applied in a cosmetic. For example, coal tar colors are subject to strict government regulations and each batch must be certified by the FDA as "harmless and suitable for use." However, some of the colors previously certified are harmful. Violet 1 was removed in the early 1970s, and, in 1976, one of the most widely used of all colors, FD & C No. 2, was removed because is was found to cause tumors in rats. In 1960 the federal government required all manufacturers to retest all artificial colors to determine safety. At present, five are permanently listed as safe. Among them FD & C Blue No. 1 and FD & C Green No. 33 have been shown to cause tumors at the site of injection in animals, but the FDA does not consider this significant because the experiments concerned injection by needle and not ingestion in food or application to the skin. FD & C Red No. 40 is also being questioned because many scientists feel that it should not have been given permanent listing based solely on the manufacturer's tests.

Almost all cosmetics are colored, but until recently it was frequently impossible for FDA scientists to detect specific colors and quantities employed. Now, with newly developed techniques, FDA scientists are able to analyze finished products and to determine the colors and quantities used. This is expected to lead to better enforcement and to more adequate epidemiological information.

Among the natural colors widely used in cosmetics are alkanet, annatto, carotene, chlorophyll, cochineal, saffron, and turmeric.

Flavorings

More than 2,000 flavoring additives are available for use in cosmetics, foods, and drugs. Of these, some 500 are natural. That is, they are derived from a wide variety of spices, plant extracts, and essential oils. The balance is synthetics such as amyl acetate, benzaldehyde, and ethyl acetate. Cosmetic products in which flavorings are important include lipsticks, dentifrices, and mouthwashes. Flavorings are usually employed in amounts ranging from a few parts to three hundred parts per million.

Fragrances

In the entire cosmetic industry, perhaps the greatest number of creative people are in the production of fragrances. It is an ancient art and the formulas are closely guarded. Even the new federal labeling regulations recognize this and require only the words "perfume" or "fragrance" be added to the label. There may be more than two hundred ingredients in a single scent. Pleasant aromas are derived from a spectacular number of substances, including plant materials and synthetic chemicals. Perfumers can even improve on nature. Certain natural flower scents, for instance, cannot be extracted, yet the experts using various chemicals can reproduce the same aroma we smell from the actual blossom. Because of the complexity of perfume formulas, it is difficult for competitors to break them down and reproduce them, even with newly developed analytical techniques. Since fragrances are intended to vaporize, and they do contain plant and floral derivatives as well as many other chemicals, they frequently cause allergic reactions. A less frequent side effect of perfume is a skin pigmentation called berloque dermatitis (see under its alphabetical listing).

Processing Aids

Many cosmetic ingredients fall into this category. One of the largest includes surface-active agents, compounds that reduce the work between two surfaces. A large subdivision of surface-active agents consists of emulsifiers and emulsion stabilizers. Such ingredients help maintain a mixture and assure consistency. They also influence smoothness, volume, and uniformity. Sodium lauryl sulfate and alumina gel are examples used in moisture creams and lotions. Another division of surface-active agents includes solubilizers. They mix oil and water. Sodium sulfonate, for instance, is used to disperse oils in shampoos. An emulsifier may be a texturizer, but a texturizer is not necessarily an emulsifier. Texturizers are added to products to give them a desired feel and appearance. For example, acacia is used in hairdressings to thicken them and also to help them hold unruly hair in place. Clarifying and chelating agents are other processing aids that remove extraneous matter from liquids. Tannin, for instance, is used for removing extraneous matter from liquids. Ethylenediamine tetraacetic acid is used to remove calcium, magnesium, and iron soaps from shampoo solutions. Opacifiers, on the other hand, are added to liquids to darken them. The higher alcohols, such as stearyl and cetyl, are frequently used in shampoos for this purpose. Foaming agents, such as dodecylbenzene sulfonic acid, are added to make shampoos foamy.

For further ease of use, the dictionary also lists alphabetically products by general use. For example, you can look up eye shadow, mascara, lipstick, foundations, face masks and packs, powder, eyebrow pencils, rouge, and any such appearance-improving products to see what is in them. Or you may be interested in grooming products, such as dentifrices, mouthwash, nail polish, perfume, toilet water, eyewashes, preshaving and after-shave lotions, deodorants, depilatories, hair rinses, hair bleach, and so on. Anyone looking for treatment aids would check under cleansing creams and lotions, emollients, astringents, hand creams and lotions, permanent waves, hair straighteners, skin bleaches, and any other corrective treatment products. In addition, all terms used in this dictionary that might be unfamiliar are also listed alphabetically, such as polymer, reagent, and so on.

While unique in content, this dictionary follows the format of most standard dictionaries. The following are examples of entries with any explanatory notes that may be necessary:

ABIETIC ACID. Sylvic Acid.   Chiefly a texturizer in the making of soaps. A widely available natural acid, water-insoluble, prepared from pine rosin, usually yellow, and comprised of either glassy or crystalline particles. Used also in the manufacture of vinyls, lacquers, and plastics. Little is known about abietic acid toxicity; it is harmless when injected into mice but causes paralysis in frogs and is slightly irritating to human skin and mucous membranes.

We have learned that abietic acid is also known as sylvic acid, that it is a naturally occurring rosin acid, which as a texturizer maintains a smooth consistency in soaps, and we discovered its noncosmetic uses and its toxicity. Source material for the comments on toxicity is indicated in the notes at the end of the dictionary.

ALLANTOIN.   Used in cold creams, hand lotions, hair lotions, after-shave lotions, and other skin-soothing cosmetics because of its ability to help heal wounds and skin ulcers and to stimulate the growth of healthy tissue. Colorless crystals, soluble in hot water, it is prepared synthetically by the oxidation of uric acid (*see*) or by heating uric acid with dichloroacetic acid. It is nontoxic.

Allantoin we can see is a synthetic product derived from uric acid. By looking up uric acid we learn that it derives from urine and is used in sunburn preventatives.

What to Do If You Have an Adverse Response to a Cosmetic

• Before using any cosmetic, read the label carefully and follow directions exactly. This is especially important when using antiperspirants, depilatories, hair dyes and colorings, home permanents, freckle creams, and skin packs.
• To determine whether you are allergic to a cosmetic, apply a small amount on the inside of your forearm. Leave it on for 24 hours. If you see any adverse effect such as redness, blisters, or itching, don't use it again.
• If a cosmetic causes any adverse effect—burning, breaking out, stinging, or itching—stop using it. If you are not sure whether it was a cosmetic that gave you your problem or which cosmetic it was that affected you adversely, stop the use of all cosmetics. Shampoo your hair with a bland soap in order to remove all hair preparations. Stop the use of all creams, including cleansing creams, foundation creams, and cold creams. Wash your face with unscented soap. Remove all nail polish.
• If the condition does not clear up or is very uncomfortable, bring the offending or suspected cosmetics to your physician for testing. This includes cosmetic sponges and powder puffs used to apply cosmetics.
• If you have recently visited a beauty parlor and have had an adverse reaction, return to the shop and obtain the name of the brands used and samples of them.

- If the lips are not involved, the use of lipstick may be continued.
- The cosmetic responsible for your problem may be a relatively new one, or it may be one that you have used for years. The fact that all cosmetics have been applied for a long time does not rule out an adverse reaction from any one of them. The development of allergic hypersensitivity may occur at any time. Also, some ingredients in the product may have been changed by the manufacturer.
- Do not let children play with cosmetics. As you will read within this dictionary, some ingredients are deadly poisons while others would not hurt an adult but might harm children.
- Be especially careful in the use of eye cosmetics to avoid possible chemical and mechanical damage to the eyes.
- Report any adverse effects from cosmetics to the manufacturer of the product, to the FDA, and to the store where you purchased it. Look up the local Food and Drug Administration office under "United States" in your telephone directory. If you cannot find a local office, write directly to the FDA in Washington, D.C.

Terminology generally has been kept to a middle road between technician and the average interested consumer, while at the same time avoiding oversimplification of data. Once again, if in doubt, look up alphabetically any term listed that seems unfamiliar or whose meaning has been blunted by overuse, such as isolate, extract, demulcent, emollient, or even shampoo.

With *A Consumer's Dictionary of Cosmetic Ingredients,* you will be able to work with current and future labels to determine the purpose and desirability or toxicity of the ingredients listed. For the first time you will have the knowledge to choose the best cosmetics for you. By checking out a product's ingredients, as listed on the label, you can eliminate many products and choose those that are harmless, even beneficial, and you can save money, and reward those manufacturers who deserve your purchases. For the first time, with the aid of this book, you will really know what is in the cosmetics you have been using.

A

ABIETIC ACID. Sylvic Acid.   Chiefly a texturizer in the making of soaps. A widely available natural acid, water-insoluble, prepared from pine rosin, usually yellow, and comprised of either glassy or crystalline particles. Used also in the manufacture of vinyls, lacquers, and plastics. Little is known about abietic acid toxicity; it is harmless when injected into mice but causes paralysis in frogs and is slightly irritating to human skin and mucous membranes.

ABIETYL ALCOHOL.   See Abietic Acid.

ABSOLUTE.   The term refers to a plant-extracted material that has been concentrated, but that remains essentially unchanged in its original taste and odor. For example, see Jasmine Absolute. Often called "natural perfume materials" because they are not subjected to heat and water as are distilled products. See Distilled.

ABSORPTION BASES.   Compounds used to improve the water-absorbing capacity and stability of creams, lotions, and hairdressings. Lanolin-type absorption bases are made of mixtures of lanolin alcohols, mineral oil, and petrolatum *(see all)*. Also used as bases are cholesterol and beeswax *(see both)*.

ACACIA. Gum Arabic. Catechu.   Used in toilet preparations as a thickener, colloidal stabilizer, and emulsifier. Odorless, colorless, tasteless, dried gummy exudate of the stems of the acacia tree grown in Africa, the Near East, India, and the southern United States. Its most distinguishing quality among the natural gums is its ability to dissolve rapidly in water. Unground acacia occurs as white or yellow teardrops. It is also used medicinally as a demulcent to soothe and relieve irritations of the mucous membranes. Oral toxicity is low but it can cause allergic skin rashes and asthma attacks. See Catechu Black.

ACEROLA.   Used as an antioxidant. Derived from the ripe fruit of the West Indian or Barbados cherry grown in Central America and the West Indies. A rich source of ascorbic acid. Used in Vitamin C. No known toxicity.

ACETAL.   A volatile liquid derived from acetaldehyde *(see)* and alcohol and used as a solvent in synthetic perfumes such as jasmine. Also used in fruit flavorings (it has a nutlike aftertaste) and as a hypnotic in medicine. It is a central nervous system depressant, similar in action to paraldehyde but more toxic. Paraldehyde is a hypnotic and sedative whose side effects are respiratory depression, cardiovascular collapse, and possible high blood pressure reactions. No known skin toxicity.

ACETALDEHYDE. Ethanal. An intermediate (*see*) and solvent in the manufacture of perfumes. A flammable, colorless liquid, with a characteristic odor, occurring naturally in apples, broccoli, cheese, coffee, grapefruit, and other vegetables and fruits. Also used in the manufacture of synthetic rubber and in the silvering of mirrors. It is irritating to the mucous membranes, and ingestion of large doses may cause death by respiratory paralysis. Inhalation, usually limited by intense irritation of lungs, can also be toxic. Skin toxicity not identified.

ACETAMIDE MEA. N-Acetyl Ethanolamine. Used as a solvent, plasticizer, and stabilizer (*see all*). Crystals absorb water. Odorless when pure but can have a mousy odor. A mild skin irritant with low oral toxicity.

ACETANILID. Acetanilide. A solvent in nail polishes used in liquid powders to give an opaque mat finish. Usually made from aniline and acetic acid (*see both*), it is of historic interest because it was the first coal tar analgesic and antifever agent introduced into medicine. It is sometimes still used in medicines but is frowned upon by the American Medical Association since there are other related products with less toxicity. It can cause a depletion of oxygen in the blood upon ingestion and eczema when applied to the skin.

ACETATE. Salt of acetic acid (*see*) used in perfumery and as a flavoring. No known toxicity.

ACETIC ACID. Solvent for gums, resins, and volatile oils. Styptic (stops bleeding) and a rubefacient (*see*). A clear colorless liquid with a pungent odor, it is used in freckle-bleaching lotions, hand lotions, and hair dyes. It occurs naturally in apples, cheese, cocoa, coffee, grapes, skimmed milk, oranges, peaches, pineapples, strawberries, and a variety of other fruits and plants. Vinegar is about 4 to 6 percent acetic acid and essence of vinegar about 14 percent. In its glacial form (without much water) it is highly corrosive and its vapors are capable of producing lung obstruction. Less than 5 percent acetic acid in solution is mildly irritating to the skin.

ACETOLAMIDE. N-Acetyl Ethanolamine. Used in hair-waving solutions and in emulsifiers. See Ethanolamines.

ACETONE. A colorless ethereal liquid derived by oxidation or fermentation and used as a solvent in nail polish removers and nail finishes. It is obtained by fermentation and is frequently used as a solvent for airplane dope, fats, oils, and waxes. It can cause peeling and splitting of the nails, skin rashes on the fingers and elsewhere, and nail brittleness. Inhalation may irritate the lungs, and in large amounts it is narcotic, causing symptoms of drunkenness similar to ethanol (*see*).

ACETOPHENETIDIN.   See Phenacetin.

ACETYL ETHYL TETRAMETHYL TETRALIN.   A solvent and degreasing agent obtained from glycol and ammonia. It smells like benzene and menthol. It may be irritating to the skin, eyes, and mucous membranes.

ACETYL TRIBUTYL CITRATE.   See Citric Acid.

ACETYL TRIETHYL CITRATE.   A clear oily, essentially odorless liquid used as a solvent. See Citric Acid.

ACETYL TRIOCTYL CITRATE.   Salt of Citric Acid. See Citric Acid.

ACETYL TRIOCTYL CITRATE PECTIN. Citrus Pectin.   A jelly-forming powder obtained from citrus peel and used as a texturizer and thickening agent to form gels with sugars and acids. Light in color. It has no known toxicity.

ACETYLATED.   Any organic compound that has been heated with acetic anhydride or acetyl chloride to remove its water. Acetylated lanolins are used in hand creams and lotions, for instance. Acetic anhydride produces irritation and necrosis of tissues in vapor state and carries a warning against contact with skin and eyes.

ACETYLATED HYDROGENATED COTTONSEED GLYCERIDE. See Cottonseed Oil.

ACETYLATED HYDROGENATED LARD GLYCERIDE.   See Lard.

ACETYLATED HYDROGENATED VEGETABLE GLYCERIDE. See Vegetable Oils.

ACETYLATED LANOLIN. Acetulan®.   Acetylated (*see*) lanolin alcohols are pale yellow and practically odorless and almost insoluble in water. They are used in cosmetic formulas to soften and smooth the skin or hair. They can be mixed with mineral oil, castor oil, and vegetable oil. See Lanolin for toxicity.

ACETYLATED LANOLIN ALCOHOL.   See Acetylated Lanolin.

ACETYLATED LARD GLYCERIDE.   See Lard.

ACETYLATED PALM KERNEL GLYCERIDES.   Acetylated (*see*) oil obtained from the seed of the African palm. It is a white to yellowish edible fat which resembles coconut oil and is used in the manufacture of soaps and ointments. No known toxicity.

ACETYLATED POLYVINYL ALCOHOL.   See Polyvinyl Alcohol.

ACID.   An acid is a substance capable of turning blue litmus paper red and of forming hydrogen ions when dissolved in water. An acid aqueous solution is one that has a pH (*see*) of less than 7. Citric acid (*see*) is an example of a widely used acid in cosmetics.

ACID AMMONIUM SULFATE. See Quaternary Ammonium Compounds.

ACID BLACK 2. Classed chemically as an azine color. Also called Nigrosine. It is a greenish blue black. Acid colors are made by adding acids such as adipic (*see*) and tartric to obtain various shades. Toxicity depends upon ingredients used. See Colors.

ACID BLACK 58. *Irgalan Grey BL®*. A commercial color. See Acid Black 2 and Colors.

ACID BLACK 107. *Lanamid Black BL®*. Classed chemically as a monoazo color. See Acid Black 2 and Colors.

ACID BLACK 131. See Acid Dyes.

ACID BLACK 139. See Acid Dyes.

ACID BLUE 168. *Cibalan Blue BL®*. A commercial color. See Acid Black 2 and Colors.

ACID BLUE 170. *Cibalan Blue BRL®*. A commercial color. See Acid Black 2 and Colors.

ACID BLUE 188. *Irgalan Navy Blue 5 RL®*. Classed chemically as a monoazo color. See Acid Black 2 and Colors.

ACID BLUE 209. *Vialon Fast Blue FFG®*. A commercial color. See Acid Black 2 and Colors.

ACID BROWN 19. *Irgalan Brown BL®*. A commercial color. See Acid Black 2 and Colors.

ACID BROWN 44. *Irgalan Brown 2 GL®*. A commercial color. See Acid Black 2 and Colors.

ACID BROWN 46. See Acid Dyes.

ACID BROWN 48. See Acid Dyes.

ACID BROWN 224. *Cibalan Brown 2 GL®*. Classed chemically as a monoazo color. See Acid Black 2 and Colors.

ACID DYES. The ability of these dyes to color and to remain fast during washing and exposure to light varies greatly. The ones that give the best water and light fastness are the compounds that are combined with metals. They are widely used as inexpensive dyes for plastics, varnishes, and some pigments.

ACID GREEN 5. *Light Green SF Yellowish*. Classed chemically as a triphenylmethane color. Formerly FD & C Green No. 2. See Acid Black 2 and Colors.

ACID GREEN 20. *Acid Dark Green A®*. Classed chemically as a diazo color. See Acid Black 2 and Colors.

ACID ORANGE 3. Amido Yellow EA. Classed chemically as a nitro color. See Acid Black 2 and Colors.

ACID ORANGE 86. Cibalan Orange RLN®. A commercial color. See Acid Black 2 and Colors.

ACID ORANGE 88. Cibalan Orange RL®. A commercial color. See Acid Black 2 and Colors.

ACID ORANGE 89. Vialon Fast Orange R®. A commercial color. See Acid Black 2 and Colors.

ACID RED 1. Food Red 10. Formerly Ext. D & C Red No. 11. Classed chemically as a monoazo color. See Acid Black 2 and Colors.

ACID RED 73. Formerly Food Red 6 and Ext. D & C Red No. 13. Classed chemically as a monoazo color. A bluish scarlet. See Acid Black 2 and Colors.

ACID RED 88. Formerly Ext. D & C Red No. 8. Classed chemically as a monoazo color. A yellowish red. See Acid Black 2 and Colors.

ACID RED 131. Sulfonine Brilliant Red 3 B. Classed chemically as a monoazo color. See Acid Black 2 and Colors.

ACID RED 213. Cibalan Bordeaux GRL®. A commercial color. See Acid Black 2 and Colors.

ACID RED 252. Cibalan Brilliant Red BL®. Classed chemically as a monoazo color. See Acid Black 2 and Colors.

ACID RED 259. Irgalan Red 4 GL®. Classed chemically as a monoazo color. See Acid Black 2 and Colors.

ACID VIOLET 73. See Acid Dyes.

ACID VIOLET 76. See Acid Dyes.

ACID VIOLET 99. Vialon Fast Violet RR®. A commercial color. See Acid Black 2 and Colors.

ACID YELLOW 11. Fast Light Yellow. Formerly Ext. D & C Yellow No. 3. Classed chemically as a pyrazolone color. It is greenish yellow. See Acid Black 2 and Colors.

ACID YELLOW 63. Azo Yellow A 5W®. Classed chemically as a monoazo color. See Acid Black 2 and Colors.

ACID YELLOW 114. Irgalan Yellow GL®. A commercial color. See Acid Black 2 and Colors.

ACID YELLOW 127. Cibalan Brilliant Yellow 3 GL®. Classed chemically as a monoazo color. See Acid Black 2 and Colors.

ACINTOL. See Tall Oil.

ACRYLAMIDE / ACRYLATES / BUTYLAMINOETHYL METHA-CRYLATE POLYMER. See Acrylates.

ACRYLATE/ACRYLAMIDE COPOLYMER. See Acrylates.

ACRYLATES. Salts or esters of acrylic acid used as thickening agent and as constituents of nail polishes. Strong irritants. See Acrylic Monomer.

ACRYLIC MONOMER. A tough rubbery material first used in fake nails in the cosmetic industry. They were once used as fillings for teeth. Fake nails usually consist of acrylates, a catalyst such as peroxide, and a plasticizer (*see all*). The compound to be effective must be stiff at room temperature. The acrylates if inhaled can cause allergic reactions in man. Lethal to rats when inhaled in large doses.

ACRYLIC RESINS. Polymers (*see*) of acrylics. Used in waxy oils, base coats, protective coatings, and waterproofing. Acrylates (*see*), if inhaled, can cause allergic reactions in man.

ADIPIC ACID. Hexanedioic Acid. Colorless needlelike formations fairly insoluble in water; found in beets. A buffering and neutralizing agent impervious to humidity. Used in hair color rinses, nylon manufacture, and plasticizers. Lethal to rats in large oral doses. No known human toxicity.

ADIPIC ACID DIHYDRAZIDE. See Adipic Acid.

AEROSOL SHAVING CREAMS. See Shaving Creams.

AEROSOLS. Many cosmetic sprays, particularly hair and fragrances, are in aerosol containers. The first aerosol patent was actually issued in 1899 but was not used until 1940 when insecticides were first packaged in self-dispensing gas-pressurized containers. Freon, the most commonly used group among aerosol gases, is a lung irritant, central nervous system depressant, and, in high concentrations, can cause coma. More than 100 people, mostly young Americans, have died from sniffing aerosol gases for "kicks." These gases can cause severe irregular heartbeats. In addition to Freon, hair sprays contain PVP (polyvinylpyrrolidone—*see*), or shellac. PVP is believed to be cancer causing. In addition, thesaurosis, a condition in which there are foreign bodies in the lungs, has been found in persons subjected to repeated inhalation of hair sprays. The aerosol container can become a lethal weapon: a flamethrower if near a fire and a shrapnel bomb when heated. It has been known to explode when placed too near a radiator or heater. Also, aerosol gases turn into toxic gases: fluorine, chlorine, hydrogen fluoride, and chloride or even phosgene, a military poison gas. Aerosol hair dyes and "hot" shave creams were made possible by compartmentalization of the container. However, in the case of the hot shave creams, there was unreliable mixing of the chemicals and skin rashes resulted. In powder products, the inhalation of powder, or the silicones, can damage the lungs. In 1972 the Society of Cosmetic Chemists reported that powder aerosols evidenced a high particle retention in the lungs and profound pulmonary effects. Tests showed large powder particles in 23 separate areas of the lungs. In addition, Freon, the propellant, cannot be considered inert, that is, lacking in chemical activity or in an expected biologic or pharmacologic effect.

AFTERBATH LOTIONS. See Cologne.

AFTER-SHAVE LOTIONS. See Shaving Lotions.

AGAR. Japanese Isinglass. Emulsifier and emollient. Transparent, odorless, and tasteless. Extracted from various seaweeds found in the Pacific and Indian oceans and the Sea of Japan. This first seaweed to be extracted, purified, and dried was discovered by a Japanese innkeeper around 1685 and introduced into Europe and the United States by visitors from China in the 1800s as a substitute for gelatin and as a thickener. Also used as a bulk laxative. Aside from causing an occasional allergic reaction, it is nontoxic.

AGAVE LECHUGUILLA. American Aloe. Native to the warm parts of the United States, and known by its heavy stiff leaf and tall panicle or spike of candelabralike flowers. The leaves are used for juice employed in cosmetics as an adhesive and in medicines as a diuretic. The fermented juice is popular in Mexico for its distilled spirit (mescal). Some species are cultivated for their fibers, which are used in thread and rope. No known skin toxicity.

AGE SPOTS. See Skin Bleach.

ALBUMEN. See Albumin.

ALBUMIN. A group of simple proteins composed of nitrogen, carbon, hydrogen, oxygen, and sulfur that are soluble in water. In cosmetics, albumin is usually derived from egg white. The egg white is mixed with water and when the water evaporates, it leaves a tight feeling, which is promoted in face masks and astringents as therapeutic. Albumin is also used as an emulsifier in cosmetics. May cause allergic reaction.

ALCLOXA. Aluminum Chlorhydroxy Allantoinate. See Allantoin.

ALCOHOL. Ethyl Alcohol. Ethanol. Alcohol as a solvent is widely used in the cosmetic field; many cosmetics consist largely of alcohol: after-shave lotions, bubble baths, colognes, cold cream, deodorants, freckle lotions, face packs, hair lacquers, hair tonics, liquid face powders, mouthwashes, nail polish removers, perfumes, preshaving lotions, shampoos, shaving creams, skin lotions, spray deodorants, suntan lotions and oils, and toilet waters. Alcohol is manufactured by the fermentation of starch, sugar, and other carbohydrates. It is clear, colorless, and flammable, with a somewhat pleasant odor and a burning taste. Medicinally used externally as an antiseptic and internally as a stimulant and hypnotic. *Absolute alcohol* is ethyl alcohol to which a substance has been added to make it unfit for drinking. *Rubbing alcohol* contains not less than 68.5 percent and not more than 71.5 percent by volume of absolute alcohol and a remainder of denaturants, such as perfume oils. Since it is a fat solvent, alcohol can dry the hair and skin when used in excess. Toxic in large doses.

ALDEHYDE, ALPHATIC. A class of organic chemical compounds intermediate between acids and alcohols. Aldehyde contains less oxygen than acids and less hydrogen than alcohols. Formaldehyde (*see*), a preservative, is an example of an aldehyde widely used in cosmetics. Benzaldehyde and cinnamic aldehydes are used to scent perfumes. Most are irritating to the skin and gastrointestinal tract.

ALDIOXA. Aluminum Dihydroxy Allantoinate. Astringent, antiperspirant prepared with the skin-healing salts of aluminum chlorhydroxy allantoinate (*see*). Used as astringents, keratolytics, tissue stimulants, and buffers in cosmetics. Nonsensitizing and nonirritating.

ALGAE. From seaweed and pond scum. Algae is claimed to prevent wrinkles and to moisturize the skin, but the American Medical Association denies any validity for algae's therapeutic benefits. However, seaweed products are widely used in cosmetics for many purposes. Nontoxic. See Alginates.

ALGINATES. All derivatives of alginic acid are designated "algin" (ammonium, calcium, potassium, and sodium). Gelatinous substances obtained from certain seaweeds and used as emulsifiers in hand lotions and creams, as thickening agents in shampoos, wave sets, and lotions. They are also used as barrier agents (*see*) in hand creams and lotions, in the manufacture of celluloid, as an emulsifier in mineral oil, and in mucilage. Sodium alginate from brown seaweed is used as a thickener in dentifrices, but the FDA is testing the sodium form (largest use in ice cream) for short-term mutagenic birth-deforming, reproduction, and subacute effects. Alginates are also used as stabilizers and water retainers in many foods. No known toxicity.

ALGINIC ACID. A stabilizer in cosmetics, it is obtained as a highly gelatinous precipitate. The sodium carbonate (*see*) extracts of brown dried seaweeds are treated with acid to achieve the result. Resembles albumin or gelatin (*see both*). Alginic acid is slowly soluble in water, forming a very thick liquid. No known toxicity.

ALIZARIN. Turkey Red. Wrappings on Egyptian mummies dyed with Turkey red (a bright red) from alizarin remain unfaded today.

Alizarin comes from the root of the madder plant but is produced synthetically from anthracene, a coal tar. It yields different colors, depending upon the metals mixed with it. Colors used in cosmetics are Turkey red, blue, orange, red, rose, black, violet, lilac, yellow, and dark brown. Allergic reactions have been reported but toxicity is unknown. See Colors.

ALKALI.   The term originally covered the caustic and mild forms of potash and soda. Now a substance is regarded as an alkali if it gives hydroxyl ions in solution. An alkaline aqueous solution is one with a pH (*see*) greater than 7. Sodium bicarbonate is an example of an alkali that is used to neutralize excess acidity in cosmetics.

ALKANET ROOT.   A red coloring obtained from extraction of the herblike tree root grown in Asia Minor and the Mediterranean. Used as a copper or blue coloring (when combined with metals) for hair oils and other cosmetics. It is also used as a coloring for wines, inks, and sausage casings. May be mixed with synthetic dyes for color tints. Formerly used as an astringent. No known toxicity.

ALKANNIN.   A red powder and the principal ingredient of alkanet root (*see*).

ALKANOLAMINES.   Compounds used in cold creams and eyeliners as a solvent and comprised of alcohols from alkene (a saturated fatty hydrocarbon) and amines (from ammonia). These compounds are viscous, colorless liquids that form soaps with fatty acids (*see*). No known toxicity.

ALKYL ARYLPOLYETHYLENE GLYCOL ETHER.   A dispersant for preshave lotions, but basically a wetting agent. It rarely sensitizes or irritates human skin.

ALKYL BENZENE SULFONATES.   A detergent used in bubble baths and for shampoos. Prolonged feeding to animals showed no evidence of toxicity but such agents are known to be defatting and therefore drying to the skin.

ALKYL SODIUM SULFATES.   Used in shampoos because they have cleaning power and wash out of the hair easier than soap. A basic alkyl sulfate shampoo formula: sodium lauryl sulfate, 15 percent; behenic acid, 3.5 percent (*see both*); water, 81.5 percent. These sulfates were developed by the Germans when vegetable fats and oils were scarce. A large number have been made. They are prepared from primary alcohols by treatment with chlorsulfuric or sulfuric acid. The alcohols are usually prepared from fatty acids (*see*). For example, lauric acid makes a soap effective in hard water. If it is reduced to lauryl alcohol and sulfated, it makes sodium lauryl sulfate, a widely used detergent. The alkyl sulfates are low in acute and chronic toxicity but they may cause skin irritation.

ALLANTOIN. Used in cold creams, hand lotions, hair lotions, after-shave lotions, and other skin-soothing cosmetics because of its ability to help heal wounds and skin ulcers and to stimulate the growth of healthy tissue. Colorless crystals, soluble in hot water, it is prepared synthetically by the oxidation of uric acid (*see*) or by heating uric acid with dichloroacetic acid. It is nontoxic.

ALLANTOIN ACETYL METHIONINE. See Allantoin.

ALLANTOIN ASCORBATE. Allantoin (*see*) with Ascorbic Acid (*see*) salt.

ALLANTOIN CALCIUM PANTOTHENATE. A combination of the salt of the B complex vitamin and the healing agent allantoin (*see*). Used to soothe the skin in emollients. Nontoxic.

ALLANTOIN GALACTURONIC ACID. See Allantoin.

ALLANTOIN POLYGALACTURONIC ACID. See Allantoin.

ALLANTOINATE. A salt of allantoin (*see*).

ALMOND MEAL. A powder obtained by pulverizing blanched almonds and used in various cosmetics and perfumes for its soothing properties. See Almond Oil for toxicity.

ALMOND MILK. A creamy mixture of blanched almonds, acacia (*see*), sugar, and water blended to a smooth paste and sieved. Used as a demulcent, especially in organic cosmetics. See Bitter Almond Oil.

ALMOND OIL. See Bitter Almond Oil.

ALMOND PASTE. A favorite early European cleanser. Made from the dried ripe seeds of the sweet almond. See Bitter Almond Oil for toxicity.

ALOE JUICE. See Aloe Vera.

ALOE VERA. The untreated expressed juice from the aloe plant leaf from a South African lilylike plant. Used for supposed softening benefits in skin creams. It contains 99.5 percent water, with the remaining .5 percent composed of some 20 amino acids (*see*) and carbohydrates. There is no scientific evidence that aloe vera has any benefits in cosmetics according to the American Medical Association. Used in bitters, vermouth, and spice flavorings for beverages and alcoholic drinks. It has been used as a cathartic but was found to cause severe intestinal cramps and sometimes kidney damage. No known toxicity when applied to the skin.

ALPHA OLEFIN SULFONATE. See Sulfonated Oils.

ALPHA TOCOPHEROL. See Tocopherols.

ALPHATIC ALDEHYDE. See Aldehyde.

ALTHEA ROOT. *Marshmallow Root.* A natural flavoring substance from a plant grown in Europe, Asia, and the United States. The dried root is used in strawberry, cherry, and rootbeer flavorings for beverages. The boiled root is used as a demulcent in ointments to soothe mucous membranes. The roots, flowers, and leaves are used externally as a poultice. Nontoxic.

ALUM. Potash Alum. Aluminum Ammonium. Potassium Sulfate. A colorless, odorless, crystalline, water-soluble solid used in astringent lotions, after-shave lotions, and as a styptic (stops bleeding). Also used to prevent aluminum chloride (*see*) from causing skin irritation in antiperspirants. In concentrated solutions alum has produced gum damage and fatal intestinal hemorrhages. It has a low toxicity in experimental animals but ingestion of 30 grams (an ounce) has killed an adult. It is also known to cause kidney damage. Concentrated doses have damaged gums. No specific harmful effects reported in cosmetics.

ALUMINA. The natural or synthetic oxide of aluminum occurring in nature as bauxite and corundum. The aluminum hydroxide (*see*) formed is washed, dried, and used as an extender for cosmetic colors in which opacity is not desired. High concentrations of alumina may be irritating to the respiratory tract and lung problems have been reported in alumina workers. No known skin toxicity.

ALUMINA HYDRATE. White coloring for cosmetics. See Alumina and Colors.

ALUMINUM ACETATE. Burow's Solution. A mixture including acetic acid and boric acid, with astringent and antiseptic properties, used in astringent lotions, antiperspirants, deodorants, and protective creams. Ingestion of large doses can cause nausea and vomiting, diarrhea, and bleeding. Prolonged and continuous exposure can produce severe sloughing of the skin. It also causes skin rashes in some persons.

ALUMINUM CAPRYLATE. See Aluminum Salts.

ALUMINUM CHLORHYDROXIDE. See Aluminum Chlorohydrate.

ALUMINUM CHLORHYDROXY ALLANTOINATE. Used in after-shave lotions and other astringents. Also used as a buffer. Nonsensitizing and nonirritating. See Allantoin.

ALUMINUM CHLORIDE. The first antiperspirant salt (see Aluminum Salts and Alum) to be used for commercial antiperspirant products and still the strongest available in effectiveness (and acidity). It is also antiseptic but can be irritating to sensitive skin and it does cause allergic reactions in susceptible people. Lethal to mammals upon ingestion of large doses.

ALUMINUM CHLOROHYDRATE. The most frequently used antiperspirant in the United States. Causes occasional infections of the hair follicles. May be irritating to abraded skin and may also cause allergic reactions, but it is considered by cosmetic manufacturers as one of the least irritating of the aluminum salts.

ALUMINUM CHLOROHYDRATE COMPLEX. See Aluminum Chlorohydrate.

ALUMINUM DIACETATE. See Aluminum Salts.

ALUMINUM DISTEARATE. See Aluminum Salts.

ALUMINUM FORMATE. Used as an antiperspirant to make other aluminum salts less acid and corrosive to fabrics. See Aluminum Salts and Deodorants.

ALUMINUM GLYCINATE. See Aluminum Salts.

ALUMINUM HYDRATE. Gloss White. Usually obtained as a white bulky amorphous powder. Practically insoluble in water but soluble in alkaline solution. Used as an adsorbent, emulsifier, and alkali in detergents, antiperspirants and dentifrices. Used medicinally as a gastric antacid. No known toxicity.

ALUMINUM HYDROXIDE. Mild astringent and alkali used in antiperspirants, dentifrices, and dusting powders. A white gelatinuos mass used as a drying agent, catalyst, adsorbent, and coloring agent in many cosmetic processes. A leavening agent in the production of baked goods, as well as a gastric antacid in medicine. Practically insoluble in water but not in alkaline solutions. Aluminum hydroxide has a low toxicity but may cause constipation if ingested. No known skin toxicity. See Aluminum Salts and Deodorants.

ALUMINUM LANOLATE. See Aluminum Salts.

ALUMINUM METHIONATE. See Aluminum Salts.

ALUMINUM PALMITATE. White granules, insoluble in water, used as a lubricant and waterproofing material. Employed in antiperspirants. See Aluminum Salts and Deodorants.

ALUMINUM PHENOLSULFONATE. Aluminum Sulfocarbolate. Pink powder, soluble in water, used in preshave astringent-type lotions and spray deodorants for its antiseptic and detergent properties. It is also used in dusting powder. See Aluminum Sulfate for toxicity.

ALUMINUM POWDER. A color additive composed of finely divided particles of aluminum. Used in face powders and hair colorings. Nontoxic.

ALUMINUM SALTS. Aluminum Acetate. Aluminum Caprylate. Aluminum Chloride. Aluminum Chlorohydrate. Aluminum Diacetate. Aluminum Distearate. Aluminum Glycinate. Aluminum Hydroxide. Aluminum Lanolate. Aluminum Methionate. Aluminum

Phenolsulfonate. Aluminum Silicate. Aluminum Stearate. Aluminum Sulfate. Aluminum Tristearate. These are both the strong and weak acids of aluminum used in antiperspirants to combat body odors. The smell of sweat is caused by bacterial action on the moisture. The salts are believed to prevent perspiration from reaching the skin by impeding the action of sweat and act as an antibacterial. The strong salts may cause skin irritations and damage fabrics, particularly linens and cottons. Therefore, buffering agents are added by cosmetic manufacturers to counteract such adverse effects. The salts are also styptic (*see*).

ALUMINUM SILICATE. A white mass, insoluble in water, obtained naturally from clay or synthesized, used as an anticaking and coloring agent in powders. Essentially harmless when given orally and when applied to skin. See Aluminum Salts.

ALUMINUM STARCH OCTENYLSUCCINATE. Dry Flow®. See Aluminum Phenosulfonate.

ALUMINUM STEARATE. See Aluminum Tristearate.

ALUMINUM SULFATE. Cake Alum. Colorless crystals, soluble in water, used as an antiseptic, astringent, and detergent in antiperspirants, deodorants, and skin fresheners (*see last two*); also purifies water. It may cause pimples under the arm when in antiperspirants and/or allergic reactions in some people. Lethal to mice in large oral doses.

ALUMINUM TRISTEARATE. A hard plastic material used as a thickener and coloring in cosmetics. Also used as a chewing gum base component and to waterproof fabrics. No known toxicity.

AMARANTH. See FD & C Blue No. 2.

AMBER OIL, RECTIFIED. A perfume ingredient distilled from amber, a fossil resin of vegetable origins and purified. The oil is pale yellow to yellowish brown and volatile, with a penetrating odor and acrid taste. No known toxicity.

AMBERGRIS. Concretion from the intestinal tract of the sperm whale found in tropical seas. About 80 percent cholesterol, it is a gray to black waxy mass and is used for fixing delicate odors in perfumery. It is also used as a flavoring for food and beverages. No known toxicity.

AMINES. A class of compounds derived from ammonia. Quaternary ammonium compounds (*see*) are amines.

AMINO ACIDS. The body's building blocks, from which proteins are constructed. Of the twenty-two known amino acids, eight cannot be manufactured in the body in sufficient quantities to sustain growth and health. These eight are called "essential" because they are necessary to maintain good health. A ninth, histidine, is thought to be necessary for growth only in childhood.

p-AMINOBENZOIC ACID. See Para-aminobenzoic Acid.

PARA-AMINOBENZOIC ACID. The colorless or yellowish acid found in the Vitamin B complex. In an alcohol and water solution plus a little light perfume, it is sold under a wide variety of names as a sunscreen lotion to prevent skin damage from the sun. It is also used as a local anesthetic in sunburn products. It is used medicinally to treat arthritis. However, it can cause allergic eczema and a sensitivity to light in susceptible people whose skin may react to sunlight by erupting with a rash, sloughing, and/or swelling.

AMINOETHYLACRYLATE PHOSPHATE/ACRYLATE COPOLYMER. See Acrylates.

4-AMINO-2-HYDROXYTOLUENE. Used in the manufacture of dyes. See Toluene.

AMINOMETHYL PROPANEDIOL. Crystals made from nitrogen compounds that are soluble in alcohol and mixable with water. Used as an emulsifying agent for cosmetic creams and lotions and in mineral oils. No known toxicity.

AMINOMETHYL PROPANOL. An alcohol made from nitrogen compounds; mixes with water. Soluble in alcohol and used as an emulsifying agent for cosmetic creams and lotions. Used in medicines that reduce body water. Prolonged skin exposure may cause irritation due to alkalinity, but in most commercial products the alkalinity is neutralized.

AMINOPHENOL. o-Aminophenol. p-Aminophenol. m-Aminophenol. 2-Amino-5-Nitrophenol. 4-Amino-2-Nitrophenol. 2-Amino-6-Chloro-4-Nitrophenol. p-Aminophenol HCL. Aromatic, colorless crystals derived from phenol (*see*), used as intermediates (*see*) in orange red and medium brown hair dyes. Discovered in London in 1854, aminophenols are also used in the manufacture of sulfur and azo dyes (*see*). Can cause a lack of oxygen in the blood but is less toxic than aniline (*see*) in animals. Solutions on the skin have produced restlessness and convulsions in man as well as skin irritations. May also cause skin rashes and sensitizations and inhalation may cause asthma.

2-AMINO-6-CHLORO-4-NITROPHENOL. See Aminophenol.

2-AMINO-5-NITROPHENOL. See Aminophenol.

4-AMINO-2-NITROPHENOL. See Aminophenol.

m-AMINOPHENOL. See Aminophenol.

o-AMINOPHENOL.   See Aminophenol.

p-AMINOPHENOL HCL.   See Aminophenol.

AMMONIA.   Liquid used in permanent waves (cold) and hair bleaches. Obtained by blowing steam through incandescent coke. Ammonia is also used in the manufacture of explosives and synthetic fabrics. It is extremely toxic when inhaled in concentrated vapors, and is irritating to the eyes and mucous membranes. It may cause hair breakage when used in permanent waves and hair bleach.

AMMONIA WATER.   Ammonia gas dissolved in water. Used as an alkali (*see*) in metallic hair dyes, hair straighteners, and in protective skin creams. Colorless with a very pungent odor, it is irritating to the eyes and mucous mebranes. In strong solution can cause burns and blistering.

AMMONIATED MERCURY. Mercuric Chloride Ammoniated.   A white odorless powder with a metallic taste used in ointment form to combat skin infections and to treat eye disorders. All forms of mercury are poisonous. Topical application may lead to skin rash and other allergic manifestations. Prolonged use may cause skin pigmentation and when applied too vigorously, it can be absorbed and result in systemic poisoning. Absorption or ingestion may lead to kidney damage. Ingestion also causes stomach pains and vomiting. No longer permitted in cosmetics except in small amounts as a preservative.

AMMONIUM ALGINATE.   See Alginates.

AMMONIUM ALUM.   See Alum.

AMMONIUM BICARBONATE.   Used as a buffer in thioglycolate cold permanent waving lotions. Occurs in the urine of alligators. Usually prepared by passing carbon dioxide gas through concentrated ammonia water. Shiny, hard, colorless or white crystals; faint odor of ammonia. Used in baking powder formulas, in cooling baths. Used medicinally as an expectorant and to break up intestinal gas. Also used in compost heaps to accelerate decomposition. See Ammonium Carbonate for toxicity.

AMMONIUM BISULFITE.   Colorless crystals used as a preservative in cosmetics. Sold in solution only. No known toxicity.

AMMONIUM CARBONATE.   A white solid alkali derived partly from ammonium bicarbonate (*see*) and used as a neutralizer and buffer in permanent wave solutions and creams. It decomposes when exposed to air. Also used in baking powders, for defatting woolens, in fire extinguishers, and as an expectorant. Ammonium carbonate can cause skin rashes on the scalp, forehead, or hands.

AMMONIUM CHLORIDE.   Ammonium salt that occurs naturally.

Colorless, odorless crystals or white powder, saline in taste, and incompatible with alkalies. Used as an acidifier in permanent wave solutions, eye lotions, and as a cooling and stimulating skin wash. Industrially employed in freezing mixtures, batteries, dyes, safety explosives, and in medicine as a urinary acidifier and diuretic. Keeps snow from melting on ski slopes. If ingested, can cause nausea, vomiting, and acidosis. Lethal as an intramuscular dose in rats and guinea pigs. As with any ammonia compound, concentrated solutions can be irritating to the skin.

AMMONIUM CITRATE. See Citric Acid.

AMMONIUM HYDROXIDE. Ammonia Water. A weak alkali formed when ammonia dissolves in water and exists only in solution. A clear colorless liquid with an extremely pungent odor. Used as an alkali (*see*) in metallic hair dyes, hair straighteners, and in protective skin creams. Also used in detergents and for removing stains. It is irritating to the eyes and mucous membranes. It may cause hair breakage.

AMMONIUM IODIDE. Ammonium salt prepared from ammonia and iodine. White odorless crystals with a sharp saline taste. The crystals become yellow and brown on exposure to air and light. Used in cosmetics as an antiseptic and preservative and in medicine as an expectorant. See Iodine for toxicity.

AMMONIUM LAURETH SULFATE. Ammonium Lauryl Ether Sulfate. See Sodium Lauryl Sulfate.

AMMONIUM MOLYBDATE. Colorless, green or white crystalline salt. See Ammonia.

AMMONIUM MONOOLEAMIDO. See Ammonia.

AMMONIUM MYRETH SULFATE. See Sodium Lauryl Sulfate.

AMMONIUM NONOXYNOL-4-SULFATE. See Ammonium Sulfate.

AMMONIUM PARETH-25-3 SULFATE. See Ammonium Sulfate.

AMMONIUM PERSULFATE. Ammonium salt. Colorless crystals, soluble in water, used as an oxidizer and bleach in dyes and skin lighteners. Also as a disinfectant, deodorant, and preservative. It may be irritating to the skin and mucous membranes. In cosmetics, may make hair brittle. Lethal to rats in large oral doses.

AMMONIUM PHOSPHATE. Dibasic. Ammonium salt. An odorless, white or colorless crystalline powder with a cooling taste used in mouthwashes. It is also used in fireproofing textiles, paper, and wood. No known toxicity.

AMMONIUM STEARATE. Stearic Acid. Ammonium Salt. A yellowish white powder used as a texturizer in vanishing creams. No known toxicity.

AMMONIUM SULFATE. Ammonium salt. A neutralizer in permanent wave lotions, it is odorless and colorless, either white crystals or powder. Industrially used in freezing mixtures, fireproofing fabrics, and tanning. Used medicinally to prolong analgesia. No known toxicity when used cosmetically. Rats were killed when fed large doses.

AMMONIUM SULFIDE. A salt derived from sulfur and ammonium, it is used as a neutralizer in permanent wave lotions, as a depilatory, to apply patina to bronze, and in spice flavorings. It has been reported to have caused a death when ingested in a permanent wave solution. Irritating to the skin when used in depilatories.

AMMONIUM SULFITE. Ammonium salt made with sulfuric acid. White, crystalline, soluble in water, almost insoluble in alcohol and acetone. Antiseptic. A preservative in cold permanent waves. See Ammonia for toxicity.

AMMONIUM THIOGLYCOLATE. The ammonium salt of thioglycolic acid, a liquid with a strong unpleasant odor that is readily oxidized by air. A hair straightener. It can cause severe burns and blistering of the skin. Large doses injected into the stomachs of mice killed them.

AMMONIUM VINYL ACETATE/ACRYLATES TERPOLYMER. See Acrylates.

AMMONIUM XYLENESULFONATE. Ammonium salt of xylene. A lacquer solvent used in nail polishes. Flammable, insoluble in water. It may be narcotic in high doses. Chronic toxicity or skin effects are not known.

AMPD ISOSTEARIC HYDROLYZED ANIMAL PROTEIN. See Hydrolyzed and Protein.

AMPHOTERIC-1. Amphoteric, meaning capable of reacting as either an acid or base. Formerly called Miranol®. All the amphoterics are used as surface-active agents (*see*) in detergents.

AMPHOTERIC-2. See Amphoteric-1.

AMPHOTERIC-3. See Amphoteric-1.

AMPHOTERIC-5. See Amphoteric-1.

AMPHOTERIC-6. See Amphoteric-1.

AMPHOTERIC-8. See Amphoteric-1.

AMPHOTERIC-10. See Amphoteric-1.

AMPHOTERIC-11. See Amphoteric-1.

AMPHOTERIC-12. See Amphoteric-1.

AMPHOTERIC-13. See Amphoteric-1.
AMPHOTERIC-14. See Amphoteric-1.
AMPHOTERIC-15. See Amphoteric-1.
AMSONIC ACID. Used in hair dyes and bleaching products. Manufactured from sulfonic acid. Yellow needles, slightly soluble in water, and forms salts with ammonia compounds. No known toxicity.
AMYL ACETATE. Banana Oil. Pear Oil. Obtained from amyl alcohol, with a strong fruity odor. Used in nail finishes and nail polish remover as a solvent, and as an artificial fruit essence in perfume. Also used in food and beverage flavoring and for perfuming shoe polish. Amyl acetate is a skin irritant and causes central nervous system depression when ingested. Exposure of 950 ppm for one hour has caused headache, fatigue, chest pain, and irritation of the mucous membranes.
AMYL ALCOHOL. A solvent used in nail lacquers. It occurs naturally in cocoa and oranges and smells like camphor. Highly toxic and narcotic, ingestion of as little as 30 mg has killed humans. Inhalation causes violent coughing.
AMYL BUTYRATE. Used in some perfume formulas for its apricot-like odor. It occurs naturally in cocoa and is colorless. Also used for synthetic flavorings. No known toxicity.
AMYL CINNAMIC ALDEHYDE. Liquid with a strong floral odor suggesting jasmine. Used in perfumes. See Cinnamic Acid.
AMYL DIMETHYL PABA. See Para-Aminobenzoic Acid.
AMYL GALLATE. An antioxidant obtained from nutgalls and from molds. No known toxicity.
AMYL PHENOL. Used in hair-grooming preparations. See Phenol.
AMYL SALICYLATE. , Derived from salicylic acid. A pleasant-smelling liquid used in sunscreen lotions and perfumes. Insoluble in water. See Salicylates.
AMYLASE. Used as a texturizer in cosmetics, it is an enzyme prepared from hog pancreas used in flour to break down starch into smaller sugar molecules. Used medicinally to combat inflammation. Nontoxic.
AMYLOPECTIN. Amioca. The gel constituent of starch. Used as a texturizer in cosmetics. Obtained from corn. Gives a red color when mixed with iodine and does not gel when mixed with water. No known toxicity.
ANETHOLE. A flavoring used in mouthwashes and a scent for perfumes. Obtained from anise (*see*) oil and other sources. Colorless or faintly yellow liquid with a sweet taste and a characteristic anise-

like odor. Chief constituent of anise. Anethole is affected by light and caused irritation of the gums and throat when used in a denture cream. When applied to the skin, anethole may produce hives, scaling, and blisters.

ANGELICA.   Used in expensive fragrances, toothpastes, and mouthwashes. Grown in Europe and Asia, the aromatic seeds, leaves, stems, and roots have been used in medicine for flatus (gas), to increase sweating, and reduce body water. Also used as a flavoring in food. When perfume is applied, skin may break out with a rash and swell when exposed to sunlight. The bark is used medicinally as a purgative and emetic.

ANHYDRIDE.   A residue resulting from water being removed from a compound. An oxide—combination of oxygen and an element—that can combine with water to form an acid, or that is derived from an acid by the abstraction of water. Maleic anhydride (*see*) is an example.

ANHYDROUS.   Describes a substance that contains no water.

ANILINE DYES.   A synonym for coal tar (*see*) dyes. Aniline is a colorless to brown liquid that darkens with age. Slightly soluble in water. Used in the manufacture of hair dyes, medicinals, resins, and perfumes. Intoxication may occur from inhalation, ingestion, or absorption through the skin. Serious poisoning from ingestion causes acute lack of oxygen in the blood, dizziness, headache, mental confusion, and skin lesions. Tumors have been reported in animals whose skins were painted with coal tar dye. Can cause allergy and skin reactions to light.

ANIMAL PROTEIN DERIVATIVE.   See Proteins.

ANIONIC DETERGENTS.   A class of synthetic compounds used as emulsifiers in about 75 percent of all hand creams and lotions. An anion is a negatively charged ion that is "surface active." These detergents usually consist of an alkali salt as soap, or ammonium salt of a strong acid. Can be irritating to the skin depending on alkalinity. See Emulsifiers and Ammonia Water.

ANISE.   Used in masculine-type perfumes, cleaners, and shampoos. It is obtained by steam distillation of the dried ripe fruit of a herbaceous plant grown in Asia, Europe, and the United States. Colorless to pale yellow liquid with a strong odor. It was used in biblical times to pay taxes. See Anethole for toxicity.

ANISIDINE. o-ANISIDINE. p-ANISIDINE.   Derived from anisole (*see*). Colorless needles. Used in the manufacture of azo dyes (*see*).

Can be absorbed through the skin; also an irritant that can cause allergic reactions.

ANISOLE. Used in perfumery. Colorless liquid with a phenolic, aniselike odor. Obtained by distilling anisic acid or by the action of a compound on phenol. See Anise and Phenol.

ANNATTO. A vegetable dye made from the red waxy material surrounding the seeds of a shrub found in Central America and cultivated in Brazil, Guianas, Mexico, and India. When heated, it turns reddish brown. Red to yellow colorings can be used to impart to cosmetics a cream color. Rarely used today. Generally used as a spice flavoring in beverages and foods. No known toxicity.

ANTHRANILATES. Aminobenzoates. Methyl, menthyl, phenyl, benzyl, phenylethyl, linalyl, terpinyl, and cyclohexyl esters. Used in sunscreen lotions and in dyes and perfumes. Obtained from anthranilic acid, which is white to yellow crystalline. Originally derived by fusing indigo (a blue dye from plants) with alkali (*see*). Now made from phthalates. When applied, may cause skin to break out with a rash and swell when exposed to sunlight. See Coal Tar for toxicity.

ANTHRAQUINONE. A coal tar color produced industrially from phthalic anhydride and benzene (*see both*). Light yellow slender prisms, which are insoluble in water. May cause skin irritation and allergic reactions. Being studied at the U.S. Frederick Cancer Research Center for possible cancer-causing effects. See Colors.

ANTIMONY COMPOUNDS. Antimony Potassium Tartrate. Tartar Emetic. Used in hair dyes. Obtained from ore mined in China, Mexico, and Bolivia. This silver white brittle metal can cause contact dermatitis, eye and nose irritation, and ulceration by contact, fumes, or dust. It is very toxic if mixed with hydrogen and can be fatal if ingested. When applied topically, it may cause allergic reactions. It is used medicinally as an emetic.

ANTIMONY POTASSIUM TARTRATE. See Antimony Compounds.

ANTIOXIDANT. An agent such as Vitamin E (see Tocopherols) that inhibits oxidation and thus prevents rancidity of oils or fats or the deterioration of other materials through exposure to oxygen.

ANTIPERSPIRANTS. See Deodorants.

ANTIPYRINE. A white powder, with a bitter taste, soluble in water, used as an antiseptic in eye lotions, an antipyretic (anti-itch) component in skin preparations, and as an analgesic. May cause skin eruptions and vascular collapse.

APO-CAROTENAL. Obtained from orange rind, berries, and

petals, it consists of deep red leaflets used in coloring matter. It has vitamin A activity. No known toxicity.

APPLE BLOSSOM.   Used in perfumes and colognes, it is the essence of the flowers from a species of apple tree. No known toxicity.

APRICOT. *Fruit and Oil.*   The tart orange-colored fruit. The oil is used in brilliantine and the crushed fruit as a facial mask to soften the skin. For a do-it-yourself facial mask, a cup of dried apricots is soaked in water until softened and mixed with a small bunch of grapes and 3 tablespoons of skimmed milk powder. The concoction is mixed in a blender and patted on the neck and face and allowed to remain for 15 minutes, followed with a rinse of cool water. No known toxicity.

APRICOT EXTRACT.   See Apricot.

ARACHIDONIC ACID.   A liquid unsaturated fatty acid that occurs in liver, brain, glands, and fat of animals and humans. The acid is generally isolated from animal liver. Used essentially for nutrition and to soothe eczema and rashes in skin creams and lotions. No known toxicity.

ARBITRARY FIXATIVE.   An odorous substance that lends a particular note to the perfume throughout all stages of evaporation but does not really influence the evaporation of the perfume materials in the compound. Oakmoss is an example. See Fixative and Oakmoss.

ARMENIAN BOLE.   A soft claylike red earth. The pigment is found chiefly in Armenia and Tuscany and used as a coloring material in face powder. No known toxicity.

ARNICA. *Wolf's Bane.*   Skin fresheners may contain this herb found in the Northern Hemisphere. The dried flower head has long been used as an astringent and to treat skin disorders, especially in tinctures. It has been used externally to treat bruises and sprains. Ingestion leads to severe intestinal upset, nervous disturbances, irregular heartbeat, and collapse. Ingestion of one ounce has caused severe illness but not death. Active irritant on the skin. Not recommended for use in toilet preparation and should never be used on broken skin.

AROMATIC.   In the context of cosmetics, a chemical that has an aroma.

AROMATIC BITTERS.   Usually made from the maceration of bitter herbs and used to intensify the aroma of perfume. The herbs selected for aromatic bitters must have a persistent fragrant aroma. Ginger and cinnamon are examples.

ARROWROOT.   An ingredient in dusting powders and hair dyes made from the root starch of plants. Arrowroot was used by the

American Indians to heal wounds from poisoned arrows and is still employed today in easily digestible foods for children and invalids. It may cause skin rashes and stuffy nose and inflammed eyes.

ARSENIC COMPOUNDS. Arsenic is an element that occurs throughout the universe and is highly toxic in most forms. Its compounds are used in hair tonics and hair dyes and have been employed to treat spirochetal infections, blood disorders, and skin diseases. Ingestion causes nausea, vomiting, and death. Chronic poisoning can result in pigmentation of skin and kidney and liver damage. In hair tonic and dyes it may cause contact dermatitis. The limit of arsenic in colors is 0.0002 percent. Arsenic can also cause the skin to be sensitive to light and break out in a rash or to swell.

ARTIFICIAL. In the context of cosmetics, a substance not duplicated in nature. A scent, for instance, may have all natural ingredients, but it must be called artificial if it has no counterpart in nature.

ARTIFICIAL NAILS. Plastics designed to be pasted or self-adhered to one's natural nails to give the appearance of long, lovely, undamaged fingernails. After application, the artificial nails are cut or filed to desired shape and length. Artificial nails were developed from materials used by dentists to fill teeth. The basic ingredients include a vinyl compound (methyl methacrylate is one of the most commonly used vinyls), a catalyst, and a plasticizer. Allergy and irritation to the skin may develop from ingredients in the fake nails or in the adhesive.

ASCORBIC ACID. Vitamin C. A preservative and antioxidant used in cosmetic creams, particularly bleach and lemon creams. Vitamin C is necessary for normal teeth, bones, and blood vessels. The white or slightly yellow powder darkens upon exposure to air. Reasonably stable when it remains dry in air, but deteriorates rapidly when exposed to air while in solution. Nontoxic.

ASCORBYL PALMITATE. A salt of ascorbic acid (*see*), it is used as a preservative and antioxidant in cosmetic creams and lotions to prevent rancidity. Nontoxic.

ASCORBYL STEARATE. See Ascorbyl Palmitate.

ASPARTIC ACID. DL & L Forms. Aminosuccinate Acid. A nonessential amino acid (*see*) occurring in animals and plants, sugar cane, sugar beets, and molasses. It is usually synthesized for commercial purposes. No known toxicity.

ASTRINGENT. Usually promoted for oily skin. A clear liquid containing mostly alcohol, but with small amounts of other ingredients such as boric acid, alum, menthol, and/or camphor. A typical astringent formula: ethanol, 50 percent; sorbitol, 2.5 percent (*see both*); perfume oil, 0.1 percent; menthol, 0.1 percent; boric acid, 2.0 percent (*see both*); water, 44.9 percent. In addition to making the skin feel refreshed, it usually gives a tightened feeling from the evaporation of the ingredients. According to the American Medical Association, there is no evidence that astringents tighten or shrink the pores. Usually toxic when ingested because of denatured alcohol content.

ATTAPULGITE.   See Fuller's Earth.

AVOCADO. Alligator Pear.   The various common pulpy green fruit once used as an aphrodisiac. The oil is employed in shampoos, lubricating creams, and brilliantines. For a make-it-yourself hair conditioner, mash and mix 2 tablespoons of avocado with a commercial shampoo and use as ordinarily. No known toxicity.

AZO DYES.   Used in nonpermanent hair rinses and tints. Azo dyes belong to a large category of colorings that are characterized by the way they combine with nitrogen. These are a very large class of dyes made from diazonium compounds and phenol. The dyes usually contain a mild acid, such as citric or tartaric acid. It can cause allergic reaction. People who become sensitized to permanent hair dyes containing paraphenylene diamine (*see*) also develop a cross sensitivity to azo dyes. That is, a person who is allergic to permanent p-phenylenediamine dyes will also be allergic to azo dyes. There are reports that azo dyes are absorbed through the skin.

AZULENE.   An intensely blue liquid hydrocarbon (gasoline is a mixture of hydrocarbons) contained in the essential oil distilled from chamomile flowers or cubebs. Small quantities are added to shampoos and other products to impart the characteristic odor of chamomile. Also used as a coloring agent. Reportedly an antiinflammatory agent. Nontoxic.

B

BABY CREAM.   Protects baby skin against irritation and soothes it. A typical baby cream formula would include mineral oil, paraffin, lanolin, white beeswax, and ceresin but may contain any number of the following ingredients: petrolatum, mineral wax, glyceryl monostearate, methyl and propyl parabens, extract of lanolin, sterols, hydrogenated fatty oils, and spermaceti (*see all*).

BABY LOTION.   Protects, soothes, and cleanses the delicate skin of a baby. Usually contains antimicrobials (such as oxyquinoline sulfate), emulsifiers (such as glyceryl monostearate), humectants (such as propylene glycol, glycerin, and sorbitol) to retain moisture, thickeners (such as sodium alginate), and often some perfume (*see all*). The product also may contain lanolin, mineral oil, cetyl alcohol, preservatives, and antioxidants (*see all*). Few problems are reported by consumers as far as baby lotions are concerned, except for an occasional rash. However, FDA inspectors have found bacterial contamination in lotions.

BABY OIL. Protects and soothes baby skin. Usually contains mineral oil, palmitate, lanolin (*see all*), vegetable oils, and such lanolin derivatives as lantrol, lanogene, lanosel, medulan, and isopropylan (see Lanolin Alcohols). Mineral oil or vegetable oil according to pediatricians will do the same.

BABY POWDER. Soothes, dries, and protects baby skin from irritation. Usually contains talc, kaolin, zinc oxide, starch, magnesium carbonate (*see all*), perfume oil, and—although there has been repeated warnings by physicians against it—boric acid (*see*).

BABY SOAP. Usually a mild sodium soap of coconut and/or palm oil. Some are made of polyunsaturated vegetable oils. Baby soaps may contain colloidal oatmeal, a mild soap-free sudsing agent (see Amphoteric), hypoallergenic lanolin, and a germ killer such as chlorbutanol.

BAK. See Benzalkonium Chloride.

BALM MINT. *Balm of Gilead.* The secretion of any of several small evergreen African or Asian trees with leaves that yield a strong aromatic odor when bruised. Known in ancient Palestine as a soothing medication for the skin. Used in cosmetics as an unguent, which soothes and heals the skin. It is also used for its fragrance in perfumes. No known toxicity.

BALSAM MECCA. *Balm of Gilead. Balsam of Gilead.* See Balm Mint. Obtained from a twig. Insoluble in water, soluble in alcohol. Used to scent perfume. See Balsam Peru for toxicity.

BALSAM PERU. A dark brown viscous liquid with a pleasant lingering odor and a warm bitter taste (generally recognized as safe for use in a number of flavorings) for use in face masks, perfumes, cream hair rinses, and astringents. Obtained from Peruvian balsam in Central America near the Pacific Coast. Mildly antiseptic and irritating to the skin and may cause contact dermatitis and a stuffy nose. Nontoxic when ingested.

BALSAM TOLU. An ingredient used in perfumery and soap. Extracted from a tree grown on elevated plains and mountains in South America. Yellowish brown or brown thick fluid with a strong odor and taste. Its vapor has been used as an expectorant. See Balsam Peru for toxicity.

BANANA. The common fruit, high in potassium (*see*), used for dry skin by organic cosmetic enthusiasts. A banana face mask formula: mash one ripe banana and mix thoroughly with 1 tablespoon of almond meal (*see*) plus 2 tablespoons of yogurt. Spread mixture on face and neck. Leave on for 5 to 10 minutes. Remove with lukewarm water. Nontoxic.

BARIUM HYDROXIDE. See Barium Sulfate.

BARIUM SULFATE. Blanc Fixe. The salt of the alkaline earth metal, it is a fine, white, odorless, tasteless powder used as a white coloring and as a base for depilatories and other cosmetics. Barium hydroxide is also used in a similar manner. The barium products are poisonous when ingested and frequently cause skin reactions when applied.

BARIUM SULFIDE. Used in depilatories as a base, it is a grayish white to pale yellow powder. A skin irritant, it causes rashes and chemical burns. Should never be applied on broken or inflammed skin.

BARLEY FLOUR. A cereal grass cultivated since prehistoric times. Used in the manufacture of malt beverages, as a breakfast food, and as a demulcent (*see*) in cosmetics. No known toxicity.

BARRIER AGENT. A protective for hand creams and lotions, which acts as a barrier against irritating chemicals, including water and detergents. The water-repellent types deposit a film that acts as a barrier to water and water-soluble agents that irritate the skin; oil-repellent types act as barriers against oil and oil-soluble irritants. Silicones (*see*) are widely used as barrier agents. Other skin protective ingredients in barrier agents include petrolatum, paraffin, ozokerite vegetables, beeswax, casein, various celluloses, alginic acid, zein, gum tragacanth, pectin, quince seed, bentonite, zinc oxide, zinc stearate, sodium silicate, talc, stearic acid, and titanium dioxide (*see all*). Covering one's hands with Vaseline or zinc oxide ointment will protect them well and inexpensively.

BASE COAT. Similar to a nail polish (*see*) in form and formulation but does not contain pigment and has an increased amount of resin (*see*). Applied on the nail under nail polish to help prevent chipping and to allow smoother application of the nail enamel. See nail enamel for toxicity.

BASIC DYE. A group of dyes made from soluble salts, mineral acids, and certain organic acids that form insoluble compounds with acidic fibers. They produce very bright colors but lack good fastness. See Aniline Dyes for toxicity.

BASIC BROWN 1. Bismarck Brown Y. Made from nitrous acid,

it is a blackish brown powder that turns yellow and orange in solution. See Aniline Dyes for toxicity.

BASIC BROWN 4. Basic Brown R. Bismarck Brown 53.   Prepared from toluene-2-4-diamine (*see*) with nitrous acid, it is a dark, solid brown, which turns reddish brown or violet in solution. Used in hair dyes. See Aniline Dyes for toxicity.

BASIC ORANGE 1. Chrysoidine R.   A monoazo dye that has a yellow, crystalline base and is made from aniline and meta-phenylenediamine (*see*). See Aniline Dyes for toxicity.

BASIC ORANGE 2. CI Solvent Orange 3. Chrysoidine Hydrochloride. 4-Phenyl azo-m-phenylene diamine hydrochloride.   A reddish brown, crystalline powder that turns yellow in solution. Used in dying silk, cotton, and hair. See Aniline Dyes for toxicity.

BASIC VIOLET 1. Methyl Violet.   A bright violet artificial coloring agent. See Aniline Dyes for toxicity.

BATH LOTION.   For after a bath. Usually a cologne with some emollient oil (*see*). May also contain isopropyl myristate and fatty acids (*see both*). The emollient oil also acts as a carrier for the perfume. Toxic when swallowed. May cause allergic reactions, depending upon ingredients used.

BATH OIL.   Softens and protects the skin, either in a foaming or nonfoaming oil. The concentration of perfume in bath oil is usually relatively high (about 10 percent), and the oil (from 30 to 80 percent) usually is a mineral or vegetable oil and includes a surfactant (lauryl sulfate) to cause the oil to spread on the surface of the water and to emulsify it into small particles. The oil clings to the body as the bather emerges from the water and is supposed to produce a soothing skin effect. The emulsifying oils, because they are distributed throughout the water, are believed by some manfacturers to cover the bather better while sitting in the bathtub. A common ingredient of the foaming-type oil is TEA-lauryl sulfate, and sometimes a foam stabilizer, such as saponin or methyl cellulose, is used to give the bubbles longevity; also the usual chemicals that are added are castor oil, isopropyl myristate, alcohol, lanolin (*see all*), and certified colors. Bath oils have a medium toxicity when ingested. Recent complaints to the FDA reveal an orange staining of the skin, rashes from eye irritation, and burns and eye injuries resulting in blurred vision.

BATH POWDER.   Talcum bath powder usually consists of perfumed talc to which small amounts of other powders (boric, starch, and zinc oxide) may have been added. Dusting powder usually contains mostly powdered talc. Among other materials added to bath powders may be magnesium carbonate, lanolin, titanium dioxide, zinc stearate, precipitated calcium carbonate, and colorings (iron oxides for pink, ocher for tan). The hypoallergenic talcum powder contains talc, kaolin, magnesium stearate, and titanium dioxide. But the standard product may contain methylbenzethonium chloride, magnesium stearate, and talc (*see all*). A basic formula for bath powder is: magnesium carbonate, 5 percent; talc, 60 percent; titanium dioxide, 2 percent; zinc stearate, 10 percent; zinc oxide, 12 percent; chalk (heavy), 10 percent; perfume, color, and extender, 1 percent. Bath powder is not commonly involved in bad reactions but recent FDA files show complaints about rashes and swollen feet. See Talc for toxicity.

BATH SALTS.   Used to color, perfume, and chemically soften bath water, and to perfume the skin. Usually made from rock salt or sodium thiosulfate, which has been sprayed with alcohol, dye, or perfume. Rock salt is common table salt and has been used for treating inflammation of the skin. Sodium thiosulfate ("hypo") has been used to treat certain skin rashes and has a low toxicity. The effervescent-type bath salts are due to the added sodium bicarbonate and tartaric acid. The noneffervescent type may add trisodium phosphate and sodium chloride. Among other chemicals that may be in bath salt are borax, sodium hexametaphosphate, starch, sodium carbonate, and sodium sesquicarbonate (*see all*). Phosphate and borax may cause caustic irritation of the skin and mucous membranes; boric acid may cause poisoning when ingested or absorbed through the skin.

BAY OIL. Oil of Myrcia.   Astringent and antiseptic oil used in hair lotions and dressings, after-shave lotions, Bay Rum, and perfumes. Distilled from the leaves of the bayberry, it contains 40 to 55 percent eugenol (*see*). May cause allergic reactions and skin irritations.

BAY RUM.   The alcoholic, aromatic oil distilled from the leaves of the bayberry and mixed with rum or made by mixing oil from the leaves with alcohol, water, and other oils. Widely used as an after-shave preparation and skin freshener. The basic formula for Bay Rum: bay oil, 0.20 percent; pimenta oil, 0.05 percent; ethyl alcohol, 50 percent; Jamaica rum, 10 percent; water, 39.75 percent; and caramel coloring. Can cause allergic reactions. See Eugenol for toxicity.

BAYBERRY WAX.   Acrid and astringent resin from the dried root bark of the shrub that grows from Maryland to Florida and from Texas to Arkansas. It is used as an astringent in soaps and hair tonics. Formerly used to treat skin ulcers. May be irritating to the skin and cause an allergic reaction.

BEAUTY MASKS. See Face Masks and Packs.

BEER. Used to rinse hair on the theory that it gives a feeling of increased body and manageability. The sugar and protein in the beer are probably responsible for the stiffening effect but, according to the American Medical Association, champagne would have the same effect. Beer leaves an odor on the hair that, unlike champagne, may, after a while, become quite unpleasant. Nontoxic.

BEESWAX. From virgin bees and primarily used as an emulsifier. Practically insoluble in water. Yellow beeswax from the honeycomb is yellowish, soft to brittle, and has a honeylike odor. White beeswax is yellowish white and slightly different in taste but otherwise has the same properties as yellow beeswax. Used in many cosmetics including baby creams, brilliantine hairdressings, cold cream, emollient creams, wax depilatories, eye creams, eye shadow, foundation creams and makeup, lipstick, mascara, nail whiteners, protective creams, and paste rouge. Nontoxic.

BEETROOT JUICE POWDER. The powdered stem base of the beet used for its reddish color in powders and rouges. No known toxicity.

BEHENAMIDOPROPYL DIMETHYLAMINE. See Quaternary Ammonium Compounds.

BEHENIC ACID. Docosanoic Acid. Colorless water, soluble, constituent of seed fats, animal fats, and marine animal oils. It is a fatty acid (*see*) used to opacify shampoos. No known toxicity.

BEHENTRIMONIUM CHLORIDE. See Quaternary Ammonium Compounds.

BENTONITE. A white clay found in the Midwest United States and in Canada. Used to thicken lotions, to suspend makeup pigments, emulsify oils, and used in makeup lotions, liquid makeup, and facial masks to absorb oil on the face and reduce shine. Also used as a coloring. Inert and generally nontoxic but if injected in rats it can be fatal.

BENZALDEHYDE. Artificial Almond Oil. A colorless liquid that occurs in the kernels of bitter almonds. Lime is used in its synthetic manufacture. As the artificial essential oil of almonds, it is used in cosmetic creams and lotions, perfumes, soaps, and dyes. May cause allergic reactions. Lethal in rats in large oral doses.

BENZALKONIUM CHLORIDE (BAK). A widely used ammonium detergent (see Ammonium) in hair tonics, eye lotions, mouthwashes, and after-shave lotions. It is a germicide with an aromatic odor and a very bitter taste. Soluble in water and alcohol but incompatible with most detergents and soaps. Used medicinally as a topical antiseptic and detergent. Allergic conjunctivitis has been reported when used in eye lotions. Lethal to frogs in concentrated oral doses.

BENZENE. A solvent obtained from coal and used in nail polish remover. Also used in varnishes, airplane dopes, lacquers, and as a solvent for waxes, resins, and oils. Highly flammable. Poisonous when ingested and irritating to the mucous membranes. Harmful amounts may be absorbed through the skin. Also can cause sensitivity to light in which the skin may break out in a rash or swell. Inhalation of the fumes may be toxic.

BENZOCAINE. *Ethyl Aminobenzoate.* A white crystalline powder slightly soluble in water and a local anesthetic. Used in eyebrow-plucking creams and after-shave lotions. As an anesthetic, it is reportedly low in toxicity. However, there are reports of babies suffering from methemoglobinemia (a lack of oxygen in the blood), due to absorption of benzocaine through the skin. But it is believed that the absorption was enhanced by inflammed skin or rectal fissures. Systemic central nervous system excitation has been reported in adults. However, scientists feel that concentrations in most products have no toxic significance, though there are people who are allergic to benzocaine.

BENZOIC ACID. A preservative and antimicrobial agent that occurs in berries and in almost all vertebrates and is used in mouth-washes, deodorants, protective creams, and after-shave lotions. Soluble in water. A mild irritant to the skin, eyes, and mucous membranes.

BENZOIN. *Tincture.* A reddish brown aromatic balsamic resin from trees grown in China, Sumatra, Thailand, and Cambodia. Used in nail whites, in skin protective creams, and as a preservative in ointments. Also used in freckle and bleaching creams, lipstick, skin fresheners, and as a fixative for perfumery. Tincture of benzoin is omitted from hypoallergenic cosmetics because it can cause allergic reactions.

BENZOPHENONE (1–12). A fixative (*see*) for heavy perfumes (geranium, for example) and soaps (the smell of "new mown hay"). Obtained as a white flaky solid with a delicate, persistent roselike odor, and soluble in most fixed oils and in mineral oil. Also used in the manufacture of pesticides, antihistamines, and hypnotics. Toxic if injected.

BENZOXYQUINE. *Benzoxiquine. 8-Hydroxyquinoline Benzoate.* A water-soluble salt of benzoic acid. Used as an antiseptic. Also used medicinally in the treatment of dysentery. Toxic when ingested. No known skin toxicity.

BENZYL ACETATE. A colorless liquid with a pear or flowerlike odor obtained from a number of plants, especially jasmine, for use in perfumery and soap. Can be irritating to the skin, eyes, and respiratory tract. Ingestion causes intestinal upset, including vomiting and diarrhea.

BENZYL ALCOHOL. A solvent in perfumes derived as a pure alcohol and a constituent of jasmine, hyacinth, and other plants. It has a faint sweet odor. Irritating and corrosive to the skin and mucous membranes. Ingestion of large doses causes intestinal upsets.

BENZYL BENZOATE. Plasticizer in nail polishes, solvent and fixative for perfumes. Occurs naturally in balsams Tolu and Peru and in various flower oils. Colorless, oily liquid or white crystals with a light floral scent and sharp burning taste. No known toxicity.

BENZYL CINNAMATE. Sweet Odor of Balsam. Colorless prisms, used to give artificial fruit scents to perfumes. See Balsam Peru for toxicity.

BENZYL FORMATE. A synthetic flavoring agent used for its pleasant fruit odor in perfumery. Practically insoluble in water. There is no specific data for toxicity but it is believed to be narcotic in high concentrations.

BENZYL SALICYLATE. Salicylic Acid. A fixative in perfumes and solvent in sunscreen lotions. It is a thick liquid with a light pleasant odor, and is mixed with alcohol or ether. May cause skin to break out with a rash and swell when exposed to sunlight. See Salicylates.

BENZYL TRIMETHYL AMMONIUM HYDROLYZED ANIMAL PROTEIN. See Protein and Ammonium Hydroxide.

BENZYLPARABEN. See Propylparaben.

BERBERINE HYDROCHLORIDE. Mild antiseptic and decongestant in eye lotions. Derived as yellow crystals from various plants. Relatively inactive physiologically, but ingestion of large quantities may cause fatal poisoning. Used as a dressing for skin ulcers.

BERBERIS. Holly-leaved Barberry. Oregon Graperoot. Mountain Grape. The dried roots of shrubs grown in the United States and British Columbia is used medicinally to soothe skin ulcers and to break up intestinal gas. Used in creams as a mild antiseptic and decongestant. See Berberine Hydrochloride for toxicity.

BERGAMOT, RED. Oswego Tea. An orange with a pear-shaped fruit, whose rind yields a greenish brown oil much used in perfumery and brilliantine hairdressings. It can cause brown skin stains (berloque) when exposed to sunlight and is considered a prime photo-sensitizer (sensitivity to light). See Berloque Dermatitis.

BERLOQUE DERMATITIS. Some perfumes, which contain oil of bergamot (*see*) and other photosensitizers, may produce increased pigmentation (brown spots) in the area where the perfume has been applied, especially when it is immediately exposed to sunlight. There is no effective treatment and the pigmentation generally persists for some time. The American Medical Association recommends that further use of the perfume and exposure of the pigmented area to sunlight be avoided.

BETAINE. Occurs in common beets and in many vegetables as well as animal substances. Used in resins. Has been employed to treat muscle weakness medically. No known toxicity.

BETA-NAPHTHOL. Used in hair dyes, skin-peeling preparations, and hair tonics. Prepared from naphthalene, which comes from coal tar. Also used in perfumes. Oral ingestion may cause kidney damage, eye injury, vomiting, diarrhea, convulsions, anemia, and death. Fatal poisoning from external applications have been reported. Local application may produce peeling of the skin, which may be followed by pigmentation, also contact dermatitis. See Naphthas.

BETULA. Obtained from the European white birch and a source of asphalt and tar. Used in hair tonics; it reddens the scalp and creates a warm feeling due to an increased flow of blood to the area. Also used in moisturizing creams and astringents. Betula leaves were formerly used to treat rheumatism. See Methyl Salicylate for toxicity.

BHA. See Butylated Hydroxyanisole.

BHT. See Butylated Hydroxytoluene.

BICHLORIDE OF MERCURY. See Mercury Compounds.

BINDER. A substance such as gum arabic, gum tragacanth, glycerin, and sorbitol (*see all*), which dispense, swell, or absorb water, increase consistency, and hold ingredients together. For example, binders are used to make powders in compacts retain their shape; binders in toothpaste provide for the smooth dispensing of the paste.

BIOFLAVONOIDS. *Vitamin P Complex.* Citrus-flavored compounds needed to maintain healthy blood vessel walls. Widely distributed among plants, especially citrus fruits and rose hips. Usually taken from orange and lemon rinds and used as a reducing (*see*) agent. No known toxicity.

BIOTIN. *Vitamin H. Vitamin B Factor.* A whitish crystalline powder used as a texturizer in cosmetic creams. Present in minute amounts in every living cell and in larger amounts in yeast and milk.

Vital to growth. It acts as a coenzyme in the formation of certain essential fatlike substances, and plays a part in reactions involving carbon dioxide. It is needed by humans for healthy circulation and red blood cells. Nontoxic.

BIRCH. Used as an astringent in creams and shampoos, it is an ancient remedy. The medicinal properties of the plant tend to vary, depending upon which part of the tree is used. It has been used as a laxative, as an aid for gout, to treat rheumatism and dropsy, and to dissolve kidney stones. It is supposedly good for bathing skin eruptions. The oil is used in food flavorings. See Betula.

BISABOL. *Opopanax.* A myrrh-type gum resin obtained from African trees. No known toxicity.

N,N-BIS(2-HYDROXYETHYL)-p-PHENYLENDIAMINE SULFATE. See p-Phenylenediamine.

BISMUTH COMPOUNDS. *Subgallate, Subnitrate, Oxychloride.* Bismuth is a gray white powder with a bright metallic luster. It occurs in the earth's crust and for many years was used to treat syphilis. Bismuth subgallate, a dark gray, odorless, tasteless form, is used as an antiseptic and in dusting power. Bismuth subnitrate is odorless and tasteless and is used in bleaching and freckle creams and hair dyes. Bismuth oxychloride is "synthetic pearl" and is used in cosmetics to impart a "frost," or "shine." A bismuth subcarbonate is used as a skin protective. Most bismuth compounds used in cosmetics have a low toxicity when ingested but may cause allergic reactions when applied to the skin.

BISMUTH OXYCHLORIDE. See Bismuth Compounds.

BISMUTH TRIOXIDE. See Bismuth Compounds.

BISULFITES. Bisulfite straighteners or curl relaxers are used instead of the thioglycolates (*see*). They produce changes in the chemical bonds in the hair. The effectiveness of the bisulfite relaxers is similar to that from hot combing, but it is more permanent. The result is also equivalent to the caustic alkali straighteners and superior to the thioglycolate method. Less irritating to the scalp and less damaging to the hair than other methods, but should not be used if the scalp or skin is sensitive, scaly, scratched, sore, or tender. Harmful effects frequently result from not following directions. See also Sodium Bisulfite.

BITHIONOL. Used as a germicide in cold creams, emollients, hair tonics, after-shave lotions, and in medicated cosmetics. It is closely related to hexachlorophene, which has been banned by the FDA.

Bithionol has been removed from many products sold in the United States because it causes a sensitivity to light; the skin breaks out with a rash and may swell.

BITTER ALMOND OIL. Almond Oil. Sweet Almond Oil. Expressed Almond Oil. A colorless to pale yellow, bland, nearly odorless, essential, and expressed oil from the ripe seed of the small sweet almond grown in Italy, Spain, and France. It has a strong almond odor and a mild taste. Used in the manufacture of perfumes and as an oil in hair creams, nail whiteners, nail polish removers, eye creams, emollients, soaps, and perfumes. It is distilled to remove the very toxic hydrocyanic acid (prussic acid). Essentially nontoxic without the prussic acid, but many users are allergic to cosmetics with almond oil. It causes stuffy nose and skin rashes.

BITTER ORANGE OIL. The pale yellow volatile oil expressed from the fresh peel of a species of citrus and used in perfumes and flavorings. May cause skin irritation and allergic reactions.

BLACK. Inorganic carbon black and iron oxide used to color face powders. Carbon black from carbon or charcoal. Not subject to certification. Used in coloring candy. See Colors.

BLACK COHOSH. Cimicifuga. Snakeroot. Bugbane. Used in astringents, a perennial herb with a flower that is supposedly distasteful to insects. Grown from Canada to North Carolina and Kansas. It had the reputation for curing snakebites. It is used in ginger ale flavoring. A tonic and antispasmodic. It has no known toxicity.

BLACKBERRY LEAVES. The boiled and strained leaves of the blackberry plant used by organic cosmetic enthusiasts to add to the bath to refresh and soothe the skin. No known toxicity.

BLADDER WRACK EXTRACT. Fucus. Sea Wrack. A common black rockweed used in cosmetics. No known toxicity.

BLANC FIXE. See Barium Sulfate.

BLEACH. See Hair Bleach; Skin Bleach.

BLEMISH COVER. Pimple and undereye covers may be in stick or cream form. Based on oil, wax, and alcohol. Usually contains titanium dioxide (see) and pigments. Applied before makeup for covering marks, dark circles under the eyes, or other minor blemishes.

BLUE COHOSH. Squawroot. Blueberry Root. Papooseroot. A tall herb of eastern North America and Asia, it has three pointed leaves and a small greenish yellow or purple flower. It produces large blueberrylike fruits. The roots were formerly used as an antiseptic.

BLUE NO. 1. See FD & C Blue No. 1.

BLUE VIOLET. *Ultramarine Blue. Ultramarine Violet.* Used in ivory face powders. Originally made from lapis lazuli. See Ultramarine Blue.

BLUSHER. Used to put color on cheeks and on other parts of the face. Powder blushers are similar to pressed powder in composition but include lake colors (*see*). Stick blushers are similar in composition to lipsticks (*see*).

BODY-NOTE. The main and characteristic overall odor of the perfume. It has a much longer life than the Top-Note (*see*) and usually contributes to the Dry-Out (*see*).

BOIS DE ROSE OIL. A fragrance from the chipped wood of the tropical rosewood tree obtained through steam distillation. The volatile oil is colorless, pale yellow, with a light camphor odor. It is also used as a food flavoring. No known toxicity.

BORATES. Widely used as antiseptic agents and preservatives in cosmetics in spite of repeated warnings of medical scientists. Acute poisonings have followed ingestion, injection, enemas, lavage of body cavities, and application of powders and ointments to burned and abraded skin. Affects the central nervous system, the gastrointestinal tract, the kidneys, liver, and skin.

BORAX. *Sodium Borate.* A mild alkali found in the Far West, particularly in Death Valley, California. Used in cold creams, foundation creams, hair color rinses, permanent waves, and shaving creams. It is used as a water softener, as a preservative, and as a texturizer in cream products. Also used to prevent irritation of the skin by the antiperspirant aluminum chloride (*see*). See Boric Acid for toxicity.

BORIC ACID. An antiseptic with bactericidal and fungicidal properties used in baby powders, bath powders, eye creams, liquid powders, mouthwashes, protective creams, after-shave lotions, soaps, and skin fresheners. It is still widely used despite repeated warnings from the American Medical Association of possible toxicity. Severe poisonings have followed both ingestion and topical application to abraded skin.

BORNEOL. Used in perfumery, it has a peppery odor and a burning taste. Occurs naturally in coriander, ginger oil, oil of lime, rosemary, strawberries, thyme, citronella, and nutmeg. Toxicity is similar to camphor (*see*).

BRAZILWOOD. *Redwood. Pernambuco Wood.* Grown in Brazil and used in the manufacture of red lake pigment, which produces warm brown shades in hair colorings. See Colors.

BREATH FRESHENERS. Most breath fresheners contain flavoring, artificial sweeteners, water, and alcohol. They are used in glass or plastic bottles that measure out small amounts, or sprayed from aerosols. However, the propellants in the aerosols may be toxic when used in excess. The spray is really propelled mouthwash.

BRILLIANTINES.   Hairdressings that impart a shine to the hair. Cream brilliantines are usually made of mineral oil (25 percent), beeswax, triethanolamine stearate, and water (65 percent). Liquid brilliantine is composed of mineral oil (75 percent) and isopropyl myristate. Solid brilliantines are made of mineral oil, petrolatum, and paraffin. So-called two-layer dressings contain mineral oil, alcohol, and water. They also may contain antiseptics such as hexachlorophene (banned by the FDA), cetyl alcohol, cholesterol, gums such as tragacanth, lanolin, oil of bergamot, and other essential oils, olive oil, synthetic oils, synthetic thickeners, and tars. Toxicity depends upon individual ingredients.

BROMATES.   A salt of bromic acid, used in permanent wave neutralizers. Bromates are used as maturing agents and conditioners in bread. Severe poisoning has followed ingestion and topical applications to abraded skin.

BROMO ACID.   See D & C Red No. 21.

2-BROMO-2-NITROPROPANE-1,3-DIOL.   Bronopol®.   Solvent used for nail polishes, fats, oils, and dyes. Also used as an intermediate (*see*) in the manufacture of cosmetics and as a propellant. Mildly irritating to the mucous membranes but not to the skin. However, persons exposed to the vapor at work report loss of appetite, nausea, vomiting, diarrhea, and headache. It is also reported to cause a lack of oxygen in the blood and kidney damage.

BRONZE POWDER.   Any metal such as a copper alloy or aluminum in fine flakes, and used as a pigment to give the appearance of a metallic surface. Used in hair coloring to give a shine and as a "frost," or "pearl," in other cosmetics. No known toxicity.

BRUCINE SULFATE.   Salt of the poison taken from the seeds of the strychnos shrub. It has a very bitter taste and is used primarily for denaturing alcohols and oils used in cosmetics, and has been patented. As poisonous as strychnine when ingested. On the skin toxicity is unknown.

BRUSHLESS LATHER.   See Shaving Creams.

BRUSHLESS SHAVING CREAM.   Not a soap like lather shaving cream, but a vanishing or cold cream with additional lubricants added. Because lather creams soften the beard and brushless creams do not, one has to wet the face first to effect some softening. Brushless creams usually contain 10 to 20 percent stearic acid (*see*), 3 to 13 percent mineral oil, .5 to 2 percent base, up to 5 percent lanolin, up to 0.5 percent gums and thickeners, 6 to 75 percent water, and .2 percent preservative. Nontoxic.

BUBBLE BATH.   Foams, perfumes, and softens bath water and generally makes bathing something of a special event. Liquid bubble bath may contain TEA-dodecylbenzene sulfonate, fatty acid alkanolamides, perfume, water, and methylparaben. Powdered bubble bath may contain sodium lauryl sulfate, sodium chloride, and perfume. The products may also contain any of the following: alcohol, alkyl benzene sulfonate, various colorings, dioctyl sodium sulfosuccinate, propylene glycol, sodium hexametaphosphate, sodium sulfate, and sodium tripolyphosphate. (See all ingredients above under separate listings.) Ingestion of bubble baths may cause gastrointestinal disturbances and skin irritations have been reported, especially in children. Recent reports to the FDA concern skin irritation, urinary and bladder infections, toxic encephalopathy with brain damage, stomach distress, irritation and bleeding of the genital area, inflammation of the genitals, and eye injury.

BUCKTHORN. Frangula.   A shrub or tree grown on the Mediterranean Coast of Africa, it has thorny branches and often contains a purgative in the bark or sap. Its fruits are used as a source of yellow and green dyes. No known toxicity.

BUFFER.   Usually a solution with a relatively constant acidity-alkalinity ratio, which is unaffected by the addition of comparatively large amounts of acid or alkali. A typical buffer solution would be hydrochloric acid and sodium hydroxide (*see*).

BUTANE.   A flammable, easily liquefiable gas derived from petroleum. Used as a propellant or aerosol in cosmetics. The principal hazard is that of fire and explosion, but it may be narcotic in high doses and cause asphyxiation.

BUTCHER'S-BROOM.   A shrub native to Europe, with stiff prickle-tipped, flattened stems resembling true leaves, for use in cosmetics. Formerly used as a broom by butchers. No known toxicity.

BUTOXYDIGLYCOL.   See Glycols.

BUTOXYETHANOL. Butyl Cellosolve®.   A solvent for nitrocellulose (*see*), resins, grease, oil, and albumin. See polyethylene Glycol for toxicity.

BUTTER.   In cosmetology, substances that are solid at room temperature but that melt at body temperature are called "butters." Cocoa butter is one of the most frequently used in both foods and cosmetics. Newer butters are made from natural fats by hydrogenation (*see*), which increases the butter's melting point or alters its plasticity. Butters may be used in stick or molded cosmetics such as lipsticks or to give the proper texture to a variety of finished products. Nontoxic.

BUTTERMILK.   The fluid remaining after butter has been formed from churned cream. It can also be made from sweet milk by the addition of certain organic cultures. Used as an astringent right from the bottle. Apply liberally and let dry about 10 minutes. Rinse off with cool water.

BUTYL ACETATE. Acetic Acid. Butyl Ester.   A colorless liquid with a fruity odor used in perfumery, nail polish, and nail polish remover. Also used in the manufacture of lacquer, artificial leather, plastics, and safety glass. It is an irritant and may cause conjunctivitis, is narcotic in high concentrations, and toxic to man when inhaled at 200 ppm.

BUTYL ACETYL RICINOLEATE.   See Ricinoleate.

BUTYL ALCOHOL.   A colorless liquid, with an unpleasant odor, used as a clarifying agent (*see*) in shampoos; also a solvent for waxes, fats, resins, and shellac. It may cause irritation of the mucous membranes, headache, dizziness, and drowsiness when ingested. Inhalation of as little as 25 ppm causes pulmonary problems in man. It can also cause contact dermatitis when applied to the skin.

t-BUTYL ALCOHOL.   See Butyl Alcohol.

BUTYL ESTER OF ETHYLENE/MALEIC ANHYDRIDE CO-POLYMER.   A resin (*see*) made from ethylene and maleic anhydride (*see*). Used in hair sprays, setting lotions, and as a thickener in cosmetics. No known toxicity.

BUTYL ESTER OF PVM/MA COPOLYMER. Butyl Ester of Poly (Methyl Vinyl Ether, Maleic Acid). Spirit Gum.   Plastic material. Formed from vinyl methyl ether and maleic anhydride. Used in hair sprays, setting lotions, and as a thickener. No known toxicity.

BUTYL GLYCOLATE.   A plasticizer in nail lacquers. See Butyl Acetate.

BUTYL MYRISTATE.   A fatty alcohol used in nail polishes and nail polish removers, lipsticks, and face and protective creams. It is derived from myristic acid (*see*) and butyl alcohol (*see*). More irritating than ethanol (*see*), but less so than some other alcohols.

BUTYL PALMITATE.   Used in shampoos to leave a gloss on the hair. See Palmitic Acid.

BUTYL PHTHALYL BUTYL GLYCOLATE.   See Butyl Glycolate.

BUTYL STEARATE. Stearic Acid. Butyl Ester. Used in nail polish, lipsticks, bath oils, and protective creams. Slightly soluble in water. See Stearic Acid.

BUTYLATED HYDROXYANISOLE (BHA). A preservative and antioxidant in cosmetics, foods, and beverages. White to slightly yellow waxy solid with a faint characteristic odor. Insoluble in water. Can cause allergic reactions.

BUTYLATED HYDROXYTOLUENE (BHT). A preservative and antioxidant in cosmetics, foods, and beverages. A white crystalline solid with a faint characteristic odor. Prohibited as a food additive in England. Chemically similar to BHA and can cause allergic reactions.

BUTYLATED UREA-FORMALDEHYDE RESIN. A resin made from urea (*see*) and formaldehyde (*see*).

BUTYLENE GLYCOL. Butanediol. A hygroscopic liquid used chiefly as a humectant and plasticizer. Made from acetylene formaldehyde and hydrogen. See Polyethylene Glycol for toxicity.

BUTYLPARABEN. p-Hydroxybenzoic Acid n-Butyl Ester. Most widely used preservative in cosmetics. It is a crystal powder that arrests the growth of bacteria and fungi. Also used as a flavoring agent in food. Slightly soluble in water. See p-Hydroxybenzoic Acid.

BUTYRIC ACID. A clear, colorless liquid present in butter at four to five percent. It has a strong, rancid butter odor, and is used in butterscotch, caramel, and fruit flavorings. It is used in chewing gums and margarines, as well as cosmetics. It is found naturally in apples, geraniums, rose oil, grapes, strawberries, and wormseed oil. It has a low toxicity but can be a mild irritant.

BUTYROLACTONE. Butanolide. Liquid lactone used chiefly as a solvent for resins. It is also an intermediate (*see*) in the manufacture of polyvinylpyrrolidone (*see*) and as a solvent for nail polish. Human toxicity is unknown.

C

C10-13 ISOPARAFFIN. Cosmetic liquid. See Paraffin.

C11-13 ISOPARAFFIN. Cosmetic liquid. See Paraffin.

C12-14 ISOPARAFFIN. See Paraffin.

C13-16 ISOPARAFFIN. Cosmetic liquid. See Paraffin.

C12-15 ALCOHOLS. See Alcohol.

CADMIUM CHLORIDE. A white powder, soluble in water, used in photography and in dye, particularly hair dye. Inhalation of the dust is highly toxic and ingestion can cause death.

CAFFEINE. Guaranine. Methyltheobromine. Theine.   An odorless white powder with a bitter taste that occurs naturally in coffee, cola, guarana paste, tea, and kola nuts. Obtained as a by-product of caffeine-free coffee. Its current use in cosmetics has not been identified but it is used as a flavoring in beverages and other foods. It is a central nervous system, heart, and respiratory system stimulant. Can alter blood sugar release and cross the placental barrier.

CAKE MAKEUP.   See Foundation Makeup.

CAKE MASCARA.   Mascara (*see*) based on fats or soap molded forms. It is applied with a brush dipped in water. A more liquid product is used in a cylinder into which a brush is inserted and pulled out, coated with mascara. A typical cake mascara formula: triethanolamine stearate, 54.0 percent; carnauba wax, 25.0 percent; paraffin, 12.5 percent; lanolin, 4.5 percent; carbon black, 3.8 percent; propylparaben, 0.2 percent; other, 1.0 percent. (See ingredients above under separate listings.) See Mascara for toxicity.

CALAMINE.   Zinc oxide with about 5 percent ferric oxide that occurs as a pink powder. Used in protective creams, astringents, lotions, ointments, washes, and powders in the treatment of skin diseases; also to impart a flesh color. Some calamine formulations contain significant amounts of phenol (*see*), and ingestion or repeated applications over large areas of skin may cause phenol poisoning.

CALCIUM ACETATE. Brown Acetate of Lime.   A white amorphous powder that has been used medicinally as a source of calcium. Used cosmetically for solidifying fragrances and as an emulsifier and firming agent. Also used in the manufacture of acetic acid and acetone (*see both*) and in dyeing, tanning, and curing skins as well as a corrosion inhibitor in metal containers. Low oral toxicity.

CALCIUM ALGINATE.   See Alginates.

CALCIUM BENZOATE.   See Benzoic Acid.

CALCIUM CARBONATE. Chalk.   Absorbent that removes shine from talc. A tasteless, odorless powder that occurs naturally in limestone, marble, and coral. Used as a white coloring in cosmetics and food, an alkali to reduce acidity, a neutralizer and firming agent, and a carrier for bleaches. Also used in dentifrices as a tooth polisher, in deodorants as a filler, in depilatories as a filler, and in face powder as a buffer. A gastric antacid and antidiarrhea medicine, it may cause constipation. No known toxicity.

CALCIUM CARRAGEENAN.   See Carrageenan.

CALCIUM CHLORIDE. The chloride salt of calcium. Used in its anhydrous *(see)* form as a drying agent for organic liquids and gases. An emulsifier and texturizer in cosmetics and an antiseptic in eye lotions. Also used in fire extinguishers, to preserve wood, and to melt ice and snow. Employed medicinally as a diuretic and a urinary acidifier. Ingestion can cause stomach and heart disturbances. No known toxicity as a cosmetic.

CALCIUM HYDROXIDE. Limewater. Lye. Used in cream depilatories; also in mortar, plaster, cement, pesticides, fireproofing, as an egg preservative, and as a depilatory. Employed as a topical astringent and alkali in solutions or lotions. Accidental ingestion can cause burns of the throat and esophagus; also death from shock and asphyxia due to swelling of the glottis and infection. Calcium hydroxide also can cause burns of the skin and eyes.

CALCIUM LIGNOSULFONATE. See Lignoceric Acid.

CALCIUM OXIDE. Lime. Quicklime. White or gray crystals or powder commercially obtained from limestone. Used as an alkali in cosmetics, as an insecticide and fungicide, and for dehairing hides. A strong caustic that may cause severe irritation of the skin and mucous membranes and can cause both thermal and chemical burns.

CALCIUM PANTOTHENATE. Pantothenic Acid Calcium Salt. Vitamin B5. The calcium salt of pantothenic acid, found in liver, rice, bran, and molasses, and essential for metabolism of carbohydrates, fats, and other important substances. Sweetish taste with a slightly bitter aftertaste, soluble in water, it is a member of the B-complex family of vitamins. It is also found in large amounts in the jelly of the Queen Bee, the so-called royal jelly of cosmetic advertising fame. It is used as an emollient and to enrich creams and lotions. No known toxicity.

CALCIUM PHOSPHATE. White odorless powder used as an anticaking agent in cosmetics and foods. Employed in toothpaste and tooth powder as an abrasive. Practically insoluble in water. No known toxicity.

CALCIUM PYROPHOSPHATE. A fine white, odorless, tasteless powder used as a nutrient, an abrasive in dentifrices, a buffer, and a neutralizing agent in foodstuffs. No known toxicity.

CALCIUM SACCHARIN. See Saccharin.

CALCIUM SILICATE. Okenite. An anticaking agent, white or slightly cream-colored, free-flowing powder used in face powders because it has extremely fine particles and good water absorption. Also used as a coloring agent. Up to 5 percent in baking powder and

2 percent in table salts. Constituent of lime glass and cement; used in road construction. Practically nontoxic orally, except that inhalation may cause irritation of the respiratory tract.

CALCIUM STEARATE. Prepared from limewater (*see*), it is an emulsifier used in hair-grooming products. Also used as a coloring agent, in waterproofing, and in paints and printing ink. Nontoxic.

CALCIUM STEARYL LACTYLATE. Lanegin. Stearic Acid, Ester with Lactate of Lactic Acid. Calcium Salt. A free-flowing powder used as a texturizer to improve powder flow and to improve whipping of emulsions. No known toxicity.

CALCIUM SULFATE. Plaster of Paris. A fine, white to slightly yellow, ordorless, tasteless powder used in toothpaste and tooth powders as an abrasive and firming agent. Also used as a coloring agent in cosmetics. Used in creamed cottage cheese as an alkali and employed industrially in cement, wall plaster, and insecticides. Because it absorbs moisture and hardens quickly, its ingestion may result in intestinal obstruction. Mixed with flour, it has been used to kill rodents. Has no known toxicity on the skin.

CALCIUM SULPHIDE. A yellow powder formed by heating gypsum with charcoal at 1000°F. Employed in depilatories. Used in acne preparations. Also used as a food preservative and in luminous paints. It can cause allergic reactions.

CALCIUM THIOGLYCOLATE. Used in cream depilatories and permanent wave lotions. Odorless or with a faint odor. Also used to tan leather. Chronic application has led to thyroid problems in experimental animals. Some people develop skin problems on the hands or scalp with hemorrhaging under the skin.

CALENDULA. Dried flowers of pot marigolds grown in gardens everywhere. Formerly used to soothe inflammation of skin and mucous membranes, now used in "natural" creams, oils, and powders for babies. No known toxicity.

CALOMEL. Mercurous Chloride. A white, odorless, tasteless heavy powder used in bleach and freckle creams. It slowly decays in sunlight into mercuric chloride and metallic mercury. Banned July 1973, when the FDA ordered all mercury cosmetics (except for mercury preservatives in eye products) off the market.

CAMELLIA OIL. A tropical Asiatic evergreen shrub or small tree with reddish or white flowers. Used to scent perfumes. No known toxicity.

CAMOMILE. See Chamomile.

CAMPHOR. Used in emollient creams, hair tonics, eye lotions, preshave lotions, after-shave lotions, and skin fresheners as a preservative and to give a cool feeling to the skin. It occurs naturally in trees at least 50 years old grown in Japan, Formosa, Brazil, and Sumatra, but is usually made synthetically today. Also used in embalming fluid, as a moth repellent, and topically as an antiseptic and anesthetic. Camphor is readily absorbed through the skin. Ingestion may cause symptoms ranging from dizziness to death. Produces sensation of warmth and slight local anesthesia. May cause rashes and allergic reaction.

CANDELILLA WAX. Obtained from candelilla plants for use in lipsticks, solid fragrances, and liquid powders to give them body. Brownish to yellow brown, hard, brittle, easily pulverized, practically insoluble in water, slightly soluble in alcohol. Also used in the manufacture of rubber, phonograph records, in waterproofing and writing inks, and hardens other waxes. No known toxicity.

CANTHARIDES TINCTURE. Spanish Fly. Obtained from blister beetles that thrive in Southern and Central Europe and powdered for use in hair tonics and lotions to stimulate the scalp. A powerful irritant to the skin and causes blistering. If ingested, it can cause severe intestinal upset, kidney damage, and death. Long reputed for its aphrodisiac effect.

CANTHAXANTHIN. A color additive. See Carotene.

CAPRACYL BROWN 2R. See Colors; D & C Brown No. 1.

CAPRAMIDE DEA. See Capric Acid.

CAPRIC ACID. Obtained from a large group of American plants. Solid crystalline mass with a rancid odor used in the manufacture of artificial fruit flavors, in lipsticks, and to scent perfumes. No known toxicity.

CAPRYL BETAINE. See Caprylic Acid and Betaine.

CAPRYLAMINE OXIDE. See Caprylic Acid and Capric Acid.

CAPRYLIC/CAPRIC TRIGLYCERIDE. See Caprylic Acid and Capric Acid.

CAPRYLIC ACID. An oily liquid made by the oxidation of octanol (*see*) for use in perfumery. Occurs naturally as a fatty acid in sweat, fusel oil, in the milk of cows and goats, and in palm and coconut oil. No known toxicity.

CAPSICUM. The dried ripe fruit of the capsicum or African chili plant used in hair tonics to stimulate the scalp. Medicinally to soothe irritated skin and an internal gastric stimulant. May cause skin irritation and allergic reaction.

CAPTAN. A preservative used in cosmetics. It is a fungicide of low toxicity, but in large doses can cause diarrhea and weight loss. No human poisonings are known.

CARAMEL. Used as a coloring in cosmetics and a soothing agent in skin lotions. Burnt sugar with a pleasant, slightly bitter taste. Made by heating sugar or glucose and adding small quantities of alkali or a trace mineral acid during heating. Used in food as a flavoring and coloring. The FDA has given caramel priority for testing its mutagenic, teratogenic, subacute, and reproductive effects as a food additive.

CARAWAY OIL. The colorless to pale yellow volatile oil distilled from the dried ripe fruit and used to perfume soap. A characteristic aroma and taste of caraway. Has been used to treat upset stomachs. May cause allergic reaction and skin irritation.

CARBAMIDE. See Urea.

CARBITOL®. Carbide. Carbon. A solvent for nail lacquers and enamels. Absorbs water from the air and is mixable with acetone, benzene, alcohol, water, and ether. More toxic than polyethylene glycol (*see*).

CARBOMER. Carbopol. Carboxypolymethylene. A white powder, slightly acidic, that reacts with fat particles to form thick stable emulsions of oils in water. Used as a thickening, suspending, dispersing, and emulsifying agent in the cosmetic field. No known toxicity.

CARBON BLACK. Carbon, Amorphous. A coloring in eye shadow, eyebrow pencils, and mascaras; a deodorant in some cosmetics with an off odor; and an emulsifier. Obtained by several processes, including the charring of animal bones, meat, and blood, and from the incomplete combustion of natural gas. Used medicinally as an antidote for many ingested poisons and to treat diarrhea. Carbon black, which was not subject to color certification (see Colors), was finally banned in 1976. Can cause cancer. In fact, the relationship between occupation and cancer was first made with chimney sweeps in England who had constant contact with soot during their work. Eyebrow pencils containing carbon have caused eye irritations and skin rash.

CARBON DIOXIDE. Colorless, odorless, noncombustible gas with a faint acid taste. Used as a pressure-dispensing agent in gassed creams. Also used in the carbonation of beverages and as dry ice for refrigeration in the frozen food industry. Used on stage to produce harmless smoke or fumes. May cause shortness of breath, vomiting, high blood pressure, and disorientation if inhaled in sufficient amounts.

CARBOPOL. See Carbomer.

CARBOWAX®. See Polyethylene Glycol.

CARBOXYMETHYL CELLULOSE. Sodium. A synthetic gum used in bath preparations, beauty masks, dentifrices, hair-grooming aids, hand creams, rouge, shampoos, and shaving creams. As an emulsifier, stabilizer, and foaming agent, it is a barrier agent (*see*) made from cotton by-products, and occurs as a white powder or in granules. Employed as a stabilizer in ice cream, beverages, and other foods; and medicinally as a laxative or antacid. It has been shown to cause cancer in animals when ingested. Its toxicity on the skin is unknown.

CARBOXYMETHYL HYDROXYETHYLCELLULOSE. See Carboxymethyl Cellulose.

CARBOXYPOLYMETHYLENE. See Carbomer.

CARDAMOM OIL. Grains of Paradise. A natural flavoring and aromatic agent from the dried ripe seeds of trees common to India, Ceylon, and Guatemala. Used in perfumes and soaps, in butter, chocolate, and other food flavorings. As a medicine, it breaks up intestinal gas. No known toxicity.

CARMINE. Cochineal. A crimson pigment derived from a Mexican and Central American species of a scaly female insect that feeds on various cacti. The dye is used in cosmetic lakes (*see*), red apple sauce, and other foods. May cause allergic reaction.

CARMINIC ACID. Natural Red No. 4. Used in mascaras, liquid rouge, paste rouge, and red eye shadows. It is the glucosidal coloring matter from a scaly insect (see Carmine). Color is deep red in water and violet to yellow in acids. May cause allergic reactions. See Colors.

CARNATION. The essential oil of the double-flowered variety of clove pink. Pale green solid that does not have the characteristic odor of carnations until diluted. Used in fragrances. No known toxicity.

CARNAUBA WAX. The exudate from the leaves of the Brazilian wax palm tree used as a texturizer in foundation makeups, mascara, cream rouge, lipsticks, liquid powders, depilatories, and deodorant sticks. It comes in a hard greenish to brownish solid and rarely causes allergic reactions.

CAROTENE. Provitamin A. Beta Carotene. Found in all plants and in many animal tissues. It is the chief yellow coloring matter of carrots, butter, and egg yolk. Extracted as red crystals or crystalline powder. It is used as a coloring in cosmetics. Also used in the manufacture of Vitamin A. Too much carotene in the blood can lead to carotenemia, a pale yellow red pigmentation of the skin that may be mistaken for jaundice. It is a benign condition, and withdrawal of carotene from the diet cures it. Nontoxic on the skin.

CARRAGEENAN. Irish Moss. A stabilizer and emulsifier, seaweed-like in odor, derived from Irish moss, used in oils in cosmetics and foods. It is completely soluble in hot water and not coagulated by acids. Used medicinally to soothe the skin. Nontoxic.

CARROT JUICE POWDER. See Carrot Oil.

CARROT OIL. Either of two oils from the seeds of carrots. A light yellow essential oil which has a spicy odor and is used in liqueurs, flavorings, and perfumes. Rich in Vitamin A, it is also used as a coloring. No known toxicity.

CARVONE (d or l). Oil of Caraway. A colorless liquid with a characteristic caraway smell used in perfumery and soaps. Found naturally in caraway seed and dill seed oils. Used medicinally to break up intestinal gas and as a stimulant. No known toxicity.

CASCARA. A natural flavoring derived from the dried bark of a plant grown from northern Idaho to northern California. Cathartic. Used in butter, caramel, and vanilla flavoring. Formerly used to treat skin diseases. Used to soothe skin in lotions and creams. No known toxicity.

CASEIN. The principal protein of cow's milk used in protective cream and as the "protein" in hair preparations to make the hair thicker and more manageable. It is a white water-absorbing powder without noticeable odor and is used to make depilatories less irritating and as a film-former in beauty masks. It is also used as an emulsifier in many cosmetics and in special diet preparations. Nontoxic.

CASSIA OIL. Cloves. Chinese Oil of Cinnamon. Darker, less agreeable, and heavier than true cinnamon. Obtained from a tropical Asian tree and used in perfumes, poultices, and as a laxative. It can cause irritation and allergy such as a stuffy nose.

CASTILE SOAP. A fine, hard, bland soap, usually white or cream-colored, but sometimes green, named for the region of Spain where it was originally made. Made from olive oil and sodium hydroxide (*see*). No known toxicity.

CASTOR. Castoreum. Used in perfumes as a fixative (*see*). A creamy orange brown substance with a strong penetrating odor and bitter taste that consists of the dried perineal glands of the beaver and their secretion. The glands and secretions are taken from the area between the vulva and anus in the female beaver and from the scrotum and anus in the male beaver. Professional trappers use castor to scent bait. No known toxicity.

CASTOR OIL. Palma Christi Oil. Used in bath oils, nail polish removers, solid perfumes, face masks, shaving creams, lipsticks, and many men's hairdressings. Also a plasticizer in nail polish. Obtained from the castor bean. It forms a tough shiny film when dried. More than 50 percent of the lipsticks in the United States use a substantial amount of castor oil. Ingestion of large amounts may cause pelvic congestion and abortion. Soothing to the skin.

CATALYST. A substance that causes or speeds up a chemical reaction but does not itself change.

CATECHOL. Catechin. A modifier in hair colorings used as a drabber. It is a phenol alcohol found in catechu black (*see*).

CATECHU BLACK. A preparation from the heartwood of the acacia catechu used in toilet preparations and for brown and black colorings. Used as an astringent. May cause allergic reaction.

CATIONIC. A group of synthetic compounds employed as emulsifiers, wetting agents, and antiseptics in special hand creams. Their positively charged ions (cations) repel water. Any class of synthetic detergents usually consisting almost entirely of quaternary ammonium compounds (*see*) with carbon and nitrogen. Used also as wetting and emulsifying agents in acid to neutralize solutions or as a germicide or fungicide. Toxicity depends upon ingredients used.

CAUSTIC SODA. See Sodium Hydroxide.

CEDAR. The oil from write, red, or various cedars obtained by distillation from fresh leaves and branches and used in perfumes, soaps, and in sachets for its warm woodsy scent. Often used as a substitute for oil of lavender. There is usually a strong camphor odor that repels insects. Cedar oil can be a photosensitizer, causing skin reactions when the skin is exposed to light.

CEDRO OIL. See Lemon Oil.

CELLULOID®. A nail finish composed essentially of cellulose nitrate and camphor (*see both*) or other plasticizers. Also used for brushes and combs as well as for photographic film and various household products. No known toxicity.

CELLULOSE. Chief constituent of the fiber of plants. Cotton contains about 90 percent. It is the basic material for cellulose gums (*see*). Used as an emulsifier in cosmetic creams. No known toxicity.

CELLULOSE GUMS. Any of several fibrous substances consisting of the chief part of the cell walls of plants. Ethylcellulose is a film-former in lipstick. Methylcellulose (Methocel®) and hydroxyethylcellulose (Cellosize®) are used as emulsifiers in hand creams and lotions. They are resistant to bacterial decomposition and give uniform viscosity to products. No known toxicity.

CELLULOSE NITRATE. Nitrocellulose. Used in nail polish. The fibrous substance constituting the chief part of the cell walls of plants, mixed with nitrates. It is also used to make paper, cotton, linen, and explosives. No known toxicity.

CERESIN. Ceresine®. Earth Wax. Used in protective creams. It is a white or yellow hard, brittle wax made by purifying ozokerite (*see*), found in the Ukraine, Utah, and Texas. It is used as a substitute for beeswax and paraffin (*see both*); also used to wax paper and cloth, as a polish, and in dentistry for taking wax impressions. May cause allergic reaction.

CETALKONIUM CHLORIDE. Derived from ammonium, it is an antibacterial agent used in cosmetics. Soluble in water, alcohol acetone, and ethyl acetate. See Quaternary Ammonium Compounds.

CETAMINE OXIDE. A suds and foam stabilizer that is used in hair and body shampoos and in various types of household detergents. It also has mild conditioning properties, and in some instances it may be used as an emulsifier. See Quaternary Ammonium Compounds for toxicity.

CETEARETH-3. Cetyl/Stearyl Ether. An oily liquid distilled from a combination of cetyl alcohol made from spermaceti (*see*) and stearyl alcohol made from sperm whale oil. The compound is used as an emollient, an emulsifier, an antifoam agent, and a lubricant in cosmetics. Nontoxic.

CETEARETH-4. See Ceteareth-3.

CETEARETH-5. See Ceteareth-3.

CETEARETH-6. See Ceteareth-3.

CETEARETH-8. See Ceteareth-3.

CETEARETH-10. See Ceteareth-3.

CETEARETH-12. See Ceteareth-3.

CETEARETH-15. See Ceteareth-3.

CETEARETH-17. See Ceteareth-3.

CETEARETH-20. See Ceteareth-3.

CETEARETH-27. See Ceteareth-3.

CETEARETH-30. See Ceteareth-3.

CETEARYL ALCOHOL. Cetostearyl Alcohol. Emulsifying wax. A mixture chiefly of the fatty alcohols—cetyl and stearyl (*see both*) —and used primarily in ointments as an emulsifier. No known toxicity.

CETEARYL OCTOATE. See Caprylic Acid.

CETETH-1. See Ceteth-2.

CETETH-2. Polyethylene (2) Cetyl Ether. A compound of derivatives of cetyl, lauryl, stearyl, and oleyl alcohols (*see*) mixed with ethylene oxide, a gas used as a fungicide and a starting material for detergents. Oily liquids or waxy solids. Used as surface-active agents (*see*) in cosmetics. See individual alcohols for toxicity.

CETETH-4. See Ceteth-2.

CETETH-6. See Ceteth-2.

CETETH-10. See Ceteth-2.

CETETH-20. See Ceteth-2.

CETETH-30. See Ceteth-2.

CETRIMONIUM BROMIDE. A cationic (*see*) detergent and antiseptic. Medicinally a topical antiseptic, disinfectant, and cleansing agent in skin-cleaning products and shampoos. Can be fatal if swallowed. Can be irritating to the skin and eyes.

CETRIMONIUM CHLORIDE. See Quaternary Ammonium Compounds.

CETRIMONIUM TOSYLATE. A quaternary ammonium compound (*see*).

CETYL ALCOHOL. An emollient and emulsion stabilizer used in many cosmetic preparations including baby lotion, brilliantine hairdressings, deodorants and antiperspirants, cream depilatories, eyelash creams and oils, foundation creams, hair lacquers, hair strighteners, hand lotions, lipsticks, liquid powders, mascaras, nail polish removers, nail whiteners, cream rouges, and shampoos. Cetyl alcohol is waxy, crystalline, and solid, and found in spermaceti (*see*). It has a low toxicity for both skin and ingestion and is sometimes used as a laxative.

CETYL AMMONIUM. An ammonium compound, germicide, and fungicide used in cuticle softeners, deodorants, and baby creams. Medicinally an antibacterial agent. See Quaternary Ammonium Compounds for toxicity.

CETYL ARACHIDATE. An ester produced by the reaction of cetyl alcohol and arachidic acid. The acid is found in fish oils and vegetables, particularly peanut oil. A fatty compound used as an emulsifier and emollient in cosmetic creams. Nontoxic.

CETYL BETAINE. Occurs in the common beet and many vegetable and animal substances. Colorless deliquescent crystals with a sweet taste. See Quaternary Ammonium Compounds.

CETYL LACTATE. An emollient to improve the feel and texture of cosmetic and pharmaceutical preparations. Produced by the reaction of cetyl alcohol and lactic acid (*see both*). No known toxicity.

CETYL MYRISTATE. Produced by the reaction of Cetyl Alcohol and Myristic Acid (*see both*).

CETYL PALMITATE.   Produced by the reaction of cetyl alcohol and palmitic acid. Used in the manufacture of soaps and lubricants. Nontoxic.

CETYL STEARATE.   See Ceteareth-3.

CETYL STEARYL GLYCOL.   A mixture of cetyl glycol and stearyl glycol, fatty alcohols that are used as emulsifiers and emollients in cosmetic creams. Nontoxic.

CETYLPYRIDINIUM CHLORIDE.   A white powder soluble in water and alcohol. The quaternary salt of pyridine and cetyl chloride. A white powder used as an antiseptic and disinfectant in mouthwashes and topical antiseptics. See Quaternary Ammonium Compounds for toxicity.

CHALK.   Purified calcium carbonate (*see*) used in nail whiteners, powders, and liquid makeup to assist in spreading and to give characteristic smooth feeling. A grayish white amorphous powder usually molded into cones for the cosmetic industry. Used medicinally as a mild astringent and antacid. Nontoxic.

CHAMOMILE. Roman, German, and Hungarian Chamomile. The daisylike white and yellow heads of these flowers provide a coloring agent known as apigenin. The essential oil distilled from the flower heads is pale blue due to its content of azulene (*see*) and is added to shampoos to impart the odor of chamomile. Powdered flowers are used to bring out a bright yellow color to the hair, and such shampoos supposedly brighten light hair. Also used in rinses and skin fresheners. The powdered flowers were popular in ancient times as a tonic and pain reliever. Extracts have been used as a poultice to help bring down external swelling, inflammation, and pain. It reputedly has a healing effect on mucous membranes and on the skin. It is used in cosmetics and ointments to soothe skin irritations. Ingestion of large amounts may cause vomiting, but there is no known skin toxicity.

CHARCOAL BLACK.   A black pigment consisting of a charred substance such as wood charcoal or bone black for use in eye shadow. Nontoxic. See Carbon Black.

CHEILITIS.   Dermatitis of the lip attributed to lipsticks. The symptoms are dryness, chapping, cracked and peeling lips. Sometimes this is accompanied by swelling and blistering. About 95 percent of the symptoms have been found to be caused by the indelible dyes used in most lipsticks. The lips are more susceptible to irritation and allergic problems than other parts of the body due to the absence of the horny or dead layer of skin that protects the rest of the body. Even minute amounts of lipstick can cause gastrointestinal problems such as gastritis, enteritis, and colitis in susceptible women. Many allergic women are able to solve the problem of cheilitis merely by changing brands of lipstick. Others may be able to use hypoallergenic lipsticks (*see*) that do not contain the common sensitizers, lanolin and perfume, plus the staining dye, dibromofluorescein (*see*).

CHELATING AGENT. Any compound, usually that binds and precipitates metals, such as ethylenediamine tetraacetic acid (EDTA), which removes trace metals. See Sequestering Agent.

CHERRY PIT OIL. A natural lipstick flavoring and fragrance extracted from the pits of sweet and sour cherries. Also a cherry flavoring for beverages, ice cream, and condiments. No known toxicity.

CHINA CLAY. See Kaolin.

CHLORACETAMIDE. See Quaternary Ammonium Compounds.

CHLORAL HYDRATE. A bitter, colorless crystalline compound formed by treating chloral (a caustic liquid) with water. Used as a rubefacient (*see*) in hair tonics and dandruff preparations. It penetrates the skin and has a peculiar pungent odor. Used in the manufacture of DDT. By oral administration, it produces sleep. Chloral hydrate can cause gastric disturbances and skin eruptions; it is a skin irritant and when ingested is narcotic. The lethal dose in man is 10 grams.

CHLORAMINE-T. Sodium p-Toluenesulfonchloramide. A preservative and antiseptic used in nail bleaches, dental preparations, and mouthwashes. White crystals, fairly soluble in water, which lose moisture at 100°F. It is a powerful antiseptic and is used for washing wounds. May be irritating to the skin and cause allergic reactions.

CHLORHEXIDINE. A white crystalline powder used as a topical antiseptic and skin sterilizing agent in liquid cosmetics. Strongly alkaline. No known toxicity.

CHLORHEXIDINE DIGLUCONATE. See Chlorhexidine.

CHLOROACETIC ACID. Made by the chlorination of acetic acid (*see*) in the presence of sulfur or iodine. Used in the manufacture of soaps and creams. It is irritating to the skin and mucous membranes and can be toxic and corrosive when swallowed.

CHLOROBUTANOL. A white crystalline alcohol used as a preservative in eye lotions and as an antioxidant in baby oils. It has a camphor odor and taste. Formerly used medicinally as a hypnotic and sedative; today it is employed as an anesthetic and antiseptic. A central nervous system depressant, it is used as a hypnotic drug. No known toxicity for the skin.

p-CHLORO-m-CRESOL. See Cresol.

CHLOROFORM.   Used as a solvent for fats, oils, waxes, resins, and as a cleansing agent. Complaints received by the FDA about blisters and inflammation of the gums caused by toothpaste were found to be due to the amount of chloroform in the product. The manufacturer was asked to reduce the amount of the substance. Large doses may cause low blood pressure, heart stoppage, and death. In April, 1976, the FDA determined that chloroform may cause cancer and asked drug and cosmetic manufacturers who have not already done so to discontinue using it immediately, even before it is officially banned. The National Cancer Institute has made public in June, 1976, the finding that chloroform has been found to cause liver and kidney cancers in test animals.

CHLOROMETHOXYPROPYLMERCURIC ACETATE.   Preservative. See Mecury Compounds.

2-CHLORO-p-PHENYLENEDIAMINE.   See *p*-Phenylenediamine.

CHLOROPHYLL.   The green coloring matter of plants, which plays an essential part in the plant's photosynthesis process. Used in antiperspirants, dentifrices, deodorants, and mouthwashes as a deodorizing agent. It imparts a greenish color to certain fats and oils, notably olive oil and soybean. Can cause a sensitivity to light.

CHLOROPHYLLIN. Copper Derivative.   Used as a deodorant agent in mouthwashes, breath fresheners, and body deodorants. Derived from chlorophyll, the green coloring matter of plants. See Chlorophyll.

CHLOROPHYLLIN COPPER COMPLEX.   See Chlorophyllin.

4-CHLORORESORCINOL.   See Resorcinol.

CHLOROTHYMOL.   A chloro derivative of thymol (*see*) and a powerful germicide used in mouthwashes, hair tonics, and baby oils. It kills staph germs and is used topically as an antibacterial. Can be irritating to the mucous membranes and can possibly be absorbed through the skin.

CHLOROXYLENOL.   See p-Chloro-m-Xylenol.

p-CHLORO-m-XYLENOL.   A white crystalline solid used as an antiseptic, germicide, and fungicide in hair tonics, deodorants, bath salts, and brushless shave creams. Penetrates the skin but has no apparent irritating effects when diluted at 5 percent.

CHOLESTEROL.   A fat-soluble crystalline steroid alcohol (*see*) occurring in all animal fats and oils, nervous tissue, egg yolk, and blood. Used as an emulsifier and lubricant in brilliantine hairdressings, eye creams, shampoos, and other cosmetic products. It is important in metabolism but has been implicated as contributing to hardening of the arteries and subsequently heart attacks. Nontoxic to the skin.

CHONDRUS. See Carrageenan.

CHROMIUM COMPOUNDS. Oxides. Chromium occurs in the earth's crust. Chromic oxide is used for green eye shadow and chromium oxide for greenish mascara. Inhalation of chromium dust can cause irritation and ulceration. Ingestion results in violent gastro-intestinal irritation. Application to the skin may result in allergic reactions.

CHROMIUM HYDROXIDE GREEN. See Chromium Compounds.

CHROMIUM OXIDE GREENS. See Chromium Compounds.

CHYPRE. A nonalcoholic type of perfume containing oils and resins.

CINNAMAL. Cinnamaldehyde. Cinnamic Aldehyde. A synthetic yellowish oily liquid with a strong odor of cinnamon isolated from a wood-rotting fungus. Occurs naturally in cassia bark extract, cinnamon bark, and root oils. Used for its aroma in perfume and for flavoring in mouthwash and toothpaste. Also to scent powder and hair tonic. It is irritating to the skin and mucous membranes, especially if undiluted.

CINNAMIC ACID. Used in suntan lotions and perfumes. Occurs in storax, balsam Peru, cinnamon leaves, and coca leaves. Usually isolated from wood-rooting fungus. It may cause allergic skin rashes.

CINNAMON. Used to flavor toothpaste and mouthwash and to scent hair tonic and powder. Obtained from the dried bark of cultivated trees. See Cinnamal for toxicity. Extracts have been used to break up intestinal gas and to treat diarrhea, but can be irritating to the gastro-intestinal system.

CINNAMON OIL. Oil of Cassia. Chinese Cinnamon. Yellowish to brown volatile oil from the leaves and twigs of cultivated trees. About 80 to 90 percent cinnamal (*see*). It has the characteristic odor and taste of cassia cinnamon and darkens and thickens upon aging or exposure to air. Cinnamon oil is used to scent perfumes and as a flavoring in dentifrices. May cause allergic reactions.

CINNAMYL ALCOHOL. Occurs in storax, balsam Peru, cinnamon leaves, and hyacinth oil. A crystalline alcohol with a strong hyacinth odor used in synthetic perfumes and in deodorants. See Cinnamic Acid for toxicity.

CINOXATE. See Cinnamic Acid.

CITRAL. Used in perfumes, soaps, and colognes for its lemon and verbena scents. Occurs naturally in grapefruit, orange, peach, ginger, grapefruit oil, oil of lemon, and oil of lime. Either isolated from citral oils or made synthetically. A light oily liquid. No known toxicity.

CITRIC ACID.   One of the most widely used acids in the cosmetic industry, it is derived from citrus fruit by fermentation of crude sugars. Employed as a preservative, sequestering agent (*see*), to adjust acid-alkali balance; as a foam inhibitor and plasticizer. It is also used as an astringent alone or in astringent compounds. Among the cosmetic products in which it is frequently found are freckle and nail bleaches, bath preparations, skin fresheners, cleansing creams, depilatories, eye lotions, hair colorings, hair rinses, and hair-waving preparations. The clear, crystalline, water-absorbing chemicals are also used to prevent scurvy, a deficiency disease; and as a refreshing drink with water and sugar added. No known toxicity.

CITRONELLA OIL.   A natural food flavoring extract from fresh grass grown in Ceylon. Used in perfume, toilet water, and perfumed cosmetics; also an insect repellent. Ingestion causes vomiting, shock, and death. May cause allergic reactions such as stuffy nose, hay fever, asthma, and skin rash when used in cosmetics.

CITRONELLOL.   Used in perfumes. It has a roselike odor. Occurs naturally in citronella oil, lemon oil, lemon grass oil, tea, rose oil, and geranium oil. A mild irritant.

CITRUS OILS. Eugenol. Eucalyptol.   Anethole, irone, orris, and menthol (*see all*).

CIVET.   A fixative in perfumery. It is the civet cat's unctuous secretion from between the anus and genitalia of both male and female. Semisolid, yellowish to brown mass, with an unpleasant odor. No known toxicity.

CLARIFYING AGENT.   A substance that removes from liquids small amounts of suspended matter. Butyl alcohol (*see*), for instance, is a clarifying agent for clear shampoos.

CLARY. Clary Sage.   A fixative (*see*) for perfumes. A natural extract of an aromatic herb grown in southern Europe and cultivated widely in England. A well-known spice in food and beverages. No known toxicity.

CLAY PACK.   See Face Masks and Packs.

CLAYS. Bentonite. Veegum®. China Clay.   Used for color in cosmetics, as a clarifying agent (*see*) in liquids, as an emollient, and as a poultice. Nontoxic.

CLEANSING CREAMS AND LOTIONS.   The aim of skin cleansing creams and lotions is to dissolve sebum, loosen particles of grime, and facilitate the removal of dirt. There are three types: cold cream, liquefying, and washing. Cold cream contains water-soluble materials, which evaporate to give a cooling "cold" effect. A typical cold cream usually contains mineral oil, beeswax, borax (*see all*), and water. Liquefying cream is a variation of cold cream. A typical formula contains a mixture of oils such as mineral, petrolatum, and paraffin (*see all*), which melt on contact with warm skin. This oily film is intended especially to dissolve sebum and loosen grime. Liquefying cream usually includes about 10 percent water, along with most of the ingredients of the various cleansing creams. So-called washing creams are a variation of the former. All contain almost the same ingredients, but the other cleansing creams are removed with a facial tissue or soft towel because just rinsing with water will not remove their oil residues. A washing cream, however, can be rinsed off. Cleansing lotions, which serve the same purpose as cleansing creams, usually contain mineral oil, triethanolamine stearate (*see both*), and water. Among other ingredients in cleansing creams and lotions are alcohol, alkanolamines, allantoins, antibacterials, and preservatives (such as hexachlorophene or bithionol), methyl and propyl parabens, fatty alcohols (such as cetyl, stearyl, or oleyl), lanolin, perfume, polyol (such as glycerol or propylene glycol), fatty oils, thickeners, and waxes. A basic formula for cleansing cream includes mineral oil, 65 percent; petrolatum, 12 percent; paraffin, 18 percent; cetyl alcohol, 1 percent; and spermaceti, 4 percent. A widely used cold cream contains water, mineral oil, waxes, borax, synthetic gum, preservative, and perfume. A well-known hypoallergenic cold cream contains liquid petrolatum, spermaceti, borax, and depollenized beeswax. The American Medical Association and dermatologists say that soap and water will serve the same purpose as cleansing creams and lotions at less expense and with less risk of allergy. However, cleansing creams and lotions can be beneficial when used on dry skin because of the oil content they leave behind and because soap may add to the dryness of the skin.

CLOFLUCARBAN. See Aniline Dyes.

CLOVE OIL. Used as an antiseptic and flavoring in tooth powders and as a scent in hair tonics. The pale yellow volatile oil from the dried flower of a tropical tree. It is 82 to 87 percent eugenol (*see*) and has the characteristic clove odor and taste. It darkens and thickens upon exposure to air or upon aging. Can cause allergic reactions. It is used medicinally as a local anesthetic in toothache, and to break up intestinal gas. It is strongly irritating to the skin and its use in perfumes and cosmetics is frowned upon, although in very diluted forms it is innocuous.

COAL TAR. Thick liquid or semisolid tar obtained from bituminous coal and used to make cosmetic colors. Contains numerous constituents such as benzene, xylenes, naphthalene, pyridine, quinoline, phenol, and cresol. Dyes made from coal tar have been found to cause cancer in animals. Colors made from coal tar, therefore, are under government regulations. See Colors.

COBALT CHLORIDE. A metal used in hair dye. Occurs in the earth's crust; gray, hard, and magnetic. Excess administration can produce an overproduction of red blood cells and gastrointestinal upset. See Metallic Hair Dyes.

COBALT NAPHTHENATE.   See Cobalt Chloride.

COCAMIDE (DEA, MEA).   See Coconut Oil.

COCAMIDE MIPA.   See Coconut Oil.

COCAMIDE BETAINE.   See Coconut Oil.

COCAMIDOPROPYL BETAINE.   See Coconut Oil.

COCAMIDOPROPYL DIMETHYLAMINE.   See Coconut Oil.

COCAMIDOPROPYL OXIDE.   See Coconut Oil.

COCAMIDOPROPYL SULTAMINE.   See Coconut Oil.

COCAMIDOPROPYLAMINE OXIDE.   See Coconut Oil.

COCAMINE OXIDE.   See Coconut Oil.

COCAMINOBUTYRIC ACID.   See Coconut Oil and Butyric Acid.

COCAMINOPROPIONIC ACID.   See Coconut Oil.

COCETH-6.   See Coconut Oil.

COCHINEAL.   See Carmine.

COCO SULTAINE.   See Coconut Oil.

COCOA BUTTER. Theobroma Oil. Softens and lubricates the skin. A solid fat expressed from the roasted seeds of the cocoa plant that is used in eyelash creams, lipsticks, nail whiteners, rouge pastes, soaps, and emollient creams as a lubricant and skin softener. Frequently used in massage creams and in suppositories because it softens and melts at body temperature. May cause allergic reactions.

COCO-BETAINE.   See Coconut Oil.

COCOMORPHOLINE OXIDE.   See Coconut Oil.

COCONUT ACIDS.   See Coconut Oil.

COCONUT ALCOHOLS.   See Coconut Oil.

COCONUT OIL. The white, semisolid, highly saturated fat expressed from the kernels of the coconut. Used in the manufacture of baby soaps, shampoos, shaving lathers, preshaving lotions, hairdressings, soaps, ointment bases, and massage creams. Stable when exposed to air. Lathers readily and is a fine skin cleanser. Usually blended with other fats. May be irritating to skin and cause skin rashes.

COCOTRIMONIUM CHLORIDE. Coconut Trimethylammonium Chloride. See Quaternary Ammonium Compounds.

COCOYL SARCOSINE. Formed from caffeine by decomposition with barium hydroxide. Used to make antienzyme agents for toothpastes that help to prevent decay. No known toxicity.

COD-LIVER OIL. The fixed oil expressed from fresh livers used in skin ointments and special skin creams to promote healing. Pale yellow, with a bland slightly fishy odor. Contains Vitamins A and D, which promote healing of wounds and abscesses. No known toxicity.

COLD CREAM. The forerunner of all modern creams, both therapeutic and cosmetic, supposedly developed by the Greek physician Galen. The original formula consisted of a mixture of olive oil, beeswax, water, and rose petals. The product was called cold cream because after it was applied to the skin, the water evaporated and gave a feeling of coolness. The oil and wax, which liquefied on the warm skin, cleansed it by removing particles of dirt, dead skin, and other debris. Cold cream is still used, although the olive oil has been replaced with mineral or other oils that do not so easily become rancid. See Cleansing Creams and Lotions.

COLLAGEN. Protein substance found in connective tissue. In cosmetics it is usually derived from animal tissue and is one of the newer ingredients because chemists have only recently been able to stabilize it sufficiently for use. The collagen fibers in connective tissue of the skin undergo changes from aging and overexposure to the sun that contribute to the appearance of wrinkles and other outward signs of age. Cosmetic manufacturers have heralded it as a new wonder ingredient, but according to medical experts it cannot affect the skin's own collagen. No known toxicity.

COLLODION. A mixture of nitrocellulose, alcohol, and ether. A syrupy liquid, colorless or slightly yellow, clear or slightly opalescent used in cosmetics as a skin protectant. Also used as a corn remover, in the manufacture of lacquers, artificial pearls, and cement. May block perspiration and would be harmful if spread over a large area of skin. May cause allergic reactions.

COLLYRIUM. A commercial preparation for local application to the eye, usually a wash or lotion. No known toxicity.

COLOCYNTH. Bitter Apple. A denaturant used in alcohols for cosmetics. Derived from the dried pulp of a fruit grown in the Mediterranean and Near East regions. It is a supercathartic if ingested and has caused deaths. Has also caused allergic problems in cosmeticians.

COLOGNE. Named originally for the town in Germany in which it was made. It is similar to toilet water (*see*) and is often used synonymously. However, cologne is usually limited to citrus and floral bases. It has a higher alcohol content than perfume, usually is applied more liberally, and leaves a cooling, refreshing feeling on the skin. It is also currently made as a paste or semisolid stick. Cologne can be toxic if ingested but is rarely fatal. Nontoxic on the skin but may cause allergic reaction depending on ingredients.

COLOGNE, SOLID. Solid colognes are used in sticks or in small containers. Such products consist of 80 percent alcohol, about 10 percent sodium stearate, some sorbitol, cologne essence, and water. Gel colognes consist of 60 to 70 percent alcohol, perfume oils, emulsifiers, and about 30 percent water.

COLORS. A color additive is a term used to describe any dye, pigment, or other substance capable of coloring a food, drug, or cosmetic on any part of the body. The word "pigment," however, usually means a colored or white chemical compound that is insoluble in a particular solvent. The word "dye" generally refers to a chemical compound, most often of coal tar origin, which is soluble. Cosmetic manufacturers have unique problems with coloring their products. They must choose a color substance that is not only safe and stable in a product, but one that will psychologically entice the customer into buying the product. For instance, most hand lotions are either white, pink, cream, or blue. Research sponsored by cosmetic companies has shown that women over twenty-five years of age want pink shades while teen-agers prefer blue hand lotions. Many natural colors derived from plants and animals have been in use since humans first started trying to make themselves look better with makeup. Examples of such naturally derived colors are annatto, saffron, chlorophyll, and carotene (*see all*). Inorganic colors used in cosmetics include iron oxides, carbon blacks, ultramarines, chrome oxide greens, and a number of white products such as titanium dioxide, barium sulfate, and zinc oxide (*see all*). However, widely used and under FDA scrutiny are the coal tar colors. In 1900 there were more than 80 dyes in use in cosmetics, foods, and drugs. There were no regulations and the same dye used to color clothes could also be used to color candy or cosmetics. In 1906 the first comprehensive legislation for food colors was passed. There were only seven colors that, when tested, were shown to be composed of known ingredients that demonstrated no harmful effects. A voluntary system of certification for batches of color dyes was set up. In 1938 new legislation was passed, superseding the 1906 act. The colors were given numbers instead of chemical names and every batch had to be certified. The manufacturers must submit to the government samples from every batch of coal tar color. Each sample is analyzed for purity. The lot test number must then accompany the colors through all subsequent packaging. The manufacturer must pay 15¢ a pound and not less than $100 for each batch tested. Each petition for listing of a new color additive must be accompanied by a deposit of $2,600 for cosmetics. To amend a listing asking for a new use of a color, the government requires a check of $1,800. If you want to object or request public hearings on a color, it will cost you $250. What is considered a safe color? According to the FDA: "Safety for external color additives will normally be determined by tests for acute oral toxicity, primary irritation, sensitization, subacute skin toxicity on intact or abraded skin and carcinogenity (cancer causing) by skin application." The FDA commissioner may waive any of such tests if data before him establishes otherwise that such a test is not required to determine safety. Here are the certified colors classified into the following categories according to their chemical ancestry: 1. Nitro Dyes. Containing one atom of nitrogen and two of oxygen, there are only a few certified because they can be absorbed through the skin and are toxic. Ext. D & C Yellow is one. See Nitro.   2. Azo (monoazo). This includes the largest number. They are all characterized by the presence of the azo bond. See Azo Dyes.   3. Triphenylmethane. FD & C Blue No. 1 is the most popular dye of this group and is widely used. See Triphenylmethane Group.   4. Xanthene. This group contains very brilliant, widely used lipstick colors. D & C Orange is one. See Xanthene Group.   5. Quinoline. There are only two certified in this category, D & C Yellow Nos. 10 and 11. They are bright greenish yellows. See Quinoline.   6. Anthraquinone. Widely used in cosmetics because it is not affected by light. Ext. D & C Violet No. 2 is one. See Anthraquinone.   7. Indigo. These dyes have been in use a long time. D & C Blue No. 6 is an example. See Indigo. There are a few other miscellaneous dyes. Today, there are six permanently listed coal tar colors considered safe. Others are used on the "provisional" list, meaning the FDA is awaiting further proof of safety or toxicity. Some have been on the provisional list for more than two decades. When the letters FD & C precede a color, it means the color can be used in a food, drug, or cosmetic. When D & C precedes the color, it signifies that it can only be used in drugs or cosmetics, but not in food. Ext. D & C before a color means that it is certified for external use only in drugs and cosmetics and may not be used on the lips or mucous membranes. No coal tar colors are permitted for use around the eyes. In fact, the FDA does not allow any color additive to be applied around the area of the eye unless specifically approved for that purpose. There is still a great deal of controversy about the use of coal tar colors because almost all have been shown to cause cancer when injected into the skins of mice. Furthermore, many people are allergic to coal tar products.

COLTSFOOT. Wild Ginger. Used for its soothing properties in shampoos and astringents. From an herb used historically to fight colds and asthma, it reputedly opens pores and allows sweating. It has been used also as a soothing ointment. No known toxicity.

CONCRETES. Waxlike substances prepared from natural raw materials, almost exclusively vegetable in origin, such as bark, flower, herb, leaf and root and used in perfumes and stick deodorants. No known toxicity.

CONDITIONERS. See Hair Conditioners.

CONDITIONING CREAMS. See Emollients.

COPAL. A resin obtained as a fossil or as an exudate from various species of tropical plants. Must be heated in alcohol or other solvents. Used in nail enamels. May cause allergic reaction and skin rash.

COPOLYMER. Result of polymerization (*see* polymer), which includes at least two different molecules, each of which is capable of polymerizing alone. Together they form a new, distinct molecule. They are used in the manufacture of nail enamels and face masks.

COPPER, METALLIC POWDER, AND VERSENATE. Used as a coloring agent in cosmetics. One of the earliest known metals. An essential nutrient for all mammals. Naturally occurring or experimentally produced copper deficiency in animals leads to a variety of abnormalities including anemia, skeletal defects, and muscle degeneration. Copper deficiency is extremely rare in man. The body of an adult contains from 75 to 150 mg of copper. Concentrations are highest in the brain, liver, and heart. Copper itself is nontoxic, but soluble copper salts, notably copper sulfate, are highly irritating to the skin and mucous membranes and when ingested cause serious vomiting.

CORIANDER OIL. The volatile oil from the dried ripe fruit of a plant grown in Asia and Europe. Used as a flavoring in dentifrices. Colorless or pale yellow liquid with a taste and odor characteristic of coriander, which is also used as a condiment. Can cause allergic reactions.

CORN ACID. See Corn Oil.

CORN FLOUR. A finely ground powder. Used in face and bath powders. See Corn Oil.

CORN OIL. Used in emollient creams and toothpastes. Obtained as a by-product by wet milling the grain for use in the manufacture of corn starch, dextrins, and yellow oil. It has a faint characteristic odor and taste and thickens upon exposure to air. No known toxicity, but can cause skin reaction in the allergic.

CORN SYRUP. Corn Sugar. Dextrose. Used as a texturizer and carrying agent in cosmetics. Also used for envelopes, stamps, and sticking tapes, aspirin, and many food products. May cause allergic reactions.

CORNCOB MEAL. Powder made from the ear of Indian corn. Used in face and bath powders. See Corn Oil.

CORNMEAL PLUS OATMEAL. Cornmeal, made from white or yellow corn, and oatmeal, from oats, blended by cosmeticians as a skin treatment. The recipe is ½ cup oatmeal and ½ cup cornmeal mixed with hot water to make a paste. It is applied to the face, avoiding the area around the eyes, allowed to dry, massaged off briskly, rinsed with warm water, then with cool water, and the face patted with an astringent such as witch hazel. No known toxicity.

CORNSTARCH. Used in depilatories, dusting powders, face and foot powders, bath preparations, and as a thickener in cosmetics. Also used as a coloring agent. Absorbs water and is soothing to the skin. It can cause allergic reactions such as inflamed eyes, stuffy nose, and perennial hay fever.

COSTUS. A fixative in perfumes. The volatile oil is obtained by steam distillation from the dried roots of an herb. Light yellow to brown viscous liquid, with a persistent violetlike odor. Used also as a food flavoring. No known toxicity.

COTTONSEED ACID. See Cottonseed Oil.

COTTONSEED GLYCERIDE. See Cottonseed Oil.

COTTONSEED OIL. The fixed oil from the seeds of the cultivated varieties of the plant. Pale yellow, oily, odorless liquid used in the manufacture of soaps, creams, baby creams, nail polish removers, and lubricants. Known to cause allergies, but because of its wide use in many cosmetics and food products it is hard to avoid.

COUMARIN. Used in perfumes, soaps, and suntan lotions. It has the odor of new-mown hay and is found in many plants such as the tonka bean and sweet clover. At one time used as a food flavoring, it has been banned by the FDA because it caused liver injury in experimental animals. No known toxicity on the skin.

COUNTERIRRITANT. An agent applied locally to produce superficial inflammation with the object of reducing existing inflammation in deeper adjacent structures. Iodine (*see*) is an example of a counterirritant.

CREAM RINSE. Creme Rinse. Conditioners (*see*) that are poured on the hair after shampooing and then rinsed with water. A typical formula for a cream rinse: lanolin, 10 percent; mineral oil and lanolin esters, 5 percent; cholesterol, 0.25 percent; sorbitan stearate, 3 percent; preservative, 0.15 percent; distilled water, 78.60 percent; and perfume.

CREAMS. See Emollients; Hand Creams and Lotions; Cold Cream; and Hormone Creams and Lotions.

CREOSOTE. Obtained from wood tar, either almost colorless or yellowish. Used locally as an antiseptic, internally as an expectorant. It has a smoky odor and a caustic, burning taste. Large doses internally may cause stomach irritation, heart problems, and death. It is also used as a mild insect repellent.

CRESOL. Used in hair-grooming preparations and in eye lotions. Obtained from coal tar and wood. An antiseptic and disinfectant. Chronic poisoning may occur from oral absorption or through the skin. It also may produce digestive disturbance and nervous disorders, with fainting, dizziness, mental changes, skin eruptions, jaundice, uremia, and lack of urine.

o-CRESOTIC ACID. White to slightly reddish odorless crystals used in the manufacture of dyes. Slightly soluble in cold water, completely soluble in alcohol. See Salicylic Acid for toxicity.

CUCUMBER JUICE. From the succulent fruit of the vine and used as an astringent by many "natural" cosmetic fans. It has a pleasant aroma and imparts a cool feeling to the skin. Nontoxic.

CUMINALDEHYDE. Used to make perfumes. Colorless to yellowish, oily, with a strong lasting odor. It is a constituent of eucalyptus, myrrh, cassia, cumin, and other essential oils, but often is made synthetically for fragrances. No known toxicity.

CUPRIC CHLORIDE. Copper Chloride. A copper salt used in hair dye. A yellow to brown water-absorbing powder that is soluble in diluted acids. It is also used in pigments for glass and ceramics and as a feed additive, disinfectant, and wood preservative. Irritating to the skin and mucous membranes. Irritating when ingested, causing vomiting.

CUPRIC SULFATE. Copper sulfate occurs in nature as hydrocyanite. Grayish white to greenish white crystals. Used as agricultural fungicide, herbicide, and in the preparation of azo dyes (*see*). Used in hair dyes as a coloring. Very irritating if ingested. No known toxicity on the skin and is used medicinally as a skin fungicide.

CUTICLE REMOVERS. Cuticle is the dead skin that covers the base of the nail. It can either be pushed back, cut, or chemically removed. Chemical removers either plasticize or dissolve the cuticle. Alkalies (*see*) are used as cuticle softeners and removers. Lye, for example, is widely used. A typical formula for a cuticle remover is: coconut oil, 10 percent; potassium phosphate, 4 percent; potassium hydroxide, 2 percent; triethanolamine, 8 percent; water, 76 percent. (See ingredients above under separate listings.) In a recent case reported to the FDA, after using a cuticle softener made by a drug company, a woman's fingernails fell off and then her new nails were deformed when they grew in.

CYCLAMATES. Sodium Cyclamate and Calcium Cyclamate. Artificial sweetening agents about 30 times as sweet as refined sugar, removed from the food market on September 1, 1969, because they were found to cause bladder cancer in rats. At the time 175 million Americans were swallowing cyclamates in significant doses in many products ranging from chewing gum to soft drinks. Still permitted by prescription and in certain drugs and cosmetics.

CYCLAMIC ACID. Fairly strong acid with a sweet taste. It is the acid from which artificial sweeteners, cyclamates, were derived. See Cyclamates for toxicity.

CYCLOHEXANEDIAMINE TETRAACETIC ACID. See Acetic Acid.

CYCLOMETHICONE. Volatile Silicone. See Silicones.

CYCLOMETHICONE-4. See Silicones.

CYCLOMETHICONE-5. See Silicones.

O-CYMEN-3-OL. See p-Cymene.

p-CYMENE. Used as a solvent. A synthetic flavoring, a volatile hydrocarbon solvent that occurs naturally in star anise, coriander, cumin, mace oil, oil of mandarin, and origanum oil. Used in fragrances; also in citrus and spice flavorings for beverages, ice cream, candies, and baked goods. Its ingestion pure may cause a burning sensation in the mouth, and nausea, salivation, headache, giddiness, vertigo, confusion, and coma. Contact with the pure liquid may cause blisters of the skin and inflammation of mucous membranes.

CYSTEINE, L-Form.   An essential amino acid (*see*), it is derived from hair and used in hair products and creams. Soluble in water, it is used in bakery products as a nutrient. It has been used to promote wound healing. On the list of FDA additives to be studied.

D

D & C BLUE NO. 1 ALUMINUM LAKE. Brilliant Blue Lake.   Insoluble pigment prepared from FD & C Blue No. 1 (*see*). A coal tar derivative, this brilliant blue is used as a coloring in hair dyes and powders, among other cosmetics; also used in soft drinks, gelatin desserts, and candy. May cause allergic reactions. It will produce malignant tumors at the site of injection in rats. On the FDA permanent list of color additives. Rated 1A for toxicology by the World Health Organization, meaning it is completely acceptable for use in foods and cosmetics. See Colors.

D & C BLUE NO. 2 ALUMINUM LAKE. Acid Blue 74. Indigetine 1A. Indigo Carmine.   An indigoid dye (*see*).

D & C BLUE NO. 4. Acid Blue 9 (Ammonium Salt).   Bright greenish blue. A coal tar, triphenylmethane color used in hair rinses primarily. See Colors.

D & C BLUE NO. 6. Indigo.   An indigoid, it is used in lipstick, rouges, soaps, hair-waving fluids, and bath salts. See Colors.

D & C BROWN NO. 1. Resorcin Brown. Capracyl Brown®. Acid Orange 24.   Light orange brown. A diazo color (see Colors) permitted for use only in preformed hair colors. But the cosmetic industry has petitioned the FDA to allow wider use. Resorcin is irritating to the skin and mucous membranes. Absorption can cause a depletion of oxygen in the body and death. Also used as an antiseptic and fungicide.

D & C GREEN NO. 3 ALUMINUM LAKE. Food Green 3.   A brilliant but not fast dye. See Aniline Dyes for toxicity.

D & C GREEN NO. 5. Acid Green 25.   Dullish blue green. Classed chemically as an anthraquinone color (see Colors). Used in suntan oils, bath salts, shampoos, hair rinses, toothpastes, soaps, and hair-waving fluids. Low skin toxicity but may cause skin irritation and sensitivity.

D & C GREEN NO. 6. Solvent Green 3.   Dull blue green. Classified chemically as an anthraquinone color. Used in hair oils and pomades. See Colors.

D & C GREEN NO. 8. Solvent Green 7.   Yellowish green. Classified chemically as a pyrene color. Used in shampoos. See Colors.

D & C ORANGE NO. 4. Acid Orange 7.   Bright orange. Transparent orange used in lipstick and face powders. Classed chemically as a monoazo color. See Colors.

D & C ORANGE NO. 4 ALUMINUM LAKE. Persian Orange.   Insoluble pigment prepared from D & C Orange No. 4 (*see*). See Colors and Lakes.

D & C ORANGE NO. 5. Acid Orange 11. Solvent Red 72. Dibromofluorescein (see).   Reddish orange. An orange stain used in lipsticks, face powders, and talcums. See Colors.

D & C ORANGE NO. 5 ALUMINUM LAKE. Dawn Orange. Manchu Orange.   Insoluble pigment prepared from D & C Orange No. 5 (*see*). See Colors and Lakes.

D & C ORANGE NO. 5 ZIRCONIUM LAKE. Petite Orange. Dawn Orange. Acid Red 26. Ponceau R.   See Lake and Zirconium. A monoazo dye. See Azo Dyes.

D & C ORANGE NO. 10 ALUMINUM LAKE. Solvent Red 73. Erythrosine G.   A xanthene color (*see*).

D & C ORANGE NO. 10. Solvent Red 73. Diiodofluorescein. Reddish orange. Classed chemically as a fluoran color. Orange red powder used in lipsticks and other cosmetics. See Colors.

D & C ORANGE NO. 11.   Clear red. Classed chemically as a xanthene color. It is the conversion product of D & C Orange No. 10 (*see*) to the sodium or potassium salt. See Colors.

D & C ORANGE NO. 17. Permanent Orange. Pigment Orange 5. Bright orange. Classed chemically as a monoazo color. See Colors.

D & C ORANGE NO. 17 LAKE. Permanent Orange. Solvent Red 23. Sudan III.   A diazo dye (*see*). Insoluble pigment prepared from D & C Orange No. 17 (*see*) and an approved substrate. See Colors and Azo Dyes.

D & C RED NO. 2 ALUMINUM LAKE.   Insoluble pigment prepared from FD & C Red No. 2 (*see*) and an approved substrate. See Colors.

D & C RED NO. 3 ALUMINUM LAKE.   Insoluble pigment prepared from FD & C Red No. 3 (*see*) and aluminum. See Colors.

D & C RED NO. 4 ALUMINUM LAKE. Food Red 1.   A monoazo color. See Azo Dyes.

D & C RED NO. 6. Lithol Rubin B.   Medium red. Classed chemically as a monoazo color. It is the calcium salt of D & C Red No. 7

(*see*). Lithol is a topical antiseptic. Nontoxic. See Colors.

D & C RED NO. 6 ALUMINUM LAKE. Pigment Red 57. Lithol Rubine.   A monoazo color. See Azo Dyes.

D & C RED NO. 6 BARIUM LAKE. Rubine Lake. Pigment Red 57. Lithol Rubine B.   A monoazo dye. An insoluble pigment prepared from D & C Red No. 6 (*see*) and barium. See Colors and Azo Dyes.

D & C RED NO. 7. Lithol Rubin B Ca.   Bluish red. Classed chemically as a monoazo color. Used in nail lacquers and lipsticks. Lithol is a topical antiseptic. Nontoxic. See Colors.

D & C RED NO. 7 ALUMINUM LAKE. Pigment Red 57.   See Azo Dyes.

D & C RED NO. 7 BARIUM LAKE.   Insoluble pigment prepared from D & C Red No. 7 (*see*). See Colors and Lakes.

D & C RED NO. 7 CALCIUM LAKE. Pigment Red 57. Lithol Rubine B.   A monoazo dye. An insoluble pigment prepared from D & C Red No. 7 (*see*) and calcium. See Colors and Azo Dyes.

D & C RED NO. 7 ZIRCONIUM LAKE. Pigment Red 57. Lithol Rubine B.   A monoazo dye. See Azo Dyes.

D & C RED NO. 8. Lake Red C. Pigment Red 53.   Orange. Classed chemically as a monoazo color. See Colors.

D & C RED NO. 8 BARIUM LAKE. Acid Red 88. Fast Red A.   A monoazo color. See Azo Dyes.

D & C RED NO. 8 SODIUM LAKE.   Insoluble pigment prepared from D & C Red No. 8 (*see*). See Colors and Lakes.

D & C RED NO. 9. Lake Red C Ba.   Scarlet coloring. It is the barium salt of D & C Red No. 8 (*see*). Used in face powders. See Colors.

D & C RED NO. 9 BARIUM LAKE.   The insoluble pigment prepared from D & C Red No. 9 (*see*) and barium. See Colors and Lakes.

D & C RED NO. 9 ZIRCONIUM STRONTIUM LAKE.   Similar to D & C Red No. 8 (*see*).

D & C RED NO. 10. Lithol Red.   Yellowish red. Classed chemically as a monoazo color. A light orange red, practically insoluble in water, used in lipstick and rouge. See Colors.

D & C RED NO. 10 ALUMINUM LAKE. Lithol Red.   See Azo Dyes.

D & C RED NO. 10 SODIUM LAKE.   An insoluble pigment prepared from D & C Red No. 10 (*see*) and sodium. See Colors and Lakes.

D & C RED NO. 11. Lithol Red Ca.   Bright red. Classed chemically as a monoazo color. It is the calcium salt of D & C Red No. 10 (*see*). Very popular in lipsticks. It is also used in face powders. See Colors.

D & C RED NO. 11 CALCIUM LAKE.   Insoluble pigment prepared from D & C Red No. 11 (*see*). See Colors and Lakes.

D & C RED NO. 12. *Lithol Red Ba.*   Classed chemically as a monoazo color. It is a medium red popular in lipsticks and face powders. See Colors.

D & C RED NO. 12 ALUMINUM LAKE. *Lithol Red.*   A monoazo color. See Azo Dyes.

D & C RED NO. 12 BARIUM LAKE. *Bali Red.*   Insoluble pigment prepared from D & C Red No. 12 (*see*). See Colors and Lakes.

D & C RED NO. 13. *Strontium Lithol.*   Classed chemically as a monoazo color. It is the strontium salt of D & C Red No. 10. A medium bright red used in lipsticks and powders. See Colors.

D & C RED NO. 13 ALUMINUM LAKE. *Strontium Lithol.*   A monoazo color. See Azo Dyes.

D & C RED NO. 13 BARIUM LAKE. *Strontium Salt of D & C Red 10.*   See Azo Dyes.

D & C RED NO. 13 STRONTIUM LAKE.   Insoluble pigment prepared from D & C Red No. 13 (*see*) and strontium. See Colors and Lakes.

D & C RED NO. 17. *Toney Red.*   Classed chemically as a diazo color. It is used in soaps, suntan oils, hair oils, and pomades. See Colors.

D & C RED NO. 19. *Rhodamine B.*   Magenta. Classed chemically as a xanthene color. Its greenish crystals or yellow powder turns violet in solution. Used in lipstick, rouges, soaps, bath salts, nail enamel, toothpaste, hair-waving fluids, and face powders. See Colors.

D & C RED NO. 19 ALUMINUM LAKE.   Insoluble pigment prepared from D & C Red No. 19 (*see*). See Colors and Lakes.

D & C RED NO. 19 BARIUM LAKE. *Rhodamine B. Magenta.*   Violet in solution. A xanthene dye (*see*).

D & C RED NO. 19 ZIRCONIUM LAKE. *Vat Red 1. Thioindigo Pink R.*   A thioindigoid dye (*see*).

D & C RED NO. 21. *Solvent Red 43. Tetrabromofluorescein* (see). Classed chemically as a fluoran color. A bluish pink stain used in lipstick, rouges, and nail enamels. Insoluble in water but used to color oils, resins, and lacquers. See Colors.

D & C RED NO. 21 ALUMINUM LAKE.   Insoluble pigment prepared from D & C Red No. 21 (*see*) and aluminum. See Colors and Lakes.

D & C RED NO. 21 ZIRCONIUM LAKE. Solvent Red 43. Merry Pink. A xanthene dye (*see*).

D & C RED NO. 22. Eosine YS. Yellowish pink. Classed chemically as a xanthene color. It is used in soaps, hair rinses, lipsticks, and nail polishes. Red crystals with a bluish tinge or a brownish red powder, freely soluble in water. Lethal dose in animals is quite small. See Colors.

D & C RED NO. 27. Solvent Red 48. Philoxine B. Veri Pink. A xanthene dye (*see*). Classed chemically as a fluoran color. A deep bluish red stain used in lipsticks and rouges. See Colors.

D & C RED NO. 27 ALUMINUM LAKE. Tetrabromo Tetrachloro Fluorescein Lake. Insoluble pigment prepared from D & C Red No. 27 (*see*) and aluminum. See Colors and Lakes.

D & C RED NO. 27 BARIUM LAKE. Solvent Red 48. Petite Pink. A xanthene dye (*see*).

D & C RED NO. 27 ZIRCONIUM LAKE. Solvent Red 48. A xanthene dye (*see*), deep bluish red. Used in lipsticks and rouges.

D & C RED NO. 28. Phloxine B. Acid Red 92. Classed chemically as a xanthene color. It is the conversion product of D & C Red No. 27 (*see*) to the sodium salt. See Colors.

D & C RED NO. 30. Helindone Pink CN. Vat Red 1. Bluish pink. Classed chemically as an indigoid color. It is used in face powders, talcums, lipsticks, rouges, and soaps. See Colors.

D & C RED NO. 30 ALUMINUM LAKE. Vati Red 1. Thioindigo Pink R. A thioindigoid color (*see*). A red vat dye made from indigo and sulfur (*see both*).

D & C RED NO. 30 CALCIUM LAKE. Permanent Pink. Vat Red 1. Thioindigo Pink R. A thioindigo dye (*see*).

D & C RED NO. 30 LAKE. Insoluble pigment prepared from D & C Red No. 30 (*see*) with an approved metal. See Colors and Lakes.

D & C RED NO. 31. Brilliant Lake Red R. Classed chemically as a monoazo color. It is used in lipsticks and nail enamels. See Colors.

D & C RED NO. 31 CALCIUM LAKE. Brilliant Lake Red R. Monoazo color used in lipsticks and nail enamels. See Azo Dyes.

D & C RED NO. 33. Acid Red 33. Dull bluish red. Classed chemically as a monoazo color. It is used in lipsticks, rouges, soaps, bath salts, and hair rinses. See Colors.

D & C RED NO. 34. Fanchon Maroon. Deep Maroon. Classed chemically as a monoazo color. It is used in face powders, talcums, nail lacquers, lipsticks, rouges, toothpastes, and soaps. See Colors.

D & C RED NO. 34 CALCIUM LAKE.   Insoluble pigment prepared from D & C Red No. 34 (*see*). See Colors and Lakes.

D & C RED NO. 36. Pigment Red 4. Tiger Orange.   A monoazo dye. It is bright orange used in lipsticks, rouges, face powders, and talcums. See Colors and Azo Dyes.

D & C RED NO. 36 BARIUM LAKE. Pigment Red 4. Permanent Red 12.   Orange hue. A monoazo color. See Azo Dyes.

D & C RED NO. 36 LAKE. Chlorinated Para Lake. Tang Orange.   Insoluble pigment prepared from D & C Red No. 36 (*see*). See Colors and Lakes.

D & C RED NO. 36 ZIRCONIUM LAKE. Pigment Red 4.   See D & C Red No. 36 Barium Lake.

D & C RED NO. 37. Rhodamine B-Stearate. Solvent Red 49.   Bluish pink. Classed chemically as a xanthene color. It is used in soaps. See Colors.

D & C RED NO. 37 CALCIUM LAKE. Rhodamine B. Stearate Solvent.   See D & C Red No. 37.

D & C RED NO. 39.   An azo dye containing benzoic acid (*see*). Used for coloring quaternary ammonium compound (*see*) germicidal solutions for external application only. Must not exceed 0.1 percent by weight of the finished product. Must be certified. See Colors.

D & C RED NO. 40. Bluish pink.   Classed chemically as a xanthene color (*see*). Used in soaps.

D & C VIOLET NO. 2. Alizurol Purple SS. Solvent Violet 13.   Classed chemically as an anthraquinone color. It is a dull bluish violet used in suntan oils, pomades, and hair colors. See Colors.

D & C YELLOW NO. 5 ALUMINUM LAKE.   Greenish yellow. Insoluble pigment prepared from FD & C Yellow No. 5 (*see*) and aluminum. See Colors and Lakes.

D & C YELLOW NO. 5 ZIRCONIUM LAKE.   An insoluble pigment prepared from FD & C Yellow No. 5 (*see*) and zirconium. See Colors and Lakes.

D & C YELLOW NO. 6 ALUMINUM LAKE.   Insoluble pigment prepared from FD & C Yellow No. 6 (*see*) and aluminum. See Colors and Lakes.

D & C YELLOW NO. 7. Acid Yellow 73. Fluorescein.   Classed chemically as a fluoran color. It is a water-absorbing, yellowish red powder freely soluble in water. The fluorescence disappears when the solution is made acid and reappears when it is made neutral. No toxic action on fish and believed to be nontoxic to humans. See Colors.

D & C YELLOW NO. 8. Uranine. Sodium Fluorescein. Naphthol Yellow S. Classed chemically as a xanthene color. It is the sodium salt of D & C Yellow No. 7 (*see*). Light yellow or orange yellow powder soluble in water. See Colors.

D & C YELLOW NO. 10. Acid Yellow 3. Quinoline Yellow. Classed chemically as a quinoline color. It is a bright greenish yellow used in hair-waving fluids, toothpastes, bath salts, soaps, and shampoos. See Colors.

D & C YELLOW NO. 10 ALUMINUM LAKE. Insoluble pigment prepared from D & C Yellow No. 10 (*see*) and aluminum. See Colors and Lakes.

D & C YELLOW NO. 11. Solvent Yellow 33. Classed chemically as a quinoline color. It is a bright greenish yellow used in soaps, shampoos, suntan oils, hair oils, and pomades. See Colors.

DAMMAR. Resin used to produce a gloss and adhesion in nail lacquer. It is the yellowish white semitransparent exudate from a plant grown in the East Indies and the Philippines. Comes in varying degrees of hardness. It has a bitter taste. Also used for preserving animal and vegetable specimens for science laboratories. May cause allergic reactions.

DANDELION LEAF AND ROOT. Lion's Tooth. Used as a skin refreshing bath additive. Obtained from the Taraxacum plants that grow abundantly in the United States. No known toxicity.

DANDRUFF SHAMPOOS AND TREATMENTS. There are two basic types of dandruff: one associated with excessive scaling and drying of the scalp, and one that involves excessive oiliness. An effective shampoo should have some control over dandruff because it helps wash away the flakes and eliminate oil and dirt. There are also preshampoo products that combine detergents with dry skin dissolvers. They are usually put on the hair for about 20 minutes before a shampoo. There are also medicated shampoos for dandruff. These usually contain sulfur, salicylic acid, resorcinol, and hexachlorophene or bithionol (*see all*). There are also aftershampoo dandruff rinses, which usually contain a quaternary ammonium compound (*see*). And there are scalp lotions with antiseptics and stimulants such as resorcinol and/or chloral hydrate or tincture of capsicum (*see all*). Hairdressings with zinc and cetalkonium chloride (*see both*) are also used to treat dandruff. Among other ingredients in dandruff products are allantoin for its healing properties and salicylanlide (*see both*). A typical antidandruff formulation contains zinc pyrithione and an anionic detergent (*see*), whereas another contains salicylic acid, sulfur, lanolin, cholesterol, and petrolatum (*see all*). In recent years reports of scalp irritation due to dandruff shampoos and treatments have been made to the FDA. However, when dandruff is mild, any number of commercial dandruff products will work. But some people are allergic to the sulfur, tar, and/or salicylic acid (*see all*) in many of the products.

DEA-LAURETH SULFATE. See Quaternary Ammonium Compounds.

DEA-LAURYL SULFATE. See Quaternary Ammonium Compounds.

DEA-LINOLEATE. See Linoleic Acid.

DEA-METHYL MYRISTATE SULFONATE. Biterge. See Quaternary Ammonium Compounds.

DEA-OLETH-3. See Oleth-20.

DECANOIC ACID. A synthetic flavoring agent that occurs naturally in anise, butter acids, oil of lemon, and oil of lime, and used in cosmetic fragrances. Also used to flavor butter, coconut, fruit, liquor, and cheese. No known toxicity.

DECYL ALCOHOL. An intermediate (*see*) for surface-active agents, an antifoam agent, and a fixative in perfumes. Occurs naturally in sweet orange and ambrette seed. Derived commercially from liquid paraffin (*see*). Colorless to light yellow liquid. Used also for synthetic lubricants and as a synthetic fruit flavoring. Low toxicity in animals. No known toxicity for the skin.

DECYL OLEATE. See Decyl Alcohol.

DECYL SUCCINATE. Decyl Hydrogen Succinate. Produced by the reaction of decyl alcohol (*see*) and succinic acid (*see*). Used in the manufacture of perfumes and in cosmetic creams as a buffer and neutralizing agent. No known toxicity in humans.

DECYL TETRADECANOL. See Decanoic Acid.

DECYLAMINE OXIDE. See Amines.

DEHYDRATED. With the water removed.

DEHYDROACETIC ACID. DHA. Sodium Dehydroacetate. A weak acid that forms a white odorless powder with an acrid taste. Used as an antienzyme agent in toothpastes to prevent tooth decay and as a preservative for shampoos. Also used as a fungi and bacteria-destroying agent in cosmetics. The presence of organic matter decreases its effectiveness. Not irritating or allergy-causing, but it is a kidney-blocking agent and can cause impaired kidney function. Large doses can cause vomiting, imbalance, and convulsions.

DEMULCENT. A soothing, usually thick, oily or creamy substance used to relieve pain in inflamed or irritated mucous surfaces. The gum acacia, for instance, is used as a demulcent.

DENATONIUM BENZOATE. A denaturant for alcohol that is to be used in cosmetics. It is intended to make alcohol unpalatable for drinking purposes and, therefore, is unpleasant to smell and taste. No known toxicity. See Denatured Alcohol.

DENATURANT. A poisonous or unpleasant substance added to alcoholic cosmetics to make them undrinkable. It is also considered a substance that changes another substance's natural qualities or characteristics.

DENATURED ALCOHOL. Ethyl alcohol must be made unfit for drinking before it can be used in cosmetics. Various substances such as denatonium benzoate (*see*) are added to alcohol to make it malodorous and obnoxious in order to completely prevent its use or recovery for drinking purposes.

DENTIFRICES. Their primary purpose is to clean accessible surfaces of the teeth with a toothbrush. Such cleansing is important to the appearance of teeth and gum health and it prevents mouth odor. Dentifrices usually come in the form of a paste or powder. Despite the brand claims, most dentifrices contain similar ingredients: binders, abrasives, sudsers, humectants, flavors, unique additives, and liquids. Binders include karaya gum, bentonite, sodium alginate, methylcellulose, carrageenan, and magnesium aluminum silicate. Among the abrasives are calcium carbonate, dibasic calcium phosphate, calcium sulfate, tricalcium phosphate, and sodium metaphosphate hydrated alumina. Sudsers include hard soap and the detergents sodium lauryl sulfate, sodium lauryl sulfoacetate, dioctyl sodium sulfosuccinate, sulfocolaurate, and sodium lauroyl sarcosinate. Humectants include glycerin, propylene glycol, and sorbitol. The most popular flavors are spearmint, peppermint, wintergreen, and cinnamon, but there are also such odd ones as bourbon, rye, anise, clove, caraway, coriander, eucalyptus, nutmeg, and thyme. Fluorides are added to reduce decay; also added are antienzyme ingredients (sodium dehydroacetate) and tooth whiteners (sodium perborate). Still other ingredients in dentifrices are sodium benzoate, ammonium antispetics, sodium coconut monoglyceride sulfonate, sodium copper chlorophyllin, chloroform, starch, sodium chloride, calcium sulfate, strontium chloride, *p*-hydroxybenzoate as a preservative, and sodium dehydroacetate. Toothpastes promoted for sensitive teeth are questionable according to the American Dental Association. The most popular toothpaste contains sodium fluoride, calcium pyrophosphate, glycerin, sorbitol, and a blend of anionic surfactants (see Anionic Detergents) ; its competitor contains sodium *n*-lauroyl sarcosinate (Gardol), and sodium monofluorophosphate (MFP). Complaints to the FDA during the past two years about dentifrices include sore mouth and gums, tooth enamel worn away, sore tongue, and sloughing of mucous membranes. Some toothpastes were reported to be contaminated with a foreign substance and some contained too much chloroform, which was reduced by the manufacturer upon the FDA's request.

DEODORANTS. Includes Antiperspirants. It is not the normal secretions of the skin that produce an objectionable odor but the action of bacteria and chemicals on sweat that create the unpleasant smell. The difference between deodorants and antiperspirants is in sequence. Deodorants control perspiration odors but antiperspirants retard the flow of perspiration. Deodorants inhibit the growth of microorganisms, which produce the malodors; antiperspirants, which contain a hydrolyzing metal salt, develop a low pH (increased acidity) and inhibit moisture. The inhibiting action may be enhanced by antiseptics that deodorize. Aluminum salts are the most widely used for inhibiting perspiration; urea (*see*) may be added to neutralize the fabric-damaging acidity of the metal. Organic compounds such as hexachlorophene and bithionol (*see both*) inhibit the growth of skin microorganisms. Such antiseptics may be incorporated into deodorant soaps. Deodorants, formerly called "unscented toilet waters" and "sanitary liquid preparations," once contained formaldehyde or benzoic acid, which have been replaced with quaternary ammonium compounds (*see*). Deodorant-action liquid antiperspirants today usually contain aluminum chloride, urea, propylene glycol, and about 75 percent water. Deodorant-action cream antiperspirants contain aluminum chlorhydroxide, sorbitan monostearate, poloxamers, stearic acid, boric acid, petrolatum, perfume, propylene glycol, and water. Roll-on deodorants and antiperspirants (lotion type) contain cetyl alcohol, poloxamers, and aluminum chlorhydroxide, urea, perfume, and about 45 percent water. Deodorant sticks, without antiperspirant action, may contain sodium stearate, sorbitol, hexachlorophene, alcohol, and water. Spray deodorants have the same ingredients as liquid ones but are mixed with a propellant. The aluminum, alcohol, and zinc salts in deodorants and antiperspirants can cause skin and gastrointestinal irritations, and the hexachlorophene and bithionol can cause photosensitivity. Deaths from intentional inhalation of deodorant sprays have been reported. Vision has been affected from spray in the eyes. With all deodorants there can be stinging and burning, itching, sebaceous cysts, enlarged sweat glands, pimples under the arms, and lung and throat irritation. Seven cases of lung tumors attributed to underarm deodorant sprays were reported at the

1971 American Thoracic Society meeting in Los Angeles. See Vaginal Deodorants.

DEODORIZED KEROSENE. Deo-Base. Derived from petroleum, it is a mobile, water-white transparent liquid that has been deodorized and decolorized by washing kerosene with fuming sulfuric acid. It is a solvent used in brilliantines, emulsified lotions and creams, and as a constituent of hand lotions. It is a skin irritant, and dermatitis often occurs. Because of its solvent action on fats, it can cause a defatting and drying of the skin. In cosmetics, however, when it is used with fatty substances, its fat-solvent action is minimized and it is considered innocuous.

DEPILATORIES. The most effective chemical hair removers yet discovered are the sulfides (see), particularly hydrogen sulfide, but they have an unpleasant odor that is hard to mask. Most sulfides have been replaced with salts of thioglycollic acid (see), which take more time to act but smell better and are not as irritating as sulfides. However, persons who have difficulty with detergent hands or ammonia or strong soaps often have difficulty with thioglycollic depilatories. Also ingestion of thioglycollic depilatories may cause severe gastrointestinal irritation. Cream depilatores that act by dissolving the hair usually contain calcium thioglycolate, calcium carbonate, calcium hydroxide, cetyl alcohol, sodium lauryl sulfate (a detergent), water, and a strong perfume (so as to remain stable in an alkali medium). Another type of depilatory made of wax acts by hardening around the hair and pulling it out. Such products usually contain rosin, beeswax, paraffin, and petrolatum. (See above ingredients under separate listings.) Among injuries recently reported to the FDA concerning depilatories were skin irritation, headaches, scars on legs, skin burns, and rash.

DETERGENT. Any of a group of synthetic, organic, liquid, or water-soluble cleansing agents that, unlike soap, are not prepared from fats and oils and are not inactivated by hard water. Most of them are made from petroleum derivatives but vary widely in composition. The major advantage of detergents is that they do not leave a hard water scum. They also have wetting agent and emulsifying agent properties. Quaternary ammonium compounds (see), for instance, through surface action, exert cleansing and antibacterial effects. Phisoderm is an example of a liquid detergent and Dove is an example of a solid detergent. Toxicity of detergents depends upon alkalinity. Dishwasher detergents, for instance, can be dangerously alkaline while detergents used in cosmetic products have an acidity-alkalinity ratio near normal skin, 5 to 6.5 pH.

DEXTRAN. A term applied to polysaccharides produced by bacteria growing on sugar. Used as a thickening agent in cuticle removers, it is also employed as a foam stabilizer in beer. Injection into the skin has caused cancer in rats.

DEXTRIN. British Gum. Starch Gum. White or yellow powder produced from starch. Used as a diluting agent for dry extracts and for emulsions and as a thickener in cream and liquid cosmetics. May cause an allergic reaction.

DIACETONE ALCOHOL. Used as a solvent for nail enamels, fats, oils, waxes, and resins. Also used as a preservative. Prepared by the action of an alkali such as calcium hydroxide on acetone (*see*). Highly flammable with a pleasant odor, it mixes easily with other solvents. May be narcotic in high concentration and has caused kidney and liver damage, as well as anemia in experimental animals when given orally.

DIACETYL. A catalyst (*see*) in the manufacture of fake nails. It occurs naturally in cheese, cocoa, pears, coffee, raspberries, strawberries, and cooked chicken, but is usually prepared by a special fermentation of glucose. It is a yellowish green liquid. Also used as a carrier of aroma of butter, vinegar, coffee, and to flavor oleomargarine. Diacetyl compounds have been associated with cancer when ingested by experimental animals.

DIAMINONAPHTHALINE. A black dye. See Coal Tar.

DIAMINOPHENOL. A brown dye. See Phenol.

DIAMINOPHENOL HYDROCHLORIDE. A black brown dye. See Phenol.

2,4-DIAMINOPHENOL. Manufactured from aniline (*see*) and used in hair dye. For toxicity see *p*-Phenylenediamine.

2,6-DIAMINOPYRIDINE. See Pyridine.

DIAMMONIUM CITRATE. Ammonium Salt of Citric Acid, Dibasic. See Citric Acid.

DIAMMONIUM PHOSPHATE. See Ammonium Phosphate.

DIATOMACEOUS EARTH. Kieselguhr. A porous and relatively pure form of silica formed from fossil remains of diatoms—one-celled algae with shells. Inert when ingested. Used in pomades, dentifrices, nail polishes, face powders, as a clarifying agent, and as an absorbent for liquids because it can absorb about four times its weight in water. The dust can cause lung damage after long exposure to high concentrations. Not recommended for use on teeth or skin because of its abrasiveness.

DIAZO DYES. Coloring agents that contain two linked nitrogen atoms united to an aromatic group and to an acid radical. See Heliotropin.

DIBROMOFLUORESCEIN. Used in indelible lipsticks, it is made by heating resorcinol and phthalic anhydride (*see both*) to produce fluorescent orange red crystals. Ingestion can cause gastrointestinal symptoms. Skin application can cause skin sensitivity to light, inflamed eyes, skin rash, and even respiratory symptoms. See Colors.

DIBROMSALAN. *4,5-Dibromosalicylanilide.* An antibacteria agent used as an antiseptic and fungicide in detergents, toilet soaps, creams, lotions, and powders. No oral toxicity reported in man but has caused skin sensitivity to light, causing rash and swelling.

DIBUCAINE. *Nupercaine.* Bitter, water-absorbing crystals. Used as a local anesthetic for the skin, particularly in wax depilatories to prevent pain. Similar to cocaine when applied to the skin. Highly toxic when injected into the abdomen of rats; only one part per kilogram of body weight is lethal. No toxicity reported in humans.

DIBUTYL PHTHALATE. The ester of the salt of phthalic acid (*see*), which is isolated from a fungus. The colorless liquid is used as a plasticizer in nail polish, as a perfume solvent, fixative, and antifoam agent. It is also an insect repellent. Has a low toxicity but if ingested can cause gastrointestinal upset. The vapor is irritating to the eyes and mucous membranes.

DIBUTYL SEBACATE. *Sebacic Acid.* A synthetic fruit flavoring usually obtained from castor oil and used for beverages, ice cream, and baked goods. Used in fruit-fragrance cosmetics. No known toxicity.

DIBUTYLENE TETRAFURFURAL. See Tetrahydrofurfuryl Alcohol.

DI-t-BUTYLHYDROQUINONE. See Hydroquinol and Phenol.

DICALCIUM PHOSPHATE. Tooth polisher for dentifrices. See Calcium Phosphate.

DICHLORO-m-XYLENOL. Crystals from petroleum ether used as a bacteria killer in soaps and as a mold inhibitor and preservative in creams and lotions. See Coal Tar for toxicity.

DICHLOROPHENE. See Phenol.

DIETHANOLAMINE. Colorless liquid or crystalline alcohol. It is used as a solvent, emulsifying agent, and detergent. Also employed in emollients for its softening properties and as a dispersing agent and humectant in other cosmetic products. It may be irritating to the skin and mucous membranes. See Ethanolamines.

DIETHANOLAMINE BISULFATE. See Ethanolamines.

DIETHYL PALMITOYL ASPARTATE.   See Aspartic Acid.
DIETHYL PHTHALATE.   Made from ethanol and phthalic acid (*see both*). Used as a solvent, a fixative for perfume, and a denaturant (*see*) for alcohol. It has a bitter and unpleasant taste. Irritating to mucous membranes. Produces central nervous system depression when absorbed through the skin.
DIETHYLAMINE.   Used in detergent soaps. Prepared from methanol (*see*) and ammonia (*see*), very soluble in water, and forms a strong alkali. Has a fishy odor. Irritating to skin and mucous membranes.
DIETHYLAMINO METHYL COUMARIN.   See Coumarin.
DIETHYLAMINOETHYL STEARAMIDE.   See Diethylamine.
DIETHYLAMINOETHYL STEARATE.   See Stearic Acid and Amines.
DIETHYLENE GLYCOL.   Made by heating ethylene oxide and glycol. A clear, water-absorbing, almost colorless liquid; it is mixable with water, alcohol, and acetone. Used as a solvent, humectant, and plasticizer in cosmetic creams. A wetting agent (*see*) that enhances skin absorption. Can be fatal if swallowed. Not usually irritating to the skin, but can be absorbed through the skin and the use of glycols on extensive areas of the body is considered hazardous.
N,N-DIETHYL-m-TOLUAMIDE.   Made from *m*-toluoyl chloride and diethylamine in benzene or ether. A liquid soluble in water, it is used as an insect repellent. Irritating to the eyes and mucous membranes but not to the skin. Ingestion can cause central nervous system disturbances.
DIFFUSIVE.   A term used to describe a perfume compound odor which spreads quickly and widely. This quality is good in perfumes but may be disliked in other products such as hair sprays and deodorants.
DIGALLOYL TRIOLEATE.   From digallic acid and oleic acid. An oily sunscreen ingredient devoid of anesthetic properties and stable under long periods of ultraviolet radiation. It may cause the skin to break out and redden when exposed to light.
DIHEPTYL SODIUM SULFOSUCCINATE.   Available as a waxlike solid. Used as a wetting agent in bath oil preparations. No known toxicity to the skin.
DIHEPTYLUNDECYL ADIPATE.   See Adipic Acid.
DIHYDROABIETYL ALCOHOL.   See Abietyl Alcohol;Abietic Acid.
DIHYDROABIETYL METHACRYLATE.   See Abietyl Alcohol.
DIHYDROCHOLESTEROL.   See Cholesterol.

DIHYDROXYACETONE. The Food and Drug Administration declared in 1973 that this color additive is safe and suitable for use in cosmetics or drugs that are applied to color the skin. A white powder that turns colorless in liquid form, it colors the skin an orange brown shade, giving it a suntanned appearance. It is an ingredient in some suntan lotions for use indoors without sunlight. Obtained by the action of certain bacteria on glycerol, it has a sweet taste and characteristic odor. It is a strong reducing agent (*see*). It is converted by alkali to the fruit sugar fructose. Lethal when injected in large doses into rats. No known skin toxicity and the FDA has exempted it from color additive certification, which means there is no need to test each batch as a means of protecting consumers as there is with coal tar colors.

DIHYDROXYETHYL COCAMINE OXIDE. See Coconut Oil.

DIHYDROXYETHYL STEARAMINE OXIDE. See Stearic Acid.

DIHYDROXYETHYL TALLOW AMINE OXIDE. See Tallow.

DIIODOTYROSINE. See Cinnamic Acid.

DIISOCETYL ADIPATE. See Adipic Acid.

DIISOPROPYL ADIPATE. See Adipic Acid.

DIISOPROPYL SEBACATE. See Sebacic Acid.

DIISOPROPYLAMINE. DIPA. Contained in Vitamin B_{15}. Used as a yeast inhibitor and preservative in cosmetics. Has been used to treat skin fungal infections. May be irritating to the skin and mucous membranes.

DILAURYL THIODIPROPIONATE. An antioxidant. White crystalline flakes with a sweet odor. No known toxicity.

DILUENT. Any component of a color additive mixture that is not of itself a color additive and has been intentionally mixed therein to facilitate the use of the mixture in coloring cosmetics or in coloring the human body, food, and drugs. The diluent may serve another functional purpose in cosmetics, as, for example, emulsifying or stabilizing. Ethylcellulose is an example.

DIMETHICONE. Dimethicone Copolyol. A silicone (*see*) oil, white, viscous, used as an ointment base ingredient, as a topical drug vehicle, and as a skin protectant. Very low toxicity.

DIMETHICONE COPOLYOL. See Dimethicone.

DIMETHICONOL. See Dimethicone.

DIMETHOXANE. A liquid with a mustardlike odor that mixes with water. Used in cosmetics as a preservative for resins and emulsions. Also used as a preservative for cutting oils and in water-based paints. Low in toxicity; a 1 percent solution produces no irritation or sensitivity.

DIMETHYL COCAMINE. See Coconut Oil.
DIMETHYL LAURAMINE. See Lauric Acid.
DIMETHYL MYRISTAMINE. See Myristic Acid.
DIMETHYL OCTYNEDIOL. See Citronellol.
DIMETHYL PALMITAMINE. See Palmitic Acid.
N,N-DIMETHYL-p-PHENYLENE DIAMINE. See *p*-Phenylenediamine.
DIMETHYL PHOSPHATE. See Phosphoric Acid.
DIMETHYL PHTHALATE. Phthalic Esters. A colorless, aromatic oil insoluble in water. A solvent, especially for musk (*see*). Used to compound calamine lotion and as an insect repellent. See Phthalic Acid for toxicity.
DIMETHYL STEARAMINE. See Stearic Acid.
DIMETHYL SULFATE. Sulfuric Acid. Dimethyl Ester. Colorless, oily liquid used as a methylating agent (to add methyl) in the manufacture of cosmetic dyes, perfumes, and flavorings. Methyl salicylate is an example (*see*). Extremely hazardous, dimethyl sulfate has delayed lethal qualities. Liquid produces severe blistering, necrosis of the skin. Sufficient skin absorption can result in serious poisoning. Vapors hurt the eyes. Ingestion can cause paralysis, coma, prostration, kidney damage, and death.
DIMETHYL TALLOW AMINE. See Tallow.
DIMETHYL-o-TOLUIDINE. Coal tar derivative. Light yellow liquid becoming reddish brown when exposed to air. Used in the manufacture of hair dyes. See Aniline Dyes for toxicity.
DIMETHYLAMINE. Prepared from methanol (*see*) and ammonia (*see*), it is very soluble in water and in alcohol. Used in the manufacture of soaps and detergents. Irritating to the skin and mucous membranes.
DIMETHYLAMINE. Prepared from methanol and ammonia, it promotes hardening of plastic nails. It is also used in detergent soaps. Irritating to the skin and mucous membranes.
DIMETHYLAMINOETHYL METHACRYLATE. See Acrylates.
DIMETHYLAMINOPROPYL OLEAMIDE. See Oleic Acid.
DIMETHYLAMINOPROPYL STEARAMIDE. See Stearic Acid.
3-DIMETHYLAMINOPROPYLAMINE. See Propyl Alcohol.
2,5-DINITROPHENOL. Yellow crystals made from dinitrobenzene. Used in the manufacture of hair dyes. See *p*-Phenylenediamine for toxicity.
DINKUM OIL. See Eucalyptus Oil.

DIOCTYL-. Containing two octyl groups. Octyl is obtained from octane, a liquid paraffin found in petroleum.
DIOCTYL ADIPATE. See Adipic Acid.
DIOCTYL PHTHALATE. An oily liquid ester (*see*) used chiefly as a plasticizer, solvent, and fixative in perfumes and nail enamels. Because of its bitter taste, also used as a denaturant for alcohol (*see*). Irritating to mucous membranes, and a central nervous system depressant if absorbed through the skin.
DIOCTYL SEBACATE. See Sebacic Acid, of which it is a salt.
DIOCTYL SODIUM SULFOSUCCINATE. Sulfosuccinic Acid bis (2-Ethylhexyl) Ester S-Sodium Salt. A waxlike solid used in foods and beverages as a dispersing and solubilizing agent for gums and hard to wet materials. Used in bubble baths in solution; also as a wetting agent in other cosmetic preparations such as cleansing lotions. It is a stool softener in laxatives. It has caused irritation when used in eye preparations.
DIOCTYL SUCCINATE. A white wax, soluble in water, it is a wetting agent used in compounding calamine lotion. No known skin toxicity.
DIOCTYLAMINE. Di-2-Ethylhexyl-Amine. See Amines.
DIPENTENE. See Limonene.
DIPERODON HYDROCHLORIDE. Obtained by condensing piperidine and glycerol chlorohydrin with an alkali. Bitter taste. Soluble in alcohol. Used as an anesthetic in solution. No known toxicity.
DIPHENOLIC ACID. Prepared by condensing phenol (*see*) with another acid. Soluble in hot water. It is an intermediate for lubricating oil additives. Used in cosmetics as a surfactant and plasticizer. See Phenol for toxicity.
DIPHENYL METHANE. Benzyl Benzene. Used chiefly as a perfume in soaps. Prepared from methylene chloride and benzene with aluminum chloride as a catalyst. Smells like oranges and geraniums. A petroleum distillate and like all such substances can, when imposed, produce local skin irritation and more rarely a skin reaction to sunlight, which includes prickling, swelling, and sometimes pigmentation.
DIPHENYLENE SULFIDE. Dibenzothiophene. Used in dandruff treatment shampoos and products. Colorless crystals made from alcohol and chloroform and sulfur. Used as a psychopharmaceutical to treat mental disorders. When ingested can affect central nervous system, the blood, and blood pressure. However, no known toxicity when applied to the skin.

DIPOTASSIUM PHOSPHATE. A sequestrant. A white grain, very soluble in water. Used as a buffering agent to control the degree of acidity in solutions. It is used medicinally as a saline cathartic. No known toxicity.

DIPROPYLENE GLYCOL. See Propylene Glycol.

DIPROPYLENE GLYCOL SALICYLATE. Used in sunscreen preparations. See Salicylates.

DIRECT BLACK 38. Direct Deep Black E.W. See Direct Dyes and Azo Dyes.

DIRECT BLACK 131. Columbia Black EAW. See Direct Dyes and Azo Dyes.

DIRECT BLUE 6. Benzo Blue BB. A diazo dye. See Azo Dyes and Direct Dyes.

DIRECT BROWN 1. Benzochrome. Brown G. Benzamine Brown. See Azo Dyes and Direct Dyes.

DIRECT BROWN 2. Diamine Brown M. A diazo dye. See Azo Dyes and Direct Dyes.

DIRECT BROWN 31. See Direct Dyes.

DIRECT BROWN 154. Erie Brown 3GN. Classed chemically as a triazo color. See Colors.

DIRECT DYES. These compounds need salts to be effective. When combined with aniline, they improve in fastness. They are used in hair dyes and in some pigments. See Aniline Dyes for toxicity.

DIRECT ORANGE 6. Erie Orange Y. No information available.

DIRECT RED 23. Fast Scarlet 4BSA. Classed chemically as a diazo color. See Colors.

DIRECT RED 81. Benzo Fast. Red 8 BL. A diazo dye. See Azo Dyes and Direct Dyes.

DIRECT VIOLET 48. A diazo dye. See Azo Dyes and Direct Dyes.

DIRECT YELLOW 12. Chrysophenine G. A diazo dye. See Azo Dyes and Direct Dyes.

DISELENIUM SULFIDE. An antidandruff agent used in prescription items and in over-the-counter brands. See Selenium Sulfide.

DISODIUM EDTA. See Ethylenediamine Tetraacetic Acid (EDTA).

DISODIUM EDTA-COPPER. Copper Versenate. Used as a sequestering agent. See Ethylenediamine Tetraacetic Acid for toxicity.

DISODIUM LAURIMINODIPROPIONATE. See Lauric Acid.

DISODIUM MONOCETEARYL SULFOSUCCINATE. See Sodium Sulfonate.

DISODIUM MONOCOCAMIDOSULFOSUCCINATE.   See Dioctyl
Sodium Sulfosuccinate.
DISODIUM MONOLAURETHSULFOSUCCINATE.   See Dioctyl
Sodium Sulfosuccinate.
DISODIUM MONOLAURYLAMIDOSULFOSUCCINATE.   See Di-
octyl Sodium Sulfosuccinate.
DISODIUM MONOLAURYLSULFOSUCCINATE.   See Dioctyl
Sodium Sulfosuccinate.
DISODIUM MONOMYRISTAMIDOSULFOSUCCINATE.   See Di-
octyl Sodium Sulfosuccinate.
DISODIUM MONOOLEAMIDOSULFOSUCCINATE.   See Dioctyl
Sodium Sulfosuccinate.
DISODIUM MONONDECYLENAMIDO MEA-SULFOSUCCINATE.
See Sodium Sulfonate.
DISODIUM MONORICINOLEAMIDO MEA-SULFOSUCCINATE.
See Sodium Sulfonate.
DISODIUM MYRISTAMIDO MEA-SULFOSUCCINATE.   See Di-
octyl Sodium Sulfosuccinate.
DISODIUM OLEAMIDO MIPA-SULFOSUCCINATE.   See Dioctyl
Sodium Sulfosuccinate.
DISODIUM PHOSPHATE. Phosphate of Soda.   Absorbs moisture
from the air. Used as a buffer in cosmetics, and in the manufacture
of ceramics and detergents. Without water, it may cause a slight irri-
tation of the skin and mucous membranes.
DISPERSANT.   A dispersing agent, such as polyphosphate, for pro-
moting the formation and stabilization of a dispersion of one substance in another. An emulsion, for instance, would consist of a dispersed substance and the medium in which it is dispersed.
DISPERSE BLACK 9. Nacelan Diazine Black JS.   Classed chemically as an azo color. See Colors.
DISPERSE BLUE 1. 1,4,5,8–Tetraaminoanthraquinone.   Classed
chemically as an anthraquinone color. See Colors.
DISPERSE BLUE 3. Disperse Fast Blue.   An anthraquinone dye.
See Anthraquinone and Disperse Dyes.
DISPERSE BLUE 3:1. Nacelan Brilliant Blue NR.   Classed chemically as an anthraquinone color. See Colors.
DISPERSE DYES.   These compounds are only slightly soluble in
water but are readily dispersed with the aid of sulfated oils. Used on
nylon knit goods, sheepskins, and furs, they are in human hair dyes
as well as resins, oils, fats, and waxes. Not permanently listed as safe.

DISPERSE RED 1. Nacelan Scarlet CSB. Classed chemically as a monoazo color. See Colors.

DISPERSE RED 11. Solvent Violet 26. Classed chemically as an anthraquinone color. See Colors.

DISPERSE RED 17. Nacelan Red AB. A commercial color. See Colors.

DISPERSE VIOLET 4. Solvent Violet 12. Classed chemically as an anthraquinone color. See Colors.

DISPERSE VIOLET 11. Nacelan Violet 5RL. Classed chemically as an anthraquinone color. See Colors.

DISPERSE YELLOW 1. Disperse Fast Yellow PR. See Disperse Dyes.

DISPERSE YELLOW 3. Disperse Fast Yellow. Yellow G. A monoazo dye. See Azo Dyes and Disperse Dyes.

DISTILLED. The result of evaporation and subsequent condensation of a liquid, as when water is boiled and steam is condensed.

DI-TEA-PALMITOYL ASPARTATE. See Aspartic Acid.

DM HYDANTOIN. See DMHF.

DMDM HYDANTOIN. 1,3-Dimethylol-5,5-Dimethyl Hydantoin. See DMHF.

DMHF. Dimethyl Hydantoin Formaldehyde Resin. A compound that liberates formaldehyde slowly. It consists of crystals that are freely soluble in water and is used as a preservative in cosmetics. See Formaldehyde for toxicity.

2-DODECYL TETRADECANOL. See Myristic Acid.

DODECYLBENZENE SULFONIC ACID. A sulfonic acid anionic (*see*) detergent. Made from petroleum. May cause skin irritation. If swallowed will cause vomiting.

DOLOMITE. A common mineral, colorless to white or yellowish gray, containing calcium, phosphorus, and magnesium. It is one of the most important raw materials for magnesium and its salts. It is used in toothpaste as a whitener. No known toxicity.

DOMIPHEN BROMIDE. Clear, colorless, odorless crystalline powder with a slightly bitter taste. Soluble in water, but incompatible with soap, it is used as an antiseptic and detergent in cosmetics. No known toxicity.

DROSERA. Common Sundew. A dried flowering plant that grows in Europe, Asia, and in North America as far as Florida. Formerly used to treat chest disorders. Used as a mild astringent in skin lotions and in perfumes. No known toxicity.

DRY SHAMPOOS. Usually consists of a water-absorbent powder such as talc (*see*) and a mild alkali. The product is placed in the hair and then brushed out, carrying with it any oil or dirt. Many women use baby powder or bath powder to "dry" wash their hair. See Shampoos.

DRY-OUT.   Just as the Top-Note (*see*) is the first impression of a perfume, this is the last impression. It may begin to become apparent after an hour or several hours or even the next day. The Dry-Out notes show the fixative (*see*) effects of the components and will reveal the Body-Note (*see*). The Dry-Out depicts the tenacity of the composition and the fixative's ability to hold the scent. The better the perfume, usually the better the Dry-Out.

DUSTING POWDER.   See Powder.

E

EDTA.   See Ethylenediamine Tetraacetic Acid.

EGG POWDER.   Used in many cosmetics including shampoos, ointments, creams, face masks, and bath preparations. Dehydrated egg powder is often incorporated into shampoo on the theory that protein is beneficial to damaged hair. There is little scientific evidence to substantiate this, but the egg coating does make the hair more cohesive and more manageable. The oil of egg yolk, which mixes easily with other oils, is used in ointment bases and cosmetic creams. Egg albumin is used in facial masks to give that tight feeling. For a homemade egg treatment four beaten eggs are required, with a jigger of rum mixed in. Then the solution is massaged into the scalp, followed by a rinse with cold (never hot) water; the hot water would make the egg sticky. For persons not allergic to egg products, the ingredient is harmless.

ELASTOMERS.   Used for face masks. Rubberlike substances that can be stretched from twice to many times their length. Upon their release they return rapidly to almost their original length. Synthetic elastomers have similar properties and are actually superior to the natural ones. They have been in use since 1930. Thiokol was the first commercial synthetic elastomer. It is a condensation polymer (*see*), for example, neoprene, and silicone rubber.

ELDER FLOWERS. Sambucus.   Extracted from the honey-scented flowers of the elder tree. Used in skin and eye lotions and bath preparations. Mildly astringent, it supposedly keeps the skin soft and clean. Old-time herb doctors used it. Elder flowers increase perspiration and therefore reduce body water. Used to scent perfumes and lotion. No known toxicity.

ELDERBERRY JUICE POWDER. Dried powder from the juice of the edible berry of a North American elder tree. Used for red coloring. Nontoxic.

ELEMI. A soft, yellowish, fragrant plastic resin from several Asiatic and Philippine trees. Slightly soluble in water but readily soluble in alcohol. Used for gloss and adhesion in nail lacquer and to scent soaps and colognes. No known toxicity.

EMOLLIENTS. *Creams, Lotions, Skin Softeners, and Moisturizers.* An emollient by whatever designation—night cream, hand cream, eye cream, skin softener, moisturizer, and so on—remains an emollient. The selection of a cream, spray, or lotion is really a matter of taste and the influence of advertising and packaging. The AMA's Committee on Cutaneous Health finds little difference between liquid, cream, lotion, drop, or dew emollients since they all perform the same function. These preparations do help to make the skin feel softer and smoother, to reduce the roughness and cracking and irritation of the skin, and they may possibly help retard the fine wrinkles of aging. However, in any application of oil to the skin, what happens is that the roughened, scaly surface is coated with a smooth film, cementing down the dry flakes. And although the oil retards the evaporation of water, as far as the oil penetrating the skin, dermatologists say this has been overemphasized. Any dryness would be in the layer known as the stratum corneum and it is due to insufficient water in the skin. Exposure to low humidities in artificially heated or cooled rooms, aging, and heredity may all contribute to dry skin. The ancient Greek physician Galen is credited with making the first emollient of beeswax, spermaceti, almond oil, borax, and rosewater (*see all*). Most emollients today are still a mixture of oils. If the oils have a low melting point, the emollient will feel greasy; with a high melting point, it disappears from the skin. Because emollients are usually colorless, and seem to be absorbed rapidly, they are called vanishing creams. But, according to the AMA, it is the water in such creams and not the oil that benefits dry skin. Experiments with a specimen of calloused skin placed in oils for three years could not make it flexible again. However, when a brittle piece of callous is placed in water, it soon becomes flexible. Most emollients are intended to remain on the skin for a significant period of time, including overnight. Petrolatum (Vaseline) is one of the least expensive and one of the most efficient emollients. It tends to keep the loss of natural moisture from the skin at a minimum. Next in efficiency and also inexpensive is zinc oxide (see). Mineral oil, vegetable oil, and shortening also work well. All may be found on your supermarket shelf. Vitamin A and hormone creams (see both) are added to keep the skin moist and supple. How effective they are in doing so is a matter of medical controversy. Glycerin (see) is widely used in emollients and has been found to work best in humid air because it draws moisture from the air. (When the humidity is high, most people do not need emollients.) A simple condition or emollient cream may contain lanolin, petrolatum, and oil of sweet almond. A moisturizing cream may contain mineral oil, stearic acid, lanolin, beeswax, sorbitol, and polysorbates (see all). Among other ingredients in emollients and lotions are natural fatty oils such as olive, coconut, corn, peach kernel, peanut, and sesame oils in hydrogenated form; natural fats such as cocoa butter and lard; synthetic fatty oils such as butyl stearate and diglycol laurate; hydrocarbon solids such as paraffin; alcohols such as cetyl, stearyl, and oleyl; emulsifiers, preservatives, and antioxidants, including Vitamin E and paraben; and antibacterials and perfumes, especially menthol and camphor (see all). Among the problems with creams and lotions reported to the FDA recently were body and hand rashes, swelling of the eyes and face, blood vessels on the surface of the nose, red and painful eyes, burning of the face, and skin eruptions and irritations.

EMULSIFIERS.   Agents used to assist in the production of an emulsion. Among common emulsifiers in cosmetics are stearic acid soaps such as potassium and sodium stearates, sulfated alcohols such as sodium lauryl sulfate, polysorbates, poloxamers, and pegs; and sterols such as cholesterol. (See all under separate listings.)

EMULSION.   What is formed when two or more nonmixable liquids are shaken so thoroughly together that the mixture continues to appear to be homogenized. Most oils form emulsions with water.

ENCAPSULATION.   Scents can be encapsulated in gelatin and are released when a fragrance product is placed in hot water. Some microencapsulated products contain coated perfume granules that are so small they give the impression of free-flowing powder.

ENFLEURAGE.   The technique of making perfumes from flowers, such as roses and orange blossoms that cannot be subjected to steam distillation. It includes the use of glass trays that are lined with lard, on which flowers picked early in the morning are scattered. The trays are stacked on one another. The next day the flowers are removed from the fat and replaced with fresh ones. The cycle is repeated for several weeks. The lard is then scraped from the trays and mixed with alcohol. The alcohol in turn is removed by distillation, leaving behind the flower-scented essential oil, or "absolute." The process usually takes 36 days and is therefore expensive and done only for fine perfumes.

EOSINE YELLOW. See Tetrabromofluorescein.

EPICHLOROHYDRIN. A colorless liquid with an odor resembling chloroform. It is insoluble in water but mixes readily with alcohol or ether. Used as a solvent for cosmetic resins and nitrocellulose (*see both*) and in the manufacture of varnishes, lacquers, and cements for celluloid articles; also a modifier for food starch. A strong skin irritant and sensitizer. Daily administration of 1 milligram per kilogram of body weight to skin killed all of a group of rats in four days, indicating a cumulative potential. Chronic exposure is known to cause kidney damage. A 30-minute exposure to air concentrations of 8,300 parts per million was lethal to mice. Poisoned animals showed cyanosis, muscular relaxation or paralysis, convulsions, and death.

EPILATORIES. Waxlike products that are softened by heat and applied when cool and then "yanked" off, taking embedded hair with them. (Some epilatories do not have to be heated.) They may be formulated from roses, paraffin, beeswax, ceresin, carnauba wax, mineral and linseed oils, and petrolatum. (See ingredients under separate listings.) Sometimes benzocaine is added in low concentrations for its local anesthetic effect. Nontoxic. See Depilatories.

ERYTHORBIC ACID. Isoascorbic Acid. Antioxidant. White, slightly yellow crystals, which darken on exposure to light. Isoascorbic acid contains 1/20th the vitamin capacity of ascorbic acid (*see*). Nontoxic.

ERYTHROSINE. Sodium or potassium salt of tetraiodofluorescein, a coal tar derivative. A brown powder that becomes red in solution. FD & C Red No. 3 is an example. It is used in rouge. See Coal Tar for toxicity.

ESCULIN. Occurs in the bark and leaves of the horse chestnut tree. It has been used as a skin protectant in ointments and creams. No known toxicity.

ESSENCE. An extract of a substance that retains its fundamental or most desirable properties in concentrated form, such as a fragrance or flavoring.

ESSENCE OF MIRBANE. Nitrobenzene. Used to scent cheap soap. A colorless to pale yellow, oily, poisonous liquid (nitric acid and benzene). It is rapidly absorbed through the skin. Workers are warned not to get it in their eyes or on their skin or clothing. They are also warned not to breathe the vapor. Exposure to essence of mirbane may cause headaches, drowsiness, nausea, vomiting, lack of oxygen in the blood (methemoglobinemia), and cyanosis.

ESSENTIAL OIL. The oily liquid obtained from plants through a variety of processes. The essential oil usually has the taste and smell of the original plant. Essential oils are called volatile because most of them are easily vaporized. The only theories for calling such oils essential are (1) the oils were believed essential to life and (2) they were the "essence" of the plant. The use of essential oils as preservatives is ancient. A large number of oils have antiseptic, germicidal, and preservative action; however, they are primarily used for fragrances and flavorings. No known toxicity when used on the skin. A teaspoon may cause illness in an adult and less than an ounce may kill.

ESTER. A compound formed from an alcohol and an acid by elimination of water, as ethyl acetate (*see*). Usually, fragrant liquids used for artificial fruit perfumes and flavors. Toxicity depends on the ester.

ESTRADIOL. Most potent of the natural estrogenic female hormones. See Hormone Creams and Lotions.

ESTRADIOL BENZOATE. See Estradiol.

ESTRAGON OIL. Tarragon. An aromatic and flavoring agent from the oil of cloves. Used in perfumes to improve the note (*see*) of chypre-type products (*see*). No known toxicity.

ESTROGEN. A female hormone. See Hormone Creams and Lotions.

ESTRONE. A follicular hormone that occurs in the urine of pregnant women and mares, in human placenta, and in palm kernel oil (*see*). Used in creams and lotions as a "hormone" to improve the skin. Usually, there is not enough in the creams to have an effect. It can have harmful systemic effects if used by children.

ETHANOL. Ethyl Alcohol. Rubbing Alcohol. Ordinary Alcohol. An antibacterial used in mouthwashes, nail enamel, astringents, liquid lip rouge, and many other cosmetic products. Clear, colorless, and very flammable, it is made by fermentation of starch, sugar, and other carbohydrates. Used medicinally as a topical antiseptic, sedative, and vessel dilator. Ingestion of large amounts may cause nausea, vomiting, impaired perception, stupor, coma, and death. When it is deliberately denatured (*see*), it is poisonous.

ETHANOLAMIDE OF LAURIC ACID. Used in soapless shampoos,

it is derived from coconut oil. It is a mild irritant but does not cause allergic reactions. See Lauric Acid.

ETHANOLAMINE DITHIODIGLYCOLATE.   See Ethanolamines.

ETHANOLAMINE THIOGLYCOLATE.   See Ethanolamines.

ETHANOLAMINES.   Three compounds—monoethanolamine, diethanolamine, and triethanolamine—with low melting points, colorless and solid, which readily absorb water and form viscous liquids and are soluble both in water and alcohol. They have an ammonia smell and are strong bases. Used in cold permanent wave lotions as a preservative. Also form soaps with fatty acids (*see*) and are widely used as detergents and emulsifying agents. Very large quantities are required for a lethal oral dose in mice (2,140 milligrams per kilogram of body weight). They have been used medicinally as sclerosal agents for varicose veins. Can be irritating to skin if very alkaline.

ETHER.   An organic compound. Acetic ether (see ethyl acetate) is used in nail polishes as a solvent. Water insoluble, fat insoluble liquid with a characteristic odor. It is obtained chiefly by the distillation of alcohol with sulfuric acid and is used chiefly as a solvent. A mild skin irritant. Inhalation or ingestion causes central nervous system depression.

ETHOXYDIGLYCOL.   A liquid solvent prepared from ethylene oxide, a petroleum product. It is used as a solvent and thinner in nail enamels. Absorbs water. More toxic orally in animals than polyethylene glycol (*see*). No specific human data is available. It is nonirritating and nonpenetrating when applied to human skin.

ETHOXYDIGLYCOL ACETATE. Carbitol Acetate.   Used as a solvent and plasticizer for nail enamels and resins and gums. Less toxic than ethoxydiglycol alone by ingestion but is more toxic when applied to the skin.

ETHOXYETHANOL. Cellosolve. Ethylene Glycol Monoethyl Ether. A solvent for nail enamels and a stabilizer in cosmetic emulsions. Obtained by heating ethylene chloride with alcohol and sodium acetate. Colorless and practically odorless. Acute toxicity is several times greater than polyethylene glycol (*see*) in animals. Produces central nervous system depression and kidney damage. Can penetrate the intact skin.

ETHOXYETHANOL ACETATE. Cellosolve Acetate.   Used to give high gloss to nail polish and to retard evaporation. A colorless liquid with a pleasant odor. Somewhat less toxic than ethoxyethanol alone, it is a central nervous system depressant but does not cause as much kidney damage. It can be readily absorbed through the skin.

ETHYL ACETATE. A colorless liquid, with a pleasant fruity odor that occurs naturally in apples, bananas, grape juice, pineapple, raspberries, and strawberries. A very useful solvent in nail enamel and nail polish remover. Also an artificial fruit essence for perfumes. It is a mild local irritant and central nervous system depressant. The vapors are irritating and prolonged inhalation may cause kidney and liver damage. Irritating to the skin. Its fat solvent action produces drying and cracking and sets the stage for secondary infections.

ETHYL ALCOHOL. See Ethanol.

ETHYL BENZOATE. Essence de Niobe. An artificial fruit essence used in perfumes. Almost insoluble in water. Also used in strawberry and raspberry flavorings. No known toxicity.

ETHYL BUTYRATE. Pineapple Oil. An ingredient in perfumes, colorless, with a pineapple odor. It occurs naturally in apples and strawberries. Also used in synthetic flavorings such as blueberry and raspberry. No known toxicity.

ETHYL CARBONATE. Carbonic Acid Diethyl Ester. Pleasant odor. Practically insoluble in water. Solvent for nail enamels. No known toxicity.

ETHYL CINNAMATE. An almost colorless oily liquid with a faint cinnamon odor. Used as a fixative for perfumes; also to scent heavy oriental and floral perfumes in soaps, toilet waters, face powders, and perfumes. Insoluble in water. Also used as a synthetic food flavoring. No known toxicity for the skin.

ETHYL DIISOPROPYLCINNAMATE. See Cinnamic Acid.

ETHYL MORRHUATE. Lipinate. Salt of morrhuic acid, a fatty acid obtained from cod liver oil. Used in creams and lotions. No known toxicity.

ETHYL OLEATE. An ingredient in nail polish remover; yellowish, oily, insoluble in water. It is made from carbon, hydrogen, oxygen, and oleic acid (*see*) and used as a synthetic butter and fruit flavoring. No known toxicity.

ETHYL PERSEATE. Fatty acid derived from either apricot kernel or peach kernel oil. See Apricot and Peach Kernel Oil.

ETHYL PHENYLACETATE. A fixative for perfumes, colorless, or nearly colorless liquid, with a sweet honey rose odor. Also a synthetic flavoring agent in various foods. No known toxicity.

ETHYL PHTHALYL ETHYL GLYCOLATE. Aromatic ester. A solvent, a fixative for perfumes and a denaturant. See Polyethylene and Phthalic Acid for toxicity.

ETHYL SALICYLATE. Used in the manufacture of artificial perfumes. Occurs naturally in strawberries and has a pleasant odor. Also a synthetic flavoring agent in fruit, drinks, baked goods, and so on. At one time it was used to treat rheumatics. It may, when ingested, interact harmfully with medications such as anticoagulants, antidepressants, and medications for cancer such as methotrexate. It may also cause allergic reactions in those persons allergic to other salicylates, such as those used in sunscreen lotions.

ETHYL VANILLIN. An ingredient in perfumes. Colorless flakes, with an odor and flavor stronger than vanilla. Also a synthetic food flavoring. No known toxicity.

ETHYL CELLULOSE. Cellulose Ether. Binding, dispersing, and emulsifying agent used in cosmetics, particularly nail polishes and liquid lip rouge. Prepared from wood pulp or chemical cotton by treatment with an alkali. Also used as a diluent (*see*). Not susceptible to bacterial or fungal decomposition. No known toxicity.

ETHYLENE/ACRYLATE COPOLYMER. See Acrylates and Copolymers.

ETHYLENE GLYCOL. A slightly viscous liquid with a sweet taste. Absorbs twice its weight in water. Used as an antifreeze and humectant (*see*); also as a solvent. Toxic when ingested, causing central nervous system depression, vomiting, drowsiness, coma, respiratory failure, kidney damage, and possibly death.

ETHYLENE/MALEIC ANHYDRIDE COPOLYMER. Plastic material made from ethylene and maleic anhydride. Maleic anhydride is a powerful irritant causing burns. Contact with skin should be avoided. Ethylene is used in the manufacture of plastics and alcohols. High concentration can cause unconsciousness.

ETHYLENE UREA. See Urea.

ETHYLENE/VA COPOLYMER. See Polyethylene.

ETHYLENEDIAMINE TETRAACETIC ACID (EDTA). An important compound in cosmetics used primarily as a sequestering agent (*see*), particularly in shampoos. It may be irritating to the skin and mucous membranes and cause allergies such as asthma and skin rashes. Also used as a sequestrant in carbonated beverages. When ingested, it may cause errors in a number of laboratory tests, including those for calcium, carbon dioxide, nitrogen, and muscular activity. It is on the FDA list of food additives to be studied for toxicity.

ETHYLPARABEN. See Propylparaben.

EUCALYPTOL. A chief constituent of eucalyptus and cajeput oils. Occurs naturally in allspice, star anise, bay, calamus, and peppermint oil. An antiseptic, antispasmodic, and expectorant. Used to flavor toothpaste and mouthwash and to cover up malodors in depilatories. It is not used in hypoallergenic cosmetics. Fatalities followed ingestion of doses as small as 3 to 5 milliliters (about equivalent to a teaspoon), and recovery has occurred after doses as large as 20 to 30 milliliters.

EUCALYPTUS EXTRACT. See Eucalyptus Oil.

EUCALYPTUS OIL. Dinkum Oil. Used in skin fresheners. The colorless to pale yellow volatile liquid from the fresh leaves of the eucalyptus tree. It is 70 to 80 percent eucalyptol (*see*) and has a spicy cool taste and a characteristic aromatic, somewhat camphorlike odor. Used as a local antiseptic. It can cause allergic reactions, and fatalities have followed ingestion of doses as small as 3 to 5 milliliters (about equal to a teaspoon), and as little as 1 milliliter has caused coma.

EUGENOL. An ingredient in perfumes and dentifrices obtained from clove oil (*see*). Occurs naturally in allspice, basil, bay leaves, calamus, pimento, and laurel leaves. It has a spicy, pungent taste. Used as a fixative in perfumes and flavorings. Eugenol also acts as a local antiseptic. When ingested, may cause vomiting and gastric irritation. Because of its potential as an allergen, it is left out of hypoallergenic cosmetics.

EUPHRASIA. Eyebright Herbs. A derivative from any of several herbs and regarded as a remedy for eye ailments. It is used to soothe the eyes in a rinse. No known toxicity.

EXALTING FIXATIVES. A material that acts as an odor carrier, improving and fortifying transportation of the vapors of other perfume materials. Musk and civet are examples. See Fixatives.

EXT. D & C GREEN NO. 1. Acid Green 1. A dull, weak green. Classed chemically as a nitroso color. Used in hair-waving fluids, bath salts, and soaps, among other cosmetics. See Colors.

EXT. D & C VIOLET No. 2. Classed chemically as an anthraquinone color. Bluish scarlet. Permitted only for use in preformed hair colors but textbooks list use in bath salts, soaps, and hair-waving fluids as well. The cosmetics industry has petitioned the FDA to allow wider use. See Colors.

EXT. D & C YELLOW NO. 1. Acid Yellow 36. Classed chemically as a monoazo color, it is used in bath salts, soaps, hair rinses, shampoos, as well as other cosmetics. A brownish yellow powder, it is soluble in water and alcohol. No known toxicity. See Colors.

EXT. D & C YELLOW NO. 7. Formerly FD & C Yellow No. 1. Greenish yellow. A coal tar color. Classed chemically as a nitro color.

It is the disodium salt of 2,4-Dinitro-1-Naphthol-7-Sulfonic Acid. Used in hair rinses and shampoos. See Colors.

EXT. D & C YELLOW NO. 7 ALUMINUM LAKE. *Naphthol Yellow Lake.* A coal tar color. Light yellow or orange yellow powder. An insoluble pigment prepared from Ext. D & C Yellow No. 7 (*see*). See Colors.

EXTENDER. A substance added to a product, especially a diluent or modifier (*see both*). Petroleum jelly would be an example.

EXTRACT. The solution that results from passing alcohol or an alcohol-water mixture through a substance. Examples of extracts would be the alcohol-water mixtures of vanillin, orange, or lemon extracts found among the spices and flavorings on the supermarket shelf. Extracts are not as strong as essential oils (*see*).

EYE CREAMS. *Eye Wrinkle Creams.* So-called eye creams are slightly modified emollient creams (*see*), usually with the perfume omitted. There is less subcutaneous fat in the skin around the eyes and it is likely for this reason that wrinkles first begin to develop there. According to the American Medical Association, eye creams will not prevent wrinkles but may make them less noticeable. Most eye creams contain essentially the same ingredients: lecithin, cholesterol, beeswax, lanolin, sodium benzoate, boric acid, mineral oil, ascorbyl palmitate, and almond oil (*see all*).

EYE MAKEUP REMOVER. Pads saturated with ingredients to remove eye makeup. They may contain a solvent such as acetone (*see*), an oil and/or lanolin (*see*), and perfume. Hypoallergenic (*see*) cosmetic manufacturers use cotton pads saturated with pure mineral oil. Eye irritations from eye makeup removers have been reported to the FDA within the past several years.

EYE MASCARA. Mascara is used to color and thicken eyelashes. Early mascara was composed of a pigment and soap. Today it still contains a salt of stearic acid (*see*) with pigments and/or lanolin, paraffin and carnauba wax (*see all*). Within the past two years there has been a number of complaints of itching, burning, and swelling of eyes and eye irritation due to mascara.

EYE SHADOW. Shades of blue, green, brown, red, yellow, and white are used to color the lid and area under the eyebrow to highlight the eyes. The waterless type of eye shadows uses colors mixed with a lightening agent such as titanium dioxide (*see*) and are then mixed with petrolatum (*see*) on a roller mill. Eye shadows may also contain lanolin, beeswax, ceresin, calcium carbonate, mineral oil, sorbitan oleate, and talc (*see all*). The iridescent effect is achieved by adding very pure aluminum. There have been reports in recent years of eye irritation from eye shadow and one complaint of a package shattering in the eye and another of a sharp foreign article in the product applicator.

EYEBRIGHT HERBS.   See Euphrasia.

EYEBROW DYES.   See Eyelash Dyes.

EYEBROW PENCILS.   Usually contain lampblack, petrolatum, and paraffin (*see all*) and sometimes aluminum silicate and stearic acid (*see both*). The use of eyeliner pencils applied to the upper and lower border of the eyelids inside the lashes rather than to the eyelid behind the lashes is not recommended by physicians. According to a report by an eye specialist quoted by the American Medical Association, this may lead to various problems, including permanent pigmentation of the mucous membrane lining of the inside of the eye, moderate redness and itching, tearing and blurring of vision.

EYEBROW PLUCKING CREAM.   Used to soften the skin to allow the hair to be pulled more easily and to alleviate the discomfort. Most eyebrow plucking creams contain benzocaine, a pain killer, and cold cream (*see both*). Nontoxic if uncontaminated.

EYEDROPS, LOTIONS, AND WASHES.   Soothe and clear eyes of redness. Work by constricting the blood vessels in the eyes, by anesthetizing and soothing the eyes with anesthetics and emollients. Mild astringents such as boric acid or sodium chloride are used. Mild anesthetics used are antipyrine hydrastine hydrochloride and berberine hydrochloride. To contract blood vessels tetrahydrozoline hydrochloride is used. Included for their pleasant smell are camphor, peppermint, or witch hazel. Among the preservatives used are phenols, cresols, and formaldehydes. A wetting agent such as benzylkonium is also usually included. Reports of eye irritations are infrequent from eye treatment products, but the largest danger is from contamination because eye solutions are good mediums for the growth of bacteria and molds; therefore, they must be kept sterile.

EYELASH CREAMS.   Used to make the lashes soft and shiny. Such creams usually contain lanolin, cocoa butter, paraffin, cetyl alcohol, and peach kernel oil (*see all*). Nontoxic if uncontaminated. However, ingredients may cause reactions in persons who are allergic to specific ingredients.

EYELASH DYES. Includes Eyebrow Dyes.   Brown, black, and blue certified oil-soluble dyes are used. Because of possible damage to the eyes, only certain ingredients and colors may be used in these preparations (see Colors). The U.S. Food and Drug Administration forbids the use of coal tar dyes (*see*) in the area of the eye. Highly purified inorganic pigments must be used; among them carbon black, charcoal black, black iron oxide, and ultramarine blue for black and blue shades. Iron oxides are used also for yellow and brown shades, carmine for red, chromic oxides for green, and titanium dioxide or zinc oxide for white (*see all*). See Colors for toxicity.

EYELASH OILS. Used to make the lashes soft and shiny. Such oils usually contain lanolin, cocoa butter, cetyl alcohol, alcohol water, and olive oil. Nontoxic if uncontaminated. However, reactions may occur in persons allergic to specific ingredients.

EYELINERS. Used to outline and accentuate the eyes, eyeliners may be in pencil or liquid form or in the newer pencil-brush container. Eyeliners usually contain an alkanolamine, a fatty alcohol, polyvinylpyrrolidone, cellulose ether, methylparaben, antioxidants, perfumes, and titanium dioxide (*see all*). Waterproof eyeliners resist tears, moisture in the air, and perspiration. Some also resist ordinary soap and water. Most of the waterproof eyeliners are made of a pigment suspended in a gum or resin solution or a pigmented waxy base dissolved in a volatile solvent. Waterproof eyeliners must be removed with a solvent such as mineral oil or similar oils. Most facial cleansing lotions and creams contain such solvents. The U.S. Food and Drug Administration has found a persistent problem of bacterial contamination in some liquid eyeliners. Since bacterial infections around the eyes can lead to serious problems, it is probably better to purchase nonliquid eyeliners. There are also a significant number of persons allergic to eyeliners and other such products. The American Medical Association recommends that women stop using an eyeliner or eye makeup product if their skin becomes red, itchy, or swollen whenever an eye cosmetic is applied. The AMA also points out that because eyelids are easily irritated, eye makeup, particularly eyeliner, should be removed with care. It also cautions against repeatedly applying eye makeup at one session because of the possibility of irritation. There have been a number of reports of swollen eyelids and eye irritation from well-known products.

EYEWASHES. See Eyedrops, Lotions, and Washes.

F

FACE MASKS AND PACKS. Claims are made for face masks and for the thicker face packs that they shrink pores, remove wrinkles, and relieve tension. Only the last may be true. According to the American Medical Association, there is no evidence that any cosmetic can safely shrink pores and only surgery removes wrinkles. However, the apparent cooling or tight feeling derived from their use may induce a cleansing feeling. Clay face masks usually contain purified siliceous earth, kaolin, glycerin, and water. Face packs usually contain zinc stearate, zinc oxide, tragacanth, alcohol, glycerin, and limewater. Both masks and packs may also contain acacia, balsam Peru, glyceryl monostearate, hexachlorophene, magnesium carbonate, wax, salicylic acid, spermaceti, Turkey-red oil, talc, titanium oxide, and/or zinc sulfate. (See ingredients above under separate listings.) Recent complaints to the FDA about face masks and packs include a burning sensation, swelling, blisters and lumps, eye ailments, skin irritation, and corneal ulcers.

FAKE NAILS.   See Artificial Nails.

FALSE EYELASHES.   False eyelashes have become popular in recent years. They are made of real or synthetic hair on a thin stringlike base that is pasted over the natural eyelashes on the eyelid. There have been cases of eye irritation and one case of blindness reported to the FDA. Whether the problems were the result of the adhesive used, the dye on the eyelashes, or other materials, the FDA has not made public.

FARNESOL.   Used in perfumery to emphasize the odor of sweet floral perfumes such as lilac. Occurs naturally in ambrette seed, star anise, cassia, linden flowers, oils of musk seed, citronella, rose, and balsam. Also a food flavoring. No known toxicity.

FATIGUE.   Everyone's nose becomes "fatigued" when smelling a certain smell. No matter how much you like a fragrance, you can only smell it for a short interval. It is nature's way of protecting humans from overstimulation of the olfactory sense.

FATTY ACID ESTERS.   See Ester. The fatty acid esters of low molecular weight alcohols are widely used in hand products because they are oily but nongreasy when applied to the skin. They are emollients and emulsifiers. No known toxicity.

FATTY ACIDS.   Fatty acids are used in bubble baths and lipsticks, but chiefly for making soap and detergents. One or any mixture of liquid and solid acids, capric, caprylic, lauric, myristic, oleic, palmitic, and stearic. In combination with glycerin, they form fat. Necessary for normal growth and healthy skin. In foods they are used as emulsifiers, binders, and lubricants. See Stearic Acid. No known toxicity.

FATTY ALCOHOLS. Cetyl, Stearyl, Lauryl, Myristyl. Solid alcohols made from acids and widely used in hand creams and lotions.
Cetyl and stearyl alcohols form an occlusive film to keep skin mois-
tuer from evaporating and they impart a velvety feel to the skin.
Lauryl and myristyl are used in detergents and creams. Very low
toxicity.
FD & C BLUE NO. 1. Brilliant Blue FCF. A coal tar derivative,
triphenylmethane, used for hair colorings, face powders, and other
cosmetics. Also used as a coloring in bottled soft drinks, gelatin desserts,
cereals, and other foods. May cause allergic reactions and will produce
malignant tumors at the site of injections in rats. On the FDA permanent list of color additives. Rated 1A, that is, completely acceptable
for nonfood use, by the World Health Associaton. See Colors.
FD & C BLUE NO. 1 ALUMINUM LAKE. Aluminum salt of certified FD & C Blue No. 1 (*see*). See Colors and Lakes.
FD & C BLUE NO. 2. Indigo Carmine. Used in hair rinses. Almost
always contains sodium chloride, which is common table salt. A dark
blue powder sensitive to light. Also used in bottled soft drinks, foods,
and dry drink powders. Employed as a dye in kidney tests and in
testing milk. On the provisional list of approved colors. It is omitted
from hypoallergenic cosmetics because it frequently causes allergic
reactions. See Indigo and Colors.
FD & C BLUE NO. 2 ALUMINUM LAKE. Aluminum salt of certified FD & C Blue No. 2 (*see*). See Colors and Lakes.
FD & C GREEN NO. 3. Fast Green FCF. Moderate bright green.
A coal tar derivative, triphenylmethane, used in hair rinses and in
mint-flavored jelly, frozen desserts, candy, confections, and cereals. It
is a sensitizer in the allergic. On the provisional list of approved color
additives. Produces malignant tumors at the site of injection when
introduced under the skin of rats. See Colors.
FD & C RED NO. 2. Amaranth. Formerly one of the most widely
used cosmetic and food colorings. A dark, reddish-brown powder that
turns bright red when mixed with fluid. A monoazo color, it was
used in lipsticks, rouges, and other cosmetics as well as in cereals,
maraschino cherries, and desserts. The safety of this dye was questioned by American scientists for more than twenty years. Two
Russian scientists found that FD & C Red No. 2 prevented some preg-
nancies and caused some stillbirths in rats. The FDA ordered manufacturers using the color to submit data on all food, drug and cosmetic products containing it. Controversial tests at the FDA's National
Center for Toxicological Research in Arkansas showed that in high
doses Red No. 2 caused a statistically significant increase in a variety

of cancers in female rats. The dye was banned by the FDA in January, 1976.

FD & C RED NO. 2 ALUMINUM LAKE.   The aluminum salt of certified FD & C Red No. 2 (*see*). See Colors and Lakes.

FD & C RED NO. 3. Erythrosine.   Bluish pink. A coal tar derivative, a xanthene color, used in toothpaste and in canned fruit cocktail, fruit salad, and cherry pie mixes as well as maraschino cherries. On the provisional list of approved colors (*see*).

FD & C RED NO. 3 ALUMINUM LAKE.   The aluminum salt of certified FD & C Red No. 3 (*see*). See Colors and Lakes.

FD & C RED NO. 4.   A monoazo color and a coal tar dye. Used in mouthwashes, bath salts, and hair rinses. It was banned in food by the FDA in 1964 when it was shown to damage the adrenal glands and bladders of dogs. The agency relented and gave it a provisional license for use in marachino cherries. However, it was finally banned in 1976 for foods but is still permitted in cosmetics for external use. See Colors.

FD & C RED NO. 40. Allura Red AC.   Newest color. Expected to have wide use in the cosmetic industry. Approved in 1971, Allied Chemical has an exclusive patent on it. It will probably be substituted for FD & C Red No. 4 in many cosmetic, food, and drug products. Permanently listed because, unlike the producers of "temporary" colors, this producer supplied reproductive data. However, many American scientists feel that the safety of Red 40 is far from established, particularly because all the tests were conducted by the manufacturer. Therefore, the dye should not have received permanent safety rating. See Colors.

FD & C VIOLET NO. 1.   A coal tar derivative, triphenylmethane, used in hair rinses, lipsticks, gelatin desserts, ice cream, sherbets, carbonated beverages, dry drink powders, candy, and other foods. Dropped from the provisionally approved list. A Canadian study published in 1962 showed the dye caused cancer in 50 percent of the rats fed it in food. The FDA did not consider this valid evidence since the exact nature of the dye used could not be determined, and all records and specimens are lost and not available for study. Furthermore, previous and subsequent studies have not confirmed evidence of Violet 1 causing cancer in rats. However, a two-year study with dogs did show noncancerous lesions on the dogs' ears after being fed Violet 1. The FDA again felt the study was not adequate but that the ear lesions did appear to be dye-related and that perhaps two years may be too short a period to determine their eventual outcome. The

FDA ruled on October 28, 1971, that Violet 1 should remain provisionally listed pending the outcome of a new dog study. However, it was finally banned in 1973. See Colors.

FD & C VIOLET NO. 1 ALUMINUM LAKE. The aluminum salt of the certified FD & C Violet No. 1 (*see*). See Colors and Lakes.

FD & C YELLOW NO. 5. *Tartrazine*. A pyrazole color used in hair rinses, hair-waving fluids, and in bath salts. A coal tar derivative, it is also found in prepared breakfast cereals, imitation strawberry jelly, and bottled soft drinks. Causes allergic reactions in persons sensitive to aspirin. The certified color industry petitioned for permanent listing of this color in February 1965, with no limitations other than good manufacturing practice. However, in February 1966, the FDA proposed the listing of this color with a maximum rate of use of 300 ppm in food. The color industry objected to the limitation and FD & C Yellow No. 5 is still on the list of provisionally approved color additives. See Colors.

FD & C YELLOW NO. 5 ALUMINUM LAKE. See FD & C Yellow No. 5, Colors, and Lakes.

FD & C YELLOW NO. 6. *Sunset Yellow FCF*. A coal tar, a monoazo color, used in hair rinses as well as other cosmetics, carbonated beverages, gelatin desserts, and dry drink powders. It is not used in products that contain fats and oils. May cause allergic reactions. On the provisional list of approved color additives. See Colors.

FD & C YELLOW NO. 6 ALUMINUM LAKE. See FD & C Yellow No. 6, Colors, and Lakes.

FEMININE HYGIENE SPRAYS. See Vaginal Deodorants.

FENNEL. One of the earliest known herbs from the tall beautiful shrub. Used in astringents and perfumes. The fennel flowers appear in June and are bright yellow. Compresses of fennel tea are used by organic cosmeticians to soothe inflamed eyelids and watery eyes. May cause allergic reactions.

FENUGREEK SEED. *Greek Hay*. An annual herb grown in southern Europe, North Africa, and India, and used in hair tonic supposedly to prevent baldness; also added to powders, poultices, and ointments. The seeds are used in making curry. Nontoxic.

FERRIC CHLORIDE. Brownish yellow or orange iron compound. Absorbs water readily. Used as a styptic and astringent. Irritating to the skin and not suitable for wide use.

FERRIC FERROCYANIDE. *Prussian Blue*. Dark blue powder (or lumps of) and iron compound. Used as a coloring. No known toxicity.

FERROUS SULFATE. *Green or Iron Vitriol*. Pale bluish green, odorless crystals, efflorescent in dry air. An astringent and deodorant.

Used in hair dyes. A source of iron used medicinally. No known toxicity.

FINGERNAIL POLISH.   See Nail Polish.

FINGERNAIL POLISH REMOVER.   See Nail Polish Remover.

FISH GLYCERIDES.   See Fish Oil and Glycerin.

FISH OIL (Hydrogenated).   A fatty oil from fish or marine mammals used in soap making.

FIXATIVE.   A chemical that reduces the tendency of an odor or flavor to vaporize, by making the odor or flavor last longer. An example is musk (*see*), which is used in perfume.

FLEXIBLE COLLODION.   A mixture of collodion, camphor, and castor oil (*see all*).

FLORAL BOUQUETS.   One of the basic perfume types, it is a blending of flower notes with no particular standouts. For balance and body, it may contain a medley of basic notes such as amber, musk, vetiver, as well as a touch of the aromatic, but there is definitely the scent of a bouquet of flowers.

FLUORESCEIN.   A yellow granular or red crystalline dye giving a brilliant yellow green fluorescence in an alkaline solution. Very visible. See Tetrabromofluorescein for toxicity.

FLUORESCENT BRIGHTENERS (46, 47, 52).   Colorless, water- or solvent-soluble aromatic compounds with an affinity for fibers. They are usually violet, blue, or blue green colors, and are capable of increasing both the blueness and the brightness of a substrate with a resulting marked whitening effect. They improve the brightness of tints and are included in detergents of all kinds to enhance cleansing action.

FLUORIDE.   An acid salt used in toothpaste to prevent tooth decay. See Stannous Fluoride.

FLUROSALAN.   A salicylide used as an antiseptic agency. See Salicylides.

FOLIC ACID.   A yellowish orange compound and member of the Vitamin B-complex, used as a nutrient. Used in cosmetic emollients. Occurs naturally in liver, kidney, mushrooms, and green leaves. Aids in cell formation, especially red blood cells. No known toxicity.

FOOD RED 6. Formerly Ext. D & C Red No. 15, FD & C Red No. 1, and Ponceau 3R.   One of the first approved certified coal tar colors, Food Red 6 was delisted as a food additive as possibly harmful. Dark red powder, it changes to cherry red in solution. See Colors.

FOREST BLENDS.   One of the basic perfume types, these blends are woody, mossy-leafy, or resinous. They either stand out alone with the aromatic notes of an individual nature, such as sandalwood, rose-wood, the balsams, or cedarwood, or they have a combination of these notes. Quite often, the more pungent notes of geranium, lavender, fern, and herbs are added to give an earthy quality.

FORMALDEHYDE. A colorless gas obtained by the oxidation of methyl alcohol and generally used in watery solution. Vapors are intensely irritating to mucous membranes. It is used in nail hardeners, nail polish, soap, and hair-growing products. Formaldehyde generally is known as a disinfectant, germicide, fungicide, defoamer, and preservative, and is used in embalming fluids. Ingestion can cause severe abdominal pain, internal bleeding, loss of ability to urinate, vertigo, coma, and death. One ounce taken by mouth causes death within two hours. Skin reactions after exposure to formaldehyde are very common because the chemical can be both irritating and allergy causing. Products to prevent the nails from chipping, fragmenting, and peeling often contain formaldehyde. Physicians have reported severe reactions to such nail hardeners, including discoloration, bleeding under the nail, dryness, and even loss of the nails. The cuticle and surrounding skin have also been involved.

FORMIC ACID. Used as a rubefacient (*see*) in hair tonics; also a synthetic food flavoring. Colorless, pungent, highly corrosive, it occurs naturally in apples and other fruits. Also used as a decalcifier and for dehairing hides. Chronic absorption is known to cause albuminuria—protein in the urine.

FOUNDATION MAKEUP. The purpose of foundation makeup is to dry out oily skin (or to oil dry skin), cover blemishes, protect the skin from wind and cold, and give a glowing, healthy look to the skin. There is a cream-type foundation that vanishes from the skin but leaves a smooth, protective base for the application of pigmented makeup. Such creams are usually about 75 percent water, 15 percent stearic acid (*see*), and the remainder either sorbitan stearate or sorbitol (*see*). The pigmented foundation creams, which are designed to tint and cover the skin, usually contain about 50 percent water, mineral oil, stearic acid, lanolin, cetyl alcohol, propylene glycol, triethanolamine, borax, and insoluble pigments. They may also contain emulsifiers and detergents; humectants to absorb and retain water such as propylene glycol, glycerin, and sorbitol; lanolin derivatives; perfume; preservatives such as paraben; special barrier agents such as zinc stearate; cellulose derivatives and silicone; synthetic esters; thickeners such as sodium alginate, gum tragacanth, quince seed, and mucilage; and such waxes as beeswax and spermaceti. Stick-type makeup is made from isopropyl myristate, beeswax, carnauba wax, mineral oil, perfume, and dry pigment. Cake makeup, which is used by applying a wet sponge to the material and then applying the sponge to the face, is usually made of finely ground pigment, talc, kaolin, zinc, titanium oxide, precipitated calcium carbonate, and such inorganic pigments as iron oxides. To these may be added sorbitol, propylene glycol, lanolin, mineral oil, and perfume (*see all*). Cake makeup usually is the best of the makeups for covering defects. Liquid makeup preparations contain suspensions of such pigments as zinc oxide and inorganic pigments in alcohol and water solution. The instructions require the user to "shake well." However, bentonite (*see*) now helps keep the product in suspension. Emulsified lotions contain pigments plus glyceryl monostearate, propylene glycol, monostearate, mineral oil, stearic acid, water, triethanolamine, bentonite, kaolin, and sodium lauryl sulfate mixed with pigment (*see all*). Problems reported recently to the FDA concerning makeup include rashes on the face, arms, and chest, skin swelling and eruptions, swollen eyes, inflammation and itching of the face.

FRANGIPANI.   An essential oil for a perfume derived from or imitating the odor of the flower of the red jasmine. Nontoxic.

FRECKLE CREAMS, LOTIONS, AND REMOVERS.   See Skin Bleach.

FREON. Arcton.   Trademark used for a group of nonliquid paraffins (*see*), usually based on methane and containing one or more atoms of fluorine. Widely used as noncorrosive, supposedly nontoxic propellants and refrigerants in aerosols, particularly for hair sprays. See Aerosols for toxicity.

FRESHENER.   See Skin Freshener.

FRUITY BLENDS.   One of the basic perfume types, fruity blends have other notes present but are noted for their clean, fresh citrus notes, or a smooth, mellow, peachlike warmth.

FULLER'S EARTH.   Used in dry shampoos, hair colorings, beauty masks, and as a dusting powder; also used for lubricants and soaps. A white or brown naturally occurring earthy substance. A nonplastic variety of kaolin (*see*) containing an aluminum magnesium silicate. Used as an absorbent and to decolorize fats and oils. No known toxicity.

FURFURAL. Artificial Ant Oil.   Used as a solvent, insecticide, fungicide, to decolor resins, and as a synthetic flavoring in food. A colorless liquid with a peculiar odor. Occurs naturally in angelica root, apples, coffee, peaches, skim milk. Darkens when exposed to air.

It irritates mucous membranes and acts on the central nervous system. Causes tearing and inflammation of the eyes and throat. Ingestion or absorption of .06 grams produces persistent headache. Used continually, it leads to nervous disturbances and eye disorders.

G

GARDENIA. The white or yellow flowers used in fragrances. Obtained from a large genus of Old World tropical trees and shrubs. No known toxicity.

GEL. A semisolid, apparently homogenous substance that may be elastic and jellylike (gelatin) or more or less rigid (silica gel) and that is formed in various ways such as by coagulation or evaporation.

GELATIN. Used in protein shampoos because it sticks to the hair and gives it "more body," peelable face masks, and as a fingernail strengthener. Gelatin is a protein obtained by boiling skin, tendons, ligaments, or bones with water. It is colorless or slightly yellow, tasteless, and absorbs 5 to 10 times its weight of cold water. Also used as a food thickener and stabilizer and a base for fruit gelatins and puddings. Employed medicinally to treat malnutrition and brittle fingernails. No known toxicity.

GENTIAN. The yellow or pale bitter root of central and southern European plants used in cosmetics as an astringent and in conditioning creams. Also used in food flavorings, as an appetite stimulant, and by people who want to stop smoking. Used medicinally as a bitter tonic. No known toxicity.

GERANIOL. Used in perfumery to compound artificial attar of roses and artificial orange blossom oil. Also used in depilatories to mask odors. Oily, sweet, with a rose odor, it occurs naturally in apples, bay leaves, cherries, grapefruit, ginger, lavender, and a number of other essential oils. Geraniol is omitted from hypoallergenic cosmetics. Can cause allergic reactions.

GERANIUM OIL. Used in perfumery, dusting powder, tooth powder, and ointments. It is the light yellow to deep yellow oil of plants of the genus *Pelargonium* or of rose geranium leaves, with the characteristic odor of rose and geraniol (*see*). A teaspoon may cause illness in an adult and less than an ounce may kill. No known skin toxicity except for those allergic to geraniums.

GINSENG. Root of the ginseng plant grown in China, Korea, and the United States. It produces a resin, a sugar starch, glue, and volatile oil. Widely used in Oriental medicine as an aromatic bitter. It is used in American cosmetics as a demulcent (*see*).

GLAUBER'S SALT.   Crystalline sodium sulfate (*see*) used as an opacifier in shampoos and as a detergent in bath salts. Named for a German chemist, Johann R. Glauber, who died in 1668. Also used as a laxative medicinally. Skin irritations may occur.

GLOSS WHITE.   See Barium Sulfate.

GLUCOSE.   Used as a flavoring, to soothe the skin, and as a filler in cosmetics. Occurs naturally in blood, grape, and corn sugars. A source of energy for plants and animals. Sweeter than sucrose. No known toxicity in cosmetics but confectioners frequently suffer erosions and fissures around their nails and the nails loosen and sometimes fall off.

GLUCOSE GLUTAMATE.   Used as a humectant in hand creams and lotions, it occurs naturally in animal blood, grape, and corn sugars, and is a source of energy for plants and animals. It is sweeter than sucrose. Glucose syrup is used to flavor sausage, hamburger, and other processed meats. Also used as an extender in maple syrup and medicinally as a nutrient. Glutamate is the salt of glutamic acid and is used to impart meat flavor to foods and to enhance other natural food flavors. The FDA has asked for further studies as to its potential mutagenic, teratogenic, subacute, and reproductive effects. No known skin toxicity.

GLUTAMATE.   Ammonium and monopotassium salt of glutamic acid (*see*). Used to impart meat flavor to foods, to enhance other natural foods and flavors, and to improve the taste of tobacco. It is used as an antioxidant in cosmetics to prevent spoilage. It is being studied by the FDA for mutagenic, teratogenic, subacute, and reproductive effects.

GLUTAMIC ACID.   A white, practcially odorless, free-flowing crystalline powder, a nonessential amino acid (*see*) usually manufactured from vegetable protein. A salt substitute, it has been used to treat epilepsy and to correct stomach acids. It is used to impart meat flavor to foods. Used as an antioxidant in cosmetics and as a softener in permanent wave solutions to help provide against hair damage. It is being studied by the FDA for mutagenic, teratogenic, subacute, and reproductive effects.

GLUTARAL. Glutaraldehyde.   An amino acid (*see*) that occurs in green sugar beets. Used in creams and emollients. It has a faint agreeable odor. See Glutaric Acid.

GLUTARIC ACID. Pentanedioic Acid.   A crystalline fatty acid that occurs in green sugar beets, sweat, and in crude wood. Very soluble in alcohol and ether. Used in creams and emollients. See Fatty Acids.

GLYCERETH-26. Liponic EG-1.   See Glycerin.

GLYCERIDES.   Any of a large class of compounds that are esters (*see*) of the sweet alcohol, glycerol. They are also made synthetically. They are used in cosmetic creams as a texturizer and emollient. No known toxicity.

GLYCERIN. Glycerol.   A by-product of soap manufacture, it is a sweet, warm tasting, oily fluid obtained by adding alkalies (*see*) to fats and fixed oils. A solvent, humectant, and emollient in many cosmetics, it absorbs moisture from the air and, therefore, helps keep moisture in creams and other products, even if the consumer leaves the cap off the container. Also helps the products to spread better. A humectant in foods and a solvent for food colors and flavors. Among the many products containing glycerin are cream rouge, face packs and masks, freckle lotions, hand creams and lotions, hair lacquers, liquid face powder, mouthwashes, protective creams, skin fresheners, and toothpastes. In concentrated solutions it is irritating to the mucous membranes.

GLYCERYL p-AMINOBENZOATE.   A semisolid waxy mass or syrup with a faint aromatic odor, liquefying and congealing very slowly, used in cosmetic sunscreen preparations. See Benzoic Acid for toxicity.

GLYCERYL COCONATE.   See Glycerin.

GLYCERYL DILAURATE.   See Glycerin.

GLYCERYL ERUCATE.   See Glycerin.

GLYCERYL HYDROSTEARATE.   See Glyceryl Monostearate.

GLYCERYL ISOSTEARATE.   See Glyceryl Monostearate.

GLYCERYL MONOSTEARATE.   An emulsifying and dispersing agent used in baby creams, face masks, foundation cake makeup, liquid powders, hair conditioners, hand lotions, mascara, and nail whiteners. It is a mixture of two glyceryls, a white waxlike solid, or beads, and is soluble in hot organic solvents such as alcohol. Lethal when injected in large doses into mice. No known skin toxicity.

GLYCERYL MYRISTATE.   See Glycerin.

GLYCERYL OLEATE.   See Glycerin.

GLYCERYL RICINOLEATE.   See Glycerin.

GLYCERYL SESQUIOLEATE.   See Glycerin.

GLYCERYL STARCH.   See Starch and Glycerols.

GLYCERYL STEARATE.   See Glycerin.

GLYCERYL STEARATE SE.   See Glyceryl Monostearate.

GLYCERYL TRIMYRISTATE.   See Glycerin.

GLYCINE.   Used as a texturizer in cosmetics. An amino acid (*see*) classified as nonessential. Made up of sweet-tasting crystals, it is used as a dietary supplement and as a gastric antacid. No known toxicity.

GLYCOL DISTEARATE.   Alcohol from glycol. See Glycols.

GLYCOL STEARATE SE.   See Glycols.

GLYCOLIC ACID.   Contained in sugar cane juice, it is an odorless, slightly water-absorbing acid used to control the acid/alkali balance in cosmetics and whenever a cheap organic acid is needed. It is also used in copper brightening, decontamination procedures, and in dyeing. It is a mild irritant to the skin and mucous membranes.

GLYCOLS. Propylene Glycol. Glycerin. Ethylene Glycol. Carbitol. Diethylene Glycol.   Literally it means "glycerin" plus "alcohol." A group of syrupy alcohols derived from hydrocarbons (*see*) and widely used in cosmetics as humectants. The FDA cautions manufacturers that glycols may cause adverse reactions in users. Propylene glycol and glycerin (*see both*) are considered safe. Other glycols in low concentrations may be harmless for external application but ethylene glycol, carbitol, and diethylene glycol are hazardous in concentrations exceeding 5 percent even in preparations for use on small areas of the body. Therefore, in sunscreen lotions and protective creams where the area of application is extensive, they should not be used at all. Wetting agents (*see*) increase the absorption of glycols and therefore their toxicity.

GLYCRETH-26. Liponic.   See Glycerin.

GLYCYRRETINIC ACID.   Used as a flavoring, to soothe skin, and as a carrier. Prepared from licorice root, it is soluble in chloroform, alcohol, and acetic acid (*see*). It has been used medicinally to treat a disease of the adrenal gland. No known toxicity when used in cosmetics.

GLYCYRRHIZIC ACID.   Used as a flavoring, coloring, and to soothe the skin in cosmetics. Extracted from licorice, the crystalline material is soluble in hot water and alcohol. See Glycyrretinic Acid.

GLYOXAL.   An anesthetic and deodorant. A reactive yellow, low-melting aldehyde (*see*) made from ethylene glycol. Easily polymerized (*see*). See Ethylene Glycol for toxicity.

GLYOXYLIC ACID.   Used as a coloring. Syrup or crystals that occur in unripe fruit, young leaves, and baby sugar beets. Malodorous and strongly corrosive. Forms a thick syrup, very soluble in water, sparingly soluble in alcohol. It absorbs water from the air and condenses with urea to form allantoin (*see*) and gives a nice blue color with sulfuric acid. It is a skin irritant and corrosive.

GOLD.   Used as a coloring and to give shine to cosmetics. The soft yellow metal occurring in the earth's crust and used in jewelry, gold plating, and in medicine to treat arthritis. The pure metal is nontoxic but the gold salts can cause allergic skin reactions.

GRAPEFRUIT OIL. An ingredient in fragrances obtained by expression from the fresh peel of the grapefruit. The yellow, sometimes reddish, liquid is also used in fruit flavorings. No known toxicity.

GRAPE-SEED OIL. Expressed from grape seeds and used widely in hypoallergenic lubricating creams because it does not cause problems with the allergic. Also used as a lubricant for fine watches. Nontoxic.

GRAPHITE. Black Lead. Obtained by mining, especially in Canada and Ceylon. Usually soft, black, lustrous scales. A pigment for cosmetics. Also used in lead pencils, stone polish, and as an explosive. The dust is mildly irritating to the lungs. No known skin toxicity.

GRAY HAIR RINSES. To cover yellowish tinge that often appears in gray hair. Usually compounded with acids such as adipic or citric (*see both*) and color rinses such as Acid Violet 99 and Acid Black 2 (*see both*).

GREEN. Chrome oxide green used in face powders. See Colors.

GRINDELIA. A coarse, bumpy, or resinous herb grown in Western America. It has flower heads with spreading tips. The dried leaves and stumps of these various gum weeds are used internally as a remedy in bronchitis and topically to soothe poison ivy rashes. Grindelia contains resin and an oil used in cosmetics. No known toxicity.

GUAIACOL. Obtained from hardwood tar or made synthetically. White or yellow crystalline mass with a characteristic odor. Darkens when exposed to light. Used as an antiseptic both externally and internally. Ingestion causes irritating of the intestinal tract and heart failure. Penetrates the skin. Produces pain and burning and then loss of sensitivity when applied to mucous membranes. Causes the nose to run and the mouth to salivate. Deep irritant on the skin.

GUANIDINE CARBONATE. Used to adjust pH (*see*) and to keep cosmetics moist. Colorless crystals, soluble in water, found in turnip juice, mushrooms, corn germ, rice hulls, mussels, and earthworms. Occurs as water-absorbing crystals, which are very alkaline. Used in organic synthesis and as a rubber accelerator. It is a muscle poison if ingested. No known toxicity to the skin.

GUANINE. Obtained from scales of certain fish, such as alewives and herring, by scraping. It is mixed in water and used in nail polish. However, it has been greatly replaced with either synthetic pearl (bismuth oxychloride, see Bismuth Compounds) or aluminum and bronze particles. Lethal when injected into the abdomens of mice but no known skin toxicity in humans. See Pearl Essence.

GUAR GUM.   Used in emulsions, toothpastes, lotions, and creams. From ground nutritive seed tissue of plants cultivated in India, it has 5 to 8 times the thickening power of starch. Employed also as a bulk laxative, appetite suppressant, and to treat peptic ulcers. A stabilizer in foods and beverages. No known toxicity.

GUM ARABIC. Acacia Gum.   The exudate from acacia trees grown in the Sudan used in face masks, hair sprays, setting lotions, rouge, and powders for compacts. Serves as an emulsifier, stabilizer, and gelling agent. It may cause allergic reactions such as hay fever, dermatitis, gastrointestinal distress, and asthma.

GUM BENZOIN.   Used as a preservative in creams and ointments and as a skin protective. It is the balsamic resin from benzoin grown in Thailand, Cambodia, Sumatra, and Cochin China. Also used to glaze and polish confections. No known toxicity.

GUM DAMMAR.   See Dammar.

GUM GUAIAC.   Resin from the wood of the guaiacum used widely as an antioxidant in cosmetic creams and lotions. Brown or greenish brown. Formerly used in treatment of rheumatism. No known toxicity.

GUM KARAYA. Sterculia Gum.   Used in hair sprays, beauty masks, setting lotions, depilatories, rouge, powder for compacts, shaving creams, denture adhesive powder, hand lotions, and toothpastes. It is the dried exudate of a tree native to India. Karaya came into wide use during World War I as a cheaper substitute for gum tragacanth (*see*). Karaya swells in water and alcohol, but does not dissolve. It is used in finger wave lotions, which dry quickly and are not sticky. Because of its high viscosity at low concentrations, its ability to produce highly stable emulsions, and its resistance to acids, it is widely used in frozen food products. In 1971, however, the FDA put this additive on the list of chemicals to be studied for teratogenic, mutagenic, subacute, and reproductive effects. It can cause allergic reactions such as hay fever, dermatitis, gastrointestinal distress, and asthma. It is omitted from hypoallergenic cosmetics.

GUM ROSIN.   See Rosins.

GUM SUMATRA.   See Gum Benzoin.

GUM TRAGACANTH.   An emulsifier used in brilliantines, shaving creams, toothpastes, face packs, foundation creams, hair sprays, mascara, depilatories, compact powder, rouge, dentifrices, setting lotions, eye makeup, and hand lotions. It is the gummy exudate from a plant grown in Iran and Asia Minor. Its acid forms a gel. It may cause allergic reactions such as hay fever, dermatitis, gastrointestinal distress, and asthma.

GUMS. The true plant gums are the dried exudates from various plants obtained when the bark is cut or otherwise injured. They are soluble in hot or cold water, and sticky. Today the term gum usually refers to water-soluble thickeners, either natural or synthetic; thickeners that are insoluble in water are called resins. Gums are used in perfumes, dentifrices, emollient creams, face powders, hair-grooming aids, hair straighteners, hand creams, rouges, shampoos, skin bleach creams, and wave sets. No known toxicity other than individual allergic reactions to specific gum.

GUTTA-PERCHA. Gummi Plasticum. The purified, coagulated, milky exudate of various trees grown in the Malayan archipelago. Related to rubber; on exposure to air and sunlight, it becomes brittle. Used in dental cement, in fracture splints for broken bones, and to cover golf balls. No known toxicity.

H

HAIR BLEACH. Among the most ancient of cosmetic preparations the Roman maidens used were various native minerals such as quicklime, mixed with old lime, to produce reddish gold tresses. The most widely used bleach today is simply hydrogen peroxide. It has been employed to bleach hair since 1867. A typical modern formula for a hair bleach includes a 3 percent hydrogen peroxide, 97.1 percent; quaternary ammonium compound, 1.5 percent; adipic acid, 0.8 percent; and a sodium stannate, 0.6 percent (*see all*). Recent reports of problems with hair bleach include nausea, hives, burned scalp, severe life-threatening allergic reaction, and swelling of the face.

HAIR COLOR RINSES. This is a temporary hair color that covers the cuticle layer of the hair only and does not affect natural color pigment inside the hair shaft. Used after shampooing, it is usually washed out with the next shampooing. There are color shampoos formulated with a synthetic detergent and color, and there are powders, crayons, wave sets, and lacquers that are also used for temporary coloring. The most common color rinses today combine azo dyes (*see*). Acids used in hair color rinses are usually citric and tartaric (*see both*). The rinses may also contain fatty acids, alcohols or amides, borax, glycols, thickening agents, and isopropyl alcohol (*see all*). Recent complaints to the FDA about hair rinses include ear numbness, headaches, and hair turning the wrong color. One of the problems with hair rinses is that when customers are allergic to permanent dyes, they become allergic to rinses, although the chemicals are not the same.

HAIR COLORING.   Permanent hair-coloring products change the color of the hair. They cannot be shampooed away, but remain until the hair grows out or is cut off. The root hair must be "retouched" as it grows in. There are basically three types: natural organics, synthetics, and metallics. Natural organics such as henna and chamomile (*see both*) have been used for centuries to color hair. Such dyes are placed on the hair and removed when the desired shade has been obtained. They are more difficult to apply, less reliable than manufactured dyes, and less predictable as far as color is concerned. Except for occasional allergic reactions to specific natural ingredients, they are harmless. Synthetic dyes such as para or amino derivatives work by oxidation, that is, they are applied cold and depend on the development of the shade by the action of a compound such as hydrogen peroxide to liberate oxygen. The first synthetic dye to be used on human hair was pyrogallol (*see*), used for brown shades. The first of the amino dyes and the one most commonly used today in the United States is *p*-phenylenediamine (*see*). This dye and the other synthetic oxidation dyes frequently cause dermatitis and other allergic skin reactions, and the laws in most states require that patch testing be done before use. This means applying the dye to the skin 24 hours in advance to see if any irritation or reaction occurs. This precaution is rarely observed. Furthermore, there is evidence that *p*-phenylenediamine products cause skin cancer in animals and many European countries will not permit its use. Dyes in use today contain not only the dye itself and the oxidizer, but hair conditioners, color modifiers, antioxidants, stabilizers, and other compounds to "treat" the hair. The compounds used as bases are called "intermediates" because their actual dyeing ability comes to the fore only upon oxidation. See HC colors. Modifiers are used to develop the desired shade. Antioxidants protect the compound against unwanted reaction with oxygen, and alkalizers are used because synthetic dyes work best in an alkaline medium. Developers are added to speed up the dyeing process. Permanent hair dye is usually mixed just before application and then left on the hair for a specified amount of time. It can be applied by shampooing or by an aerosol foam. However, the lightening action of these one-step hair colorings is not strong enough to change a dark brunette into a platinum blonde. This requires two steps—bleaching out the natural color and applying the desired shade. Metallic hair dyes are usually applied gradually in a hair lotion or by a coated comb, similar to a crayon. Use of metal salts to color hair is mentioned in the literature of ancient Rome. Cosmeticians of the times darkened hair by passing it through a lead comb that had been dipped in vinegar. Because the metallic dyes are incompatible with permanent wave solutions and oxidation dyes, they are not widely used by American women. However, American men use them as a subtle method of changing hair coloring. Lead, silver, and copper are most often used, although they are not recommended for moustaches because of the danger of ingestion or inhalation of the metals, which can be toxic. How do you know which class of dye you are purchasing? The permanent hair dyes are almost always para or amino dyes; the labels carry the warning to patch-test; the dye and developer are in separate containers and must be mixed just before use. Semipermanent dyes, which also carry a warning to patch-test, require no mixing before use; there is also a notice that they will last only for four or five shampoos. The packaging of temporary hair colorings clearly indicates they are temporary. Metallic hair dyes offer no shade selection and directions indicate they develop gradually with each use. Recent reports of injuries from hair coloring to the FDA include scalp irritation, hair breakage, contact dermatitis, hair falling out, swelling of the face, itching, and explosion of the bottles of hair dye. There were also complaints of headache, possible lead poisoning, and loss of sight.

HAIR CONDITIONERS.   Hair conditioners try to undo the damage from other hair preparations, particularly bleaches and dyes, and from the drying effects of the sun as well as the aging process. They include humectants, finishing agents, and emulsions. Hair is softened by water. Consequently, humectants bring moisture into the hair and reduce brittleness. Glycerin, propylene glycol, sorbitol, and urea (*see all*) help retain moisture and keep water from evaporation and consequently keep hair softer. Finishing agents, which include cream rinses, are added to shampoos or applied after shampooing. They leave a film on the hair to make it feel soft and look shiny. Isopropyl myristate and balsam are examples (*see both*). Emulsions, including cream and protein conditioners, are applied before, during, or after shampooing and sometimes between shampoos. They should be nonsticking and if rubbed between the hands, they should disappear. Such products usually contain lanolin, alcohols, sterols, glyceryl monostearate, spermaceti, glycerin, mineral oil, water, and perfume (*see all*). The aerosol type of hair conditioner is made by preparing a "concentrate" from lanolin, isopropyl palmitate (*see*), perfume oil, and some propellant. Protein conditioners contain a protein (*see*) such as beer or egg, aimed at replacing lost protein. However, according to the American Medical Association, there is little, if any evidence, to substantiate this. There is no proof that protein from hair conditioners can penetrate the hair shaft and reconstruct healthy hair. If there is any affect, it is merely a coating similar to those of cream rinses (*see*). Except for individual allergies, hair conditioners are nontoxic.

HAIR LACQUERS AND SPRAYS.   These products "hold the set" and keep the hair looking as if it were just done at the beauty parlor. Once strictly a woman's product, men now freely spray their hair. Hair lacquers usually come in either a plastic squeeze bottle or an aerosol. The early products contained shellac, and many still do. The shellac type is made by dissolving perfume in alcohol and then adding shellac (the excretion of certain insects) and then adding a mixture of triethanolamine (*see*) and water. Pegs, lanolin alcohols, and castor oil may also be included in the mixture (*see all*). The early shellacs made hair shine but caused it to be brittle to the touch. The addition of lanolin, castor oil, and glycol counteract this effect. The newer hair lacquers contain a product used as a blood extender in medicine—polyvinylpyrrolidone (PVP). Related to plastics and similar to egg albumin in texture, it slightly stiffens the hair to keep it in place. PVP is dissolved in ether and then in glycerin and perfume is added. The solution may also include polyethylene glycol, cetyl alcohol, and lanolin alcohols (*see all*). Pressurized hair sprays contain PVP, alcohol, sorbitol, and water. Additional ingredients may be lanolin, perfume, shellac, silicone, sodium alginate, or vegetable gums such as gum karaya, acacia, or gum tragacanth (*see all*). The propellant is usually freon, the same one used as a coolant in air conditioners. Most hair lacquer mixtures are 20 percent alcohol and 72.5 percent water. Hair sprays can cause eye and lung damage and should be used with caution. Recent complaints to the FDA about hair sprays include headache, hair loss, rash, change in hair color, throat irritation, suspected lung lesion, and death. In one case the hair ignited after a cigarette was lit.

HAIR LOTIONS.   See Hair Tonics, Lotions, and Thickeners.

HAIR RINSES.   Aimed at improving the feel and appearance of hair. Usually made of a water-soluble material that can be dissolved and dispersed after application. When water has evaporated, a deposit is left behind, which forms a film. Among ingredients used are gums, certain protein derivatives, and synthetic polymers. A basic cream rinse contains glyceryl monostearate, 3 percent; benzalkonium chloride, 3 percent; water, about 94 percent; perfume, and coloring. The American Medical Association maintains that cream rinses cannot repair damaged hair as claimed in advertisements. See Hair Conditioners.

HAIR SPRAYS. See Hair Lacquers and Sprays.

HAIR STRAIGHTENERS. Half the population wants its hair curled, the other half wants it straightened. There are three methods, none perfect, for strightening hair: pomades that coat the hair and glue it straight; the much advertised hot combs and irons; and chemical straighteners. Pomades, of course, are the least effective but the least damaging. Heating the hair, when done properly at 300° to 500° F, does straighten the strands when tension is applied. Burns of the scalp are not uncommon, and the hair is dried out and may become very brittle. Chemical straighteners are effective but can cause burns, irritations, and hair damage. They usually contain either thioglycolic acid compounds (*see*) or alkalies such as sodium hydroxide as well as polyethylene glycol, cetyl alcohol, stearyl alcohol, a triethanolamine, propylene glycol (*see all*), perfume, and water. The glycols and alcohols may be caustic. The thioglycolate curl relaxers require the application of a neutralizer to the hair to stop the straightening process. Although there are home hair-straightening kits, there is a fine line between enough straightening and too much. If possible, the procedure should be done by a professional. The alkali curl relaxants, which are more effective for kinky hair, straighten the hair in about 5 to 10 minutes while a comb is run through. The hair is then rinsed with water to stop the chemical action. Again, there is a fine line between enough and too much, and the procedure should be done by a professional. Alkali straighteners contain strong burning ingredients, and first to third degree chemical burns can occur. They can also cause allergic reactions and swelling of the face and scalp. The greatest danger from these products is eye damage. Extreme caution must be used to avoid contact with the eyes. The hair will become fragile with any form of chemical or heat straightening. Bleached hair is particularly susceptible and straightening of bleached hair is usually not recommended. Recent reports to the FDA of injuries include scalp irritation, loss of hair, and scalp burns.

HAIR THICKENERS. See Hair Tonics, Lotions, and Thickeners.

HAIR TONICS, LOTIONS, AND THICKENERS. Hair tonics and

lotions are designed to keep the hair in place and looking healthy. There are three basic types: alcoholic, emulsion, and drug/tonic. Alcoholics may consist of an oil mixed with alcohol, glycerin (*see*), and perfume. Emulsions may be made by heating mineral oil and stearic acid (*see*), mixing it with hot water and triethanolamine (*see*), and adding perfume. The tonic or drug-type hairdressing usually contains antiseptics and may affect the function or structure of the human body or they are designed to treat a diseased condition. They also contain low concentrations of rubefacients (these are products that cause a reddening and thus stimulation of the skin). Antiseptics employed may be cresols, phenols, chlorothymol, or resorcinol (*see all*). There is another type of hairdressing, used mostly by men, which is similar to a wave set common to women. It contains natural gums such as tragacanth, and karaya, or sodium alginate with alcohol, water, perfume, and glycerol. Among other chemicals in hair tonics and lotions are benzalkonium chloride, beta-naphthol, bithionol, camphor, cantharides tincture, chloral hydrate, hexachlorophene, phosphoric acid, pilocarpine, glycols, quinine, sorbitan derivatives, salicylic acid, and tars (*see all*). Hair thickeners contain oils and proteins that coat the hair with an invisible film, thus giving it body. The thickeners make the hair feel smoother and it is more manageable. A common hair tonic formula contains resorcinol, 0.8 percent; chloral hydrate, 1.5 percent; ethanol, 80 percent; beta-naphthol, 0.8 percent; Turkey-red oil, 16.9 percent; perfume; and color (*see all*). Recent complaints to the FDA about hair conditioners and dressings include loss of hair, eye irritation, pimples, inflammed scalp, hair shrunk into knots, face irritation, dryness, and rash.

HAMAMELIS WATER.   See Witch Hazel.

HAND CREAMS AND LOTIONS.   These are emollients, which must apply easily and not leave a sticky feeling. They must soften the skin of the hands and leave a pleasant odor. Most contain lanolin and stearic acid (*see both*) and water. They may also contain cetyl alcohol, mineral oil, glycerin, potassium hydroxide, perfume, and glyceryl monostearate (*see all*). The newer formulas also contain healing agents (*see*) such as allantoin (*see*) to promote healing, and water-repellent silicones (*see*) to protect the hands against further irritation from water, detergents, or wind. Most leading hand creams and lotions are uncolored, though surveys show that pink or blue hand creams are preferred; women over 25 years prefer pink and teen-agers, blue. The pH level (*see*) of most hand creams and lotions is between 5 and 8. A typical formula for hand cream contains cetyl alcohol,

2 percent; lanolin, 1 percent; mineral oil, 2 percent; stearic acid, 13 percent; glycerin, 12 percent; methylparaben, 0.15 percent; potassium hydroxide, 1 percent; water, 68 percent; and perfume in sufficient amounts (*see all*). A typical hand lotion contains cetyl alcohol, 0.5 percent; lanolin, 1 percent; stearic acid, 3 percent; glycerin, 2 percent; methylparaben, 0.1 percent; triethanolamine, .75 percent; water, 85 percent; and perfume in sufficient amounts (*see all*). Among problems reported recently to the FDA concerning hand preparations were rash, blisters, and swollen feet.

HANDKERCHIEF PERFUME. A woman's perfume in a retail shop. The name was dervied from the practice of dabbing scent on a handkerchief to allow the sniffer to distinguish between perfume compounds.

HC BLACK NO. 1. Calcozine Black CBF. Commerical hair coloring. See Colors.

HC BLUE NO. 1. N^4,N^4-Bis(2-Hydroxyethyl)-N^1-Methyl-2-Nitro-p-Phenylenediamine. Commercial hair coloring. See *p*-Phenylenediamine and Colors.

HC BLUE NO. 2. N^1,N^4,N^4-(2-Hydroxyethyl)-2-Nitro-p-Phenylenediamine. Commercial hair coloring. See *p*-Phenylenediamine and Colors.

HC BLUE NO. 3. Cibalan Blue FBL. Commercial hair coloring. See Colors.

HC BROWN NO. 1. Capracyl Brown 2R. Commercial hair coloring. See Colors.

HC ORANGE NO. 1. 2-Nitro-4-Hydroxydiphenylamine. Commercial hair coloring. See *p*-Phenylenediamine and Colors.

HC RED NO. 1. 4-Amino-2-Nitrodiphenylamine. Commercial hair coloring. See *p*-Phenylenediamine and Colors.

HC RED NO. 3. N^1-(2-Hydroxyethyl)-2-Nitro-p-Phenylenediamine. Commercial hair coloring. See *p*-Phenylenediamine and Colors.

HC RED NO. 6. Formerly FD & C Red No. 1 and Food Red 6. A monoazo dye. See Azo Dyes.

HC YELLOW NO. 2. N-(2-Hydroxyethyl)-2-Nitroaniline. Commercial hair coloring. See Aniline Dyes and Colors.

HC YELLOW NO. 3. N^1-Tris(Hydroxymethyl)-Methyl-4-Nitro-o-Phenylenediamine. Commercial hair coloring. See *p*-Phenylenediamine and Colors.

HC YELLOW NO. 4. N,N-Bis(2-Hydroxyethyl)-2-Amino-5-Nitrophenol. Commercial hair coloring. See *p*-Phenylenediamine and Colors.

HC YELLOW NO. 5. N¹-(2-Hydroxyethyl)-4-Nitro-o-Phenylenedi-
amine. Commercial hair coloring. See *p*-Phenylenediamine and
Colors.

HEALING AGENTS. Medications added to hand creams and lotions
(*see*) to treat chapped and irritated hands. Allantoin (*see*) is probably the most widely used healing agent in hand creams and lotions.
Urea (*see*) has also been used.

HECTORITE. An emulsifier and extender. A clay consisting of silicate of magnesium and lithium, it is used in the chill-proofing of
beer. The dust can be irritating to the lungs. No known toxicity on
the skin.

HELIOTROPIN. Piperonal. A purple diazo dye (*see*) used in perfumery and soaps. Consists of colorless, lustrous crystals that have a
heliotrope odor. Usually made from oxidation of piperic acid. Ingestion of large amounts may cause central nervous system depression.
Applications to the skin may cause allergic reactions and skin irritation. Not recommended for use in cosmetics or perfumes.

HENNA LEAVES. An ancient hair cosmetic Cleopatra supposedly
used. Mohammed allegedly dyed his beard with it. It is a greenish
powder ingredient in many auburn to red hair rinses (*see*) and obtained from ground-up dried leaves and stems of a shrub found in
North Africa and the Near East. A paste of henna and water is applied directly to the hair and a reddish hair color is produced. There
is no known toxicity, but allergic skin rashes have been reported in
users. However, those who are allergic to other dyes may be able to
use henna without problems. Although it is rather messy and un-
predictable to use, there is renewed interest in the dye because of the
desire to return to "natural" products rather than using man-made
cosmetics. The FDA ruled that henna is safe for coloring hair only.
It may not be used for coloring eyelashes or eyebrows or in the area
of the eyes.

HEPTANOIC ACID. Enanthic Acid. Found in various fusel oils
and in rancid oils, it has the faint odor of tallow. It is made from
grapes and is a fatty acid used chiefly in making esters (*see*) for
flavoring materials. No known toxicity.

2-HEPTANONE. Used in perfumery as a constituent of artificial
carnation oils. Found in oil of cloves and in cinnamon bark oil. It has
a peppery fruity odor that is very penetrating. Heptanone is responsible for the peppery odor of Roquefort cheese. Can be irritating to
human mucous membranes and is narcotic in high doses.

HERBAL SHAMPOOS. Renewed interest in natural cosmetic products has caused renewed consumer interest in herbal shampoos. Saponin products used in many regular shampoos (*see*) are extracted from quillaja bark or soaproot. Saponin is a class of substances found in many plants that possess the common properties of foaming, or making suds when agitated in water. They also hold resins and fatty substances in suspension in water. These products clean the scalp and reduce scaliness. Here is a typical formula for herbal shampoo: quillaja bark, powdered, 5 percent; ammonium carbonate, 1 percent; borax, 1 percent; bay oil, 1 percent (*see all*); and water, 92 percent. Saponins can be irritating when applied to the skin, and when given internally can cause nausea. Toxicity of herbal shampoos depends on ingredients and amounts used.

HEXACHLOROPHENE. An antibacterial used in baby oil, baby powder, brilliantine hairdressings, cold creams, emollients, deodorants, antiperspirants, face masks, hair tonics, shampoos, medicated cosmetics, after-shave lotions, skin fresheners, soaps, and many other cosmetic products. In 1969 scientists reported microscopically visible brain damage in rats from small concentrations of the antibacterial. The company that had the patent on hexachlorophene, the Swiss-based Givaudan Corporation, sold the chemical only to those companies that could demonstrate a safe and effective use for it. Givaudan refused to sell hexachlorophene for use in toothpastes and mouthwashes. However, when the patents expired in the mid-1960s, the FDA allowed hexachlorophene to be used in toothpastes and mouthwashes. In 1971 the chemical was the ingredient of nearly 400 products ranging from fruit washes to baby lotion. Chloasma, a pigmenting of the face, was reported in 1961 in persons who used hexachlorophene-containing products. Coma in burn patients washed in hexachlorophene products was reported in 1968. On March 29, 1971, August Curley and Robert E. Hawk of the U.S. Environmental Protection Agency presented a paper in Los Angeles at the American Chemical Society meeting stating that hexachlorophene has been found toxic to experimental animals, capable of penetrating the skin, and present in the blood of some human beings. Tests on 13 human volunteers showed hexachlorophene levels of one part in a billion parts of blood to 89 ppb. Curley, chief research chemist at the Environmental Protection Agency, said that the agency thought the material was absorbed through the skin. He pointed out: "For over two decades, hexachlorophene has been widely used as a bactericide in the United States. However, relatively little quantitative data is available concerning its dermal absorption in either experimental animals or humans." On May 17, 1971, the American Academy of Pediatrics warned that products containing hexachlorophene that are intended for oral use, such as certain toothpastes or throat lozenges, may be poisonous to children. In December 1971 the FDA curbed the use of hexachlorophene-containing detergents and soaps for total body bathing. Winthrop, the makers of pHisohex, which contained 3 percent hexachlorophene, sent out further information to doctors saying that the product should not be used as a lotion, left on the skin after use, used as a wet soak or compress, or transferred to any other container that would allow for misuse. It should always be rinsed thoroughly from the skin after any use, should be used in strict accordance with directions, and it should always be kept out of reach of children. Eventually, the FDA is expected to ban hexachlorophene in cosmetics. In the meantime it has limited it up to 0.75 percent. Products containing up to 0.75 percent will be able to continue on the market with the warning: "Contains hexachlorophene. For external use only. Rinse thoroughly."

HEXADECYL METHICONE.   A silicone wax. See Silicones.

HEXAMETHYL DISILOXANE.   See Silicones.

1,2,6-HEXANETRIOL.   An alcohol used as a solvent. No known skin toxicity.

HEXANOL. Hexyl Alcohol.   Used as an antiseptic and preservative in cosmetics, it occurs as the acetate (*see*) in seeds and fruits of *Heracleum sphondylium* and *Umbelliferae.* Colorless liquid, slightly soluble in water, it is miscible with alcohol. No know toxicity.

HEXYL LAURATE.   See Lauric Acid.

HEXYLENE GLYCOL.   See Polyethylene Glycol.

4-HEXYLRESORCINOL.   Used in mouthwashes and sunburn creams. A pale yellow heavy liquid that becomes solid upon standing at room temperature. It has a pungent odor and a sharp astringent taste and has been used medicinally as an antiworm medicine and antiseptic. It can cause severe gastrointestinal irritation; bowel, liver, and heart damage has been reported. Concentrated solutions can cause burns of the skin and mucous membranes.

HOMOSALATE. Heliophan.   See Cresol.

HONEY.   Used as a coloring, flavoring, and emollient in cosmetics. Formerly used in hair bleaches. The common, sweet, viscous material taken from the nectar of flowers and manufactured in the sacs of various kinds of bees. The flavor and color depend upon the plants from which it was taken. May cause allergic reaction in persons allergic to pollen.

HONEYSUCKLE.   The common fragrant tubular flowers, filled with honey, which are used in perfumes. No known toxicity.

HOPS.   Used in perfumes and flavorings. Derived from the carefully dried pineconelike fruit of the hop plant grown in Europe, Asia, and North America. Light yellow or greenish, it is an oily liquid with a bitter taste and aromatic odor. Used also in beer brewing and for food flavorings. Hops at one time was used as a sedative. Can cause allergic reactions.

HOPS OIL.   See Hops.

HORMONE CREAMS AND LOTIONS.   The cosmetic manufacturers claim that hormone creams containing estrogen or progesterone are cosmetics, and many dermatologists and some staff members of the U.S. Food and Drug Administration maintain they are drugs. Cosmetic manufacturers, ever aware of the human desire to stay young forever, have advertised the hormone creams as wrinkle preventatives and youthful skin restoratives. According to the American Medical Association, there is little scientific evidence that locally applied hormones can thicken the thinning skin of the aging and that simple emollient creams may do a better job. In a review of the experimental data on the use of sex steroids in cosmetics, there was some evidence that topically applied steroidal hormones, both active and inactive biologically, do cause a slight thickening of aged skin. However, the effects are negligible, and in the amounts considered safe to use in cosmetics, topically applied hormones have no effect on human oil glands and oil secretion. Estrogen may be added at not more than 10,000 international units per ounce. Progesterone content may not exceed 5 mg per ounce. Prices of hormone creams range from $5 to $50.

HORSE CHESTNUT.   The seeds of *Aesculus hippocastanum.* A tonic, natural astringent for skin, and fever-reducing substance that contains tannic acid (*see*). No known toxicity

HORSERADISH EXTRACT. Scurvy Grass.   A condiment ingredient utilizing the grated root from the tall, coarse, white-flowered herb native to Europe. Often combined with vinegar or other ingredients. Contains ascorbic acid (*see*) and acts as an antiseptic in cosmetics. No known toxicity.

HORSETAIL.   Used in herbal shampoos for its supposedly soothing quality. It is derived from the plant that has been used medicinally to reduce body water and as an astringent. It has a historical reputation for being able to cure dropsy and kidney infections. Supposedly stops wounds from bleeding and heals them. No known toxicity.

HOT OIL TREATMENT.   Used to restore luster to bleach-damaged hair. The hair is completely doused with oil and then heated by a lamp or an electric cap. Oils include mineral and vegetable.

HUMECTANT.   A substance used to preserve the moisture content of materials, especially in hand creams and lotions. The humectant of glycerin and rose water, in equal amounts, is the earliest known hand lotion. Glycerin, propylene, glycol, and sorbitol (*see all*) are widely used humectants in hand creams and lotions. Humectants are usually found in antiperspirants, baby preparations, beauty masks, dentifrices, depilatories, hair-grooming aides, and wave sets. See individual substances for toxicity.

HYACINTH.   Used in perfumes and soaps. It is the extract of the very common fragrant flower. Also used as a flavoring for chewing gum. Dark green liquid with a penetrating odor, the juice of hyacinth is very irritating to the skin. It can also cause allergic reactions.

HYBRID SAFFLOWER OIL. FD & C Yellow 6. Food Yellow 3. A monoazo dye. See Azo Dyes.

HYDRATED.   Combined with water.

HYDRATED SILICA.   See Silica and Hydrated.

HYDROABIETYL ALCOHOL.   Used in eyebrow pencils. See Abietic Acid.

HYDROCARBONS.   A large class of organic compounds containing only carbon and hydrogen. Petroleum, natural gas, coal, and bitumens are common hydrocarbon products. Hydrocarbons such as petrolatum, mineral oils, paraffin wax, and ozokerite have been used in sunscreen hand creams, lotions, and nail polish. They are believed to work by forming a water-repellent film that keeps water from evaporating from the skin. Toxicity depends upon the hydrocarbons used.

HYDROCHLORIC ACID.   Acid used in hair bleaches to speed up oxidation in rinses and to remove color. Also a solvent. A clear, colorless, or slightly yellowish, corrosive liquid, it is a water solution of hydrogen chloride of varying concentrations. Inhalation of the fumes causes choking and inflammation of the respiratory tract. Ingestion may corrode the mucous membranes, esophagus, and stomach, and cause diarrhea.

HYDROGEN PEROXIDE.   A bleaching and oxidizing agent, a detergent, and antiseptic. Used in skin bleaches, hair bleaches, cold creams, mouthwashes, toothpastes, and in cold permanent waves. An unstable compound readily broken down into water and oxygen. It is made from barium peroxide and diluted phosphoric acid. Generally recognized as safe as a preservative and germ killer in cosmetics as well as in milk and cheese. A 3 percent solution is used medicinally as an antiseptic and germicide. A strong oxidizer, undiluted it can cause burns of the skin and mucous membranes.

HYDROGENATED CASTOR OIL. See Castor Oil and Hydrogenation.

HYDROGENATED COCONUT OIL. See Coconut Oil and Hydrogenation.

HYDROGENATED COTTONSEED GLYCERIDE. See Cottonseed Oil and Hydrogenation.

HYDROGENATED COTTONSEED OIL. See Cottonseed Oil and Hydrogenation.

HYDROGENATED FATTY OILS. Used in baby creams and lipstick. See Fatty Acids and Hydrogenation.

HYDROGENATED LENETH-5. See Lauric Acid and Hydrogenation.

HYDROGENATED LANETH-20. See Lauric Acid and Hydrogenation.

HYDROGENATED LANETH-25. See Lauric Acid and Hydrogenation.

HYDROGENATED LANOLIN. See Lanolin and Hydrogenation.

HYDROGENATED LANOLIN ALCOHOL. See Lanolin and Hydrogenation.

HYDROGENATED LARD GLYCERIDE. See Lard and Hydrogenation.

HYDROGENATED PALM KERNEL OIL. See Palm Kernel Oil and Hydrogenation.

HYDROGENATED PALM OIL. See Palm Oil and Hydrogenation.

HYDROGENATED POLYISOBUTENE. See Isobutryic Acid and Hydrogenation.

HYDROGENATED SHARK-LIVER OIL. See Shark Liver and Hydrogenation.

HYDROGENATED SOY GLYCERIDE. See Soybean Oil and Hydrogenation.

HYDROGENATED TALLOW ACID. See Tallow and Hydrogenation.

HYDROGENATED TALLOW AMINE. See each separately.

HYDROGENATED TALLOW GLYCERIDE. See Tallow and Hydrogenation.

HYDROGENATED VEGETABLE GLYCERIDE. See Vegetable Oils and Hydrogenation.

HYDROGENATED VEGETABLE OILS. See Vegetable Oils and Hydrogenation.

HYDROGENATION. The process of adding hydrogen gas under high pressure to liquid oils. It is the most widely used chemical process in the edible fat industry. Used in the manufacture of petrol from coal, and in the manufacture of margarine and shortening. Used primarily in the cosmetic and food industries to convert liquid oils to semisolid fats at room temperature. Reduces the amount of acid in the compound and improves color. Usually, the higher the amount of hydrogenation, the lower the unsaturation in the fat and the less possibility of flavor degradation or spoilage due to oxidation. Hydrogenated oils still contain some unsaturated components that are susceptible to rancidity. Therefore, the addition of antioxidants is still necessary.

HYDROLYZED. Subject to hydrolysis or turned partly into water. Hydrolysis is derived from the Greek *hydro,* meaning "water," and *lysis,* meaning "a setting free." It occurs as a chemical process in which the decomposition of a compound is brought about by water, resolving into a simpler compound. Hydrolysis also occurs in the digestion of foods. The proteins in the stomach react with water in an enzyme reaction to form peptones and amino acids (*see*).

HYDROLYZED ANIMAL PROTEIN. See Proteins and Hydrolyzed.

HYDROLYZED MILK PROTEIN. See Milk and Hydrolyzed.

HYDROQUINOL. An alkaline solution that turns brown in air and is made up of white leaflets that are soluble in water. Used as an antiseptic and reducing agent (*see*) in cosmetics. Has caused skin cancer in mice.

HYDROQUINONE. Used in bleach and freckle creams and in suntan lotions. A white crystalline phenol (*see*) that occurs naturally but is usually manufactured in the laboratory. Hydroquinone combines with oxygen very rapidly and becomes brown when exposed to air. Death has occurred from the ingestion of as little as 5 grams. Ingestion of as little as one gram (1/30th of an ounce) has caused nausea, vomiting, ringing in the ears, delirium, a sense of suffocation, and collapse. Industrial workers exposed to the chemical have suffered clouding of the eye lens. Application to the skin may cause allergic reactions.

p-HYDROXYANISOLE. See Guaiacol.

o-HYDROXYBENZOIC ACID. See Salicylic Acid.

p-HYDROXYBENZOIC ACID. Prepared from *p*-bromophenol. Used as a preservative and fungicide. See Benzoic Acid for toxicity.

HYDROXYCITRONELLAL. Laurine®. Colorless liquid obtained by the addition of water to citronellol (*see*). Used as a fixative (*see*) and a fragrance in perfumery for its sweet lilylike odor. It has been known to cause allergic reactions.

HYDROXYETHYLCELLULOSE. See Ethylcellulose.

HYDROXYLAMINE HCL. An antioxidant for fatty acids and soaps. Soluble in water and alcohol. It is made from sodium bisulfite (*see*) and sodium nitrite (*see*). May be slightly irritating to skin, eyes, and mucous membranes, and may cause a depletion of oxygen in the blood when ingested. In the body it is reportedly decomposed to sodium nitrite.

HYDROXYLAMINE SULFATE. A hair-waving component in permanent wave solutions, it is a crystalline ammonium sulfate compound. It is also used for dehairing hides, in photography, as a chemical reducing agent, and to purify aldehydes (*see*) and ketones (*see*). No known toxicity to the skin. The lethal dose given in the abdomens of rats is small.

HYDROXYPROPYL CELLULOSE. See Cellulose Gums.

HYDROXYPROPYL METHYLCELLULOSE. See Cellulose Gums.

HYDROXYPROPYLAMINE NITRITE. See Isopropanolamine Nitrite.

HYDROXYQUINOLINE. See Oxyquinoline Sulfate.

HYDROXYSTEARIC ACID. See Stearic Acid.

HYPERICUM. Hypericin. Blue black needles obtained from pyridine (*see*). The solutions are red or green with a red cast. Small amounts seem to be a tranquilizer and have been used as an antidepressant in medicine. It can produce a sensitivity to light.

HYPO. Prefix from the Greek, meaning "under," or "below," as in hypoacidity—acidity in a lesser degree than is usual or normal.

HYPOALLERGENIC. A term for cosmetics supposedly devoid of common allergens that most frequently cause allergic reactions. However, spokesmen for both the FDA and the AMA find insufficient the claims of scientific proof for their efficacy. When first marketed in the 1930s, these cosmetics were called nonallergic, which implied they could not cause an allergic reaction. The term was abandoned because there are always people who will be allergic to almost any substance. The term "hypoallergenic" means least likely to cause a reaction. Not only the user, but his or her companion may suffer allergic reaction to cosmetics. For instance, a wife to her husband's shaving lotion; a child to its mother's hair spray.

I

ICHTHAMMOL. Pale yellow or brownish black, thick viscous

liquid, which smells like coal. It mixes with water, glycerol, fats, oils, and waxes, and is used medicinally as a topical antiseptic. It has slight bacteria-killing properties and is used in ointments for the treatment of skin disorders. It is also a feeble skin irritant. Formerly used medicinally as an expectorant. Large doses caused stomach upset and diarrhea.

IMIDAZOLIDINYL UREA.   See Urea.

IMINO-BIS-PROPYLAMINE.   See Propylamine.

IMITATION.   With reference to a fragrance, containing all or some portion of nonnatural materials. For instance, unless a strawberry flavoring used in lipsticks is made entirely from strawberries, it must be called imitation.

INDIGO.   Probably the oldest known dye. Prepared from various *Indigofera* plants native to Bengal, Java, and Guatemala. Dark blue powder with a coppery luster. No known skin irritation but continued use on hair can cause the hair to become brittle.

INDOLE.   A white, lustrous, flaky substance with an unpleasant odor, occurring naturally in jasmine oil and orange flowers and used in perfumes. Also extracted from coal tar and feces; in highly diluted solutions the odor is pleasant. Large doses have been lethal in dogs. No known toxicity on the skin.

INOSITOL.   A dietary supplement of the Vitamin B family used in emollients. Found in plant and animal tissue. Isolated commercially from corn. A fine, white, crystalline powder, it is odorless with a sweet taste. Stable in air. No known toxicity.

INTERMEDIATE.   A chemical substance found as part of a necessary step between one organic compound and another, as in the production of dyes, pharmaceuticals, or other artificial products that develop properties only upon oxidation. For instance, it is used for hair-dye bases that have dyeing action only when exposed to oxygen.

IODINE.   Discovered in 1811 and classed among the rarer earth elements, it is found in the earth's crust as bluish black scales or plates. Used as an antiseptic and germicide in cosmetics. The solid element is intensely irritating to the eyes, skin, and mucous membranes. The diluted element is used as a counterirritant (*see*).

IONONE.   Irisone®. Used as a scent in perfumery and as a flavoring agent in foods, it occurs naturally in *Boronia,* an Australian shrub. Colorless to pale yellow with an odor reminiscent of cedarwood or violets. It may cause allergic reactions.

IPECAC.   Used as a denaturant in alcohol. From the dried rhizome and roots of a creeping South American plant with drooping flowers. Used to induce vomiting in poisonings. Fatal dose in humans is as low as 20 milligrams per kilogram of body weight. Irritating when taken internally but no known toxicity on the skin.

IRISH MOSS.   See Carrageenan.

IRON OXIDES.   Used to color cosmetics. Any of several natural or synthetic oxides of iron (that is, iron combined with oxygen), varying in color from red to brown, black to orange or yellow, depending on the degree of water added, and the purity. Ocher, sienna, and iron oxide red are among the colors used to tint face powders, liquid powders, and foundation creams. Black iron oxide is used for coloring eye shadow. See Colors for toxicity.

IRONE.   The fragrant principle of violets, usually isolated from the iris, and used in perfumery. A light yellow viscous liquid, it gives off the delicate fragrance of violets when put in alcohol. It is also used to flavor dentifrices. See Orris for toxicity.

ISO.   Greek for "equal." In chemistry, it is a prefix added to the name of one compound to denote another composed of the same kinds and numbers of atoms but different from each other in structural arrangement.

ISOBORNYL ACETATE.   A synthetic pine odor in bath preparations. Also used as a synthetic fruit flavoring for beverages. No known toxicity.

ISOBUTANE.   A constituent of natural gas and illuminating gas, colorless and insoluble in water, and used in refrigeration plants. See Paraffin and Propellants.

ISOBUTOXYPROPANOL.   See Isopropyl Alcohol.

ISOBUTYL PABA. Isobutyl-p-Aminobenzoate.   See Propylparaben.

ISOBUTYL PALMITATE.   See Palmitate.

ISOBUTYL SALICYLATE.   See Salicylates.

ISOBUTYLENE/ISOPRENE COPOLYMER.   Unstable liquid, miscible with water and alcohol, and used in the manufacture of plastics and synthetic elastics. Used in nail enamels. Irritating to the skin and mucous membranes.

ISOBUTYLENE/MALEIC ANHYDRIDE COPOLYMER.   Antioxidant and fungicide. Used in the manfacture of plastics and creams. See Maleic Anhydride for toxicity.

ISOBUTYRIC ACID.   A pungent liquid that smells like butyric acid (*see*). A mild irritant used chiefly in making fragrances materials.

ISOCETYL ALCOHOL.   See Cetyl Alcohol.

ISOCETYL ISODECANOATE.   See Cetyl Alcohol.

ISOCETYL PALMITATE.   See Palmitate.

ISOCETYL STEARATE.   See Stearic Acid.

ISODECYL HYDROXYSTEARATE.   See Decyl Alcohol and Stearic Acid.

ISODECYL ISONONANOATE.   See Decyl Alcohol.

ISODECYL MYRISTATE.   See Decyl Alcohol and Myristic Acid.

ISODECYL NEOPENTANOATE.   See 1-Pentanol.

ISODECYL OLEATE.   See Decyl Alcohol and Oleic Acid.

ISODECYL PALMITATE.   See Decyl Alcohol and Palmitic Acid.

ISOEUGENOL.   An aromatic liquid phenol oil obtained from eugenol (*see*) by mixing with an alkali. Used chiefly in perfumes but also employed in hand creams and in making vanillin (*see*). Strong irritant. Not recommended for use.

ISOHEXYL LAURATE.   See Lauryl Alcohol.

ISOHEXYL PALMITATE.   See Palmitic Acid.

ISONONYL ISONONANOATE.   The ester produced by the reaction of nonyl alcohol with nonanoic acid. Used in fruit flavorings for lipsticks and mouthwashes. Occurs in cocoa, oil of lavender. No known toxicity.

ISOPENTANE.   Volatile flammable liquid hydrocarbon found in petroleum and used as a solvent in cosmetics. A skin irritant. Narcotic in high doses.

ISOPROPYL ALCOHOL. Isopropanol.   An antibacterial, solvent, and denaturant (*see*). Used in hair color rinses, body rubs, hand lotions, after-shave lotions, and many other cosmetics. It is prepared from propylene, which is obtained in the cracking of petroleum. Also used in antifreeze compositions and as a solvent for gums, shellac, and essential oils. Ingestion or inhalation of large quantities of the vapor may cause flushing, headache, dizziness, mental depression, nausea, vomiting, narcosis, anesthesia, and coma. The fatal ingested dose is around a fluid ounce. No known toxicity on the skin.

ISOPROPYL ISOSTEARATE.   See Stearic Acid.

ISOPROPYL LANOLATE.   See Lanolin.

ISOPROPYL LAURATE.   See Lauric Acid.

ISOPROPYL LINOLEATE.   See Linoleic Acid.

ISOPROPYL METHOXYCINNAMATE.   See Cinnamic Acid.

ISOPROPYL MYRISTATE.   A mixture of myristate with small amounts of fatty acids used in foundation makeup, mascara, preshave lotions (oily type), bath preparations, and other cosmetics. Used in cosmetics and topical medicines where good absorption through the skin is desired. Withstands exudation and usually does not become rancid. Practically insoluble in water and dissolves many waxes such as lanolin and cholesterol. One commercial product is actually jellied isopropyl myristate. No known toxicity.

ISOPROPYL NITRITE. Prepared by treating isopropyl alcohol with nitrosyl chloride. A pale yellow oil used as a jet propellant. Inhalation can cause a lack of oxygen in the blood. Severe poisoning can result in fatal shock.

ISOPROPYL OLEATE. See Oleic Acid.

ISOPROPYL PALMITATE. A sticky substance obtained from fats and used in aerosol hair conditioner sprays and in bath preparations, hair creams, and rouge. Lethal dose injected into the abdomens of mice is small. No known toxicity to the skin.

ISOPROPYL STEARATE. See Stearic Acid.

ISOPROPYLAMINE. An emulsifier used in hair-grooming creams and lotions. A colorless, flammable liquid with an ammonia odor and made from acetone. May be irritating to the skin, eyes, and mucous membranes.

4,4'-ISOPROPYLIDENEDIPHENOL. See Phenol.

ISOSTEARAMIDE DEA. See Stearic Acid.

ISOSTEARETH-2. See Stearyl Alcohol.

ISOSTEARETH-3. See Stearyl Alcohol.

ISOSTEARETH-10. See Stearyl Alcohol.

ISOSTEARETH-20. See Stearyl Alcohol.

ISOSTEARIC ACID. See Stearic Acid.

ISOSTEARIC HYDROLYZED ANIMAL PROTEIN. Used in creams. See Protein and Hydrolyzed.

ISOSTEARYL ALCOHOL. See Stearyl Alcohol.

ISOSTEARYL ISOSTEARATE. See Stearyl Alcohol.

ISOTRIDECYL ISONONANOATE. See Tridecyl Alcohol.

IVY EXTRACT. Extract of climbing plant with evergreen leaves native to Europe and Asia. Produces a color that ranges from dark grayish green to yellowish. No known toxicity.

J

JABORANDI. Pilocarpus. A tincture from the leaves of the pilocarpus plant grown in South America. It supposedly stimulates the sebaceous glands and scalp and was formerly used to induce sweating. Used in hair tonics. A source of pilocarpine (*see*). Poisonous when ingested. No known toxicity on the skin.

JAGUAR GUM. See Guar Gum.

JALAP RESIN. A resin (*see*) used in cosmetics. The dried purgative, tuberous root of a Mexican plant. Was once used as a drastic cathartic. No known toxicity on the skin.

JAPAN WAX. Vegetable Wax. Japan Tallow. A fat squeezed from the fruit of a tree grown in Japan and China. Pale yellow flat cakes, disks or squares, with a fatlike rancid odor and taste. Used as a substitute for beeswax in cosmetic ointments; also floor waxes and polishes. May cause allergic reactions. Contains an irritant similar to the one in poison ivy.

JASMINE. Used in perfumes. The essential oil extracted from the extremely fragrant white flowers of the tall climbing, semievergreen jasmine shrub. May cause allergic reactions.

JASMINE ABSOLUTE. Oil of jasmine obtained by extraction with volatile or nonvolatile solvents. Sometimes called the "natural perfume" because the oil is not subjected to heat and distilled oils. See Absolute. May cause allergic reactions.

JUGLONE. A coloring for hair dyes. Yellow needles, slightly soluble in hot water but soluble in alcohol. It is the active coloring principle in walnuts. When mixed in solution with an alkali, it gives a purplish red color. It has antihemorrhaging activity. The lethal oral dose in mice is only 2.5 milligrams per kilogram of body weight. No known skin toxicity.

JUNIPER TAR. Oil of Cade. The volatile oil from the wood of a pine tree. Dark brown, viscous, with a smoky odor and acrid, slightly aromatic taste. Very slightly soluble in water. It is used as a skin peeler and antiitching factor in hair preparations and as a scent in perfumes. Less corrosive than phenol (*see*).

K

KAOLIN. China Clay. Aids in the covering ability of face powder and in absorbing oil secreted by the skin. Used in baby powder, bath powder, face masks, foundation cake makeup, liquid powder, face powder, dry rouge, and emollients. Originally obtained from Kaoling Hill in Kiangsi Province in Southeast China. Essentially a hydrated aluminum silicate (*see*). It is a white or yellowish white mass or powder, insoluble in water and absorbent. Used medicinally to treat intestinal disorders, but in large doses it may cause obstructions, perforations, or granuloma formation. It is also used in the manufacture of porcelain, pottery, bricks, and color lakes (*see*). No known toxicity for the skin.

KARAYA GUM. See Gum Karaya.

KERATIN. Protein (*see*) obtained from the horns, hoofs, feathers, quills, and hairs of various creatures. Yellowish brown powder. Insoluble in water, alcohol, or ether but soluble in ammonia. Used in permanent wave solutions and hair rinses. Nontoxic.

KEROSENE. See Deodorized Kerosene.

KETONES. Acetone, Methyl, or Ethyl. Aromatic substances obtained by the oxidation of secondary alcohols. Ethereal or aromatic odor, generally insoluble in water, but soluble in alcohol or ether. Solvents used in nail polish and nail polish removers. The intraperitoneal (into the abdomen) intermediate dosages injected in rats is lethal. See Acetone for skin toxicity.

KRAMERIA EXTRACT. Bhatany Extract. A synthetic flavoring derived from the dried root of either of two American shrubs. Used in raspberry, bitters, fruit, and rum flavorings. Used in cosmetics as an astringent. Low oral toxicity. Large doses may produce gastric distress. Can cause tumors and death after injection, but not after ingestion.

L

LABDANUM. Synthetic Musk. Used in perfumes, especially as a fixative, it is a volatile oil obtained by steam distillation from gum extracted from various rockrose shrubs. Golden yellow, viscous, with a strong balsamic odor and a bitter taste. Also used as a synthetic flavoring in foods. No known toxicity.

LACTIC ACID. Used in skin fresheners. Odorless, colorless, usually a syrupy product normally present in blood and muscle tissue as a product of the metabolism of glucose and glycogen. Present in sour milk, beer, sauerkraut, pickles, and other food products made by bacterial fermentation. Also an acidulant. It is caustic in concentrated solutions when taken internally or applied to the skin.

LACTOSE. Milk Sugar. Used widely as a base in eye lotions. Present in the milk of mammals. Stable in air but readily absorbs odors. Used in preparing food for infants, in tablets, as a general base and diluent in pharmaceutical and cosmetic compounding, and in baked goods. In large doses it is a laxative and diuretic but generally nontoxic.

LAKES, COLOR. A lake is an organic pigment prepared by precipitating a soluble color with a form of aluminum, calcium, barium, potassium, strontium, or zirconium, which then makes the colors insoluble. Not all colors are suitable for making lakes.

LAMPBLACK. Used in eye makeup pencils. It is a bluish black fine soot deposited on a surface by burning liquid hydrocarbons (*see*) such as oil. It is duller and less intense in color than other carbon blacks and has a blue undertone. It is also used in pigments for paints, enamels, and printing inks. See Carbon Black for toxicity.

LANETH-5. See Lanolin Alcohols.

LANETH-9 ACETATE. See Lanolin Alcohols.

LANETH-10. See Lanolin Alcohols.

LANETH-10 ACETATE. See Lanolin Alcohols.

LANETH-15. See Lanolin Alcohols.

LANETH-16. See Lanolin Alcohols.

LANETH-20. See Lanolin Alcohols.

LANETH-25. See Lanolin Alcohols.

LANETH-40. See Lanolin Alcohols.

LANOLIN. Wool Fat. Wool Wax. A product of the oil glands of sheep. Used in lipstick, liquid powder, mascara, nail polish remover, protective creams, suntan preparations, hand lotions, baby lotions, baby oil, bath oil, rouge, eye shadow, foundation creams, foundation cake makeup, hair conditioners, eye creams, cold creams, brilliantine hairdressings, ointment bases, and emollients. A water-absorbing base material and a natural emulsifier, it absorbs and holds water to the skin. Chemically a wax instead of a fat. Contains about 25 to 30 percent water. Mixes with about twice its weight of water. Lanolin has been found to improve the emollient effect of creams and ointments, and it does help to prevent excessive dryness of the skin and decreases the drying properties of detergents (although it makes them less effective when in shampos). Advertisers have found that the words "contains lanolin" help to sell a product and have promoted it as being able to "penetrate the skin better than other oils," although there is little scientific proof of this. Lanolin has been found to be a common skin sensitizer, causing allergic contact skin rashes. It will not prevent or cure wrinkles, and it will not stop hair loss. It is not used in pure form today because of its allergy-causing potential. The products derived from it do not usually cause allergic reactions.

LANOLIN ACID. See Lanolin.

LANOLIN ALCOHOLS. Sterols. Triterpene Alcohols. Aliphatic Alcohols. Derived from lanolin (*see*), lanolin alcohols are available commercially as solid waxy materials that are yellow to amber in color or as pale to golden yellow liquids. When acetylated (*see*), they repel water, cling to the skin, but are nonsticky. They are widely used as emulsifiers (*see*) and emollients (*see*) in hand creams and lotions. See Lanolin for toxicity.

LANOLIN LINOLEATE. See Lanolin Alcohols.

LANOLIN OIL. Lanogene®. Used as the oil in baby oils, it consists of 15 to 17 percent cholesterol, with the remainder liquid lanolin. See Lanolin for toxicity.

LANOLIN RICINOLEATE. See Lanolin Alcohols.

LANOLIN WAX. See Lanolin.

LANOLINAMIDE DEA. See Lanolin.

LANOSTEROL. A widely used skin softener in hand creams and lotions, it is the fatty alcohol derived from the wool fat of sheep. See Lanolin for toxicity.

LANTHANUM CHLORIDE. An inorganic salt. A rare earth mineral that occurs in cerite, monazite, orthite, and certain fluorspars, and used as a reagent (*see*) and catalyst (*see*) in cosmetic preparations. No known toxicity from topical use but a small oral dose is lethal in rats.

LAPIS LAZULI See Colors.

LAPYRIUM CHLORIDE. See Quaternary Ammonium Compounds.

LARD. Easily absorbed by the skin, it is used as a lubricant, emollient, and base in shaving creams, soaps, and various cosmetic creams. It is the purified internal fat from the abdomen of the hog. It is a soft white unctuous mass, with a slight characteristic odor and a bland taste. Insoluble in water. No known toxicity.

LARD GLYCERIDE. See Lard.

LATEX. Synthetic Rubber. The milky usually white juice or exudate of plants obtained by tapping. Used in beauty masks (see Face Masks and Packs) for its coating ability. Any of various gums, resins, fats, or waxes in an emulsion of water and synthetic rubber or plastic are now considered latex. Ingredients of latex compounds can be poisonous, depending upon which plant products are used. Can cause skin rash.

LATHER. Produced by action of air bubbles in a soap solution. For satisfactory shaving, a lather must be dense. The air bubbles must be fine and stable for the duration of the shave. In bubble baths the air bubbles must be large and light.

LAURALKONIUM CHLORIDE. See Quaternary Ammonium Compounds.

LAURAMIDE DEA. Lauric Acid Diethanolamide. See Lauric

Acid.
LAURAMIDE MEA.   See Lauric Acid.
LAURAMIDOPROPYL DIMETHYLAMINE.   See Lauric Acid and Dimethylamine.
LAURAMINE OXIDE.   See Lauric Acid.
LAURAMINOPROPIONIC ACID.   See Propionic Acid.
LAURETH-1.   See Lauryl Alcohol.
LAURETH-4.   See Lauryl Alcohol.
LAURETH-9.   See Lauryl Alcohol.
LAURETH-12.   See Lauryl Alcohol.
LAURETH-23.   See Lauryl Alcohol.
LAURIC ACID. n-Dodecanoic Acid.   A common constituent of vegetable fats, especially coconut oil and laurel oil. Its derivatives are widely used as a base in the manufacture of soaps, detergents, and lauryl alcohol (*see*) because of their foaming properties. Has a slight odor of bay and makes large copious bubbles when in soap. A mild irritant but not a sensitizer.
LAURIC ALDEHYDE.   See Lauric Acid.
LAUROYL SARCOSINE.   See Sarcosines.
LAURTRIMONIUM CHLORIDE.   See Quaternary Ammonium Compounds.
LAURYL ALCOHOL. 1-Dodecanol.   A colorless, crystalline compound that is produced commercially from coconut oil. Used to make detergents because of its sudsing ability. Has a characteristic fatty odor. It is soluble in most oils but is insoluble in glycerin. Used in perfumery. See Lauric Acid for toxicity.
LAURYL AMINE.   See Lauric Acid.
LAURYL BETAINE.   See Lauric Acid.
LAURYL ISOQUINOLINIUM BROMIDE.   A quaternary ammonium compound (*see*) active against a microorganism believed to cause a type of dandruff. Used in hair tonics and cuticle softeners. Slightly greater toxicity than benzalkonium chloride in rats. No skin irritation or sensitization in concentrations of 0.1 percent and lower. Used also as an agricultural fungicide.
LAURYL LACTATE.   See Lauric Acid.
LAURYL METHACRYLATE.   See Lauric Acid.
LAURYL PYRIDINIUM CHLORIDE.   See Quaternary Ammonium Compounds.
LAURYL SULFATE.   Derived from lauryl alcohol (*see*). Its potassium, zinc, magnesium, sodium, calcium, and ammonium salts are

used in shampoos because of their foaming properties. See Sodium Lauryl Sulfate.

LAVANDIN OIL.   Used in soaps and perfumes. It is the essential oil of a hybrid related to the lavender plant. Fragrant, yellowish, with a camphor lavender scent. No known toxicity.

LAVENDER OIL.   Used in skin fresheners, powders, shaving preparations, mouthwashes, dentifrices, and perfumes. The volatile oil from the fresh flowering tops of lavender. Also used in a variety of food flavorings. It can cause allergic reactions and has been found to cause adverse skin reactions when the skin is exposed to sunlight.

LEAD ACETATE. Sugar of Lead.   Colorless white crystals or grains with an acetic odor. Bubbles slowly. It has been used as a topical astringent but is absorbed through the skin, and therefore might lead to lead poisoning. Also used in hair dyeing and printing colors and in the manufacture of chrome yellow (see Colors). Still used to treat bruises and skin irritations in animals. Not recommended for use because of the possibility of lead buildup in the body.

LEAD COMPOUNDS.   Used in ointments and hair dye pigments. Lead may cause contact dermatitis. It is poisonous in all forms. It is one of the most hazardous of toxic metals because its poison is cumulative and its toxic effects are many and severe. Among them are leg cramps, muscle weakness, numbness, depression, brain damage, coma, and death. Ingestion and inhalation of lead cause the most severe symptoms.

LECITHIN.   From the Greek, meaning "egg yolk." A natural antioxidant and emollient used in eye creams, lipsticks, liquid powders, hand creams and lotions, soaps, and many other cosmetics. Also a natural emulsifier and spreading agent. It is found in all living organisms, and is frequently obtained for commercial purposes from eggs and soybeans. Usually naturally white or light yellow, but turns brown upon exposure to air. Insoluble in water but swells when immersed. Egg yolk is 8 to 9 percent lecithin. Nontoxic.

LEMON.   The common fresh fruit and fruit extract is the most frequently used acid in cosmetics. It is 5 to 8 percent citric acid. Employed in cream rinses, hair color rinses, astringents, fresheners, skin bleaches, and for reducing alkalinity of many other products. Do-it-yourselfers can squeeze 2 lemons into a strainer, add the juice to 1 cup of water, and use it as a rinse after shampooing to remove scum and to leave a shine on the hair. Lemon can cause allergic reactions.

LEMON BALM. Sweet Balm. Garden Balm.   Used in perfumes and as a soothing facial treatment. An Old World mint cultivated for its lemon-flavored, fragrant leaves. Often considered a weed, it has been used by herbalists as a medicine and to flavor foods and medicines. It reputedly imparts long life. Also used to treat earache and toothache. Nontoxic.

LEMON EXTRACT.   See Lemon Oil.

LEMON JUICE.   See Lemon.

LEMON OIL. Cedro Oil.   Used in perfumes and food flavorings, it is the volatile oil expressed from the fresh peel. A pale yellow to deep yellow, it has a characteristic odor and taste of the outer part of fresh lemon peel. It can cause an allergic reaction and has been suspected of being a co-cancer-causing agent.

LEMONGRASS OIL. Indian Oil of Verbena.   Used in perfumes, especially those added to soap. It is the volatile oil distilled from the leaves of the lemon grasses. A yellowish or reddish brown liquid, it has a strong odor of verbena. Also used in insect repellents and in fruit flavorings for foods and beverages. Death reported when taken internally, and autopsy showed lining of the intestines was severely damaged. Skin toxicity unknown.

LICORICE.   Used as a coloring in cosmetics. Extract from the Mediterranean plant, used in fruit, licorice, anise, maple, and root beer flavoring. Used to soothe the skin. Some people known to have eaten licorice candy regularly and generously have had raised blood pressure, headaches, and muscle weakness. No known skin toxicity.

LIDOCAINE.   Needles from benzene or alcohol, insoluble in water. A local anesthetic, it relieves itching, pain, soreness, and discomfort due to skin rashes, including eczema and minor burns. Can cause an allergic reaction.

LIGNOCERIC ACID.   Obtained from beechwood tar or by distillation of rotten oak wood. Occurs in most natural fats. Used in shampoos and soaps and plastics. No known toxicity.

LIGNOL.   See Lignoceric Acid.

LILAC.   Used in perfumes. Derived from the plant, especially the European shrub variety. It has fragrant bluish to purple pink flowers. No known toxicity.

LILY OF THE VALLEY. Convallaria Flowers.   A perfume ingredient extracted from the low perennial herb. It has oblong leaves and fragrant, nodding, bell-shaped white flowers. Has been used as a heart stimulant. No known toxicity for the skin.

LIME.   A perfume ingredient from the small greenish yellow fruit of a spicy tropical tree. Its very acid pulp yields a juice used as a flavoring agent and as an antiseptic. A source of Vitamin C. Can cause an adverse reaction when skin is exposed to sunlight.

LIME SULFUR. Topical antiseptic. A brown clear liquid prepared by boiling sulfur and lime with water. Can cause skin irritation.

LIMEWATER. An alkaline water solution of calcium hydroxide that absorbs carbon dioxide from the air, forming a protective film of calcium carbonate (*see*) on the surface of the liquid. Used in medicines, as an antacid, and as an alkali in external washes, face masks, and hair-grooming products. No known toxicity.

LIMONENE. *d,l, and dl forms.* A synthetic flavoring agent that occurs naturally in star anise, buchu leaves, caraway, celery, oranges, coriander, cumin, cardamon, sweet fennel, common fennel, mace, marigold, oil of lavandin, oil of lemon, oil of mandarin, peppermint, petitgrain oil, pimento oil, orange leaf (absolute), orange peel (sweet oil), origanum oil, black pepper, peels of citrus, and hops oil. Used in lime flavorings and fragrances. A skin irritant and sensitizer.

LINALOE OIL. Bois de Rose Oil. An ingredient in perfume that is the colorless to yellow volatile essential oil distilled from a Mexican tree. It has a pleasant flowery scent and is soluble in most fixed oils. May cause allergic reactions.

LINALOOL. Linalol. Used in perfumes and soaps instead of bergamot or French lavender. It is a fragrant, colorless liquid that occurs in many essential oils such as linaloe, Ceylon cinnamon, sassafras, orange flower, and bergamot. Also used in food flavorings such as blueberry, chocolate, and lemon. May cause allergic reactions.

LINALYL ACETATE. A colorless, fragrant liquid, slightly soluble in water, it is the most valuable constituent of bergamot and lavender oils, which are used in perfumery. It occurs naturally in basil, jasmine oil, lavandin oil, lavender oil, and lemon oil. It has a strong floral scent. Also used as a synthetic flavoring in food. No known toxicity.

LINDEN EXTRACT. A natural flavoring from the flowers of the tree grown in Europe and the United States. Used in fragrances and in raspberry and vermouth flavorings. No known toxicity.

LINOLEAMIDE. Aliphatic amide of linoleic acid. See Linoleic Acid.

LINOLEAMIDE DEA. Alkyl amides produced by a diethanolamine condensation of linoleic acid. See Linoleic Acid.

LINOLEIC ACID. Used as an emulsifier. An essential fatty acid (*see*) prepared from edible fats and oils. Component of Vitamin F and a major constituent of many vegetable oils, for example, cottonseed and soybean. Used in emulsifiers and vitamins. Large doses can cause nausea and vomiting. No known skin toxicity and, in fact, may have emollient properties.

LINOLENIC ACID.   Colorless liquid glyceride found in most drying oils. Insoluble in water, soluble in organic solvents. Used to make nail polishes dry faster. Slightly irritating to mucous membranes.

LINSEED ACID.   See Linseed Oil.

LINSEED OIL.   Oil used in shaving creams, emollients, and medicinal soaps. Soothing to the skin. It is the yellowish oil expressed or extracted from flax seed. Gradually thickens when exposed to air. It has a peculiar odor and a bland taste and is also used in paint, varnish, and linoleum. Can cause allergic reactions.

LIP BRUSH.   A brush to trace a sharp outline of the lips with lipstick. Usually made of sable or other animal hair. No known toxicity.

LIP CREAM.   A mixture of oils that melt on contact with the skin to soften and soothe the lips. Almost identical to night creams or moisturizers. See Emollients.

LIP GLOSS.   Usually comes in jars, sometimes in tubes. Contains different proportions of the same ingredients as lipstick but usually has less wax and more oil to make the lips shinier. Used alone or with lipstick and applied with the fingertip.

LIP PENCIL.   A colored wax mixture in wood or metal casing for the same purpose as a lip brush.

LIP PRIMER.   A stick similar to lipstick but containing less wax used to soften the lips and to serve as a base for the lipstick. Makes the lips shinier.

LIPSTICK.   Regular, Frosted, Medicated, Sheer. Primarily a mixture of oil and wax in stick form with a red staining certified dye dispersed in oil, red pigments similarly dispersed, flavoring, and perfume. Bromo acid, D & C Red No. 21 (*see*) and related dyes are most often used. Among other common lipstick dyes are D & C Red No. 27 and insoluble dyes known as lakes such as D & C Red No. 34 Calcium Lake and D & C Orange No. 17 Lake (see D & C Colors). Pinks are made by mixing titanium dioxide (*see*) with various reds. Among the oils and fats used are olive, mineral, sesame, castor, butyl stearate, polyethylene glycol, cocoa butter, lanolin, petrolatum, lecithin, hydrogenated vegetable oils, carnauba and candelilla waxes, beeswax, ozokerite, and paraffin (*see all*). The lipstick case, a precision instrument, almost always costs more than the ingredients. Colors of lipsticks on the market remain essentially the same but the names such as "strawberry rose" are frequently changed to induce customers to buy. A typical lipstick formula contains: castor oil, about 65 percent;

beeswax, 15 percent; carnauba wax, 10 percent; lanolin, 5 percent; certified dyes, soluble; color lakes, insoluble, and perfume. Frosted lipstick includes a pearlizing agent that adds luster to the color. Such an agent may be a bismuth compound or guanine (*see both*). Medicated lipstick is used to treat or prevent chapped or sun-dried lips. It may or may not combine coloring with ingredients but usually contains petrolatum, mineral wax, and oils. It may or may not contain menthol (*see*) or a sunscreen. Sheer lipstick includes transparent coloring and no indelible dyes so as to give a more natural look to the lips. The main difficulty with lipsticks results from allergy to the dyes or to specific ingredients. There is also some evidence that some of the dyes used can cause cancer in animals and that some of the animal fats and vegetable oils and waxes contain pesticides. Among lip problems reported recently to the FDA were burns, cracks, and lacerations, excessive dryness, numbness, rash, and swollen gums as adverse reactions to lipstick products. See Cheilitis.

LIQUEFYING CREAM.   Cleansing cream designed to liquefy when rubbed into the skin. It usually contains paraffin, a wax, stearic acid, sodium borate, liquid petrolatum (54 percent) (*see all*), and water (26 percent).

LIQUID MAKEUP.   See Foundation Makeup.

LIQUID POWDER.   See Foundation Makeup.

LITHIUM CHLORIDE.   A crystalline salt of the alkali metal, used as a scavenger in purifying metals, to remove oxygen, and in soap and lubricant bases. The crystals absorb water and then become neutral or slightly alkaline. It is also used in the manufacture of mineral waters, in soldering, and in refrigerating machines. Formerly used as a salt substitute. Prolonged absorption may cause disturbed electrolyte balance in humans and impair kidney function and cause central nervous system problems.

LITHIUM HYDROXIDE.   Used in making cosmetic resins and esters (*see both*). A granular, free-flowing powder, acrid, and strongly alkaline. It is the salt of the alkaline metal that absorbs water from the air and is soluble in water. Used in photo developers and in batteries. Very irritating to the skin, and flammable in contact with the air.

LITHIUM STEARATE.   White, fatty, solid, and soluble in water and alcohol. A metallic soap used as an emulsifier, lubricant, and plasticizer in various cosmetic creams and lotions, also a coloring agent. No known toxicity.

LOCUST BEAN GUM. St. John's Bread. Carob Bean Gum.   A thickener and stabilizer in cosmetics and foods. Also used in depila-

tories. A natural flavor extract from the seed of the carob tree cultivated in the Mediterranean area. The history of the carob tree dates
back more than two thousand years when the ancient Egyptians used
locust bean gum as an adhesive in mummy binding. It is alleged that
the "locust" (through confusion of the locusts with carob) and wild
honey, which sustained John the Baptist in the wilderness, was from
this plant, thus the name St. John's Bread. The carob pods are used
as feed for stock today because of their high protein content. No
known toxicity from cosmetic use. It is on the FDA list for study of
side effects.

LOGWOOD.   An active ingredient known as hematoxylin from the
very hard brown or brownish red heartwood of a tree common to the
West Indies and Central America. It is used as a liquid or as a solid
extract obtained by evaporation in black hair colorings and for neutralizing red tones in dyed hair. It is also a mild astringent. May cause
allergic reaction in the hypersensitive.

LOVAGE.   An ingredient in perfumery from an aromatic herb native
to southern Europe and grown in monastery gardens centuries ago for
medicine and food flavoring. It has a hot, sharp, biting taste. The
yellow brown oil is extracted from the root or other parts of the herb.
It has a reputation for improving health and inciting love; Czecho-
slovakian girls reportedly wear it in a bag around their necks when
dating boys. It supposedly has deodorant properties when added to
bath water. No known toxicity.

LUBRICATING CREAM.   See Emollients.

LYCOPODIUM. Ground Pine. Ground Fir.   A dusting powder derived from erect or creeping evergreen plants grown in North America, Europe, and Asia. The plant's spores create a fine yellow powder
that sticks to the fingers when touched. It is odorless and absorbent.
It may cause a form of inflammatory (granulomatous) reaction in
wounds or exposed tissues and can cause allergic reactions such as
a stuffy nose and hay fever. It is highly flammable.

M

MACERATION.   The extraction of flower-oil production by immer-
sion in warm fats.

MAGNESIA.   A skin freshener and dusting powder ingredient.
Slightly alkaline white powder taken from any one of several ores
such as periclase. Named after Magnesia, an ancient city in Asia
Minor. An antacid. No known toxicity.

MAGNESIUM ALUMINUM SILICATE. Veegum®. A coloring agent in cosmetics. Activated magnesium silicate is a hard, porous, granular substance used in the making of antibiotics. Used chiefly as a filler or as an extender in pharmaceutical compounds. It has astringent properties. Magnesium silicate is used also in table salt and vanilla powder as an anticaking agent. Soothing to the stomach and used as an antacid. No known toxicity.

MAGNESIUM CARBONATE. Perfume carrier and coloring agent used in baby powder, bath powder, tooth powders, face masks, liquid powders, face powder, and dry rouge. It is a silver white very crystalline salt that occurs in nature as magnesite or dolomite. Can be prepared artificially and is also used in paint, printing ink, table salt, and as an antacid. Nontoxic to the intact skin but may cause irritation when applied to abraded skin.

MAGNESIUM CITRATE. Used in hair sets or hair-bodying agents. The magnesium salt of citric acid. Soluble in water. It leaves a glossy film after drying. No known toxicity.

MAGNESIUM HYDROXIDE. Used as an alkali in dentifrices and skin creams, in canned peas, and as a drying agent and color retention agent for improved gelling in the manufacture of cheese. Slightly alkaline crystalline compound obtained by hydration of magnesia (*see*) or precipitation of seawater by lime. Toxic when inhaled. Harmless to skin and in fact soothes it.

MAGNESIUM LANOLATE. Magnesium salt of lanolin. See Magnesium and Lanolin.

MAGNESIUM LAURYL SULFATE. See Sodium Lauryl Sulfate.

MAGNESIUM MONTMORILLONITE. See Montmorillonite.

MAGNESIUM OLEATE. Salt of magnesium used in liquid powders as a texturizer. It is a yellowish powder or mass that is insoluble in water. No known toxicity.

MAGNESIUM OXIDE. A white powder that occurs in the mineral periclase. Used in dentifrices as an abrasive and in antiperspirants to protect against skin irritations. Also used as a cosmetic coloring and in stomach powders as an antacid. A laxative for animals. No known toxicity.

MAGNESIUM SILICATE. An insoluble, effervescent, white powder that is slowly decomposed by acids to form a soluble salt and an insoluble silica, which has strong absorptive properties. Used to opacify shampoos; also medicinally to reduce stomach acidity, with a slow neutralizing action. Nontoxic.

MAGNESIUM STEARATE. Coloring agent used in face powder,

protective creams, and baby dusting powders. It is a white soapy powder, insoluble in water. Also used for tablet making. No known toxicity.

MAGNESIUM TRISILICATE. Coloring agent. See Magnesium Aluminum Silicate.

MAGNOLIA. Sweet Bay. Used in perfumery. A genus of North American and Asian shrubs and trees named after the French botanist Pierre Magnol. The plants have evergreen or deciduous leaves and usually showy white, yellow, rose, or purple flowers appearing in early spring. The dried bark is used in folk medicine to induce sweating and as a bitter tonic. No known toxicity.

MAKEUP BASE, FOUNDATION. See Foundation Makeup.

MALEIC ANHYDRIDE. A colorless, crystalline acid that gives rise to malic acid (*see*) on reaction with water. Used as a fungicide and plasticizer in cosmetics and in hair lacquers. Employed in the manufacture of resins and oils. A powerful irritant, it can cause burns of the skin and it is dangerous to the eyes. Inhalation causes fluid retention in the lungs. A skin irritant. Numerous cases of skin rash have been reported when used as a hair lacquer ingredient.

MALIC ACID. A colorless, crystalline compound with a strong acid taste that occurs naturally in a wide variety of fruits, including apples and cherries. An alkali in cosmetics, foods, and wines. Also used as an antioxidant for cosmetics and as an ingredient of hair lacquer. Irritating to the skin and can cause allergic reaction when used in hair lacquers.

MALLOW EXTRACT. From the herb family. A moderate purplish red that is paler than magenta rose. Used in coloring and also as a source of pectin (*see*). No known toxicity.

MALONIC ACID. An antioxidant prepared synthetically. Occurs naturally in many plants. The colorless crystals obtained from the oxidation of malic acid are used in the manufacture of barbiturates. It is a strong irritant. Large doses injected into mice are lethal.

MALT EXTRACT. Extracted from barley that has been allowed to germinate, then heated to destroy vitality, and dried. It contains sugars, proteins, and salts from barley. The extract is mixed with water and allowed to solidify. It is used as a nutrient and in cosmetics as a texturizer. No known toxicity.

MANGANESE SULFATE. Usually prepared by dissolving dolomite (*see*) or magnesite in acid. It is the salt of the element manganese, a metal ore. Its pale red crystals are used in red hair dye and to make red glazes on porcelain. Also used medicinally as a purgative and as a dressing for cotton goods. No known toxicity to the hair or scalp but very small doses injected into mice are lethal.

MANGANESE VIOLET. Burgundy Violet. Permanent Violet. Ammonium Manganese Pyrophosphate. A moderate purple that is redder and duller than heliotrope and more blue than amethyst. Toxic when inhaled.

MANNITOL. A humectant in hand creams and lotions and used in hair-grooming products as an emulsifier and antioxidant. It is widespread in plants but mostly prepared from seaweed. White, crystalline solid, odorless, and sweet tasting. Its use as a food additive is under study by the FDA because it can cause gastrointestinal disturbances. However, there is no known toxicity from its use as a cosmetic.

MARJORAM OIL. Used in hair preparations, perfumes, and soaps, it is the yellowish essential oil from sweet marjoram. Insoluble in water, soluble in alcohol and chloroform. Can irritate the skin. The redness, itching, and warmth experienced when applied to the skin are carried by local dilation of the blood vessels or by local reflex. May produce allergic reaction in the sensitive. Essential oils, such as marjoram, are believed to penetrate the skin and produce systemic effects.

MASCARA. A cosmetic for coloring the eyelashes and eyebrows. Contains insoluble pigments, carnauba wax, triethanolamine stearate, paraffin, and lanolin (*see all*). Pigments in eye makeup must be inert and are usually carbon black, iron oxides, chromium oxide, ultramarine, or carmine. Coal tar dyes are not permitted. The excipients may contain beeswax, cetyl alcohol, glyceryl monostearate, gums such as tragacanth, mineral oil, perfume, preservatives such as *p*-hydroxybenzoic acid, propylene glycol, spermaceti, and synthetics such as isopropyl myristate, as well as vegetable oils (*see all*). The newer lash extenders may carry certain tiny fibers of rayon or nylon. As the liquid of the mascara evaporates, the fibers adhere to the wet lashes making them appear longer. Mascara may cause allergic reactions. The product may become contaminated, particularly if the user spits on the material to moisten it before application. No eye makeup should be shared with another because of the danger of infection.

MATTE FINISH MAKEUP. Designed to be all-in-one makeup combining foundation and powder in one. It is a more concentrated version of standard makeup and contains more powder, pigment, and emollient than standard makeup. Effective in covering blemishes. Skin toxicity depends upon ingredients used.

MAYONNAISE. The common salad dressing. Semisolid, made with

eggs, vegetable oil and vinegar or lemon juice. Used by natural cosmeticians as a dry hair conditioner. The hair is rubbed liberally with
mayonnaise, a hot towel is wrapped around the hair and is kept on
for 15 minutes, and then removed. Two soapings and plenty of rinsing
follow. As effective as any of the more expensive products.

MDM HYDANTOIN. Monomethylol Dimethyl Hydantoin. Used
as a preservative in cosmetic preparations, the compound liberates
formaldehyde (*see*) steadily at a slow rate in the presence of water.
The resin is used in hair lacquers. See Formaldehyde for toxicity.

MEDICATED MAKEUP. Cosmetic manufacturers advertise medicated makeup that both "covers" and treats the skin simultaneously.
Such cosmetics contain antibacterials such as bithionol and tribromsalan (TBS) (*see both*). The American Medical Association frowns
on such preparations because such antiinfective agents are useful in
medical preparations for the treatment of minor cuts and abrasions,
but in cosmetics and toilet preparations they serve merely to limit the
bacterial contamination of the product during use. Furthermore, their
potential harm often outweighs their benefit because such agents may
cause allergic reactions and sensitivity to sunlight or bright lights;
when the skin is exposed, it breaks out or reddens.

MEK. Methyl Ethyl Ketone. A flammable, colorless liquid compound resembling acetone and most often made by taking the hydrogen out of butyl alcohol. Used chiefly as a solvent. Similar to, but
more irritating than, acetone; its vapor is irritating to mucous membranes and eyes. Central nervous system depression in experimental
animals has been reported, but the irritating odor usually discourages
further inhalation in humans. No serious poisonings reported in man,
except for skin irritations when nail polish was applied with MEK as
a solvent. Large doses inhaled by rats are lethal.

MELAMINE. White, free-flowing powdered resin. Used in nail
enamel. First introduced into industry in 1939, it is now used in a
wide variety of products including boil-proof adhesives and scratch-
resistant enamel finishes. Combined with urea resins, it forms the
heat-resistant amino plastics. It may cause skin rashes, but that is
believed to be caused by the formaldehyde component rather than
the melamine.

MENADIONE. Vitamin K₃. Used as a preservative in emollients.
A synthetic wtih properties of Vitamin K. Bright yellow crystals
which are insoluble in water. They are used medically to prevent
blood clotting and to prevent souring of milk products. No known
toxicity.

MENHADEN OIL. Pogy Oil. Mossbunker Oil.   Obtained along the east coast of Africa from the menhaden fish, which are a little larger then herrings. The fish glycerides of menhaden are reddish, and have a strong fishy odor. Used in soaps and creams. No known toxicity.

MENTHOL.   Used in perfumes, emollient creams, hair tonics, mouthwashes, shaving creams, preshave lotions, after-shave lotions, body rubs, liniments, and skin fresheners. It gives that "cool" feeling to the skin after use. It can be obtained naturally from peppermint or other mint oils and can be made synthetically by hydrogenation (*see*) of thymol (*see*). It is a mild local anesthetic. It is nontoxic in low doses, but in concentrations of 1 percent or more it exerts an irritant action that can, if continued long, produce changes in all layers of the mucous membrane.

MERCAPTANS. Quicksilver.   Used in depilatories. A class of compounds that contain sulfur and have a disagreeable odor. Depilatories containing mercaptans can cause irritation and allergic reactions as well as infection of the hair follicles.

MERCURY COMPOUNDS. Quicksilver.   Until July 5, 1973, mercury was widely used in cosmetics, including wax face masks, hair tonics, medicated soaps, and bleach and freckle creams. Mercury compounds are heavy, silver liquids from the metal that occurs in the earth's crust. Mercury is potentially dangerous by all portals of entry, including the skin. It may cause a variety of symptoms ranging from chronic inflammation of the mouth and gums to personality changes, nervousness, fever, rash; and, if ingested in small amounts, it may be fatal. The ban on mercury was brought about because it was found that its use in bleaching creams and other products over a long period of time caused mercury buildup in the body. Mercury is still used as a preservative in eye preparations to inhibit growth of germs. It is now the only use permitted. Because the prevention of eye infection warrants the use of mercury, eye makeup may contain up to 0.0065 percent.

METABROMSALAN.   See Bromates.

METALLIC HAIR DYES.   Metals such as copper are used to change the color of hair. They are not used very often because they tend to dull the hair. However, they are used in products that are designed for daily application over a week or so to effect color changes gradually. Combs impregnated with dye or hair lotions may contain metals for this purpose. See Hair Coloring for further information, including toxicity.

METHANOL. Methyl Alcohol. Wood Alcohol.   A solvent and

denaturant obtained by the destructive distillation of wood. Flammable, poisonous liquid with a nauseating odor. Better solvent than ethyl alcohol. See Ethanol for skin toxicity.

METHENAMINE.   An odorless white crystalline powder made from formaldehyde and ammonia (*see both*). Used as an antiseptic and bacteria killer in deodorant creams and powders, mouthwashes, and medicines. It is one of the most frequent causes of skin rashes in the rubber industry and is omitted from hypoallergenic cosmetics. Skin irritations are believed to be caused by formic acid, which occurs by the action of perspiration on the formaldehyde.

METHIONINE.   An essential amino acid (*see*) that occurs in protein. Used as a texturizer in cosmetic creams. Also used as a dietary substance and is attracted to fat. Nontoxic.

METHOXYDIGLYCOL.   See Polyethylene Glycol.

METHOXYETHANOL.   See Ethanol.

p-METHOXYPHENYL.   See Guaiacol.

4-METHOXY-m-PHENYLENEDIAMINE.   See p-Phenylenediamine.

METHYL ACETAMIDE.   See Methyl Caproate.

METHYL ACETATE. Acetic Acid.   Colorless liquid that occurs naturally in coffee, with a pleasant apple odor. Used in perfume to emphasize floral notes (*see*), especially that of rose, and in toilet waters having a lavender odor. Also naturally occurs in peppermint oil. Used as a solvent for many resins and oils. May be irritating to the respiratory tract and, in high concentrations, may be narcotic. Since it has an effective fat solvent drying effect on skin, it may cause skin problems such as chafing and cracking.

METHYL ACETYL RICINOLEATE. Flexricin Castor Oil.   See Ricinoleate.

METHYL ANTHRANILATE.   Used as an "orange" perfume for ointments, in the manufacture of synthetic perfumes, and in suntan lotions. Occurs naturally in neroli, ylang-ylang, bergamot, jasmine, and other essential oils. Colorless to pale yellow liquid with a bluish fluorescence and a grapelike odor. It is made synthetically from anthranilates (*see*). Can irritate the skin.

METHYL BENZOATE.   Essence or oil of Niobe. Made from methanol and benzoic acid (*see both*). Used in perfumes. Colorless, transparent liquid with a pleasant fruity odor. Also used as a flavoring in foods and beverages. No known toxicity.

METHYL CAPROATE. Methyl Hexanoate.   The ester produced by the reaction of methyl alcohol and caproic acid. Used as a stabilizer and plasticizer for hand and face creams. No known toxicity.

METHYL CAPRYLATE.   See Methyl Caproate.
METHYL ETHYL KETONE.   See MEK.
METHYL EUGENOL. Eugenol. Methyl Ether.   See Eugenol and Ether.
METHYL HEPTINE CARBONATE.   Derived from castor oil, it is used in perfumes, lipsticks, toilet waters, facial creams, and perfumed cosmetics because of its violet scent. Slightly yellow liquid with a powerful unpleasant odor when undiluted. However, when diluted, it has the odor of violets. It may cause allergic reactions such as a stuffy nose, hay fever, and skin rash.
METHYL HEXYL KETONE. 2-Octanone.   Colorless liquid with apple odor and camphor taste. Insoluble in water. Used in perfumery. No known toxicity.
METHYL MYRISTATE.   See Myristic Acid.
METHYL NICOTINATE.   Derived from nicotinic acid and used as a rubefacient. No known toxicity.
METHYL OLEATE.   See Oleic Acid.
METHYL PHTHALYL ETHYL GLYCOLATE.   See Phthalic Acid and Polyethylene Glycol.
METHYL ROSINATE. Cloud.   See Rosin.
METHYL SALICYLATE. Oil of Wintergreen.   A counterirritant, local anesthetic, and disinfectant used in perfumes, toothpaste, tooth powder, and mouthwash. The volatile oil obtained by maceration and subsequent steam distillation in a species of leaves, including those of sweet birch, cassie, and wintergreen. Colorless, yellow liquid, with a strong odor of wintergreen. A strong irritant to the skin and mucous membranes and may be absorbed readily through the skin. It has the typical systemic effects of salicylates (*see*), and ingestion of even small amounts may cause death.
METHYL SILICONE.   Prepared by hydrolyzing (*see*) dimethyldichlorosilane or its esters, it is used to help compounds resist oxidation. No known toxicity. See Silicones.
p-METHYLAMINOPHENOL.   See p-Methylaminophenol Sulfate.
p-METHYLAMINOPHENOL SULFATE.   Crystals that discolor in air and are soluble in water. They are used in photographic developers, for dyeing furs, and for hair dyes. May cause skin irritation, allergic reactions, and a shortage of oxygen in the blood. In solution applied to the skin, restlessness and convulsions have been produced in man.
METHYLATED SPIRIT. Toilet Quality.   Alcohol denatured with methanol (*see*). Used in fragrances and other cosmetic products in

amounts of over 85 percent ethyl alcohol, 5 percent methyl alcohol, and 5 percent water. See Ethanol for toxicity.

METHYLBENZETHONIUM CHLORIDE. Diaparene Chloride. A quaternary ammonium compound used as a germicide in cosmetics and baby products such as baby oils. Also used as a topical disinfectant. See Quaternary Ammonium Compounds for toxicity.

METHYLCELLULOSE. Cellulose Methyl Ether. A binder, thickening, dispersing, and emulsifying agent used in wave-setting lotions, foam stabilizers, bath oils, and other cosmetic products. It is prepared from wood pulp or chemical cotton by treatment with alcohol. Swells in water. Soluble in cold water and insoluble in hot. See also Carboxymethyl Cellulose. A dose injected into the abdomen of rats causes cancer. Nontoxic on the skin.

METHYLENE CHLORIDE. A solvent for nail enamels and for cleansing creams. A colorless gas that compresses into a colorless liquid of pleasant odor and sweet taste. Used as an anesthetic in medicine. High concentrations are narcotic. Damage to the liver, kidney, and central nervous system can occur, and persistent postrecovery symptoms after inhalation include headache, nervousness, insomnia, and tremor. Can be absorbed through the skin and is then converted to carbon monoxide which, in turn, can cause stress in the cardiovascular system.

METHYLPARABEN. Methyl p-Hydroxybenzoate. Used in bubble baths, cold creams, eyeliners, and liquid makeup. It is an antimicrobial and preservative made of small, odorless, colorless crystals that have a burning taste. Nontoxic in small amounts but can cause allergic skin reactions.

METHYLPHENYLPOLYSILOXANE. Cresol (*see*) with a blend of silicone (*see*) oils. An oily, fluid resin, stable over a wide temperature range, used in lubricating creams. No known toxicity.

MICA. Any of a group of minerals that are found in crystallized, thin, elastic sheets that can be separated easily. They vary in color from pale green, brown, or black to colorless. Ground and used as a lubricant and coloring in cosmetics. Nontoxic.

MICROCRYSTALLINE WAX. Any of various plastic materials that are obtained from petroleum. They are different from paraffin waxes (*see*) in that they have a higher melting point and higher viscosity and much finer crystals that can be seen only under a microscope. Used in nail polishes and in cake cosmetics. No known toxicity.

MILFOIL. See Yarrow.

MILK. Used in bath preparations and face masks as a soothing skin cleanser. Also used by natural cosmeticians as a face wash: for dry

skin, cream is used; for oily skin, they use skimmed milk. It is as
effective as many more expensive products. Nontoxic, but if not
rinsed thoroughly from the skin with water, rancidity sets in and
becomes a focus of bacteria. Consequently, the skin may break out
with pimples.

MIMOSA.   Reddish yellow solid with a long-lasting, pleasant odor
resembling ylang-ylang (*see*) used in perfumes. Derived from trees,
shrubs, and herbs native to tropical and warm regions. Mimosa
droops and closes its leaves when touched. Also used in tanning. May
produce allergic skin reactions.

MINERAL OIL. White Oil.   Used in baby creams, baby lotions, bay
oil, brilliantine hairdressings, cleansing creams, cold creams, emollients, moisturizing creams, eye creams, foundation creams and
makeup, hair conditioners, hand lotions, lipsticks, mascaras, rouge,
shaving creams, compact powders, makeup removers, suntan creams,
oils, and ointments. Also a cosmetic lubricant, protective agent, and
binder. It is a mixture of refined liquid hydrocarbons (*see*) derived
from petroleum. Colorless, transparent, odorless, and tasteless. When
heated, it smells like petroleum. It stays on top of the skin and leaves
a shiny protective surface. Nontoxic.

MINERAL SPIRITS. Ligroin.   A refined solvent of naphtha. Contains naphthenes and paraffin (*see*). Used as a solvent in cosmetic
oils, fats, and waxes. See Kerosene for toxicity.

MINERAL WAX.   See Ceresin.

MINK OIL.   Used in emollients, it supposedly softens the skin. It
became popular as a cosmetic ingredient when a mink farmer noticed
his hands were softer after handling minks. According to the American Medical Association, mink oil is no more effective than other oils
in minimizing the evaporation of moisture from the skin and smooth-
ing the surface scales of excessively dry skin. No known toxicity.

MINT.   See Spearmint Oil, Peppermint Oil, Wintergreen Oil, Sassafras Oil.

MISTLETOE.   Berries of a Eurasian shrub with greenish stems,
leathery leaves, and small yellow flowers. It is being used in cosmetics
today but its use has not been made public. Used medicinally as an
antispasmodic and narcotic. No known skin toxicity.

MIXED ISOPROPANOLAMINE LAURYL SULFATE.   See Lauryl
Sulfate.

MIXED TERPENES.   Terpenes are a classic of organic compounds
widely distributed in nature. They are components of volatile or
essential oils and are found in substantial amounts in cedarwood oil,

camphor, thymol, eucalyptol, menthol, turpentine, and pure oil. They are used in cosmetics as wetting agents and surfactants. Can cause local irritation.

MODERN BLENDS.   One of the basic perfume types, it has indefinable top-notes (*see*) which can not be linked to either the floral or the oriental. These blends contain aldehydes (*see*) meaning that whether they are basically floral or woody, they have a sparkle in their more insistent notes, which enhances all the others.

MODIFIER.   A term in cosmetics to describe a substance that induces or stabilizes certain shades in hair coloring.

MOISTURIZERS.   See Emollients.

MONOBENZONE. Hydroquinone Monobenzyl Ether.   Prepared synthetically and used as an antioxidant and to retard melanin production. Used also in bleach and freckle creams. It may cause blotchiness and allergic skin reactions.

MONOMER.   A molecule that by repetition in a long chain builds up a large structure or polymer (*see*). Ethylene, the gas, for instance, is the monomer of polyethylene (*see*).

MONTAN WAX.   Dark brown, white, or nearly white wax extracted from lignite. Used in polishes instead of carnauba wax (*see*) and in the manufacture of candles, waterproof paints, and varnishes. No known toxicity.

MONTMORILLONITE.   A clay forming the main ingredient of bentonite (*see*) and fuller's earth (*see*). Used in the petroleum industry as a carrier. Inhalation of the dust can cause respiratory irritation.

MORDANTS.   Chemicals that are insoluble compounds that serve to fix a dye, usually a weak dye to hasten the development of the desired shade or to modify it in hair colorings. Toxicity depends upon specific ingredients.

MORPHOLINE.   Used as a surface-active agent (*see*) and an emulsifier in cosmetics. Prepared by taking the water out of diethanolamine (*see*). A mobile, water-absorbing liquid that mixes with water. It has a strong ammonia odor. A cheap solvent for resins, waxes, and dyes. Also used as a corrosion inhibitor, antioxidant, plasticizer, viscosity improver, insecticide, fungicide, local anesthetic, and antiseptic. Irritating to the eyes, skin, and mucous membranes. It may cause kidney and liver injury, and can produce sloughing of the skin.

MORPHOLINE STEARATE.   A coating and preservative. See Morpholine.

MOUTHWASH.   Designed either to cleanse and refresh the mouth or to mask or overcome objectionable odors. Claims for killing cold germs and bad breath have not been proven. The two basic mouth-washes are alkalines, containing sodium bicarbonate, sodium chloride, alcohol, water, mixed flavoring oils; and certified colors and astringents containing zinc chloride, saccharin, flavoring oils, alcohol, water, and certified colors. Among other common ingredients used in mouthwashes are ammonium phosphate, benzalkonium chloride, benzoic acid, boric acid, cetylpyridinium chloride, chlorophyllin, glycerin, 4-hexylresorcinol, propylene glycol, sorbitol, urea, cinnamon oil, methyl salicylate, menthol, anethole, and thyme (*see all*). The mouthwashes are of no medicinal value but may temporarily mask the odor of bad breath. They will not, however, cure the cause.

MUCILAGE. A solution in water of the sticky principles of vegetable substances. Used as a soothing application to the mucous membranes.

MUDPACKS. Long in use as facial treatment. Today, they consist of a paste for the face composed chiefly of fuller's earth and astringents (*see both*). There is no evidence that mudpacks are effective. No known toxicity.

MUIRA PUAMA EXTRACT. A wood extract used as an aromatic resin and fat. No known toxicity.

MUSK. Used in perfumes. It is the dried secretion from the preputial follicles of the northern Asian small hornless deer, which has musk in its glands. Musk is a brown, unctuous, smelly substance associated with attracting the opposite sex and which is promoted by stores for such purposes. Also used in food flavorings and at one time was a stimulant and nerve sedative in medicine. Can cause allergic reactions.

MUSTARD OIL. Allyl Isothiocyanate. The greenish yellow, bland, fatty oil expressed from the seeds of the mustard plant. Used in soaps, liniments, and lubricants. It has an intensely pungent odor that can be irritating. It is a strong skin blisterer and is used diluted as a counterirritant (*see*) and rubefacient (*see*).

MYRCIA. Bay Rum. See Bay Rum.

MYRETH-3 CAPRATE. Myristyl Ethoxy Caprate. See Palm Oil.

MYRISTALKONIUM CHLORIDE. See Quaternary Ammonium Compounds.

MYRISTAMIDE DEA. Myristic Diethanolamide. See Myristic Acid.

MYRISTAMINE OXIDE. See Myristic Acid.

MYRISTIC ACID. Used in shampoos, shaving soaps, and creams. A solid organic acid that occurs naturally in butter acids (such as nutmeg butter to the extent of 80 percent), oil of lovage, coconut oil, mace oil, *cire d'abeille* in palm seed fats, and in most animal and vegetable fats. Also used in food flavorings. When combined with potassium, myristic acid soap gives a very good copious lather. No known toxicity.

MYRISTYL ALCOHOL.   Used as an emollient in hand creams, cold creams, and lotions to give them a smooth velvety feel. It is made up of white crystals prepared from fatty acids (*see*). Practically insoluble in water. Nontoxic.

MYRISTYL LACTATE.   See Myristyl Alcohol and Lactic Acid.

MYRISTYL MYRISTATE.   See Myristyl Alcohol and Myristic Acid.

MYRISTYL NEOPENTANOATE. Ceraphyl.   An emollient used to improve the texture and fell of cosmetics. See Valeric Acid.

MYRISTYL PROPIONATE.   See Myristic Acid.

MYRRH.   Used in perfumes, dentifrices, and skin tonics. One of the gifts of the Magi, it is a yellow to reddish brown aromatic bitter gum resin that is obtained from various trees, especially from East Africa and Arabia. Used by the ancients as an ingredient of incense and perfumes and as a remedy for localized skin problems. Also used in food and beverage flavorings. The gum resin has been used to break up intestinal gas and as a topical stimulant. No known toxicity.

MYRTRIMONIUM BROMIDE.   See Quaternary Ammonium Compounds.

N

NAIL, ARTIFICIAL.   See Artificial Nails.

NAIL BLEACHES.   Compounds designed to remove ink, nicotine, vegetable, and other stains from fingers and nails. They consist mainly of an oxidizing agent and chlorinated compounds. A typical formula includes titanium dioxide, 20 percent; talc, 20 percent; zinc peroxide, 7.5 percent; petrolatum, 26 percent; mineral oil, 26.5 percent; and perfume (*see all*). Toxicity depends upon ingredients used.

NAIL ENAMEL.   See Nail Polish.

NAIL FINISHES. Top Coat.   Usually a colorless nail polish (*see*) or it can be slightly pink. Contains celluloid, amyl acetate, and acetone (*see all*). Protects the nail by strengthening it physically, helps to keep the nail polish from chipping, and produces a shiny surface.

NAIL HARDENERS.   Keeps the nails from breaking or chipping. Most nail hardeners contain formaldehyde or silicone (*see both*).

Physicians report severe reactions to nail hardeners containing formaldehyde, ranging from cracking and discoloring to loss of nails. Recent reports to the FDA include nail peeling, burned and inflammed nails, deformed nails, and nerves affected at the base of the nails. The FDA has questioned the safety of some specific nail hardeners.

NAIL POLISH. Used to paint the nails with colors, usually some shade of red. Polishes contain cellulose nitrate (nitrocellulose), butyl acetate, ethyl acetate, toluene, dibutyl phthalate, alkyl esters (amyl, acetate, ethyl acetate), dyes, glycol derivatives, gums, hydrocarbons (aromatic and aliphatic), ketones (acetone, methyl, ethyl), lakes, and phosphoric acid (*see all*). Common colors used are D & C Red No. 19 or 31 (*see*). Skin rashes of the eyelids and neck are common in those allergic to nail polish. Among recent complaints to the FDA about nail polishes were irritation of the nail area, discolored nails, nails permanently stained black, splitting of nails, and nausea.

NAIL POLISH REMOVER. Usually a liquid, it is used to remove nail polish. It contains acetone, toluene, alcohol, amyl acetate, butyl acetate, benzene, ethyl acetate. It also contains castor oil, lanolin, cetyl alcohol, olive oil, perfume, spermaceti, synthetic oil (ethyl oleate, butyl stearate) (*see all*). Many components are very toxic and can cause central nervous system depression, especially the toluene and aliphatic acetates. A recent report to the FDA described a "tight, smothering feeling in the chest" after use of a nail polish remover.

NAIL STRENGTHENERS. See Nail Hardeners.

NAIL WHITES. The cream nail whiteners may contain titanium dioxide, beeswax, cetyl alcohol, petrolatum, cocoa butter, sodium borate, tincture of benzoin (*see all*), and water. The liquid nail whites may contain titanium dioxide, glyceryl monostearate, beeswax, almond oil, petrolatum (*see all*), and water. Toxicity is dependent upon ingredients.

NAPHAZOLINE HYDROCHLORIDE. Privine Hydrochloride. Prepared from acids, it is composed of bitter-tasting crystals, which are soluble in water. Used as a nasal and eye decongestant. It may cause sedation in infants, and high blood pressure and central nervous system excitement followed by depression in adults.

1,5-NAPHTHALENEDIOL. See Naphthas.

2,7-NAPHTHALENEDIOL. See Naphthas.

NAPHTHAS. Obtained from the distillation of petroleum, coal tar, and shale oil. It is a common diluent (*see*) found in nail lacquer. Among the common naphthas that are used as solvents are coal tar/ naphtha and petroleum/naphtha. See Kerosene for toxicity.

1-NAPHTHOL. Used in hair dyes and treatment of skin diseases.

White crystals with phenolic odor and disagreeable burning taste. Slightly soluble in water. See Naphthas.

2-NAPHTHOL.   Used as an antiseptic and modifier in hair preparations, with a tendency to darken gray hair. Sometimes used in treatment of eczema, ringworm, and psoriasis. See Phenol for toxicity.

NATURAL COSMETICS.   See Organic Cosmetics.

NATURAL RED 26. Carthamic Acid.   A red crystalline glucoside coloring constituting the coloring matter of the safflower (*see*). No known toxicity.

NEAT'S-FOOT OIL.   Lubricant used in creams and lotions. A pale yellow fatty oil made by boiling the feet and shinbones of cattle. Used chiefly as a leather dressing and waterproofing. Can cause allergic reactions in the hypersensitive.

NEOMYCIN.   Used in underarm deodorants. It is produced from the growth of a microorganism inhabiting the soil. Inhabits the growth of bacteria and, therefore, the odor from sweat. It can cause the skin to swell, redden, or break out when exposed to light and produces allergic reactions. Highly toxic to the eighth nerve, which involves hearing, and to the kidneys. The FDA does not believe the use of neomycin in deodorants is justified because it caused resistant strains of staphylococci to develop. Such staph infections are extremely difficult to treat and could be lethal.

NEROL.   A primary alcohol used in perfumes, especially in rose and orange blossom scents. Occurs naturally in oil of lavender, orange leaf, palmarosa oil, rose, neroli, and oil of petitgrain. It is colorless, with the odor of rose. Also used in food flavorings. Similar to geraniol (*see*) in toxicity.

NEROLI BIGARADE OIL.   Used chiefly in cologne and in perfumes. Named for the putative discoverer, Anna Maria de la Tremoïlle, princess of Nerole (1670). A fragrant, pale yellow essential oil obtained from the flowers of the sour orange tree. It darkens upon standing. Also used in food flavorings. No known toxicity.

NETTLES.   Used in hair tonics and shampoos. It is obtained from a troublesome weed, with stingers. It has a long history and was used in folk medicine. Its flesh is rich in minerals and plant hormones, and it supposedly stimulates hair growth and shines and softens hair. Also used to make tomatoes resistant to spoilage, to encourage the growth of strawberries, and to stimulate the fermentation of humus. No known toxicity.

NGDA.   See Nordehydroguaiaretic Acid.

NIACINAMIDE. Nicotinamide. Vitamin B.   Used as a skin stimulant. A white or yellow crystalline, odorless powder used to treat pellegra, a vitamin deficiency disease, and in the assay of enzymes or substrates. No known toxicity.

NICKEL SULFATE. Used in hair dyes and astringents. Occurs in the earth's crust as a salt of nickel. Obtained as green or blue crystals and is used chiefly in nickel plating. It has a sweet astringent taste and acts as an irritant and causes vomiting when swallowed. Its systemic effects include blood vessel, brain, and kidney damage, and nervous depression. Frequently causes skin rash when used in cosmetics.

NICOTINE REMOVERS. See Nail Bleaches.

NITRIC ACID. Used as an oxidizer in hair dyes and as a stabilizer in cosmetics. A corrosive, colorless, inorganic acid made by the action of ammonia on sulfuric acid and nitrate. Used chiefly as an oxidizing agent, in the manufacture of fertilizers, explosives, and nitroparaffin. The fumes in moist air give off a choking odor. Ingestion can cause burning and corrosion of the mouth, esophagus, and stomach, and can result in death. Chronic inhalation of vapors can cause bronchitis. Can be irritating to the skin.

NITRO-. A prefix denoting one atom of nitrogen and two of oxygen. Nitro also denotes a class of dyes derived from coal tars. Nitro dyes can be absorbed through the skin. When absorbed or ingested, they can cause a lack of oxygen in the blood. Chronic exposure may cause liver damage. See Colors.

NITROCELLULOSE. Any of several esters (*see*) obtained as white fibrous flammable solids by adding nitrate to cellulose, the cell walls of plants. Used in skin protective creams, nail enamels, and lacquers. No known toxicity.

NITROGEN. A gas that is 78 percent by volume of the atmosphere and essential to all living things. Odorless. Used as a preservative for cosmetics, in which it is nontoxic. In high concentration it can asphyxiate. Toxic concentration in man is 90 ppm; in mice, 250.

2-NITRO-p-PHENYLENEDIAMINE. See p-Phenylenediamine.

4-NITRO-o-PHENYLENEDIAMINE. See p-Phenylenediamine.

NITROUS OXIDE. Laughing Gas. A whipping agent for whipped cosmetic creams and a propellant in pressurized cosmetic containers. Slightly sweetish odor and taste. Colorless. Used in rocket fuel. Less irritating than other nitrogen oxides but narcotic in high concentrations and it can asphyxiate.

NONFAT DRY MILK. The solid residue produced by removing the water from defatted cow's milk. See Milk.

NONIONIC. A group of emulsifiers used in hand creams. They resist freezing and shrinkage. Toxicity depends upon specific ingredients.

NONOXYNOL-2. Polyoxyethylene (2) Nonyl Phenyl Ether. Used as a nonionic (*see*) surface-active agent and as a dispersing agent in cosmetics. No known toxicity. See Polyethylene Glycol.

NONOXYNOL-4. See Nonoxynol-2.

NONOXYNOL-5. See Nonoxynol-2.

NONOXYNOL-6. See Nonoxynol-2.

NONOXYNOL-7. See Nonoxynol-2.

NONOXYNOL-8. See Nonoxynol-2.

NONOXYNOL-9 IODINE. See Nonoxynol-2.

NONOXYNOL-10. See Nonoxynol-2.

NONOXYNOL-15. See Nonoxynol-2.

NONOXYNOL-20. See Nonoxynol-2.

NONOXYNOL-30. See Nonoxynol-2.

NONOXYNOL-40. See Nonoxynol-2.

NONOXYNOL-50. See Nonoxynol-2.

NONYL ACETATE. Used in perfumery. An ester produced by the reaction of nonyl alcohol and acetic acid (*see*). Pungent odor, suggestive of mushrooms, but when diluted it resembles the odor of gardenias. Insoluble in water. No known toxicity.

NONYL NONOXYNOL-9 PHOSPHATE. Polyethylene Glycol. P-nonylphenyl ether. A surfactant and dispersing agent used in perfumery. No known toxicity.

NONYL NONOXYNOL-10. See Nonoxynol-2.

NONYL NONOXYNOL-49. See Nonoxynol-2.

NORDIHYDROGUAIARETIC ACID. NGDA. An antioxidant used in brilliantines and other fat-based cosmetics. Occurs in resinous exudates of many plants. White or grayish white crystals. Lard containing .01 percent NGDA stored at room temperature for 19 months in diffused daylight showed no appreciable rancidity or color change. Canada banned the additive in food in 1967 after it was shown to cause cysts and kidney damage in a large percentage of rats tested. The FDA removed it from the generally recognized safe list of food additives in 1968. No known toxicity for use as a cosmetic.

NORVALINE. A protein amino acid (*see*), soluble in hot water and insoluble in alcohol. See Valeric Acid.

NOTE. A distinct odor or flavor. "Top" note is the first note normally perceived when a flavor is smelled or tasted; usually volatile and gives "identity." "Middle," or "main," note is the substance of the flavor, the main characteristic. "Bottom" note is what is left when top and middle notes disappear. It is the residue when an aroma or flavoring evaporates.

NUTMEG.   A natural flavoring extract from the dried ripe seed of a small tropical evergreen. Used to flavor dentifrices. It has been in common household use since the Middle Ages and is still a potentially toxic substance. Ingestion of as little as 3 whole seeds or 5 to 15 grams of grated spice can cause flushing of the skin, irregular heart rhythm, absence of salivation, and central nervous system symptoms such as euphoria and hallucinations. On the FDA list for study of short-term mutagenic, subacute, teratogenic, and reproductive effects.

NYLON.   The commonly known synthetic material used as a fiber in eyelash lengtheners and mascaras and as a molding compound to shape cosmetics. Comes in clear or white opaque plastic for use in making resins. Can cause allergic reactions. Resistant to organic chemicals but is dissolved by phenol, cresol (*see both*), and strong acids. No known toxicity.

O

OAKMOSS.   Any one of several lichens that grow on oak trees and yield a resin for use as a fixative (*see*) in perfumery. Stable green liquid with a long-lasting characteristic odor. Soluble in alcohol. No known toxicity.

OAT FLOUR.   Flour from the cereal grain that is an important crop grown in the temperate regions. Light yellowish or brown to weak greenish or yellow powder. Slight odor; starchy taste. Makes a bland ointment for cosmetic treatments, including soothing baths. No known toxicity.

OAT GUM.   A plant extract used as a thickener and stabilizer in foods and cosmetics. Also an antioxidant in butter, creams, and candy. In foods it can cause allergic reactions such as diarrhea and intestinal gas. No known toxicity.

OATMEAL.   Meal obtained by the grinding of oats from which the husks have been removed. Used through the ages by women as a face mask. Here is a modern version: put in blender 4 tablespoons of quick-cooking or regular oatmeal and 1 teaspoon of dried mint leaves and turn to high until the mix is finely ground; add enough hot water to make a spreadable paste; smooth and pat on face gently. When paste is dry, remove with lukewarm water, then rinse well with cool water. Apply chilled witch hazel. Soothing. Nontoxic.

OCOTEA CYMBARUM OIL.   An oil obtained by steam distillation from the wood of a Brazilian tree. Used chiefly as a source of safrole, a natural oil, and as a substitute for sassafras oil (*see*) in cosmetics and in inexpensive soaps. No know toxicity.

1-OCTANOL. Caprylic Alcohol.   Used in the manufacture of perfumes. Colorless, viscous liquid, soluble in water, insoluble in oil. Occurs naturally in oil of lavender, oil of lemon, oil of lime, oil of lovage, orange peel, and coconut oil. It has a penetrating, aromatic scent. May cause skin rash.

2-OCTANOL. Caprylic Alcohol.   An oily aromatic liquid, with a somewhat unpleasant odor. For use in the manufacture of perfumes and disinfectant soaps. No known toxicity.

OCTOXYNOL-1. Polyoxyethylene (1) Octylphenyl Ether.   A waxlike emulsifier, dispersing agent, and detergent used in hand creams, lotions, and lipsticks. No known toxicity.

OCTOXYNOL-3.   See Octoxynol-1.

OCTOXYNOL-5.   See Octoxynol-1.

OCTOXYNOL-9.   See Octoxynol-1.

OCTOXYNOL-13.   See Octoxynol-1.

OCTYL DIMETHYL PABA.   See P-Aminobenzoic Acid.

OCTYL DODECANOL. 2-Octyl Dodecanol.   See Stearyl Alcohol.

OCTYL HYDROXYSTEARATE.   See Stearic Acid.

OCTYL METHOXYCINNAMATE.   See Cinnamate.

OCTYL PALMITATE.   See Palmitate.

OCTYL SALICYLATE.   See Salicylates.

OCTYL STEARATE.   See Stearic Acid.

OLEAMIDE. Oleylamide.   See Oleic Acid.

OLEAMIDE DEA. Oleic Diethanolamide.   See Oleic Acid.

OLEAMIDE MIPA.   See Oleic Acid.

OLEAMINE. (Oleyl Amine).   A fatty amine derived from oleic acid and used as a stabilizer and plasticizer in creams, lotions, lipsticks, and perfumes. Not as greasy as oil-type stabilizers and plasticizers. No known toxicity.

OLEAMINE OXIDE.   See Oleamine.

OLEIC ACID.   Obtained from various animal and vegetable fats and oils. Colorless. On exposure to air, it turns a yellow to brown color and develops a rancid odor. Used in preparation of Turkey-red oil (*see*), soft soap, permanent wave solutions, vanishing creams, brushless shave creams, cold creams, brilliantines, nail polish, toilet soaps, and lipsticks. Possesses better skin penetrating properties than vegetable oils. Also employed in liquid makeup, liquid lip rouge, shampoos, and preshave lotions. Low oral toxicity, but it is mildly irritating to the skin.

OLEOYL SARCOSINE.   See Sarcosines.

OLEORESIN. A natural plant product consisting of essential oil and resin extracted from a substance, such as ginger, by means of alcohol, ether, or acetone. The solvent, alcohol, for example, is percolated through the ginger. Although the oleoresin is very similar to the space from which it is derived, it is not identical because not all the substances in the spice are extracted. Oleoresins are usually more uniform and more potent than the original product. The normal use range of an oleoresin is from one fifth to one twentieth the corresponding amount for the crude spice. Certain spices are extracted as oleoresins for color rather than for flavor. Examples of color-intensifying oleoresins are those from paprika and turmeric.

OLETH-2. See Oleyl Alcohol.

OLETH-3. See Oleyl Alcohol.

OLETH-3 PHOSPHATE. See Oleyl Alcohol and Phosphate.

OLETH-5. See Oleyl Alcohol.

OLETH-10. See Oleyl Alcohol.

OLETH-10 PHOSPHATE. See Oleyl Alcohol.

OLETH-20. Brij 98. An oily liquid derived from fatty alcohols. Used as a surface-active agent (*see*). No known toxicity.

OLETH-20 PHOSPHATE. See Oleth-20.

OLETH-25. See Oleyl Alcohol.

OLETH-50. See Oleyl Alcohol.

OLEYL ALCOHOL. Ocenol®. Found in fish oils. Oily and usually pale yellow. Gives off an offensive burning odor when heated. Chiefly used in the manufacture of detergents and wetting agents and as an antifoam agent; also a plasticizer for softening and lubricating fabrics and as a carrier for medications. No known toxicity.

OLEYL BETAINE. See Oleamine.

OLIVE OIL. Superior to mineral oils in penetrating power. Used in brilliantine hairdressings, emollients, eyelash oils, lipsticks, nail polish removers, shampoos, soaps, face powders, and hair colorings. Antiwrinkle and massage oils. It is the pale yellow or greenish fixed oil obtained from ripe olives grown around the Mediterranean Sea. When applied to dry scalp, the dandruff is made worse. May cause an allergic reaction. If instilled in the eyes, causes smarting.

OPACIFYING AGENTS. Substances such as the fatty alcohols stearyl and cetyl (*see both*) that make shampoos and other liquid cosmetics impervious to light.

ORANGE-FLOWER OIL. See Nerol.

ORANGE OIL. Sweet Orange Oil. Yellow to deep orange, highly volatile, unstable liquid with a characteristic orange taste and odor expressed from the fresh peel of the ripe fruit of the sweet orange plant species. Once used as an expectorant, it is now employed in perfumery, soaps, and flavorings. Inhalation or frequent contact with oil of orange may cause severe symptoms such as headache, dizziness, and shortness of breath. Workers who peel oranges frequently have skin problems including blisters and swelling. Perfumes, colognes, and toilet water containing oil of orange may cause allergic reaction in the hypersensitive. Omitted from hypoallergenic cosmetics.

ORGANIC COSMETICS.   Cosmetics made from only animal or vegetable products. Used as a gimmick to sell "new" cosmetics to those who believe "natural" is better, although most cosmetic ingredients are derived from natural sources.

ORIENTAL BLENDS.   One of the basic perfume types, this group gives an impression of subtlety and warmth, with an intense note of spices and incense. They usually include amber, musk, and civet. They vary between heavily floral and richly resinous. They are more insistent in their predominating notes than any other type and usually are worn at night.

ORRIS. Orrisroot Oil. White Flag. Love Root.   Distilled for use in dusting powders, perfumes, dry shampoos, toothpaste, and sachets. Made from the roots of the plant. Yellowish, semisolid, and fragrant oil. Discontinued in the United States because of the frequent allergic reactions to orris, including infantile eczema, hay fever, stuffy nose, red eyes, and asthma.

ORRIS ABSOLUTE.   One of the most widely used perfume ingredients, it is the oldest and most expensive of all natural perfume materials. It is twice the price of Rose Otto Bulgaria (*see*) and three times that of French Jasmine (*see* Jasmine). The so-called oil concrete is produced by steam distillation from the underground stems of the iris. The rhizomes are washed, dried, and then stored for three years to acquire their fragrance. Prior to distillation, they are pulverized, and the absolute is distinctly violetlike with a fruity undertone—sweet, floral, warm, and lasting. The bulk of the material is produced in Italy, distillation taking place mostly in France, and sometimes in England and Italy. See Orris for toxicity.

OURICURY WAX.   The wax exuded from the leaves of the Brazilian palm tree. The hard brown wax has the same properties and uses as carnauba wax (*see*).

OX BILE. Oxgall.   Emulsifier from the fresh bile of male castrated bovines used in cosmetic creams. Brownish green or dark green, viscous liquid, it has a characteristic odor and a bitter, disagreeable taste. No known toxicity.

OXALIC ACID. Occurs naturally in many plants and vegetables, particularly in the *Oxalis* family; also in many molds. Used in freckle and bleaching cosmetic preparations. Caustic and corrosive to the skin and mucous membranes; may cause severe intestinal upsets and kidney damage if ingested. Used industrially to remove paint, varnish, rust, and ink stains. Used in dentistry to harden plastic models. Fingernails exposed to it have turned blue, become brittle, and fallen off.

OXIDIZER. A substance that causes oxygen to combine with another substance. Oxygen and hydrogen peroxide are examples of oxidizers.

OXYQUINOLINE. 8-Hydroxyquinoline. White crystalline powder, almost insoluble in water. Used as a fungistat and for reddish orange colors when combined with bismuth. Used internally as a disinfectant. Has caused cancer in animals both orally and when injected. See Oxyquinoline Sulfate.

OXYQUINOLINE BENZOATE. 8-Quinolinol Benzoate. The salt of benzoic acid (*see*) and oxyquinoline (*see*).

OXYQUINOLINE SULFATE. Made from phenols; composed of either white crystals or powder, almost insoluble in water and ether but soluble in alcohol, acetone, and benzene. Used as a preservative in cosmetics for its ability to prevent fungus growth and to disinfect. See Phenol for toxicity.

OZOKERITE. Ceresin. A naturally occurring waxlike mineral; a mixture of hydrocarbons. Colorless or white when pure; horrid odor. Upon refining, it yields a hard white microcrystalline wax known as ceresin (*see*). Used in lipstick and cream rouge. No known toxicity.

P

PALM-KERNEL OIL. Palm Nut. The oil from palms, particularly the African oil palm tree. A white to yellowish edible fat, it resembles coconut oil more than palm oil. It is used chiefly in making soaps and ointments. No known toxicity.

PALM OIL. Palm Butter. Palm Tallow. Oil used in baby soaps, ordinary soaps, liniments, and ointments. Obtained from the fruit or seed of the palm tree. A reddish yellow to dark dirty red. A fatty mass with a faint violet odor. Also used to make candles and lubricants. No known toxicity.

PALMITAMINE OXIDE. Palmityl Dimethylamine Oxide. See Palmitic Acid and Dimethylamine.

PALMITATE. A salt of palmitic acid used as an oil in baby oils, bath oils, eye creams, hair conditioners, and cream rouges. Occurs in palm oil, butter fat, and most other fatty oils and fats. See Palmitic Acid for toxicity.

PALMITIC ACID. A mixture of solid organic acids obtained from fats consisting chiefly of palmitic acid with varying amounts of stearic acid (*see*). Used as a texturizer in shampoos, shaving soaps, and creams. It is white or faintly yellow and has a fatty odor and taste. Palmitic acid occurs naturally in allspice, anise, calamus oil, cascarilla bark, celery seed, butter acids, coffee, tea, and many animal fats and plant oils. It forms 40 percent of cow's milk. Obtained from palm oil, Japan wax, or Chinese vegetable tallow. No known toxicity to skin and hair, provided no salts of oleic or lauric acids (*see both*) are present.

PANTHENOL. Dexpanthenol. Vitamin B Complex Factor. Used in hair products and in emollients and as a supplement in foods. Employed medically to aid digestion. It is good for human tissues. No known toxicity.

PAPAIN. See Papaya.

PAPAYA. A base for organic makeup. It is a fruit grown in tropical countries. It contains an enzyme, papain, used as a meat tenderizer and, medicinally, to prevent adhesions. It is deactivated by cooking. Because of its protein-digesting ability, it can dissolve necrotic (dead) material. It may cause allergic reactions.

PARABENS. See Propylparaben.

PARAFFIN. Used in solid brilliantines, cold creams, wax depilatories, eyelash creams and oils, eyebrow pencils, lipsticks, liquefying creams, protective creams, and mascaras; also used for extracting perfumes from flowers. Obtained from the distillate of wood, coal, petroleum or shale oil. Colorless or white, odorless, greasy, and not digestible or absorbable in the intestines. Easily melts over boiling water and is used to cover food products. Implants of modest doses in mice caused cancer. Pure paraffin is harmless to the skin but the presence of impurities may give rise to irritations, eczemas, and precancerous or cancerous conditions.

PARSLEY OIL. Used as a preservative, perfume, and flavoring in cosmetics, it is obtained by steam distillation of the ripe seeds of the herb. Yellow to light brown, with a harsh odor. Parsley may cause skin to break out with a rash, redden, and swell when exposed to light. It may also cause an allergic reaction in the sensitive.

PARSLEY SEED OIL. See Parsley Oil.

PATCHOULI OIL. Used in perfume formulations to impart a long-lasting oriental aroma in soaps and cosmetics. It is the essential oil obtained from the leaves of an East Indian shrubby mint. Yellowish to greenish brown liquid, with the pleasant fragrance of summer flowers. May produce an allergic reaction in hypersensitive individuals.

PCA. 2-Pyrrolidone-5-Carboxylic Acid. Employed in the manufacture of polyvinylpyrrolidone (*see*), which goes into hair sprays. Also a high-boiling solvent in petroleum processing, and a placticizer and coalescing agent for floor polishes. No known skin toxicity.

PEACH KERNEL OIL. Persic Oil. Used as an oil base in emollients, eyelash creams, and brilliantines. It is a light yellow liquid expressed from a seed. Smells like almonds. Also a flavoring in foods. No known toxicity.

PEANUT OIL. Arachis Oil. Used in the manufacture of soaps, baby preparations, hair-grooming aids, nail dryers, shampoos, and as a solvent for ointments and liniments; also in night creams and emollients. Greenish yellow, with a pleasant odor. Prepared by pressing shelled and skinned seeds of the peanut. It is used as a substitute for almond and olive oils in cosmetic creams, brilliantines, antiwrinkle oils, and sunburn preparations. Has been reported to be a mild irritant in soap, but considered harmless to the skin.

PEANUTAMIDE MEA. Loramine Wax. See Peanut Oil.

PEARL ESSENCE. Guanine. A suspension of crystalline guanine (*see*) in nitrocellulose (*see*) and solvents. Guanine is obtained from fish scales. Used in nail polish to give it a shine. Implants of small amounts of guanine hydrochloride were lethal in mice. No known toxicity to skin or nails.

PECAN SHELL POWDER. A coloring agent used in cosmetics. Employed medicinally by the American Indians. It is the nut from a hickory of the southern central United States, with a rough bark and hard but brittle wood. Edible. No known toxicity.

PECTIN. Emulsifying agent used in place of various gums in toothpastes, hair-setting lotions, and protective creams. The pectins are found in roots, stems, and fruits of plants and form an integral part of such structures. They are used in cosmetics as a gelling and thickening agent. They are soothing and mildly acidic. Also used in foods as a "cementing agent" and as an antidiarrheal medication. No known toxicity to the skin.

PEG. See Polyethylene Glycol.

PEG-4. Carbowax 200®. Polyethylene Glycol 200.   Polymer (*see*) of ethylene oxide, a product of petroleum gas or dehydration of alcohol. Used in hand lotions, hairdressings, and various lotions. It is a binder, plasticizing agent, solvent, and softener. Improves resistance to moisture and oxidation. No known toxicity to the skin.

PEG-6.   See PEG-4.

PEG-6-32.   See PEG-4.

PEG-8.   See PEG-4.

PEG-12.   See PEG-4.

PEG-20.   See PEG-4.

PEG-32.   See PEG-4.

PEG-75.   See PEG-4.

PEG-150.   See PEG-4.

PEG-350.   See PEG-4.

PEG-5M.   See PEG-4.

PEG-7M.   See PEG-4.

PEG-14M.   See PEG-4.

PEG-90M.   See PEG-4.

PEG-8 CASTOR OIL.   See PEG-6 Dioleate.

PEG-9 CASTOR OIL. Lipal.   See Polyethylene Glycol and Castor Oil.

PEG-36 CASTOR OIL.   See PEG-6 Dioleate.

PEG-40 CASTOR OIL.   See PEG-6 Dioleate.

PEG-3 COCAMIDE.   See Polyethylene Glycol and Cocamide.

PEG-6 COCAMIDE.   See Polyethylene Glycol and Cocamide.

PEG-15 COCAMINE.   See PEG-6 Dioleate.

PEG-8 COCOATE.   See PEG-6 Dioleate.

PEG-4 DILAURATE.   See PEG-6 Dioleate.

PEG-6 DILAURATE.   See PEG-6 Dioleate.

PEG-6-32 DILAURATE.   A dispersant. See Polyethylene Glycol and Lauric Acid.

PEG-8 DILAURATE.   See PEG-6 Dioleate.

PEG-150 DILAURATE.   See PEG-6 Dioleate.

PEG-6 DIOLEATE.   Derived from oleic acid (*see*). Each PEG is a mixture of several polymers (*see*). Consistencies vary but generally are like that of petrolatum (*see*). Dissolves in water to a clear solution. Used as a carrier or base in hand lotions, hairdressings, and various other cosmetic lotions. No known toxicity.

PEG-8 DIOLEATE.   See PEG-6 Dioleate.

PEG-3 DISTEARATE.   See Polyethylene Glycol and Stearic Acid.

PEG-8 DISTEARATE.   See PEG-6 Dioleate.
PEG-12 DISTEARATE.   See PEG-6 Dioleate.
PEG-20 DISTEARATE.   See PEG-6 Dioleate.
PEG-32 DISTEARATE.   See PEG-6 Dioleate.
PEG-75 DISTEARATE.   See PEG-6 Dioleate.
PEG-150 DISTEARATE.   See PEG-6 Dioleate.
PEG-8 DITRIRICINOLEATE. *Ricinoleic Acid.*   See PEG-6 Dioleate.
PEG-20 GLYCERYL STEARATE.   See PEG-6 Dioleate.
PEG-25 HYDROGENATED CASTOR OIL.   See PEG-6 Dioleate.
PEG-40 HYDROGENATED CASTOR OIL.   See PEG-6 Dioleate.
PEG-5 HYDROGENATED LANOLIN.   See PEG-6 Dioleate.
PEG-20 HYDROGENATED LANOLIN.   See PEG-6 Dioleate.
PEG-24 HYDROGENATED LANOLIN.   See PEG-6 Dioleate.
PEG-30 HYDROGENATED LANOLIN.   See PEG-6 Dioleate.
PEG-6 ISOPALMITATE.   See Palmitate.
PEG-20 LANOLATE.   See PEG-6 Dioleate.
PEG-50 LANOLATE.   See Polyethylene Glycol and Lauric Acid.
PEG-27 LANOLIN.   See PEG-6 Dioleate.
PEG-40 LANOLIN.   See PEG-6 Dioleate.
PEG-75 LANOLIN.   See PEG-6 Dioleate.
PEG-85 LANOLIN.   See PEG-6 Dioleate.
PEG-75 LANOLIN OIL.   See PEG-6 Dioleate.
PEG-3 LAURAMIDE.   See PEG-2 Laurate.
PEG-7 LAURAMIDE.   See PEG-2 Laurate.
PEG-2 LAURATE. *Diethylene Glycol Monolaurate.*   Yellow oily liquid insoluble in water. Emulsifier in cosmetic creams and lotions. Gives an oil-in-water emulsion. No known toxicity other than allergic reactions in some persons sensitive to laurates.
PEG-4 LAURATE.   See PEG-2 Laurate.
PEG-8 LAURATE.   See PEG-2 Laurate.
PEG-12 LAURATE.   See PEG-2 Laurate.
PEG-6 METHYL ETHER.   A wax. See Polyethylene Glycol.
PEG-2 OLEATE.   Emulsifying agent in creams and lotions. Derived from oleic acid (*see*). A dark red oil that can be dispersed in water, soluble in alcohol, miscible with cottonseed oil. No known toxicity.
PEG-6 OLEATE.   See PEG-2 Oleate.
PEG-8 OLEATE.   See PEG-2 Oleate.
PEG-10 OLEATE.   See Polyethylene Glycol and Oleic Acid.
PEG-12 OLEATE.   See PEG-2 Oleate.
PEG-6 PALMITATE.   See Palmitate.
PEG-18 PALMITATE.   See Palmitic Acid and Polyethylene Glycol.

PEG-20 PENTAERYTHRITOL LAURATE. See Polyethylene Glycol and Lauric Acid.

PEG-39 PENTAERYTHRITOL OLEATE. See Polyethylene Glycol and Oleic Acid.

PEG-25 PROPYLENE GLYCOL STEARATE. Used as an emulsifying agent and dispersing agent. Carries perfume oils into nonalcohol solutions or propylene glycol water mixtures. Used in antiperspirants. No known toxicity.

PEG-2 RICINOLEATE. See Polyethylene Glycol and Castor Oil.

PEG-8 SESQUILAURATE. See PEG-6 Dioleate.

PEG-6 SORBITAN BEESWAX. Combination of polyoxyethylene glycol esters and beeswax. It is used as an emulsifying agent in the preparation of cosmetics and pharmaceuticals. No known toxicity.

PEG-8 SORBITAN BEESWAX. See PEG-6 Sorbitan Beeswax.

PEG-20 SORBITAN BEESWAX. See PEG-6 Sorbitan Beeswax.

PEG-20 SORBITAN ISOSTEARATE. See PEG-6 Dioleate.

PEG-40 SORBITAN LANOLATE. See PEG-6 Dioleate.

PEG-75 SORBITAN LANOLATE. See PEG-6 Dioleate.

PEG-10 SORBITAN LAURATE. See PEG-6 Dioleate.

PEG-40 SORBITAN PEROLEATE. See Oleic Acid.

PEG-5 SOYAL STEROL. See Polyethylene Glycol and Soybean Oil.

PEG-5 SOYAMINE. See PEG-6 Dioleate.

PEG-2 STEARATE. Diethylene Glycol Monostearate. Derived from stearic acid (*see*). Tan-colored wax. Can be dispersed in hot water, soluble in hot water, acetone, and in hot oils. Emulsifying agent in creams and lotions. No known toxicity.

PEG-4 STEARATE. See PEG-2 Stearate.

PEG-6 STEARATE. See PEG-2 Stearate.

PEG-6-32 STEARATE. See PEG-2 Stearate.

PEG-8 STEARATE. See PEG-2 Stearate.

PEG-12 STEARATE. See PEG-2 Stearate.

PEG-20 STEARATE. See PEG-2 Stearate.

PEG-30 STEARATE. See PEG-2 Stearate.

PEG-32 STEARATE. See PEG-2 Stearate.

PEG-40 STEARATE. See PEG-2 Stearate.

PEG-50 STEARATE. See PEG-2 Stearate.

PEG-75 STEARATE. See PEG-2 Stearate.

PEG-100 STEARATE. See PEG-2 Stearate.

PEG-150 STEARATE. See PEG-2 Stearate.

PEG-8 TALLATE.   See PEG-6 Dioleate.
PEG-16 TALLATE.   See PEG-6 Dioleate.
PEG-5 TALLOW AMIDE.   See PEG-6 Dioleate.
PEG-50 TALLOW AMIDE.   See PEG-6 Dioleate.
PEG-5 TALLOW AMINE.   See PEG-6 Dioleate.
PEG-20 TALLOW AMINE.   See Polyethylene Glycol and Tallow.
PENTADECALACTONE. Angelica Lactone.   Used as a cosmetic fragrance and in berry, fruit, liquor, nut, and vanilla flavorings, it is obtained from the fruit and root of a plant grown in Europe and Asia. No known toxicity.
PENTAERYTHRITOL TETRAOCTANOATE.   See Caprylic Acid.
PENTAERYTHRITOL TETRASTEARATE AND CALCIUM STEA-RATE.   See Stearic Acid.
1-PENTANOL. Pentyl Alcohol. n-Amyl Alcohol.   Liquid, with a mild odor, slightly soluble in water. Used as a solvent. Irritating to the eyes and respiratory passages, and absorption may cause a lack of oxygen in the blood.
PENTAPOTASSIUM TRIPHOSPHATE.   See Pentasodium Pentetate.
PENTASODIUM PENTETATE. Pentasodium Diethylenetriamine-pentaacetate. Sodium Tripolyphosphate.   Prepared from dehydration of mono- and disodium phosphates. An inorganic salt used as a water softener, sequestering agent (*see*), emulsifier, and dispersing agent in cosmetic cleansing creams and lotions. Moderately irritating to the skin and mucous membranes. Ingestion can cause violent purging.
PENTASODIUM TRIPHOSPHATE.   See Pentasodium Pentetate.
PENTETIC ACID. Penthanil. Diethylenetriaminepentaacetic Acid.   A chelating agent (*see*) to remove iron particles floating in cosmetic solutions. No known toxicity.
PEPPERMINT LEAVES.   See Peppermint Oil.
PEPPERMINT OIL.   Used in toothpaste and tooth powder, eye lotions, shaving lotions, and toilet waters. It is the oil made from the dried leaves and tops of a plant common to Asian, European, and American gardens. Widely used as a food and beverage flavoring. It has been used to break up intestinal gas and as a local antiseptic. Peppermint oil is thought to have mild local anesthetic properties, but it is a skin irritant especially if a dressing is applied over the oil. It can also cause allergic reactions such as hay fever and skin rash.
PERFUME.   Literally means "through smoke" because the first perfumes were incense. Thereafter, man powdered flowers, leaves,

wood, spices, and aromatic resins and used them for fragrances for religious festivals, for the home, and for the body. Egyptians developed a perfume, kyphi, which was made in the form of cones, placed on the head, and allowed to melt at body temperature, thereby perfuming the face. Colognes (*see*) are attributed to a seventeenth-century Italian barber who settled in Cologne, Germany. He developed a fragrant water he called "l'eau admirable de cité de Cologne." Perfumery today is still an art, and rife with secrets. Some perfumes have as many as 200 ingredients. The essential oils used for today's scents come from leaves, needles, roots, and peels of plants. Floral oils come from petals, whole flowers, gums, and resins. Animal exudates such as musk and ambergris are all used in perfumes. Isolates used in perfumes are made of individual factors in natural oils, which may also be treated chemically. Synthetic chemicals imitate natural aroma. There are three basic scents today: florals, fruits, and modern blends such as woodsy-mossy-leafy, spicy, and oriental. Woodsy-mossy-leafy types have a warm aromatic scent with sandalwood, cedarwood, and balsam predominating. Orientals have subtly heavier odors. Fruity perfumes have a clean fresh fragrance. No rule or standard governs how much perfume oil must be used to allow a product to be called a perfume. Generally, a perfume aroma lasts longer than a toilet water or cologne. Better perfumes use between 20 to 24 ounces of oil per gallon of alcohol, but formulas with 10 to 36 ounces have been made. Most toilet waters contain 3 to 6 ounces of perfume oil per gallon. A typical basic flower perfume (rose) would include phenylethyl alcohol, 35 percent; geraniol, 48 percent; amyl cinnamic aldehyde, 2 percent; benzyl acetate, 4 percent; ionone, 4 percent; eugenol, 2 percent; and terpineol, 5 percent (*see all*). Perfumes are frequent allergens and are left out of many hypoallergenic products. Complaints to the FDA concerning perfume include headaches, dizziness, rash, hyperpigmentation (see Berloque Dermatitis), violent coughing and vomiting, skin irritation, and the explosion of the perfume container.

PERHYDROSQUALENE.   See Squalene.

PERMANENT WAVE NEUTRALIZER.   Used to neutralize the acids that curl the hair (see Permanent Waves). May contain sodium perborate, bromates, or sodium hexametaphosphate (*see all*). Before 1940, bromate poisoning was rare but when bromate was put into permanent wave neutralizers, for home use, incidents became more common. Many manufacturers then substituted sodium perborate and sodium hexametaphosphate, a product used as a laundry detergent and in water softeners.

PERMANENT WAVES. Cold Waves.   Chemicals designed to "permanently" bend or curl the hair. Once done only in beauty parlors, kits have been developed for home use. The process in both the beauty parlor and at home consists of applying a waving lotion containing thioglycolic acid, ammonia, and 93 percent water; as well as borax, ethanolamine, or sodium lauryl sulfate (*see all*). Then, after a period of time, depending upon the lotion used and the tightness of the curl desired, a neutralizer is applied. Chemicals in the neutralizer may be sodium or potassium bromate, sodium perborate, or hydrogen peroxide. (See Permanent Wave Neutralizer.) The thioglycolates are toxic and may cause skin irritation and low blood sugar. Among injuries recently reported to the FDA were hair damage, swelling of legs and feet, eye irritation, rash in area of ears, neck, scalp, and forehead, and swelling of eyelids.

PEROXIDE.   Used in hair bleaches. It is a strong oxidant and can injure the skin and eyes. Chemists are cautioned to wear rubber gloves and goggles when handling it. May cause hair breakage and is an irritant. See Hydrogen Peroxide.

PERSIC OIL.   See Apricot and Peach Kernel Oil.

PERSULFATES.   A salt derived from persulfuric acid, a strong oxidizer. Persulfates are excellent catalysts that speed hair color changes in hair dyes. See Hydrogen Peroxide for toxicity.

PERUVIAN BALSAM.   See Balsam Peru.

PETITGRAIN OIL.   Used extensively in perfumes. It is the volatile oil obtained from the leaves and twigs and unripe fruit of the bitter orange tree. Brownish to yellow with a bittersweet odor. Also used in food flavorings. Supposedly dissolves in sweat, and under the influence of sunlight becomes an irritant. May also cause an allergic skin reaction in the hypersensitive.

PETROLATUM. Vaseline. Petroleum Jelly. Paraffin Jelly.   Used in cold creams, emollient creams, conditioning creams, wax depilatories, eyebrow pencils, eye shadows, liquefying creams, liquid powders, nail whites, lipsticks, protective creams, baby creams, and rouge. It is a purified mixture of semisolid hydrocarbons from petroleum. Yellowish to light amber or white, semisolid unctuous mass, practically odorless and tasteless, almost insoluble in water. As a lubricant in lipsticks it gives them a shine, and in creams it makes them smoother. Helps to soften and smooth the skin in the same way as any other emollient and is less expensive. The oily film helps prevent evaporation of moisture from the skin and protects the skin from irritation. However, petrolatum has the disadvantage of being harder to remove from the skin than other cosmetics, and it may feel more greasy. Creams and hairdressings containing petrolatum have been known to cause allergic skin rashes but it is generally nontoxic to the skin.

PETROLEUM DISTILLATE.   Clear, colorless, highly flammable distillates used as solvents for fats, oils, and detergents. See Kerosene for toxicity.

pH.   The scale used to measure acidity and alkalinity. pH is the hydrogen (H) ion concentration of a solution. "p" stands for the power of the hydrogen ion. The pH of a solution is measured on a scale of 14. A truly neutral solution, neither acidic nor alkaline, such as water, is 7. The pH of blood is 7.3; vinegar is 2.3; lemon juice is 8.2; and lye is 13. Skin and hair are naturally acidic. Soap and detergents are alkaline.

PHENACETIN. *Acetophenetidin.*   Obtained from phenol and salicylic acid (*see both*). Slightly bitter, crystalline powder, used in sunscreen lotions and soothing creams. Used medicinally as an analgesic and antifever agent. Less toxic than acetanilid (*see*), but may cause kidney damage in prolonged and excessive internal doses. No known toxicity on the skin.

PHENETHYL ALCOHOL. *2-Phenylethanol.*   Used as a floral scent in rose perfumes and as a preservative in cosmetics, it occurs naturally in oranges, raspberries, and tea. Used in synthetic fruit flavors. It is a possible sensitizer. No known skin toxicity in humans.

PHENOL. *Carbolic Acid.*   Used in shaving creams and hand lotions. Obtained from coal tar. Occurs in urine and has the characteristic odor present in coal tar and wood. It is a general disinfectant and anesthetic for the skin. Ingestion of even small amounts may cause nausea, vomiting, circulatory collapse, paralysis, convulsions, coma, and greenish urine as well as necrosis of the mouth and gastrointestinal tract. Death results from respiratory failure. Fatalities have been reported from ingestion of as little as 1.5 grams (30 grams to the ounce). Fatal poisoning can occur through skin absorption. Although there have been many poisonings from phenolic solutions, it continues to be used in commercial products. A concentration of 1 percent used to prevent itching from insect bites and sunburn, applied for several hours, caused gangrene resulting from spasm of small blood vessels under the skin. Swelling, pimples, hives, and other skin rashes following application to the skin have been widely reported. A concentration of 2 percent causes gangrene, burning, and numbness.

PHENOXYDIGLYCOL.   See Diethylene Glycol.

PHENOXYETHANOL.   An oily liquid with a faint sweet odor and a burning taste. Obtained by treating phenol (*see*) with ethylene oxide. Slightly soluble in water but completely soluble in alcohol. Used as a fixative (*see*) for perfumes, as a bacteria killer in conjunction with quaternary ammonium compounds (*see*), and as an insect repellent. Used medicinally as a topical antiseptic. See Polyethylene Glycol for toxicity.

PHENOXYISOPROPANOL. 1-Phenoxy-2-Propanol.   See Phenol.

PHENYL ANTHRANILATES.   See Anthranilates.

PHENYL DIMETHICONE.   See Dimethicone.

PHENYLACETALDEHYDE.   Used in perfumes. An oily colorless liquid with a harsh odor. Upon dilution, emits the fragrance of lilacs and hyacinths. Derived from phenethyl alcohol. Less irritating than formaldehyde (*see*), but a stronger central nervous system depressant. In addition, it sometimes produces fluid in the lungs upon ingestion. Because it is considered an irritant, it is not used in baby cosmetic preparations.

PHENYLACETIC ACID.   Used as a starting material in the manufacture of perfumes and soaps. Occurs naturally in Japanese mint, oil of neroli, and black pepper. It has a honeylike odor. Also used as a synthetic flavoring for foods and in the manufacture of penicillin. No known toxicity.

m-PHENYLENEDIAMINE.   See *p*-Phenylenediamine.

o-PHENYLENEDIAMINE.   See *p*-Phenylenediamine.

p-PHENYLENEDIAMINE. PPD.   Most permanent home and beauty parlor hair dyes contain this chemical or a related one such as 4-nitro-*o*-phenylenediamine. Also called oxidation dyes, amino dyes, para dyes, or peroxide dyes. PPD was first introduced in 1890 for dyeing furs and feathers. It comes in about 30 shades and is used as an intermediate (*see*) in coal tar dyes. The final color is produced by oxidizing PPD directly on the hair. The color then penetrates the hair shaft and dyes it permanently. May produce eczema, bronchial asthma, gastritis, skin rash, and death. Can crossreact with many other chemicals, including azo dyes (*see*) used for temporary hair colorings. Can also produce photosensitivity. Europeans will not allow PPD in their products but use safer *p*-toluenediamine instead. Before using permanent hair dyes, beauticians and individual users are supposed to test a patch of skin to determine if there is an adverse reaction.

p-PHENYLEPHRINE HCL. Hydrochloride.   Same as nasal decongestant Neo-Synephrine HCL®. Used topically to contract blood vessels and as a nasal decongestant; also in eye lotions to "take the red out." Prepared from *m*-hydroxy-*w*-chloroacetophenone and methylamine in water-alcohol solution. Some hypersensitive individuals may experience a mild stinging sensation. Prolonged exposure to air, metal, or strong light will cause oxidation and some loss of potency. Deeply discolored solutions, while harmless, should therefore be discarded.

PHENYLMERCURIC ACETATE.   Made by heating benzene with mercuric acetate. Metal compound; white lustrous prisms. Slightly soluble in water. Used as a germicide. Very toxic internally and blisters have been reported when it is applied to the skin.

PHENYLMERCURIC BENZOATE.   See Benzoic Acid and Mercury.

PHENYLMERCURIC BORATE.   Crystalline powder. Soluble in water and alcohol. Local external antiseptic. Much less toxic than most mercury compounds.

o-PHENYLPHENOL.   White flaky crystals with a mild characteristic odor. Prepared from phenyl ether. Practically insoluble in water. An intermediate in the manufacture of cosmetic resins. Also a germicide and fungicide in cosmetics. See Phenol for toxicity.

N-PHENYL-p-PHENYLENEDIAMINE.   *4-Aminodiphenylamine.* White crystals, very soluble in alcohol. Used in hair dyes. Intense skin irritation and blisters reported. Similar to other compounds of the group.

N-PHENYL-p-PHENYLENEDIAMINE HCL.   White crystals, slightly soluble in water. A constituent of hair dyes. Derived from diphenolic acid (*see*). Probably of moderate toxicity but reports of several skin rashes from its use have been described in the literature. It is thought to be less irritating than its parent compound.

PHENYLTHIOGLYCOLIC ACID.   See Thioglycolic Acid Compounds.

PHLOROGLUCINOL.   Prepared from various acids for use in hair dyes. Consists of white crystals with a sweet taste. Discolors in the light. The aqueous solution gives a blue violet color. See Pyrogallol for toxicity.

PHOSPHATE.   A salt or ester of phosphoric acid (*see*). Used as an emulsifier and texturizer and sequestrant in cosmetics and foods. No known toxicity.

PHOSPHOLIPIDES. Phosphatides.   Complex fat substances found in all living cells. Lecithin is an example. It is used in hand creams and lotions. Phospholipides contain phosphoric acid and nitrogen and are soluble in the usual fat solvents, with the exception of acetone (*see*). No known toxicity.

PHOSPHORIC ACID.   An acid, sequestrant, and antioxidant used in hair tonics, nail polishes, and skin fresheners. A colorless, odorless solution made from phosphate rock. Mixes with water and alcohol. No known toxicity in cosmetic use. Concentrated solutions are irritating to the skin.

PHOTOSENSITIVITY.   A condition in which the application or ingestion of certain chemicals, such as propylparaben (*see*), causes skin problems—including rash, hyperpigmentation, and swelling— when the skin is exposed to sunlight.

PHTHALIC ACID.   Obtained by the oxidation of various benzene derivatives, it can be isolated from the fungus *Gibberella fujikuroi.* When rapidly heated, it forms phthalic anhydride (*see*) and water. It is used chiefly in the manufacture of cosmetic esters, dyes, and nail polishes. Moderately irritating to the skin and mucous membranes.

PHTHALIC ANHYDRIDE.   Prepared from naphthalene by oxidation, it consists of lustrous white needles. It is used in the manufacture of cosmetic dyes and artificial resins. It is moderately irritating to the skin and mucous membranes.

PICRAMIC ACID. *4,6-Dinitro-2-Aminophenol.*   A red crystalline acid obtained from phenol (*see*) and used chiefly in making azo dyes (*see*). Highly toxic material. Readily absorbed through intact skin. Vapors absorbed through respiratory tract. Produces marked increase in metabolism and temperature, profuse sweating, collapse, and death. May cause skin rash, cataracts, and weight loss.

PIGMENT BLUE 15.   Classed chemically as a phthalocyanine (copper complex) color. See Chlorophyllin and Colors.

PIGMENT GREEN 7.   Classed chemically as a phthalocyanine (copper complex) color. See Chlorophyllin and Colors.

PILOCARPINE.   Used in hair tonic to stimulate the sweat glands. Derived from a tree grown in Brazil and Paraguay. Soluble in water, alcohol, and chloroform. White water-absorbing crystals with a bitter taste. Also an antidote for atropine poisoning. Readily absorbed through the skin from the concentrations employed in hair tonics. High concentrations are known to be irritating and toxic but no available information on toxicity in cosmetics reported.

PINE OIL.   The extract from a variety of pine trees. As a pine tar it is used in hair tonics; also a solvent, disinfectant, and deodorant. As an oil from twigs and needles, it is used in pine bath oil emulsions, bath salts, and perfumery. Irritating to the skin and mucous membranes. Bornyl acetate, a substance obtained from various pine needles, has a strong pine odor and is used in bath oils. It can cause nausea, vomiting, convulsions, and dizziness if ingested. In general, pine oil in concentrated form is an irritant to human skin and may cause allergic reactions. In small amounts it is nontoxic.

PINE TAR. A product obtained by distillation of pinewood. A blackish brown viscous liquid, slightly soluble in water. Used as an antiseptic in skin diseases. May be irritating to the skin.

PINE TAR OIL. A synthetic flavoring obtained from pine wood and used in licorice flavorings for ice cream and candy. Used as a solvent, disinfectant, and deodorant in cosmetics. May be irritating to the skin and mucous membranes, and in large ingested doses causes central nervous system depression.

PINEAPPLE JUICE. The common juice from the tropical plant. Contains a protein-digesting and milk-clotting enzyme, bromelin. An antiinflammatory enzyme, it is used in cosmetic treatment creams. It is also used as a texturizer. No known toxicity.

PIPERITONE. A snythetic flavoring agent that occurs naturally in Japanese mint. Used to give dentifrices a minty flavor and to give perfumes their peppermint scent. No known toxicity.

PIPERONAL. Heliotropin. A synthetic flavoring and perfume agent that occurs naturally in vanilla and black pepper. White crystalline powder, with a sweet floral odor. Used chiefly in perfumery. Ingestion of large amounts may cause central nervous system depression. Has been reported to cause skin rash. In lipsticks, said to produce smarting of the skin. Not recommended by some cosmetic chemists because of its ability to produce skin irritation.

PLACENTAL EXTRACT. Prepared from the placenta, the nourishing lining of the human womb that is expelled after birth. Promoted by cosmetic manufacturers as capable of removing wrinkles. The American Medical Association maintains no such evidence has been presented, nor is it likely. (Even newborn babies emerge from the womb with wrinkled skin.) Nontoxic.

PLASTICIZERS. Chemicals added to natural and synthetic resins and rubbers to impart flexibility, workability, or distensibility without changing the chemical nature of the material. Dibutyl phthalate (*see*) is a plasticizer for nitrocellulose used in nail lacquers.

PODOPHYLLUM. A bitter light brown to greenish yellow resin that is irritating to the eyes and mucous membranes. Obtained from an herb, podophyllum, and used as a cathartic. Applied externally in solution in the treatment of venereal disease, warts, and in cell research for its ability to inhibit the division of cancer cells. No known skin toxicity.

POLISH REMOVER. See Nail Polish Remover.

POLISHING AGENTS. Used in dentifrices to shine teeth. Even after removing debris and stains, teeth may still be dull. Polishing whitens and brightens teeth, and teeth that are polished are less receptive to dental plaque. Substances used to polish teeth are hydrated alumina, sodium metaphosphate, calcium phosphate, and calcium carbonate (*see all*).

POLOXAMER 101. See Poloxamer 188.

POLOXAMER 105. See Poloxamer 188.

POLOXAMER 124. See Poloxamer 188.

POLOXAMER 181. See Poloxamer 188.

POLOXAMER 182. See Poloxamer 188.

POLOXAMER 183. See Poloxamer 188.

POLOXAMER 184. See Poloxamer 188.

POLOXAMER 188. Poloxalene. A liquid nonionic surfactant polymer. If chain lengths of polyoxyethylene and polyoxypropylene are increased, the product changes from liquid to paste to solid. No known toxicity. See Polymer.

POLOXAMER 212. See Poloxamer 188.

POLOXAMER 215. See Poloxamer 188.

POLXAMER 333. See Poloxamer 188.

POLOXAMER 234. See Poloxamer 188.

POLOXAMER 238. See Poloxamer 188.

POLOXAMER 338. See Poloxamer 188.

POLOXAMER 401. See Poloxamer 188.

POLOXAMER 407. See Poloxamer 188.

POLYACRYLAMIDE. Prepared from acrylonitrile. Used in the manufacture of plastics used in nail polishes. Highly toxic and irritating to the skin. Causes central nervous system paralysis. Can be absorbed through unbroken skin.

POLYBUTENE. Indopol. Polybutylene. A plasticizer. A polymer (*see*) of one or more butylenes obtained from petroleum oils. May asphyxiate.

POLYETHYLENE. A polymer (*see*) of ethylene; a product of petroleum gas or dehydration of alcohol. One of a group of lightweight thermoplastics that have a good resistance to chemicals, low moisture absorption, and good insulating properties. Used in hand lotions, hairdressings, and various lotions. No known skin toxicity, but implants of large amounts in rats caused cancer. Ingestion of large oral doses has produced kidney and liver damage.

POLYETHYLENE GLYCOL. PEG. Used in hair straighteners, antiperspirants, baby products, fragrances, polish removers, hair tonics, lipsticks, and protective creams. It is a binder, plasticizing agent, solvent, and softener widely used for cosmetic cream bases and pharmaceutical ointments. Improves resistance to moisture and oxidation. See Polyethylene for toxicity.

POLYGLYCEROL. Prepared from edible fats, oils, and esters of fatty acids. Derived from corn, cottonseed, palm, peanuts, safflower, sesame, and soy bean oils, lard and tallow. Used as an emulsifier in cosmetics. No known toxicity.

POLYGLYCERYL-2 SESQUIOLEATE. See Polyglyceryl-4 Oleate.

POLYGLYCERYL-2 TETRASTERATE. See Polyglyceryl-4 Oleate.

POLYGLYCERYL-3 DIISOSTEARATE. See Polyglyceryl-4 Oleate.

POLYGLYCERYL-4 OLEATE. Oily liquid prepared by adding alcohol to coconut oil or other triglycerides with a polyglyceryl. Used in foods, drugs, and cosmetics as fat emulsifiers in conjunction with other emulsifiers to prepare creams, lotions, and other emulsion products. In addition, they may also be used as lubricants, plasticizers, gelling agents, and dispersants. No known toxicity.

POLYGLYCERYL-10 DECALINOLEATE. See Polyglycerly-4 Oleate.

POLYGLYCERYL-10 DECAOLEATE. See Polyglyceryl-4 Oleate.

POLYGLYCERYL-10 TETRAOLEATE. See Polyglyceryl-4 Oleate.

POLYMER. A substance or product formed by combining many small molecules (monomers). The result is essentially recurring long-chain structural units that have tensile strength, elasticity, and hardness. Examples of polymers (literally: "having many parts") are plastics, fibers, rubber, and human tissue.

POLYOXYETHYLENE COMPOUNDS. The nonionic emulsifiers used in hand creams and lotions. Usually oily or waxy liquids. No known toxicity.

POLYSORBATE-20. Polyoxyethylene (20) Sorbitan Monolaurate. Emulsifier in cosmetic creams and lotions and a stabilizer of essential oils in water. A viscous, oily liquid. A lauric acid (*see*) ester. May cause an allergic reaction in the hypersensitive but is generally considered nontoxic.

POLYSORBATE-21. Polyoxyethylene (4) Sorbitan Monolaurate. See Polysorbate-20.

POLYSORBATE-40. Polyoxyethylene (20) Sorbitan Monopalmitate. Tween 40®. Used as an emulsifier in cosmetic creams and lotions and as a stabilizer of essential oils in water; also as a detergent. Oily liquid, soluble in alcohol but insoluble in water. Palmitic acid (*see*) ester. No known toxicity.

POLYSORBATE-60. Polyoxyethylene (20) Sorbitan Monostearate. Tween 60®. Used in cosmetic creams and lotions and as a stabilizer of essential oils in water. A wax derived from a stearic acid (*see*) ester. Soluble in solvents; warm alcohol. Insoluble in water. No known toxicity.

POLYSORBATE-61. Polyoxyethylene (4) Sorbitan Monostearate. Tween 61®. See Polysorbate-60.

POLYSORBATE-65. Polyoxyethylene (20) Sorbitan Tristearate. See Polysorbate-60.

POLYSORBATE-80. Polyoxyethylene (20) Sorbitan Monoleate. Tween 80®. Emulsifier in baby lotions, cold creams, cream deodorants, antiperspirants, and suntan lotions. Also used as a stabilizer of essential oils in water in bath oil products. Viscous liquid with a faint caramel odor. Derived from sorbitol (*see*). No known toxicity.

POLYSORBATE-81. Polyoxyethylene (5) Sorbitan Monoleate. See Polysorbate-80.

POLYSORBATE-85. See Polysorbate-80.

POLYSTYRENE. Used in the manufacture of cosmetic resins. Colorless to yellowish oily liquid with a penetrating odor. Obtained from ethylbenzene by removing the hydrogen or by chlorination. Sparingly soluble in water; soluble in alcohol. May be irritating to the eyes, mucous membranes, and, in high concentrations, may be narcotic.

POLYSTYRENE LATEX. A white plastic solid derived from petroleum and used in preparing opaque hair-waving lotions. It has outstanding moisture resistance. No known toxicity.

POLYVINYL ACETATE. See Polyvinylpyrrolidone.

POLYVINYL ALCOHOL. Synthetic resins used in lipstick, setting lotions, various creams. A polymer prepared from polyvinyl acetates by replacement of the acetate groups with the hydroxyl groups. Dry, unplasticized polyvinyl alcohol powders are white to cream colored and have different viscosities. Solvent in hot and cold water but certain ones require alcohol-water mixtures. No known toxicity.

POLYVINYL METHYL ETHER. See Polyvinyl Alcohol.

POLYVINYLPYRROLIDONE. PVP. A faintly yellow solid plastic resin resembling albumin. Used to give a softer set in shampoos, hair sprays, and lacquers; also a carrier in emollient creams, liquid lip rouge, and face rouge; also a clarifier in vinegar and a plasma expander in medicine. Ingestion may produce gas and fecal impaction damage to lungs and kidneys. It may last in the system months to a year. Strong circumstantial evidence indicates thesaurosis—foreign bodies in the lung—may be produced in susceptible individuals from concentrated exposure to PVP in hair sprays. Modest intravenous doses in rats caused them to develop tumors.

POMADES.   Almost synonymous with solid brilliantines (*see*) but of older origin. Pomades were originally made with the residual fatty material left from the enfleurage process (*see*) of extracting floral odors. Poma (*apples*) were used, hence giving the hairdressing its name. Now pomades are manufactured with stearic acid, mineral, oil, paraffin (*see all*), or other waxes and oils, plus perfumes and colorings. Generally, its ingredients are nontoxic.

POPPY OIL.   A yellow to reddish oil obtained from the seeds of the poppy for use in emulsions and soaps and as a lubricant for fine machinery. Nontoxic.

POTASSIUM ALGINATE.   See Alginates.

POTASSIUM ALUM.   See Alum.

POTASSIUM BINOXALATE. Potassium Acid Oxalate. Salt of Sorrel.   White odorless crystals, which are poisonous, used in nail bleaches and as a stain remover.

POTASSIUM BIPHTHALATE. Phthalic Acid Potassium Acid Salt. A buffer used to effect alkalinity/acidity ratios. See Phthalic Acid.

POTASSIUM BORATE.   A crystalline salt used as an oxidizing agent and as a preservative in cosmetics and in flour. See Borates for toxicity.

POTASSIUM BROMATE.   Antiseptic and astringent in toothpaste, mouthwashes, and gargles as 3 to 5 percent solution. Colorless or white crystals. Very toxic when taken internally. Burns and skin irritation have been reported from its industrial uses. In toothpaste it has been reported to have caused inflammation and bleeding of gums.

POTASSIUM CARBONATE. Salt of Tartar. Pearl Ash.   Inorganic salt of potassium. Odorless, white powder, soluble in water but practically insoluble in alcohol. Used in freckle lotions, liquid shampoos, vanishing creams, setting lotions, and permanent wave lotions; also in the manufacture of soap, glass, pottery, and to finish leather. Irritating and caustic to human skin and may cause dermatitis of the scalp, forehead, and hands.

POTASSIUM CASEINATE.   See Casein.

POTASSIUM CHLORATE.   Antiseptic, astringent in mouthwashes, toothpaste, and gargles as 2 to 5 percent solution. Potassium salt.

Used in bleach and freckle lotions and in permanent wave solutions. A colorless or white powder that dissolves slowly in water. Also used in explosives, fireworks, matches, and in printing and dyeing cotton and wool black. May be absorbed through the skin. Irritating to the intestines and the kidney. Used medicinally to treat irritations in the mouth and in the vagina. Can cause dermatitis of the scalp, forehead, and hands. In toothpastes, reported to have caused inflammation of the gums.

POTASSIUM CHLORIDE. Used as a buffer in eye lotions and solid perfumes. The most important potassium salt. Colorless, crystalline, odorless, with a salty taste. A yeast food used in the brewing industry to improve brewing and fermentation and in the jelling industry. Used as a substitute for sodium chloride in low salt diet foods. More than 90 percent of the substance is used for fertilizer and the rest for producing potassium compounds. No known toxicity from cosmetic use. Small intestinal ulcers may occur with oral administration. Large doses can cause gastrointestinal collapse.

POTASSIUM COCO HYDROLYZED PROTEIN. See Proteins.

POTASSIUM COCOATE. See Coconut Oil.

POTASSIUM DODECYLBENZENE SULFONATE. See Quaternary Ammonium Compounds.

POTASSIUM GLYCOL SULFATE. See Polyethylene Glycol.

POTASSIUM GUAIACOL SULFONATE. An expectorant. See Guaiacol.

POTASSIUM HYDROXIDE. Caustic Potash. Used as an emulsifier in hand lotion, as a cuticle softener, and as an alkali in liquid soaps, protective creams, shaving preparations, and cream rouges. Prepared industrially by electrolysis of potassium chloride (*see*). White or slightly yellow lumps. It may cause irritation of the skin in cuticle removers. Extremely corrosive and ingestion may cause violent pain, bleeding, collapse, and death. When applied to the skin of mice, moderate dosages cause tumors. May cause skin rash and burning. Concentration above 5 percent can destroy fingernails as well. Good quality toilet soaps do not contain more than 0.25 percent free alkali.

POTASSIUM IODIDE. Potassium salt. A dye remover and an antiseptic. Used in table salt as a source of dietary iodine. Restricted to .01 percent. It is also in some drinking water. The lethal dose injected intravenously in rats is small. May cause an allergic reaction.

POTASSIUM LAURYL SULFATE. A water softener used in shampoos. See Sodium Lauryl Sulfate.

POTASSIUM OLEATE. Oleic Acid Potassium Salt. Used as a detergent. Yellowish or brownish soft mass. Soluble in water or alcohol. No known toxicity.

POTASSIUM PERSULFATE.   Colorless or white odorless crystals. A powerful oxidant. Soluble in water. The solution is acid and is used in the manufacture of soaps and as a germicidal preparation for the bathroom. Aqueous solutions of 2.5 to 3 percent are not irritating to humans. Twenty-five percent is irritating in animals.

POTASSIUM PHOSPHATE. Monobasic, Dibasic, and Tribasic. Used as a buffering agent in shampoos and in cuticle removers. Colorless to white powder, also used as a yeast food in brewing industries in the production of champagne and other sparkling wines. Has been used medicinally as a urinary acidifier. No known toxicity.

POTASSIUM SILICATE. Soluble Potash Glass.   Colorless or yellowish translucent to transparent glasslike particles. Used as a binder in cosmetics and in soap manufacturing. Also used as a detergent and in the glass and ceramics industries. Usually very slowly soluble in cold water. No known toxicity.

POTASSIUM SODIUM COPPER CHLOROPHYLLIN. Chlorophyllin. Copper Complex.   Used in coloring dentifrices in levels not to exceed 0.1 percent. Does not require certification. See Chlorophyllin for toxicity.

POTASSIUM SORBATE. Sorbic Acid Potassium Salt.   Used as a mold and yeast inhibitor. May cause mild irritation of the skin.

POTASSIUM STEARATE. Stearic Acid Potassium Salt.   White powder with a fatty odor. Strongly alkaline. Used in the manufacture of soap, hand creams, emulsified fragrances, lotions, and shaving creams. Acts as a defoaming agent. No known toxicity.

POTASSIUM SULFATE.   Does not occur free in nature but is combined with sodium sulfate. Colorless or white crystalline powder, with a bitter taste. Used as a reagent (*see*) in cosmetics and as a salt substitute; also a water corrective in brewing, a fertilizer, and a cathartic. Large doses can cause severe gastrointestinal bleeding. No known toxicity to the skin.

POTASSIUM SULFITE.   See Sulfides.

POTASSIUM THIOGLYCOLATE.   See Thioglycolic Acid Compounds.

POTASSIUM TOLUENE SULFONATE.   A water soluble powder that may be used in cosmetics as a solubilizing agent (*see*) in conjunction with other detergent materials. This is primarily used in household chemical products and for various industrial purposes. See Toluene for toxicity.

POTASSIUM TROCLOSENE. Troclosene. Potassium. Used in solid bleaches and detergents, and as a local anti-infective agent. No known toxicity.

POTASSIUM UNDECYLENOYL HYDROLYZED ANIMAL PROTEIN. See Protein and Hydrolyzed.

POTATO STARCH. A flour prepared from potatoes, ground to a pulp, and washed of fibers. (See Starch.) Swells in hot water to form gel on cooling. A demulcent, used in dusting powder; an emollient in dry shampoos and baby powders. With glycerin forms soothing, protective applications in eczema, skin rash, chapped skin. May cause allergic skin reactions and stuffy nose in the hypersensitive.

POWDER. Face, Compact, and Dusting. Applied to the face with a puff. Usually done at the end of the makeup process. Its objective is to remove the "shine" from the face and to give a healthy subtle glow. Face powders are either loose or compacted. Talc is the principal ingredient (about 50 percent), but face powders also include about 15 percent of a clay, kaolin, about 10 percent precipitated calcium carbonate, 10 percent zinc oxide, 10 percent zinc stearate, 5 percent magnesium carbonate (*see all*), perfume, and pigments. Also included are fractions of barium sulfate, boric acid, cetyl alcohol, titanium dioxide, rice or corn starch (*see all*). The absorbing, covering, and adherent properties of the face powder may be changed by varying the amounts of the ingredients or by elimination of some of them. For instance, eliminating titanium dioxide makes the powder more transparent. Various pigments are used for shades of face powder including yellow ocher and sienna, red ochers, umbers, burnt sienna, ultramarine blue and violet, all inorganic pigments. Organic pigments used may include D & C Red No. 7 Calcium Lake or D & C Orange No. 4 (*see both*). Problems with face powders are rare. The FDA recently recorded a concern with rash. Compact powder is similar to face powder but includes binders such as gums (*see*); cake makeup employs a binder such as lecithin. Also used in compact powder to make it keep its shape are glyceryl monostearate glycols or mineral oil (*see all*), and other oils. Dusting powder, usually used after a bath or shower, generally contains talc, perfume, and zinc stearate (*see*). Toxicity concerns mechanical blocking of pores and subsequent irritation and inhalation of the powders. See Talc and Starch for toxicity.

PPG BUTETH-55. A polymer prepared by the etherification of butyl alcohol with ethylene oxide and propylene oxide. A mixture of several polymers (*see*), it has the consistency of petroleum jelly but dissolves in water. Used in hand lotions, various other lotions, and hairdressings. No known toxicity.

PPG BUTETH-260.   See PPG Buteth-55.
PPG BUTETH-660.   See PPG Buteth-55.
PPG BUTETH-1000.   See PPG Buteth-55.
PPG BUTETH-2000.   See PPG Buteth-55.
PPG BUTETH-3520.   See PPG Buteth-55.
PPG BUTETH-5100.   See PPG Buteth-55.
PPG BUTYL ETHER-200.   Polymer (*see*) prepared from butyl alcohol with propylene glycol (*see both*).
PPG BUTYL ETHER-300.   See PPG Butyl Ether-200.
PPG BUTYL ETHER-385.   See PPG Butyl Ether-200.
PPG BUTYL ETHER-1145.   See PPG Butyl Ether-200.
PPG BUTYL ETHER-1715.   See PPG Butyl Ether-200.
PPG-10 CETYL ETHER.   See Cetyl Alcohol.
PPG-28 CETYL ETHER.   See Cetyl Alcohol and Polypropylene.
PPG-30 CETYL ETHER.   A liquid nonionic surface-active agent (*see*). No known toxicity. See Cetyl Alcohol.
PPG-2 DIBENZOATE.   See Benzoic Acid.
PPG-27 GLYCERYL ETHER.   See Glycerin.
PPG-55 GLYCERYL ETHER.   See Propylene Glycol.
PPG-30 ISOCETYL ETHER.   See Cetyl Alcohol.
PPG-3-ISOSTEARETH-9.   See Stearyl Alcohol and Polypropylene.
PPG-30 LANOLIN ETHER.   Derived from lanolin alcohols (*see*).
PPG-9 LAURATE.   See Lauric Acid.
PPG-2 METHYL ETHER.   See Propylene Glycol.
PPG-20-METHYL GLUCOSE ETHER.   See Polypropylene Glycol.
PPG-3-MYRETH-11.   See Polyethylene Glycol and Myristic Acid.
PPG-4 MYRISTYL ETHER.   See Myristyl Alcohol.
PPG-26 OLEATE. Polyoxypropylene 2000 Monooleate. Carbowax. A solid polyethylene glycol (*see*). Each PPG is a mixture of several polymers (*see*) with various consistencies. Used as a base or carrier in hand lotions, and hair dressings, various other cosmetic lotions. No known toxicity.
PPG-36 OLEATE. Polyoxypropylene (36) Monooleate. See PPG-26 Oleate.
PPG-10 OLEYL ETHER.   See PPG-26 Oleate.
PPG-30 OLEYL ETHER.   See PPG-26 Oleate.
PPG-50 OLEYL ETHER.   See PPG-26 Oleate.
PPG-12-PEG-50 LANOLIN.   See Polypropylene and Lanolin.
PPG-2 SALICYLATE.   See PPG-26 Oleate.
PPG-15 STEARYL ETHER.   See Stearic Acid and Propylene Glycol.
PPM.   Parts per million.

PRECIPITATE. To separate out from a solution or suspension. A deposit of a solid separated out from a solution or suspension as a result of a chemical or physical change, as by the action of a reagent (*see*).

PREGNENOLONE ACETATE. Derived from the urine of pregnant women. Used topically as an antiinflammatory, antiitch agent. Very slightly soluble in water. A corticosteroid. No known toxicity.

PRESERVATIVES. Because the presence of viable microorganisms in cosmetic products can lead to separation of emulsions, discoloration, the formation of gas and odors, and changes in the general properties, as well as possible infection for the users, a preservative must be effective against a wide range of microorganisms. It must not be toxic internally or externally. It must not alter the character of the product, and it is required to be long-lasting and inexpensive. Many kinds of yeasts, fungi, and bacteria have been identified in cosmetics, including pseudomonas, staphylococcus, and streptococcus. In many instances a product might show no visible evidence of microbial contamination and yet contain actively growing, potentially harmful germs. Esters of *p*-hydroxybenzoic acid (*see*) are the most widely used preservatives.

PRESHAVING LOTIONS. See Shaving Lotions.

PRISTANE. A liquid hydrocarbon obtained from the liver oil of sharks and from ambergris (*see both*). Used as a lubricant and anti-corrosive agent.

PROGESTERONE. A female sex hormone used in face cream for its supposed antiwrinkle properties. There is no proven benefit to the skin and it may be absorbed through the skin and have adverse systemic effects. See Hormone Creams and Lotions.

PROPANE. A gas heavier than air; odorless when pure. It is used as a fuel and refrigerant. Cleared for use in a spray propellant and as an aerating agent for cosmetics in aerosols. May be narcotic in high doses.

PROPELLANT 11. Trichlorofluoromethane. Freon 11®. A low pressure, odorous propellant used for hair sprays, shaving lathers, and other products with alcohol. Less toxic than carbon dioxide (*see*) but decomposes into harmful materials when exposed to flames or high heat. May be narcotic in high concentrations.

PROPELLANT 11S. A stabilized form of Propellant 11 (*see*).

PROPELLANT 12. Dichlorodifluoromethane. Freon 12®. High pressure propellant used in aerosols, particularly for foam products such as hair coloring. Frequently used for perfumes because it has no odor of its own. See Aerosols for toxicity.

PROPELLANT 114. Dichlorotetrafluoroethane. Freon 114®. Most frequently used propellant. It is a low pressure one. See Aerosols for toxicity.

PROPELLANT 142B. Chlorodifluoroethane. Freon 142B®. A propellant not frequently used because of its high pressure. See Aerosols for toxicity.

PROPELLANT 152A. Difluoroethane. Propellant used in glass, plastic, and aluminum containers. See Aerosols for toxicity.

PROPIONIC ACID. Occurs naturally in apples, strawberries, tea, and violet leaves. An oily liquid with a slightly pungent, rancid odor. Can be obtained from wood pulp, waste liquor, and by fermentation. Used in perfume bases and as a mold inhibitor, antioxidant, and preservative in cosmetics. Its salts have been used as antifungal agents to treat skin mold. Large oral dose in rats is lethal. No known toxicity when used externally.

PROPIONIC ANHYDRIDE. Used in perfume oils. It has a more pungent odor than that of propionic acid (*see*). No known toxicity to skin.

PROPYL ACETATE. Colorless liquid, soluble in water, derived from propane and acetate. It has the odor of pears. Used in the manufacture of perfumes and as a solvent for resins. It may be irritating to the skin and mucous membranes.

PROPYL ALCOHOL. Obtained from crude fusel oil. Alcoholic and slightly overpowering odor. Occurs naturally in cognac green oil, cognac white oil, and onion oil. A synthetic fruit flavoring. Used instead of ethyl alcohol as a solvent for shellac, gums, resins, oils; as a denaturant (*see*) for alcohol in perfumery. Not a primary irritant, but because it dissolves fat it has a drying effect on the skin and may lead to cracking, fissuring, and infection. No adverse effects have been reported from local application as a lotion, liniment, mouthwash, gargle, or sponge bath.

PROPYL GALLATE. A fine, white, odorless powder with a bitter taste used as an antioxidant in creams and lotions. No known toxicity.

PROPYLAMINE. 1-Aminopropane. An alkaline base for cosmetics, it is a colorless liquid with a strong ammonia odor. Miscible with water, alcohol, and ether. Strong skin irritant. May cause allergic reactions.

PROPYLENE CARBONATE. An odorless, colorless liquid that because of its solubility characteristics may be used in cosmetics as a solvent, plasticizer, solubilizer, or diluent in a variety of formulations. No known toxicity.

PROPYLENE GLYCOL. 1,2-Propanediol. A clear, colorless,

viscous liquid, slightly bitter tasting. Absorbs moisture, acts as a solvent and a wetting agent. Used in liquid makeup, foundation makeup, foundation creams, mascaras, spray deodorants, hair straighteners, liquid powders, preshave lotions, after-shave lotions, baby lotions, cold creams, emollients, antiperspirants, lipsticks, mouthwashes, stick perfumes, and suntan lotions. No adverse effects have been reported in man, but large oral doses in animals have produced central nervous system depression and slight kidney changes. However, the lethal oral dose in guinea pigs and rats is very small.

PROPYLENE GLYCOL ALGINATE. Kelcoloid®. The propylene glycol ester of alginic acid (*see*) derived from seaweed. Used as a stabilizer and defoaming agent in cosmetics and food. No known toxicity.

PROPYLENE GLYCOL CAPRYLATE. See Polyethylene Glycol and Capric Acid.

PROPYLENE GLYCOL DICAPRYLATE/DICAPRIATE. A gel. See Propylene Glycol and Capric Acid.

PROPYLENE GLYCOL DICOCONATE. Mixture of propylene glycol esters of coconut fatty acids. See Propylene Glycol.

PROPYLENE GLYCOL DIPELARGONATE. See Propylene Glycol.

PROPYLENE GLYCOL LAURATE. An ester of propylene glycol and lauric acid. An emulsifying agent for solvents, cosmetic creams and lotions; also a stabilizer of essential oils in water. Light orange oil, dispersible in water, soluble in alcohol and oils. Nontoxic but can cause allergic reactions in the hypersensitive.

PROPYLENE GLYCOL MYRISTATE. See Propylene Glycol and Myristic Acid.

PROPYLENE GLYCOL RICINOLEATE. Ester of propylene glycol and ricinoleic acid (*see both*).

PROPYLENE GLYCOL STEARATE. Cream-colored wax. Dispenses in water, soluble in hot alcohol. Lubricating agent and emulsifier in cosmetic creams and lotions. Stabilizer of essential oils. No known toxicity.

PROPYLENE GLYCOL STEARATE SE. See Propylene Glycol.

PROPYLPARABEN. Propyl p-Hydroxybenzoate. Developed in Europe, the esters of *p*-hydroxybenzoic acid are widely used in the cosmetic industry as preservatives and bacteria and fungus killers. They are active against a variety of organisms, are neutral, low in toxicity, slightly soluble, and active in all solutions, alkaline, neutral, or acid. Used in shampoos, baby preparations, foundation creams, beauty masks, dentifrices, eye lotions, hair-grooming aids, nail creams, and wave sets. Used medicinally to treat fungus infections. Can cause contact dermatitis. Less toxic than benzoic or salicylic acids (*see*).

PROTECTIVE CREAMS. Water-repellent or oil-repellent creams designed to act as barrier agents against irritating chemicals, including water. Some products such as the widely used silicones are both water and oil repellent. Among the chemicals used in protective creams are stearic acid, beeswax, glycerin, casein, ammonium hydroxide, zince stearate, titanium dioxide, butyl stearate, petrolatum, polyethylene glycol, paraffin, potassium hydroxide, magnesium stearate, aluminum compounds, benzoic acid, borates, calamine, ceresin, lanolin, salicylates, sodium silicate, talc, and triethanolamine (*see all*).

PROTEINS. The chief nitrogen-containing constituents of plants and animals—the essential constituents of every living cell. They are complex but by weight contain about 50 percent carbon, about 20 percent oxygen, about 15 percent nitrogen, about 7 percent hydrogen, and some sulfur. Some also contain iron and phosphorus. Proteins are colorless, odorless, and generally tasteless. They vary in solubility. They readily undergo putrefaction, hydrolysis, and dilution with acids or alkalies. They are regarded as combinations of amino acids (*see*). Cosmetic manufacturers, particularly makers of hair products, claim "protein enrichment" is beneficial to the hair and skin. Hair, of course, is already dead. It does consist of a type of protein, keratin (*see*), but the surface of the hair is cornified tissue that cannot be revitalized. Such products will add body to thin hair and add gloss or luster, but so will other hair conditioners (*see*). As for face creams with protein, the lubricant is more beneficial than the protein. No known toxicity.

PSORALEN®. Named from the Latin "psora," meaning itch, and derived from a plant. Used in the treatment of vitiligo (lack of skin pigment), in sunscreens to increase tanning, and in perfumes. It can cause photosensitivity (*see*).

PUMICE. Used in hand-cleansing pastes, skin-cleansing grains, toothpastes, powders, and some soaps for acne treatment. A tooth whitener in Elizabethan times. Used to rub hair from legs and as a nicotine remover paste. Light, hard, rough, porous mass of gritty, gray-colored powder of volcanic origin. Used in cosmetics for removing tough or rough skin. Pumice consists mainly of silicates (*see*) found chiefly in the Lipari islands and in the Greek archipelagos. Because of its abrasive action, daily use in dentifrices is not recommended. If used continuously on a dry sensitive skin, it may cause irritation. Reported to be an irritant when used with soapless detergents but is generally considered harmless.

PURCELLINE OIL SYN.   A synthetic mixture of fatty esters simulating the natural oil obtained from the preen glands of waterfowl. Used as a fixative in perfumes. No known toxicity.

PVP-IODINE.   Complex of polyvinylpyrrolidone and iodine (*see* both).

PYRAZOLE.   A crystalline compound used to overcome acidity of aluminum chloride in antiperspirants. Soluble in water, alcohol, ether, and benzene. No known toxicity when used externally. A modest injection into the abdomens of mice is lethal.

PYRIDINE.   Occurs naturally in coffee and coal tar. Disagreeable odor; sharp taste. Used as a solvent. Once used to treat asthma, but may cause central nervous system depression and irritation of the skin and respiratory tract. After prolonged administration, kidney and liver damage may result.

PYRIDIUM COMPOUNDS.   A toxic, water-soluble, flammable liquid with a disagreeable odor that is obtained by distillation of bone oil or as a by-product of coal tar. Used as a modifier and preservative in shaving creams, soaps, hand creams, and lotions; also a solvent, a denaturant in alcohol, and an industrial waterproofing agent. No known toxicity when used externally. The lethal dose injected into the abdomens of rats is only 3.2 milligrams per kilogram of body weight.

PRYIDOXINE.   See Pyridoxine HCL.

PYRIDOXINE DIOCTENOATE. Vitamin B_6 Dioctenoate.   See Pyridoxine HCL.

PYRIDOXINE DIPALMITATE. Vitamin B_6 Dipalmitate.   See Pyridoxine HCL.

PYRIDOXINE HCL. Vitamin B_6 Hydrochloride.   Texturizer. A colorless or white crystalline powder present in many foodstuffs. A coenzyme that helps in the metabolism of amino acids (*see*) and fats. Also soothing to skin. Nontoxic.

PYRIDOXINE TRIPALMITATE. Vitamin B_6 Tripalmitate.   See Pyridoxine HCL.

PYROCATECHOL.   Used as an antiseptic. Colorless leaflets, soluble in water, prepared by treating salicylaldehyde with hydrogen peroxide (*see*). Used in blond-type dyes as an oxidizing agent and for dyeing furs; also in photography. Very toxic when ingested. It can cause eczema and systemic effects similar to phenol (*see*).

PYROGALLOL. Antiseptic hair dye for hair restorers. The first synthetic organic dye used in human hair. Discovered in 1786 and suggested for use in hair in 1845. Solution grows darker as it is exposed to air. Consists of white odorless crystals. An aromatic alcohol of pyrogallic acid. Used medicinally as an external antimicrobial and to soothe irritated skin. Ingestion may cause severe gastrointestinal irritation, kidney and liver damage, circulatory collapse, and death. Application to extensive areas of the skin is extremely dangerous. Even with careful use, it can cause a skin rash. Its adverse effects supposedly can be reduced by adding sulfide.

PYROLIGNEOUS ACID. An acid reddish brown aqueous liquid obtained by the destructive distillation of hardwood. Contains acetic acid and methanol (see *both*), wood oil, and tars. It is corrosive and may cause epigastric pain, vomiting, circulatory collapse, and death. Used as synthetic flavoring.

PYROPHOSPHATE. Salt of Pyrophosphoric Acid. It increases the effectiveness of antioxidants in creams and ointments. In concentrated solutions it can be irritating to the skin and mucous membranes.

PYROPHYLLITE. Pencil Stone Agalmatolite. White to yellowish gray mineral consisting predominantly of a hydrous aluminum silicate (*see*) mixed with silica (*see*). Used to color cosmetics and drugs applied to the skin. No known toxicity.

Q

QUASSIN. Bitter alkaloid obtained from the wood of *Quassia amara*. Chiefly used as a denaturant for ethyl alcohol. Shavings from a plant found in Jamaica and the Caribbean islands. Yellowish white to bright yellow chips. Used to poison flies. Toxic to humans.

QUATERNARY AMMONIUM COMPOUNDS. A wide variety of preservatives, surfactants, germicides, sanitizers, antiseptics, and deodorants used in cosmetics. Benzalkonium chloride (*see*) is one of the most popular. Quaternary ammonium compounds are synthetic derivatives of ammonium chloride (*see*) and are used in aerosol deodorants, after-shave lotions, antidandruff shampoos, antiperspirants, cuticle softeners, hair colorings, hair-grooming aids, hand creams, hair-waving preparations, mouthwashes, hand creams, and regular shampoos. Diluted solutions are used in medicine to sterilize the skin and mucous membranes. All the quaternary ammonium compounds can be toxic, depending upon the dose and concentration.

Concentrated solutions irritate the skin and can cause necrosis of the mucous membranes. Concentrations as low as 0.1 percent are irritating to the eye and mucous membranes except benzalkonium chloride, which is well tolerated at such low concentrations. Ingestion can be fatal.

QUATERNIUM-1. See Quaternary Ammonium Compounds.

QUATERNIUM-2. See Quaternary Ammonium Compounds.

QUATERNIUM-3. See Quaternary Ammonium Compounds.

QUATERNIUM-4. See Quaternary Ammonium Compounds.

QUATERNIUM-5. See Quaternary Ammonium Compounds.

QUATERNIUM-5 BENTONITE. See Quaternary Ammonium Compounds and Bentonite.

QUATERNIUM-5 HECTORITE. See Quaternary Ammonium Compounds and Hectorite.

QUATERNIUM-6. See Quaternary Ammonium Compounds.

QUATERNIUM-7. See Quaternary Ammonium Compounds.

QUATERNIUM-8. See Quaternary Ammonium Compounds.

QUATERNIUM-9. See Quaternary Ammonium Compounds.

QUATERNIUM-10. See Quaternary Ammonium Compounds.

QUATERNIUM-11. See Quaternary Ammonium Compounds.

QUATERNIUM-12. See Quaternary Ammonium Compounds.

QUATERNIUM-13. See Quaternary Ammonium Compounds.

QUATERNIUM-14. See Quaternary Ammonium Compounds.

QUATERNIUM-15. See Quaternary Ammonium Compounds.

QUATERNIUM-16. See Quaternary Ammonium Compounds.

QUATERNIUM-17. Cetyl Dimethyl Ethyl Ammonium Bromide. See Quaternary Ammonium Compounds.

QUATERNIUM-18. See Quaternary Ammonium Compounds.

QUATERNIUM-19. See Quaternary Ammonium Compounds.

QUATERNIUM-20. See Quaternary Ammonium Compounds.

QUATERNIUM-21. See Quaternary Ammonium Compounds.

QUATERNIUM-22. See Quaternary Ammonium Compounds.

QUATERNIUM-30. Dodecylbenzyl Triethanolammonium Chloride. See Quaternary Ammonium Compounds.

QUATERNIUM-31. See Quaternary Ammonium Compounds.

QUATERNIUM-28 DODECYLBENZYL TRIMETHYLAMMONIUM CHLORIDE. See Quaternary Ammonuim Compounds.

QUATERNIUM-29 DODECYLXYLYL bis. Trimethyl Ammonium Chloride. See Quaternary Ammonium Compounds.

QUATERNIUM-18 HECTORITE. See Quaternary Ammonium Compounds.

QUERCITRIN.   The inner bark of a species of oak tree common in North America. Its active ingredient is quercitrin, used in dark brown hair dye shades but employed mainly for dyeing artificial hairpieces. Allergic reactions have been reported.

QUILLAJA BARK. Soapbark.   Bark of a South American tree containing saponin. Used as foam producer, in shampoos and bubble baths, and to cleanse the scalp and reduce scaliness; also an emulsifier. See Saponins for toxicity.

QUINCE SEED.   The seed of a plant grown in southern Asia and Europe for its fatty oil. Thick jelly produced by soaking seeds in water. Used in setting lotions, as a suspension in skin creams and lotions, as a thickening agent in depilatories, and as an emulsifier for fragrances, hand creams, lotions, rouges, and wave sets; medicinally as a demulcent. Has been largely replaced by cheaper substitutes. It may cause allergic reactions.

QUININE.   The most important alkaloid of cinchona bark, which grows wild in South America. White crystalline powder; almost insoluble in water. Used as a local anesthetic in hair tonics and sunscreen preparations. Used in bitters as flavoring for beverages in limited amounts. When taken internally, it reduces fever. It may cause skin rashes.

QUINOLINE.   A coal tar derivative used in the manufacture of cosmetic dyes. Also a solvent for resins. Made either by the distillation of coal tar, bones, and alkaloids or by the interaction of aniline (*see*) with acetaldehyde and formaldehyde (*see both*). Absorbs water; has a weak base. Soluble in hot water. Also used as a preservative for anatomical specimens. See Coal Tar for toxicity. See Colors.

QUINOLINE SALTS.   A colorless, oily, very hygroscopic liquid, with a disagreeable odor. Occurs in coal tar. Used in suntan preparations and perfumes as a preservative and solvent. Also a preservative for anatomical specimens. No known toxicity when used externally.

R

RAISIN-SEED OIL.   Dried grapes or berries used in lubricating creams. See Grape-Seed Oil.

RAPESEED OIL.   Brownish yellow oil from a turniplike annual herb of European origin. Widely grown as a forage crop for sheep in the United States. A distinctly unpleasant odor. Used chiefly as a lubricant, an illuminant, and in rubber substitutes; also used in soft soaps and margarine. Can cause acnelike skin eruptions.

RASPBERRY JUICE. Juice from the fresh ripe fruit grown in Europe, Asia, the United States, and Canada. Used as a flavoring for lipsticks, food, and medicines. It has astringent properties. No known toxicity.

RAYON. Regenerated cellulose. Rayon is man-made textile fibers of cellulose and yarn; produced from wood pulp. Its appearance is similar to silk. Used to give shine and body to face powders and in eyelash extenders in mascaras. No known toxicity.

REAGENT. A chemical that reacts or participates in a reaction; a substance that is used for the detection or determination of another substance by chemical or microscopical means. The various categories of reagents are colorimetric—to produce color-soluble compounds; fluxes—used to lower melting points; oxidizers—used in oxidation; precipitants—to produce insoluble compounds; reducers—used in reduction (*see*); solvents—used to dissolve water-insoluble compounds.

RED PEPPER. Cayenne Pepper. A condiment made from the pungent fruit of the plant. Used in sausage and pepper flavorings. Has been reported to stunt growth in Mexican children who eat considerable amounts of it. A stimulant in hair tonics, but may be an irritant and also may cause allergic reaction.

REDUCING AGENT. A substance that decreases, deoxidizes, or concentrates the volume of another substance. For instance, a reducing agent is used to convert a metal oxide to the metal itself. It also means a substance that adds hydrogen agents to another, for example, when acetaldehyde is converted to alcohol in the final step of alcoholic fermentation.

REDUCTION. The process of reducing by chemical or electrochemical means. The gain of one or more electrons by an ion or compound. It is the reverse of oxidation.

RESINS. The brittle substance, usually translucent or transparent, formed from the hardened secretions of plants. Among the natural resins are dammar, elemi, and sandarac. Synthetic resins include polyvinyl acetate, various polyester resins, and sulfonamide resins. Resins have many uses in cosmetics. They contribute depth, gloss, flow adhesion, and water resistance. Toxicity depends upon ingredients used.

RESORCINOL. A preservative, antiseptic, astringent, and anti-itching agent, particularly in dandruff shampoos. Also used in hair dyes, lipsticks, and hair tonics. Obtained from various resins (*see*). Resorcinol's white crystals become pink on exposure to air. A sweetish taste. Irritating to the skin and mucous membranes. It may cause allergic reactions. Used as an antifungal agent.

RESORCINOL ACETATE. See Resorcinol.

RESTHARROW EXTRACT. A European woody herb with pink flowers and long, tough roots used for medicinal purposes and in emollients. No known toxicity.

RHODINOL. Used in perfumes, especially those of the rose type. Isolated from geranium or rose oils. It has the strong odor of rose and consists essentially of geraniol and citronellol (*see*). Also used in food and beverage flavorings. No known toxicity.

RHUBARB. The common plant with large edible leaves. It is combined with henna, black tea, and chamomile for hair dye. Its active principle is chrysophanol, which produces a desirable blond shade. No known skin toxicity.

RIBOFLAVIN. Vitamin B₂. Lactoflavin. Formerly called Vitamin G. Riboflavin is a factor in the Vitamin B Complex and is used in emollients. Every plant and animal cell contains a minute amount. Good sources are milk, eggs, and organ meats. It is necessary for healthy skin and respiration, protects the eyes from sensitivity to light, and is used for building and maintaining human body tissues. A deficiency leads to lesions at the corner of the mouth and to changes in the cornea.

RICE BRAN OIL. Oil expressed from the broken coat of rice grain.

RICE POWDER. See Rice Starch.

RICE STARCH. The finely pulverized grains of the rice plant used in baby powders, face powders, and dusting powders. It is a demulcent and emollient and forms a soothing, protective film when applied. May cause mechanical irritation by blocking the pores and putrefying. May also cause an allergic reaction.

RICINOLEAMIDE. See Ricinoleic Acid.

RICINOLEATE. Salt of ricinoleic acid found in castor oil. Used in the manufacture of soaps. No known toxicity.

RICINOLEIC ACID. A mixture of fatty oils found in the seeds of castor beans. Castor oil contains 80 to 85 percent ricinoleic acid. The oily liquid is used in soaps, added to Turkey-red oil (*see*), and in contraceptive jellies. It is believed to be the active laxative in castor oil. Also used externally as an emollient. No known toxicity.

ROCHELLE SALT. Potassium Sodium Tartrate. Used in the manufacture of baking powder and in the silvering of mirrors. Translucent crystals or white crystalline powder with a cooling saline taste. Slight efflorescence in warm air. Probably used in mouthwashes, but use not identified in cosmetics. No known toxicity.

ROCK SALT CRYSTALS. See Sodium Chloride.

ROSE BENGAL. A bluish red fragrant liquid taken from the rose of the Bengal region of the subcontinent. Used to scent perfumes and as an edible color product to make lipstick dyes. Nontoxic.

ROSE GERANIUM. Distilled from any of several South African herbs grown for their fragrant leaves. Used in perfumes, and to scent toothpaste and dusting powders. No known toxicity except may cause allergic reactions.

ROSE OIL. Attar of Roses. The fragrant, volatile, essential oil distilled from fresh flowers. Colorless or yellow, with a strong fragrant odor and taste of roses. Used in perfumes, toilet waters, and ointments. Nontoxic but may cause allergic reactions.

ROSE OTTO BULGARIA. One of the most widely used perfume ingredients, it is the essential oil, steam-distilled from the flowers of Rosa Damascena. The rose flowers are picked early in the morning when they contain the maximum amount of perfume and are distilled quickly after harvesting. Bulgaria is the main source of supply, but the USSR, Turkey, Syria, and Indo-China also grow it. The liquid is pale yellow and has a warm, deep floral, slightly spicy, and extremely fragrant, red rose smell. No known toxicity other than allergic reactions.

ROSE WATER. The watery solution of the odoriferous constituents of roses made by distilling the fresh flowers with water or steam. Used as a perfume in emollients, eye lotions, and freckle lotions. No known toxicity except for allergic reactions.

ROSE WATER OINTMENT. See Cold Cream.

ROSEMARY. Used in perfumery. The flowers and leaves of the plant are a symbol of love and loyalty. Rosemary oil is the volatile oil from the fresh flowering tops of rosemary and is used in liniments and hair tonics. Colorless to yellow, with the characteristic odor of rosemary and a warm camphorlike taste. Rosemary has the folk reputation of stimulating the growth of hair and is used in rinse water. It supposedly is also beneficial for the skin. It is used internally as a tonic and astringent and by herbalists as a stimulant for the nerves. No known toxicity when used externally. A teaspoonful may cause illness in an adult, and an ounce may cause death.

ROSIN. Used in soaps, hair lacquers, wax depilatories, and ointments. It is the pale yellow residue left after distilling off the volatile oil from the oleoresin obtained from various species of pine trees chiefly produced in the United States. Also used in the manufacture of varnishes and fireworks. It can cause contact dermatitis.

ROUGE. One of the oldest types of makeup. Rouge is applied to the cheeks to give a rosy, healthy look. It is usually a finely divided form of ferric oxide generally prepared by heating ferrous sulfate.

Cake or compact rouge usually contains talc, kaolin, brilliant red lake (certified), zinc oxide, zinc stearate, liquid petrolatum, tragacanth, mucilage (*see all*), and perfume. Liquid rouge usually contains carmine coloring, ammonium hydroxide, glycerin (*see all*), and water. Liquid lip rouge, which may be substituted for lipstick, usually contains ethanol, ethylcellulose, oleic acid, monoglyceride (*see all*), and a red coloring pigment. It may also contain polyvinylpyrrolidone or sodium carboxymethyl cellulose, glycerin, color, propylene glycol (*see all*), alcohol, perfume, and water. Rouge paste may contain carmine coloring, ammonium hydroxide, beeswax, cetyl alcohol, stearic acid, cocoa butter, and petrolatum (*see all*). Cream rouge may contain erythrosine as a coloring, stearic acid, cetyl alcohol, potassium hydroxide, glycerin, and water; or sorbitol, lanolin, mineral oil, petrolatum, a color pigment, perfume, and water; or anhydrous or emulsified carnauba wax, ozokerite, isopropyl palmitate, titanium dioxide, talc, certified colors, pigments, and perfume (*see all*). Dry rouge may contain kaolin, talc, precipitated calcium carbonate, magnesium carbonate, titanium dioxide, zinc stearate, certified colors and lakes, inorganic oxides, and perfume (*see all*). A typical formula for an emulsified rouge includes white beeswax, 12 percent; petrolatum, 24 percent; spermaceti, 8 percent; mineral oil, 22 percent; borax, 0.8 percent; water, about 30 percent; pigment, 3.1 percent; *p*-hydroxybenzoic acid, 0.1 percent; and perfume (*see all*). Rouge does not figure often in FDA complaints. In recent years there have been complaints of eye irritation and fungus.

ROYAL JELLY.   Highly touted as a magic ingredient in cosmetics to restore one's skin to youthfulness. Royal jelly is the very nutritious secretion of the throat glands of the honeybee workers that is fed to the larvae in a colony, and to all queen larvae, and possibly to the adult queen. It is a mixture of proteins plus about 31 percent fats, 15 percent carbohydrates, 15 percent minor growth factors, and 24 percent water and trace elements. If stored, royal jelly loses its capacity to develop queen bees. Even when fresh, there is no proven value in a cosmetic preparation. No known toxicity.

RUBBING ALCOHOLS.   Isopropyl alcohol (*see*), probably the most common rubbing alcohol, is used in astringents, skin fresheners, colognes, and perfumes. It can be irritating to the skin. Ethanol (*see*) is used in perfumes and as a solvent for oils. It also can be irritating. Rubbing alcohols are denatured with chemicals to make them poisonous so they will not be ingested as an alcoholic beverage.

RUBEFACIENTS.   Help stimulate blood circulation to the scalp and the activity of the oil secreting glands. Pilocarpine (*see*) is an example.

RUE OIL. A spice agent obtained from the fresh aromatic blossoming plants grown in Southern Europe and the Orient. It has a fatty odor and is used in baked goods. The oil is obtained by steam distillation and is used in fragrances and in blueberry, raspberry, and other fruit flavorings. Formerly used in medicine to treat disorders and hysteria. It is on the FDA list for study of mutagenic, teratogenic, subacute, and reproductive effects.

RYE FLOUR. Used in powders. Flour made from hardy annual cereal grass. Seeds are used for feed and in the manufacture of whiskey and bread. May cause allergic reactions.

S

SACCHARATED LIME. Produced by the action of lime upon sugar. Used as a buffer (*see*) in cosmetics and as a preservative. No known toxicity.

SACCHARIN. An artificial sweetener in use since 1879. It is 300 times as sweet as natural sugar. Used as a sweetener for mouthwashes, dentifrices, and lipsticks. It sweetens dentifrices and mouthwashes in 0.05 to 1 percent concentration. On the FDA's top priority list to retest for mutagenic, teratogenic, subacute, and reproductive effects. White crystals or crystalline powder. Odorless or with a faint aromatic odor. It was used with cyclamates in the experiments that led to the ban on cyclamates. The FDA has proposed restricting saccharin to 15 milligrams per day for each kilogram of body weight or 1 gram a day for a 150-pound person.

SAFFLOWER GLYCERIDE. See Safflower Oil.

SAFFLOWER OIL. Used in creams and lotions to soften the skin. Oil is expressed from the seed of an Old World herb that resembles a thistle, with large bright red or orange flowers. Widely cultivated for its oil, which thickens and becomes rancid on exposure to air. No known toxicity.

SAFFRON. Used in perfumery and coloring in cosmetics. It is the dried stigma of the crocus cultivated in Spain, Greece, France, and Iran. Used also in bitters, liquors, and spice flavorings. Formerly used to treat skin diseases. No known toxicity.

SAFROLE. Found in certain natural oils such as star anise, nutmeg, ylang-ylang, it is a stable, colorless to brown liquid with an odor of sassafras and root beer. Used in the manufacture of heliotropin (*see*) and in inexpensive soaps and perfumes. Also used as a beverage flavoring. No known toxicity.

SAGE OIL. Obtained by steam distillation from the flowering tops of the plant believed by the Arabs to prevent dying. A pale yellow liquid that smells and tastes like camphor. Used to cover gray hair in some rinses and as an astringent in skin fresheners and steam baths. Supposedly has healing power. No known toxicity.

SALAD OIL. Any edible vegetable oil. Dermatologists advise rubbing salad oils or fats on the skin, particularly on babies and older persons. Vegetable oils are used in commercial baby preparations, cleansers, emollient creams, face powders, hair-grooming preparations, hypoallergenic cosmetics, lipsticks, nail creams, shampoos, shaving creams, and wave sets. Nontoxic.

SALICYLAMIDE. An analgesic, fungicide, and anti-inflammatory agent used to soothe the skin. White to slightly pink crystalline bitter powder. Gives a sensation of warmth on the tongue. Soluble in hot water. No known toxicity.

SALICYLANILIDE. Usually made from salicylic acid (*see*) with aniline (*see*). Odorless leaflets, slightly soluble in water, freely soluble in alcohol. Used as topical antifungal agent, in antibacterial soaps, and topical preparations. In concentrated form may cause irritation of the skin and mucous membranes. When exposed to sunlight, it can cause swelling, reddening, and/or rash of the skin.

SALICYLATES. Amyl. Phenyl. Benzyl. Menthyl. Glyceryl. Dipropylene Glycol Esters. Salts of salicylic acid used as sunburn preventatives and antiseptics. See Salicylic Acid.

SALICYLIC ACID. Occurs naturally in wintergreen leaves, sweet birch, and other plants. Synthetically prepared by heating phenol (*see*) with carbon dioxide. It has a sweetish taste and is used as a preservative and antimicrobial at 0.1 to 0.5 percent in skin softeners, face masks, hair tonics, deodorants, dandruff preparations, protective creams, hair dye removers, and suntan lotions and oils. It is antipuretic (antiitch) and antiseptic. In fact, in medicine it is used as an antimicrobial at 2 to 20 percent concentration in lotions, ointments, powders, and plasters. It is also used in making aspirin. It can be absorbed through the skin. Absorption of large amounts may cause vomiting, abdominal pain, increased respiration, acidosis, mental disturbances, and skin rashes in sensitive individuals.

SALICYLIDES. Any of several crystalline derivatives of salicylic acid (*see for toxicity*) from which the water has been removed.

SALVE. An unctuous adhesive composition or substance applied to wounds or sores; a healing ointment.

SAMBUCUS.   See Elder Flowers.
SANDALWOOD OIL.   Used in perfume. It is the pale yellow, some-what viscous volatile oil obtained by steam distillation from the dried ground roots and wood of the plant. A strong, warm, persistent odor, soluble in most fixed oils. Also used as a food flavoring. May produce skin rash in the hypersensitive, especially if present in high concentrations in expensive perfumes.
SANDARAC GUM.   Resin from a plant grown in Morocco. Light yellow, brittle, insoluble in water. Used in tooth cements, varnishes, and for gloss and adhesion in nail lacquers. Also used as an incense. No known toxicity.
SANGUINARIA. Bloodroot.   Derived from the dried roots and rhizome of the North American herb. The resin is used to soothe the skin, and its reddish juice stanches blood when used in styptic pencils. No known toxicity.
SANTALOL.   Alcohol from sandalwood used in fragrances. See Sandalwood Oil.
SAPONIFICATION.   The making of soap, usually by adding alkalies to fat, with glycerol. To saponify is to convert to soap.
SAPONIN.   Any of numerous natural glycosides—natural or synthetic compounds derived from sugars—that occur in many plants such as soapbark, soapwort, or sarsaparilla. Characterized by their ability to foam in water. Yellowish to white, acrid, hygroscopic. In powder form they can cause sneezing. Extracted from soapbark or soapwort and used chiefly as a foaming and emulsifying agent and detergent; also to reduce surface tensions, produce fine bubble lather in shaving creams, shampoos, bath oils, and dry shampoos. No known skin toxicity.
SARCOSINES.   Found in starfish and sea urchins and also formed from caffeine. Sweetish, crystalline acids used in dentifrices as an antienzyme to prevent tooth decay. Because of their excellent foaming qualities, they are also used in shampoos. No known toxicity.
SASSAFRAS OIL.   Used in dentifrices, perfumes, soaps, and powders to correct disagreeable odors. It is the yellow to reddish yellow volatile oil obtained from the roots of the sassafras. It is 80 percent safrole (*see*) and has the characteristic odor and taste of sassafras. Applied to insect bites and stings to relieve symptoms; also a topical antiseptic and used medicinally to break up intestinal gas. May produce dermatitis in hypersensitive individuals.
SD ALCOHOLS 3-A; 23-H; 38-B; 38-F; 39-B; 39-C; 40; 40-A; 40-B; 40-C; 46.   All ethyl alcohols denatured (*see*) in accordance with government regulations.

SEBACIC ACID. Decanedioic Acid.   Colorless leaflets, sparingly soluble in water and soluble in alcohol. Manufactured by heating castor oil with alkalies or by distillation of oleic acid (*see*). The esters of sebacic acid are used as plasticizers in cosmetics. No known toxicity.

SELENIUM SULFIDE. Selsun®.   Yellow, solid or brownish powder, insoluble in water. Discovered in 1807 in the earth's crust. Used in antidandruff shampoos. Can severely irritate the eyes if it gets into them while hair is being washed. Occupational exposure causes pallor, nervousness, depression, garlic odor of breath, gastrointestinal disturbances, skin rash, and liver injury in experimental animals.

SEQUESTERING AGENT.   A preservative, which prevents physical or chemical changes affecting color, flavor, texture, or appearance of a product. Ethylenediamine Tetraacetic acid (EDTA) is an example. It prevents adverse effects of metals in shampoos.

SERINE.   An amino acid (*see*), nonessential, taken as a dietary supplement. It is a constituent of many proteins. See Proteins.

SERPENTARIA EXTRACT. Snakeroot. Snakeweed.   Extracted from the roots of Rauwolfia Serpentina, its yellow rods turn red upon drying. Used in the manufacture of resins, and as a bitter tonic. No known toxicity when applied to the skin but can affect heart and blood pressure when ingested.

SESAME OIL.   An emollient extracted from the seeds of an East Indian herb. Substitute for olive and other oils in sunscreen preparations, nail bleaches, hair-grooming aids, emollients, massage creams, baby preparations, shampoos, soaps, and lubricating creams. Used also in the manufacture of edible oils and oleomargarine. No known toxicity.

SESAME SEED.   See Sesame Oil.

SETTING LOTIONS.   Wave-setting lotions, which women apply before rolling their hair in rollers or pins, depend on the hair-swelling ability of the water contained in them and the gum film that dries and holds the hair in place. The natural gums commonly used in such preparations are tragacanth, karaya, acacia, and quince seed, as well as sodium alginate from seaweed. Synthetic gums such as sodium carboxymethyl cellulose and methylcellulose are also used but tend to flake when dry (*see all*). A typical setting lotion may consist of karaya gum dissolved in ethyl alcohol and then mixed with water, glycerin, and perfume. A generally harmless product, but there have been some cases of scalp irritation reported to the FDA in recent years.

SHAMPOOS.   Shampoos are of relatively recent origin because people used to wash their hair with soap. The original products were made of coconut oil and castile soap. In 1930 the liquid detergent shampoos were introduced, followed by the cream type, and then the liquid cream shampoos. Today, shampoos are packaged in plastic tubes or bottles, aerosol cans, jars, and glass. They have various special purposes, such as mending split ends or curing dandruff. They contain a variety of ingredients ranging from eggs to herbs. A soap shampoo today still may contain about 25 percent coconut oil, some olive oil, about 15 percent alcohol, and 50 percent glycerol and water. The soapless shampoo cream may contain 50 percent sodium lauryl sulfate, some sodium stearate (*see both*), and about 40 percent water. The liquid shampoo is the most popular today and usually contains a detergent such as triethanolamine dodecylbenzene sulfonate, ethanolamide of lauric acid (*see both*), perfume, and water. Cream shampoos may have the same ingredients as the liquid but in different proportions to obtain a cream, and they usually contain lanolin. Special shampoos contain such things as dehydrated egg powder or herbs. Opacifying agents such as stearyl and cetyl alcohol (*see both*) may be added to cream lotion types. Various sequestering agents (*see*) may be used to make the water soft to remove the film, and to make the hair shinier. Various finishing agents such as mineral oil and lanolin may be added to make the hair lustrous. Water-absorbing materials such as glycerin and sorbitol (*see*) are used as conditioning agents; these two increase the water absorption of the hair and make it more pliable and less brittle. Antiseptics such as bithionol (*see*) are used to make antiseptic shampoos. Preservatives such as *p*-hydroxybenzoic acid and sodium hexametaphosphate (*see both*) may also be used. Ingestion of detergents can cause gastric irritation. Shampoos are among the most frequently cited in complaints to the FDA. Reports include eye irritation, scalp irritation, tangled hair, loss of hair, rash, shortness of breath due to product's fumes, hardened hair, swelling of hands, face, and arms, and split and fuzzy hair.

SHARK-LIVER OIL.   A rich source of Vitamin A believed to be beneficial to the skin. A brown fatty oil obtained from the livers of the large predatory fish. Used in lubricating creams and lotions. No known toxicity.

SHAVING CREAMS.   Dry hair is hard and difficult to cut with a razor. The object of a shaving cream is to make the hair softer and easier to save. Brushless shave creams are emulsions of oil and water, really vanishing creams rather than soaps. Not as efficient as the lathering type, it usually requires that the beard (or legs) be washed with soap and water. Shaving creams, which must be applied, are soaps with small but copious bubbles known as lather. They can be applied with a brush or with an aerosol. Aerosol shaving creams produce foam. This foam is applied directly to the beard and are the most popular form used today. Some men still use the older shaving creams offered in a cake or stick. The American Medical Association recommends that men with dry or soap sensitive skin use brushless shave creams that, because of their emollient properties, soothe the skin and do not dry it out. Men with oily skin, on the other hand, should use the lather-type cream applied by aerosol or brush. The AMA also points out that thorough washing and rinsing of the face in hot water or applying a hot wet towel for a few minutes before shaving will soften a beard as well as any cream.

SHAVING LOTIONS. Preshave and After-Shave.   Most preshave lotions are designed to be used before shaving with an electric razor. Some are made for a regular razor and usually contain coconut oil, fatty acids, triethanolamine, alkyl arylpolyethylene glycol ether (a dispersant), water, and perfume. Preshave preparations temporarily tighten the skin to facilitate cutting the hairs. Electric razor preshave products may contain aluminum phenolsulfonate, menthol, camphor (*see all*), water, and perfume dissolved in alcohol. An oily type of preshave lotion may contain isopropyl myristate or isopropyl palmitate (*see*), 74.5 percent alcohol, and perfume. After-shave lotions are supposed to soothe the skin, which may have been irritated by shaving. The earliest were merely substitutes for water. At the end of the nineteenth century talcum powder appeared among men's shaving products. Then barbershop preparations such as bay rum and witch hazel came into use. By 1916 manufacturers were actively promoting men's toiletries, and today perfume is as common in men's products as it is in women's. After-shave lotions fall into two categories: alcoholic and nonalcoholic. The most common ingredients of the alcoholic type are, in addition to alcohol, glycerin, water, certified color, and perfume. Menthol may be added to give that cool feeling to the skin. Some antiseptic such as hexachlorophene, bithionol, or quaternary ammonium compounds may also be added (*see all*). Alum may be used for its astringent-styptic effect; also allantoin (*see*) to promote rapid healing of razor nicks. The after-shave nonalcoholic product resembles hand lotion. In fact, hand lotion may be substituted by the consumer. Such products may be prepared from stearic acid, triethanolamine, cetyl alcohol, glycerin (*see all*), distilled water, and very small amounts of lanolin and a preservative such as *p*-hydroxybenzoic acid (*see*). Many other fats, waxes, and emulsifying agents may be added. Antiseptics and the soothing allantoin, as well as coloring and perfume, may be incorporated into this type of preparation. However, the best beard softener is still water. Reports of problems to the FDA include the product igniting on the face from a lighted cigarette, face irritation, burned skin and peeling, and eye irritation.

SHELLAC. Used in hair lacquer. It is the resinous excretion of certain insects feeding on appropriate host trees, usually in India. As processed for marketing, the lacca that is formed by the insects may be mixed with small amounts of arsenic trisulfide (for color) and with rosin. White shellac is free of arsenic. It is also used as a candy glaze and polish. May cause allergic reactions.

SHORTENINGS. See Salad Oil.

SIENNA. Used to color face powder. It is made from any of the various earthy substances that are brownish yellow when raw, and orange red to reddish brown when burnt. They are in general darker in color and more transparent in oils than ochers. No known toxicity.

SILICA. A white powder, slightly soluble in water, that occurs abundantly in nature and is 12 percent of all rocks. Sand is a silica. Upon drying and heating in a vacuum, hard transparent porous granules are formed that are used as absorbent and adsorbent material in toilet preparations, particularly skin protectant creams. Also used as a coloring agent. See Silicones.

SILICATES. Salts or esters derived from silicic acid (*see*). Any of numerous insoluble complex metal salts that contain silicon and oxygen and that constitute the largest group of minerals, and with quartz make up the greater part of the earth's crust (as rocks, soils, and clays). Contained in building materials such as cement, concrete, bricks, and glass. No known toxicity.

SILICEOUS EARTH. Purified silica (*see*) by boiling with diluted acid and washing through a filter. Used in face masks. No known toxicity.

SILICIC ACID. Silica Gel. White gelatinous substance obtained by the action of acids on sodium silicate (*see*). Odorless, tasteless, inert, white fluffy powder when dried. Insoluble in water and acids. Absorbs water readily. Used in face powders, dentifrices, creams, talcum powders as an opacifier. Soothing to skin. No known toxicity.

SILICONES. Any of a large group of fluid oils, rubbers, resins, and compounds derived from silica (*see*), and which are water repellent, skin adherent, and stable over a wide range of temperatures. Used in after-shave preparations, hair-waving preparations, nail driers, hair straighteners, hand lotions, and protective creams. Used commercially in waterproofing and lubrication. No known toxicity when used externally.

SILK POWDER.   Coloring agent in face powders and soaps obtained from the secretion of the silkworm. A white solid, which is insoluble in water. Causes severe allergic skin reactions and when inhaled, or ingested, systemic reactions.

SILVER.   White metal not attacked by water or atmospheric oxygen. Used as a catalyst (*see*) and as a germicide and coloring in cosmetics. Prolonged absorption of silver compounds can lead to a grayish blue discoloration of the skin. May be irritating to the skin and mucous membranes.

SILVER NITRATE.   A germicide, antiseptic, and astringent in cosmetics and a coloring agent in metallic hair dyes. Odorless, colorless, transparent, and poisonous. A white crystalline salt, it was used as a nineteenth-century hair dye. It darkens with exposure to light in the presence of organic matter. Silver combines readily with protein and turns brown. Disadvantages are that it may cause unpleasant off shades and make the hair stiff. It is also adversely affected by permanent waving. On the skin, it may be caustic and irritating. If swallowed, it causes severe gastrointestinal symptoms and frequently death.

SILVER SULFATE.   See Silver Nitrate.

SIMETHICONE.   An antifoam compound, a silicone oil, white, viscous, liquid. Used as an ointment base ingredient. A topical drug vehicle and skin protectant. Used medicinally to break up intestinal gas. No known toxicity.

SINGLE FLORALS.   A basic type of perfume that has a definite fragrance of one flower, such as lily of the valley, carnation, or rose. This does not mean that only one note (see Body-Note) is used. Such perfumes require skillful blending to surround the desired single floral with other notes to give it power and beauty without intruding on the single theme.

SISAL. Agave Lechuguilla.   A wax and intermediate (*see*) obtained from a plant native to the Mexican desert. The dust is irritating to the respiratory tract and may cause allergic asthma. Skin toxicity unknown.

SKATOLE.   Used in perfumery as a fixative (*see*). A constituent of beetroot, feces, and coal tar. Gives a violet color when mixed with iron and sulfuric acid. No known toxicity in humans.

SKIN BLEACH. There are a variety of products for removing freckles, age spots (chloasma), flat moles, postinflammatory changes, and even naturally dark skin. The original bleaching creams contained ammoniated mercury (*see*), and many of today's creams still do. Mercury may produce some temporary lightening of the skin by causing sloughing of the outer skin, thus reducing the number of dark pigment cells near the surface. Mercury frequently causes allergic reactions and can have adverse effects internally even though it is only applied to the skin. More efficient bleaching creams today use hydroquinone (*see*), which may cause some lightening of the skin in light- but not dark-skinned blacks. After treatment is stopped, repigmentation almost always occurs. Some powerful hydroquinone products can produce blotches, allergic reactions, and other undesirable side effects. According to the American Medical Association, bleach products are useful for treating limited areas where excessive pigmentation is the result of an abnormal process. For instance, they may be of limited use in treating melasma, "the mask of pregnancy," that is, the excessive skin pigmentation fairly common in pregnant women and women taking birth control pills. The use of bleach cream is a long-term process and often the only benefit is from the lubricating effect of the cream base, which relieves dryness of the skin. The bases of the creams and ointments are usually petrolatum, mineral oil, lanolin, or vanishing creams of the stearate type (*see all*). Active ingredients and carriers and scents include acetic acid, alcohol, bismuth compounds, citric acid, glycerin, hydrogen peroxide, hydroquinone, monobenzone, oxalic acid, potassium carbonate, potassium chlorate, rose water, borate, sugar, benzoin, zinc oxide, and zinc peroxide (*see all*). Among problems reported to the FDA were symptoms of mercury poisoning, swelling of the face and neck, jerking of hands, skin rash, burns, and stomach distress. Mercury was banned from cosmetics in 1973.

SKIN BRACER. There is little difference between shaving lotions (*see*) and skin bracers. A skin bracer may have a high alcohol content and may also be used as a body refresher after a bath or shower. It is made mostly of water, alcohol, and perfume. Toxicity depends upon ingredients.

SKIN FRESHENER. Fresheners are weaker than astringents (*see*). They are usually clear liquids designed to make the skin feel cool, "tightened," and refreshed. May contain about 60 percent witch hazel, about 15 percent camphorated alcohol, 24 percent alcohol, and 1 percent citric acid. May also contain arnica, bay rum, boric acid,

brucine sulfate, chamomile, floral scents, glycerin, lactic acid, magnesia, menthol, lavender oil, phosphoric acid, talc, benzoin, and aluminum salts (*see all*). Few complaints have been received by the FDA, but included were rash and contents of the bottle separating.
SLIPPERY ELM BARK.   Bark from the North American elm. Fragrant and sticky, it contains much mucilage and powder. Mixed with hot water, it forms a fawn-colored mass. Used as a demulcent (*see*). No known toxicity.
SOAP.   The oldest cleanser, usually a mixture of sodium salts of various fatty acids (*see*). In liquid soaps, potassium instead of sodium salts is used. Bar soaps vary in contents from brand to brand, depending on the fats or oils used. Sodium hydroxide (*see*) makes a strong soap, fatty acids a mild soap. So-called "neutral" soaps actually are alkaline, with pH (*see*) around 10 (compared to skin, which is 5 to 6.5 pH) when dissolved in water. Neutrogena soap, a clear, much-promoted mild soap, is composed of triethanolamine (*see*) instead of sodium hydroxide, and is nonalkaline. Superfatted soaps, which are among the most popular brands, are advertised as preventing dryness. They are made with an abundance of fatty acids or oils, which are supposed to serve as emollient residues on the skin. Many soaps include antibacterial ingredients to combat skin infections and odor. Hexachlorophene and salicylamides (*see both*) are used. Both may have disadvantages. Soaps are also used in toothpaste, tooth powder, and shaving creams. Soap is usually made by the saponification (*see*) of a vegetable oil with caustic soda. Hard soap consists largely of sodium oleate or sodium palmitate (*see both*) and is used medicinally as an antiseptic, detergent, or suppository. Complaints to the FDA concerning soap include finding metal particles in the soap, allergic reactions, eye irritations, and rashes.
SOAPWORT. Fuller's Herb. Saponaria.   A European and middle Asian perennial herb that has a coarse pink or white flower and foams like soap bubbles when scratched. Substituted for soap in shampoos. No known toxicity.
SODIUM ACETATE. Sodium Salt of Acetic Acid.   A preservative and alkalizer in cosmetics. Transparent crystals highly soluble in water. In industrial forms, it is used in photography and dyeing processes and in foot warmers because of its heat retention ability. Medicinally it is used as an alkalizer and as a diuretic to reduce body water. No known toxicity.
SODIUM ALGINATE.   An emollient used in baby lotions, hair lacquers, wave sets, and shaving creams. It is the sodium salt of alginic

acid extracted from brown seaweed. Occurs as a white to yellowish fibrous or granular powder, nearly odorless and tasteless. Dissolves in water to form a viscous, colloidal solution and is used in cosmetics as a stabilizer, thickener, and emulsifier. No known toxicity.

SODIUM ALUM. See Alum.

SODIUM ALUMINUM CHLORHYDROXY LACTATE. The sodium salt of lactic acid and aluminum chlorohydrate (*see both*).

SODIUM ALUMINUM LACTATE. See Lactic Acid.

SODIUM ASCORBATE. See Ascorbic Acid.

SODIUM BENZOATE. An antiseptic and preservative used in eye creams, vanishing creams, and toothpastes. White odorless powder or crystals, with a sweet antiseptic taste. Once used medicinally for rheumatism and tonsillitis. Now used as a preservative in margarine, codfish, and bottled soft drinks. No known toxicity for external use.

SODIUM BICARBONATE. *Bicarbonate of Soda. Baking Soda.* Used in effervescent bath salts, mouthwashes, and skin-soothing powders. It is an alkali. Its white crystals or powder are used in baking powder, as a gastric antacid, as an alkaline wash, and to treat burns. Used also as a neutralizer for butter, cream, fluid milk, and ice cream. Essentially harmless to the skin but when used on very dry skin in preparations that evaporate, it leaves an alkaline residue that may cause irritation.

SODIUM BISULFITE. *Sodium Acid Sulfite.* An inorganic salt used as an antiseptic, antifermentative in cosmetic creams, mouthwashes, bleaches, perfumes, and hair dyes, and to remove warts. White crystalline powder with a characteristic odor and foul taste. In its aqueous solution, it is an acid. Concentrated solutions are highly irritating to the skin and mucous membranes.

SODIUM BORATE. Used in freckle lotions, nail whiteners, liquefying (cleansing) creams, and eye lotions a as preservative and emulsifier. Hard odorless powder insoluble in water, it is a weak antiseptic and astringent for mucous membranes. Used also in bath salts, foot preparations, scalp lotions, permanent wave solutions, and hair-setting lotions. Has a drying effect on the skin and may cause irritation. Continued use of a shampoo containing it will cause the hair to become dry and brittle.

SODIUM BROMATE. In organic salt. Colorless, odorless crystals that liberate oxygen. Used as a solvent. See Potassium Bromate for toxicity.

SODIUM C14-16 OLEFIN SULFONATE. *Bioterge.* See Sulfonated Oils.

SODIUM CAPRYLATE.   See Palm Oil.

SODIUM CARBONATE. Soda Ash.   Small odorless crystals or powder that occurs in nature in ores and is found in lake brines or seawater. Absorbs water from the air. Has an alkaline taste and is used as an antacid and reagent (*see*) in permanent wave solutions, soaps, mouthwashes, shampoos, foot preparations, bath salts, and vaginal douches. Ingestion may produce corrosion of the gastrointestinal tract, vomiting, diarrhea, circulatory collapse, and death. It can cause skin or eye damage and is the cause of scalp, forehead, and hand rash when in cosmetics.

SODIUM CARBONATE PEROXIDE.   See Sodium Carbonate.

SODIUM CARBOXYMETHYL CELLULOSE.   Used in setting lotions. It is an artificial gum that dries and leaves a film on the hair. Prepared by treating alkali cellulose with sodium chloroacetate. See Cellulose Gums.

SODIUM CARRAGEENAN.   Sodium salt of carrageenan (*see*).

SODIUM CETEARYL SULFATE.   Sodium salt of a blend of cetyl and stearyl alcohol (*see both*) sulfuric acid esters. A wax used as a surface-active agent (*see*). No known toxicity.

SODIUM CETYL SULFATE.   Marketed in the form of a paste. Contains alcohol, sodium sulfate (*see*), and water. A surface-active agent (*see*). No known toxicity.

SODIUM CHLORIDE.   Common table salt. Used as an astringent and antiseptic in mouthwashes, dentifrices, bubble baths, soap, bath salts, and eye lotions. It consists of opaque white crystals. Odorless, with a characteristic salty taste, and absorbs water. Used topically to treat inflammed lesions. Diluted solutions are not considered irritating, but upon drying water is drawn from the skin and may produce irritation. Salt workers have a great deal of skin rashes. Also reported to irritate the roots of the teeth when used for a long time in dentifrices.

SODIUM CITRATE.   White odorless crystals, granules, or powder with a cool salty taste. Stable in air. Used as a sequestering agent (*see*) to remove trace metals in solutions and as an alkalizer in cosmetic products. No known skin toxicity.

SODIUM COCAMINOPROPIONATE.   See Coconut Oil.

SODIUM COCOMONOGLYCERIDE SULFATE.   See Coconut Oil.

SODIUM COCOYL ISETHIONATE.   See Cocaminopropionate.

SODIUM COCOYL SARCOSINATE.   See Sarcosines.

SODIUM COCYL GLUTAMATE.   A softener. See Glutamate.

SODIUM DECYL SULFATE. See Sodium Decylbenzene Sulfonate.
SODIUM DECYLBENZENE SULFONATE. Used in commercial detergents. May cause skin irritations.
SODIUM DEHYDROACETATE. Dehydroacetic Acid. A preservative; white, odorless, powdered, with an acrid taste. Used as a plasticizer, fungicide, and bacteria killer in cosmetics; also an antienzyme ingredient in dentifrices, allegedly to prevent decay, and a kidney tube blocking agent. Can cause impaired kidney function. Large doses can cause vomiting, ataxia, and convulsions. There are no apparent allergic skin reactions.
SODIUM DIHYDROXYETHYL GLYCINATE. See Dioctyl Sodium Sulfosuccinate.
SODIUM DODECYLBENZENESULFONATE. An anionic detergent used in cosmetic bath products and in creams. It may irritate the skin. Will cause vomiting if swallowed. See Sodium Lauryl Sulfate.
SODIUM ERYTHORBATE. A white odorless powder used as an antioxidant in cosmetics. No known toxicity.
SODIUM FLUORIDE. Used in toothpastes to prevent tooth decay and as an insecticide, disinfectant, and preservative in cosmetics. Can cause nausea and vomiting when ingested and even death, depending upon the dose. Tooth enamel mottling has also been reported. No known skin toxicity.
SODIUM GLYCERYL OLEATE PHOSPHATE. See Glyceryl Monostearate.
SODIUM HEXAMETAPHOSPHATE. Graham's Salt. Used in bath salts, bubble baths, permanent wave neutralizers, and shampoos. An emulsifier, sequestering agent (*see*), and texturizer. Used in foods and potable water to prevent scale formation and corrosion. Because it keeps calcium, magnesium, and iron salts in solution, it is an excellent water softener and detergent. No known toxicity to the skin or scalp.
SODIUM HYDROGENATED TALLOW GLUTAMATE. See Glutamate and Tallow.
SODIUM HYDROSULFITE. Sodium Dithionate. A bacterial inhibitor and antifermentative. Slight odor. White or grayish white crystalline powder that oxidizes in air. No known toxicity to the skin.
SODIUM HYDROXIDE. Caustic Soda. Soda Lye. An alkali and emulsifier in liquid face powders, soaps, shampoos, cuticle removers, hair straighteners, shaving soaps, and creams. White or nearly white pellets, flakes, or sticks. Readily absorbs water. Also a modifier for

food starch, a glazing agent for pretzels, and a peeling agent for tubers and fruits. The FDA banned use of more than 10 percent in household liquid drain cleaners. If too much alkali is used, dermatitis of the scalp may occur. Its ingestion causes vomiting, prostration, and collapse. Inhalation causes lung damage.

SODIUM IODATE. Used in dusting powder and to soothe the skin. White crystalline powder. Antiseptic, particularly to the mucous membranes. No known skin toxicity.

SODIUM IODIDE. White, odorless, water-absorbing crystals. Slowly becomes brown on exposure to air. See Sodium Iodate.

SODIUM ISETHIONATE. See Sodium Hydroxide.

SODIUM LACTATE. Plasticizer substitute for glycerin. Colorless, thick, odorless liquid miscible with water, alcohol, and glycerin. Solution is neutral. No known toxicity.

SODIUM LAURAMINOPROPIONATE. See Propionic Acid.

SODIUM LAURATE. See Sodium Lauryl Sulfate.

SODIUM LAURETH SULFATE. See Sodium Lauryl Sulfate.

SODIUM LAUROYL GLUTAMATE. A softener. See Glutamate.

SODIUM LAUROYL SARCOSINATE. See Sarcosines.

SODIUM LAUROYLISETHIONATE. See Sodium Lauryl Sulfate.

SODIUM LAURYL BENZENE SULFONATE. See Sodium Lauryl Sulfate.

SODIUM LAURYL SULFATE. A detergent, wetting agent, and emulsifier used in bubble baths, emollient creams, cream depilatories, hand lotions, cold permanent waves, soapless shampoos, and tooth-pastes. Prepared by sulfation of lauryl alcohol followed by neutralization with sodium carbonate. Faint fatty odor; also emulsifies fats. May cause drying of the skin because of its degreasing ability, but generally nontoxic to the skin.

SODIUM LAURYL SULFOACETATE. See Sodium Lauryl Sulfate.

SODIUM MAGNESIUM SILICATES. See Silicates.

SODIUM METAPHOSPHATE. A water softener, emulsifier, sequestering agent (*see*), and texturizer used in tooth powders and tooth-pastes. Colorless, glassy, transparent granules or flakes, soluble in water. Controls dandruff; soothing to the scalp. No known toxicity to the skin.

SODIUM METASILICATE. An alkali usually prepared from sand and soda ash. Used in detergents. Caustic substance, corrosive to the skin, harmful if swallowed, and cause of severe eye irritations. Preserves eggs in egg shampoos.

SODIUM METHYL COCOYL TAURATE. See Ox Bile.

SODIUM METHYL NAPHTHALENE SULFONATE. Used in solutions for peeling fruits and vegetables with a water rinse and in detergents. See Sulfonated Oils.

SODIUM METHYL OLEOYL TAURATE. See Ox Bile.

SODIUM n-METHYL-n-OLEYL TAURATE. See Ox Bile.

SODIUM MONOFLUOROPHOSPHATE. See Sodium Fluoride.

SODIUM MONOUNDECYLENAMIDO MEA-SULFOSUCCINATE. See Dioctyl Sodium Sulfosuccinate.

SODIUM MONUNDECYLENAMIDO MEA-SULFOSUCCINATE. See Sulfonated Oils.

SODIUM MYRETH SULFATE. See Myristyl Alcohol.

SODIUM MYRISTYL SULFATE. See Myristyl Alcohol.

SODIUM NITRATE. Chile Saltpeter. Colorless, transparent crystals, white granules or powder. Used as a catalyst in enamels and color fixatives. No known toxicity to the skin.

SODIUM NONOXYNOL-1 SULFATE. See Nonoxynol-2.

SODIUM NONOXYNOL-9 PHOSPHATE. See Nonoxynol-2.

SODIUM OLEATE. Sodium Salt of Oleic Acid. White powder, fatty odor, alkaline. Used in soaps. No known toxicity.

SODIUM OXALATE. Sodium Salt of Oxalic Acid. White odorless, crystalline powder used as an intermediate (*see*), in hair dyes, and as a texturizer. Toxic when ingested and may be irritating to the skin.

SODIUM PALMITATE. Sodium salt of palmitic acid (*see*).

SODIUM PCA. A naturally occurring component of human skin that is believed to be in part responsible for its moisture binding capacity. It is highly water absorbing and at high humidity dissolves in its own water hydration. Application of this compound to the skin as a humectant (*see*) is claimed to increase softness. No known toxicity.

SODIUM PERBORATE. White crystals, soluble in water, used as a reagent (*see*), antiseptic, deodorant, bleach, and in dentifrices as a tooth whitener; also in foot baths and detergents. Ulcerations of the mouth have been reported in its use in dentifrices. Strong solutions that are very alkaline are irritating if permitted on skin.

SODIUM PERSULFATE. Oxidizing agent that promotes emulsion used in hair-waving solutions. An inorganic salt; a crystalline powder, which decomposes in moisture and warmth. Can cause allergic reactions in the hypersensitive. Highly irritating to the skin and mucous membranes.

SODIUM o-PHENYL PHENATE. Sodium Salt of o-Phenylphenol. Antiseptic, germicide, fungicide, and preservative used in cosmetic creams and lotions. Yellow flakes or powder with a slight soap odor.

Soluble in water, alcohol, and acetone. A skin irritant. Regarded as more effective than phenol (*see*) and cresol (*see*) because it has greater germ-killing power and may be used in smaller concentrations and is less irritating to the skin, although it is often considered toxic by some cosmetic companies for use in products.

SODIUM PHOSPHATE.   Buffer and efflorescent used in manufacture of nail enamels and detergents. White crystalline or granular powder; stable in air. Without water, it can be irritating to the skin but has no known toxicity in cosmetics.

SODIUM PICRAMATE. Sodium Salt of Picramic Acid.   See Picramic Acid.

SODIUM POLYMETHACRYLATE.   See Acrylates.

SODIUM POLYNAPHTHALENE SULFONATE.   See Sulfonated Oils.

SODIUM PROPIONATE.   Colorless or transparent odorless crystals that gather water in moist air. Used as a preservative in cosmetics and foodstuffs to prevent mold and fungus. It has been used to treat fungal infections of the skin, but can cause allergic reactions.

SODIUM PYRITHIONE. Sodium Omadine®.   Sodium salt of pyrithione, a zinc derivative. Used as a fungicide and bacteria killer. Used in dandruff shampoos to control dandruff and as an antibacterial in soaps and detergents. No known toxicity.

SODIUM SACCHARIN.   An artificial sweetener in dentifrices, mouthwashes, and lipsticks. In use since 1879. Pound for pound it is 300 times as sweet as natural sugar but leaves a bitter aftertaste. It was used along with cyclamates in the experiments that led to the ban on cyclamates in 1969. The FDA has proposed restricting saccharin to 15 milligrams per day for each kilogram of body weight or one gram a day for a 150-pound person. On the FDA's priority list for further safety testing.

SODIUM SALICYLATE.   A white, odorless, crystalline powder used in shaving creams and in sunscreen lotions. Becomes pinkish upon long exposure to light; also used to lower fever and kill pain in animals. Mild antiseptic, analgesic, and preservative. May cause nasal allergy. See Salicylates.

SODIUM SESQUICARBONATE.   White crystals, flakes, or powder produced from sodium carbonate (*see*). Soluble in water. Used as an alkalizer in bath salts, shampoos, tooth powders, and soaps. Irritating to the skin and mucous membranes. May cause an allergic reaction in the hypersensitive.

SODIUM SILICATE. Water Glass. An anticaking agent preserving eggs, detergents in soaps, depilatories, and protective creams. Consists of colorless to white or grayish white crystallike pieces or lumps. These silicates are almost insoluble in cold water. Strongly alkaline. As a topical antiseptic can be irritating and caustic to the skin and mucous membranes. If swallowed, it causes vomiting and diarrhea.

SODIUM SOAP. See Sodium Stearate.

SODIUM STANNATE. An inorganic salt. White or colorless crystals. Absorbs water from air. Used in hair dyes. No known toxicity.

SODIUM STEARATE. 92.82 percent stearic acid (*see*). A fatty acid used in deodorant sticks, stick perfumes, toothpastes, soapless shampoos, and shaving lather. A white powder with a soapy feel and a slight tallowlike odor. Slowly soluble in cold water or cold alcohol. Also a waterproofing agent and has been used to treat skin diseases and in suppositories. One of the least allergy causing of the sodium salts of fatty acids. Nonirritating to the skin.

SODIUM STEAROYL LACTYLATE. See Lactic Acid.

SODIUM SULFATE. Salt Cake. Occurs in nature as the minerals mirabilite and thenardite. Used chiefly in the manufacture of dyes, soaps, and detergents. Also as a chewing gum base and used medicinally to reduce body water. It is a reagent (*see*) and a precipitant; mildly saline in taste. Usually harmless when applied in toilet preparations. May prove irritating in concentrated solutions if applied to the skin, permitted to dry, and then remain. May also enhance the irritant action of certain detergents.

SODIUM SULFITE. An antiseptic, preservative, and antioxidant used in hair dyes. White to tan pink, odorless or nearly odorless powder having a cooling, salty, sulfurlike taste. It has been used medicinally as a topical antifungal agent. No known skin toxicity.

SODIUM SULFONATE. A bubble bath clarifying agent and a dispersing agent used to make shampoos clear. See Sulfonated Oils.

SODIUM TALLOW SULFATE. A defoamer, emollient, intermediate (*see*), and surface-active agent. A mixture of sodium alkyl sulfates. See Tallow.

SODIUM THIOSULFATE. A germicide and bleach. A sequestrant used in hair dye. Consists of large crystals or coarse powder, which is deliquescent in moist air. Insoluble in alcohol. In photography, used under the name "hypo." Also employed in tanning, the preparation of mordants (*see*), the manufacture of other chemicals, and to prevent fermentation in dyeing. No known toxicity but it is being studied by the FDA.

SORBIC ACID   223

SODIUM TRIPOLYPHOSPHATE. STPP. Used in bubble baths and as a texturizer in soaps. It is a crystalline salt, moderately irritating to the skin and mucous membranes. Ingestion can cause violent purging. See Sodium Phosphate.

SODIUM UNDECYLENATE. A sodium salt of undecylenic acid. Occurs in sweat. A topical fungicide. Liquid or crystals with a sweaty odor prepared from castor oil. No known toxicity.

SODIUM XYLENE SULFONATE. Used as a solubilizer. An isolate from wood and coal tar. No known toxicity. See Xylene.

SOLUBILIZATION. The process of dissolving in water such substances as fats and liquids that are not readily soluble under standard conditions by the action of a detergent or similar agent. Technically, a solubilized product is clear because the particle side of an emulsion is so small that light is not bounced off the particle. Solubilization is used in colognes and clear lotions. Sodium sulfonates (see) are common solubilizing agents.

SOLUBILIZED VAT BLUE 5. A vat dye (see) in the form of a soluble sodium salt of a sulfuric acid monoester. Vat dyes are more expensive than ordinary dyes and are used in pastels. See Vat Dyes for toxicity.

SOLUBILIZED VAT DYES. These are the sodium salts of vat dyes. They are comparatively expensive but give excellent penetration and fastness. See Vat Dyes.

SOLVENT. A liquid capable of dissolving or dispersing one or more substances. Methyl ethyl ketone is an example of a solvent.

SOLVENT BLACK 5. Classed chemically as an azine color. Similar to Acid Black 2 (see).

SOLVENT BLUE 16. Classed chemically as an anthraquinone color. No further information available. See Colors.

SOLVENT BROWN 43. Irgacet Brown 2RL®. A commercial color. No further information available. See Colors.

SOLVENT DYE. Generally insoluble in water, but dissolves in varying degrees in different organic media in liquid, molten, and solid forms. These include alcohols, oils, fats, and waxes. The use of a solvent dye depends upon fastness to light and adequate solubility, in powders, resins, and plastics. Can be irritating to the skin.

SOLVENT YELLOW 63. Acetosol Yellow RLS. Classed chemically as an azo (see) color.

SOLVENT YELLOW 90. Irgacet Yellow GL. A commercial color. See Colors.

SORBETH-20. See Sorbitol.

SORBIC ACID. A white free-flowing powder obtained from the berries of the mountain ash. Also made from chemicals in the factory. Used in cosmetics as a preservative and humectant. A mold and yeast inhibitor, it is also used in foods and beverages. Used as a replacement for glycerin in emulsions, ointments, embalming fluids, mouthwashes, dental creams, and various cosmetic creams. A binder for toilet preparations and a plasticizer. Produces a velvetlike feel when rubbed on skin. In large amounts sticky. Practically nontoxic but may cause a slight skin irritation in susceptible people.

SORBITAN LAURATE. Span 20®. Oily liquid, insoluble in water, soluble in alcohol and oils. An emulsifier in cosmetic creams and lotions; a stabilizer of essential oils in water. No known toxicity.

SORBITAN OLEATE. Sorbitan Monooleate. An emulsifying agent, defoaming agent, and plasticizer. No known toxicity.

SORBITAN PALMITATE. Span 40®. Derived from sorbitol (*see*). An emulsifier in cosmetic creams and lotions; a solubilizer of essential oils in water. Light yellow wax, insoluble in water, soluble in solvents. No known toxicity.

SORBITAN SESQUIOLEATE. See Sorbitol.

SORBITAN SESQUISTEARATE. See Sorbitan Stearate.

SORBITAN STEARATE. Sorbitan Monostearate. An emulsifier in cosmetic creams and lotions, a solubilizer of essential oils in water. Used in antiperspirant deodorants, cake makeup, hand creams, hair tonics, rouge, and suntan creams. Manufactured by reacting edible commercial stearic acid with sorbitol (*see both*). Light cream to tan colored, hard, waxy, solid, with a bland odor and taste. Soluble at temperatures above its melting point in toluene, ethanol, methanol, and ether. No known toxicity.

SORBITAN TRIISOSTEARATE. See Stearic Acid.

SORBITAN TRIOLEATE. See Sorbitol.

SORBITAN TRISTEARATE. An emulsifier and alternate for sorbitan stearate (*see*). No known toxicity.

SORBITOL. A humectant. Gives a velvety feel to skin. Used as a replacement for glycerin in emulsions, ointments, embalming fluid, mouthwashes, dental creams, and various cosmetic creams. A binder for toilet preparations and a plasticizer. Also used in hair sprays, beauty masks, cuticle removers, foundation cake makeup, hand lotions, liquid powders, dentifrices, after-shave lotions, deodorants, antiperspirants, shampoos, and rouge. First found in the ripe berries of the mountain ash; it also occurs in other berries (except grapes) and in cherries, plums, pears, apples, seaweed, and algae. Consists of white hygroscopic powder, flakes, or granules, with a sweet taste. It is a texturizing agent and a sequestrant. Also used in antifreeze, in foods as a sugar substitute, in writing inks to ensure a smooth flow from the point of the pen, and to increase the absorption of vitamins in pharmaceutical preparations. Medicinally used to reduce body water and for intravenous feedings. No known toxicity if taken externally. However, if ingested in excess, it can cause diarrhea and gastrointestinal disturbances; also it may alter the absorption of other drugs making them less effective or more toxic.

SOY FLOUR. See Soybean Oil.

SOYA ACID. See Soybean Oil.

SOYA STEROL. See Soybean Oil.

SOYAMINE. See Soybean Oil.

SOYATRIMONIUM CHLORIDE. Soya Trimethyl Ammonium Chloride. See Ammonium Chloride and Soya Acid.

SOYBEAN OIL. Extracted from the seeds of plants grown in eastern Asia, especially Manchuria, and the Midwestern United States. Used in manufacture of soaps, shampoos, and bath oils. Pale yellow to brownish yellow. Also used in the manufacture of margarine and other foodstuffs. May cause allergic reactions, including hair damage and acnelike pimples.

SPEARMINT OIL. Used in perfumes, perfumed cosmetics, and toothpaste. It is the essential volatile oil obtained by steam distillation from the fresh aboveground parts of the flowering plant grown in the United States, Europe, and Asia. Consists of 50 percent carvone (*see*) and is colorless, yellow, or yellow green, with the characteristic taste and odor of spearmint. Also used as a flavoring agent in food. May cause allergic reactions such as skin rash.

SPEEDWELL. Used in shampoos. It is an herb, a common hairy perennial grown in Europe, with pale blue or lilac flowers. It has a reputation among herbalists of inducing sweating and restoring healthy body functions; also an expectorant tonic, a treatment for hemorrhages, and a medication for skin diseases. No known toxicity.

SPERMACETI. Cetyl Palmitate. Used as a base for ointments and creams, and as an emollient in cleansing creams. Also in shampoos, cold creams, and other creams to improve their gloss and increase their viscosity. Derived as a wax from the head of the sperm whale. Generally nontoxic but may become rancid and cause irritations.

SPICY BOUQUETS. One of the basic perfume types, they derive their characteristics from spice-giving ingredients, such as cinnamon, clove, vanilla, and ginger, but they may also be characterized by spiciness inherent in the flower notes of the perfume composition.

SPIKE LAVENDER OIL. French Lavender. Used in perfumes. A pale yellow stable oil obtained from a flower grown in the Mediterranean region. A lavenderlike odor. Used in cologne, toilet water, blended with lavender oil, soaps, and varnishes. Used also for fumigating to keep moths from clothes and in food and beverage flavorings. No known toxicity.

SPRAY DEODORANT. With Antiperspirant Action. Usually contains aluminum phenol sulfonate, 10 percent; propylene glycol, 5 percent; alcohol, 85 percent; and perfume. Dispenses by aerosols (*see*). See Deodorants.

SQUALANE. Obtained from shark-liver oil. Stable in air and oxygen. A lubricant and perfume fixative. Nontoxic.

SQUALENE. From shark-liver oil. Occurs in smaller amounts in olive oil, wheat germ oil, rice bran oil. A faint agreeable odor. Absorbs oxygen and becomes viscous. Practically insoluble in water but soluble in solvents. A bactericide, an intermediate (*see*) in hair dyes, and used in surface-active agents. No known toxicity.

STABILIZER. A substance added to a product to give it body and to maintain a desired texture, for instance, the stabilizer alginic acid, which is added to cosmetics.

STANNIC CHLORIDE. Tin Tetrachloride. A thin, colorless, fuming, caustic liquid, soluble in water, used as a mordant (*see*) in metallic hair dye and as a reagent (*see*) in perfumes and soaps. May be highly irritating to the eyes and mucous membranes.

STANNOUS CHLORIDE. Tin Dichloride. An antioxidant, soluble in water, and a powerful reducing agent, particularly in the manufacture of dyes. May be irritating to the skin and mucous membranes.

STANNOUS FLUORIDE. Tin Difluoride. Fluoristan. Prepared by dissolving tin in hydrofluoric acid. Used in dentifrices as a decay preventative. No known toxicity.

STANNOUS PYROPHOSPHATE. Salt of tin. It is relatively nontoxic and poorly absorbed from the gastrointestinal tract. Used as a mordant (*see*). No known toxicity when used externally. See Phosphate.

STARCH. Acid Modified. Pregelatinized and Unmodified. Starch is stored by plants and is taken from grains of wheat, potatoes, rice, corn, beans, and many other vegetable foods. Insoluble in cold water or alcohol but soluble in boiling water. Comparatively resistant to naturally occurring enzymes, and this is why processors modify starch to make it more digestible. Used in dusting powders, dentifrices, hair colorings, rouge, dry shampoos, baby powders, emollients, and bath salts. Soothing to the skin and used to treat rashes. Used internally as a gruel in diarrhea. Allergic reaction to starch in toilet goods includes stuffy nose and other symptoms due to inhalation. Absorbs moisture and swells causing blocking and distension of the pores leading to mechanical irritation. Particles remain in pores and putrefy, accelerated by sweat.

STARCH DIETHYLAMINOETHYL ETHER.   See Starch.

STEARALKONIUM CHLORIDE.   See Quaternary Ammonium Compounds.

STEARALKONIUM HECTORITE.   See Hectorite.

STEARAMIDE.   An emulsifier. Colorless leaflets, insoluble in water. No known toxicity. See Stearic Acid.

STEARAMIDE DEA. Stearic Acid Diethanolamide.   See Stearamide.

STEARAMIDE DIBA STEARATE.   See Stearamide.

STEARAMIDE MEA STEARATE.   See Stearamide.

STEARAMIDE MIPA.   See Stearamide.

STEARAMIDOPROPYL DIMETHYLAMINE.   See Dimethylamine.

STEARAMINE OXIDE.   See Stearyl Alcohol.

STEARATES.   See Stearic Acid.

STEARETH-2.   A polyoxyethylene (*see*) ether of fatty alcohol. The oily liquid is used as a surfactant. No known toxicity.

STEARETH-10.   See Steareth-2.

STEARETH-20.   See Steareth-2.

STEARETH-30.   See Steareth-2.

STEARIC ACID.   Used in deodorants and antiperspirants, liquid powders, foundation creams, hand creams, hand lotions, liquefying creams, hair straighteners, protective creams, shaving creams, and soap. Occurs naturally in butter acids, tallow, cascarilla bark, and in other animal fats and oils. A white waxy natural fatty acid, it is the major ingredient used in making bar soap and lubricants. A large percentage of all cosmetic creams on the market contains it. It gives pearliness to hand creams. It is also used as a softener in chewing gum base, for suppositories, and as a food flavoring. It is a possible sensitizer for allergic people. See Fatty Acids.

STEARIC HYDRAZIDE.   See Stearic Acid.

STEARMIDOETHYL DIETHYLAMINE.   See Diethylamine.

STEAROXY DIMETHICONE.   See Dimethicone.

STEAROYL SARCOSINE.   See Sarcosines.

STEARTRIMONIUM CHLORIDE.   See Quaternary Ammonium Compounds.

STEARYL ALCOHOL. Stenol. A mixture of solid alcohols prepared from sperm whale oil. Unctuous white flakes, insoluble in water, soluble in alcohol and ether. Can be prepared from sperm whale oil. A substitute for cetyl alcohol (*see*) to obtain a firmer product at ordinary temperatures. Used in pharmaceuticals, cosmetic creams, for emulsions, as antifoam agent, and lubricant; also in depilatories, hair rinses, and shampoos. No known toxicity.

STEARYL HEPTOATE. A solid. See Heptanoic Acid.

STEARYL LACTATE. An emulsifier that occurs in tallow and other animal fats as well as vegetable oils. No known toxicity.

STEARYLDIMETHYL AMINE. See Stearyl Alcohol.

STEROL. Any class of solid complex alcohols from animals and plants. Cholesterol is a sterol and is used in hand creams. Sterols are lubricants in baby preparations, emollient creams and lotions, emulsified fragrances, hair conditioners, hand creams, and hand lotions. No known toxicity.

STIFFENING AGENT. An ingredient to add body to shaving soaps and creams. Many of the gums, such as karaya and carrageenan (*see*), are used for this purpose.

STILLINGIA. Chinese Tallow Tree. Queen's Root. Yaw Root. Dried roots of a southeastern United States plant. An acrid resin; fixed and volatile oils. Used as a drying oil in cosmetics. Formerly used medicinally to induce vomiting. No known toxicity in cosmetics.

STONEROOT. Horse Balm. Used for its constituents of resin, saponin, and tannic acid (*see all*). An erect smooth perennial; a strong-scented herb of eastern North America with pointed leaves. It produces a chocolate-colored powder with a peculiar odor and bitter astringent taste. Soluble in alcohol. No known toxicity.

STORAX. Styrax. Sweet Oriental Gum. Used in perfumes. It is the resin obtained from the bark of an Asiatic tree. Grayish brown, fragrant semiliquid, containing also styrene and cinnamic acid (*see both*). Once used in medicine as a weak antiseptic and as an expectorant. Also used in food and beverage flavorings. Moderately toxic when ingested. Can cause urinary problems when absorbed through the skin. Can cause skin irritation, welts, and discomfort when applied topically.

STPP. See Sodium Tripolyphosphate.

STRAMONIUM. Thorn Apple. Jimpson Weed. Stinkweed. Used in antiperspirants for its antiperspirant properties. Obtained from the dried leaves and flowering tops of a plant grown in Europe, Asia, and the United States. Leaves contain 0.25 to 0.45 percent alkaloids consisting of atropine, hyoscyamine, and scopolamine. It is used medicinally to treat intestinal spasms, asthma, and Parkinson's disease. No known toxicity.

STRAWBERRY.   Fresh ripe strawberries are reputed to contain ingredients that soften and nourish the skin. Widely used in natural cosmetics today. No scientific evidence of benefit or harm.

STRONTIUM HYDROXIDE.   Used chiefly in making soaps and greases in cosmetics. Colorless, water-absorbing crystals or white powder. Absorbs carbon dioxide from the air. Very alkaline in solution. Also used in refining beet sugar and separating sugar from molasses. Irritating when applied to the skin.

STRONTIUM SULFIDE.   Used in depilatories, it is less irritating than sodium sulfide and more efficient than calcium sulfide. It is a sulfur compound that occurs free or in combination, such as in gypsum; found most often in volcanic areas. It is a gray powder with the odor of hydrogen sulfide and is slightly soluble in water. May cause skin rash, irritation, and hair breakage.

STYPTIC PENCIL.   A cylindrical stick comprised of potassium aluminum sulfate, glycerin, and talc. It has an astringent effect, tending to contract or bind. Designed to check blood flow, primarily from razor nicks. May sting but nontoxic.

STYRENE.   Obtained from ethylbenzene by taking out the hydrogen. Colorless to yellowish oily liquid with a penetrating odor. Used in the manufacture of cosmetic resins and in plastics. May be irritating to the eyes and mucous membranes, and in high concentrations it is narcotic.

STYRENE/ACRYLATE COPOLYMER.   An opacifier. See Acrylates.

STYRENE/ACRYLIC ACID COPOLYMER.   See Styrene and Acrylates.

SUCCINIC ACID.   Occurs in fossils, fungi, lichens, etc. Prepared from acetic acid (*see*). Odorless; very acid taste. The acid is used as a plant growth retardant. A germicide and mouthwash and used in perfumes and lacquers; also a buffer and neutralizing agent. Has been employed medicinally as a laxative. No known toxicity in cosmetic use. Large amounts injected under the skin of frogs kills them.

SUCCINIC ANHYDRIDE.   A starch modifier. See Succinic Acid.

SUCROSE. Sugar. Cane Sugar. Saccharose.   A sweetening agent and food, a starting agent in fermentation production, a preservative and antioxidant in pharmacy, a demulcent, and a substitute for glycerin (*see*). Workers who handle raw sugar often develop rashes and other skin problems. Sugar when it oxidizes with sweat draws water from the skin and causes chapping and cracking. Among infections, erosions and fissures around the nails can occur. No known toxicity in cosmetics.

SUCROSE ACETATE ISOBUTYRATE.   A denaturant for rubbing alcohols (*see both*).

SUCROSE OCTAACETATE.   A preparation from sucrose (*see*). A synthetic flavoring. Used in adhesives and nail lacquers; a denaturant for alcohol. No known toxicity.

SUGAR.   See Sucrose.

SULFAMIC ACID.   A cleaning agent in cosmetics and used in the manufacture of hair dyes and lakes (*see*). A strong white crystalline acid used chiefly as a weed killer, in cleaning metals, and as a flameproofing and softening agent. Moderately irritating to the skin and mucous membranes.

SULFATED CASTOR OIL.   See Turkey-Red Oil.

SULFIDES.   Inorganic sulfur compounds that occur free or in combination with minerals. They are salts of weak acids and are used as hair dissolving agents in depilatories. They are skin irritants and may cause hair breakage.

SULFONAMIDE FORMALDEHYDE.   A solvent in nail polish and the most frequent cause of nail polish dermatitis, which generally affects the neck and eyelids. Sulfonamide is the amide of a sulfonic acid. See Formaldehyde and Sulfonamide Resins.

SULFONAMIDE RESINS. Sulfanilamide.   The use of sulfonamides dates back to 1934 when the dye prontosil was shown to cure certain infections caused by bacteria. Sulfonamides are bacteria killers and are used to inhibit germ growth in cosmetics. They are also used to contribute depth, gloss, flow adhesion, and water resistance to films in nail lacquers. They may cause allergic reactions.

SULFONATED OILS. Sulfated.   Used in soapless shampoos and hair sprays as an emulsifier and wetting agent. Shampoos containing sulfonated oils were first manufactured in 1880 and were effective in hard or soft water. Sulfonated oils strip color from both natural and colored hair and can bring out streaks. Sulfated castor oil has been used to remove all types of dye. Applied to hair and heated, it is used as a hair treatment. Sulfonated oils are used in hair tonics that remain on the hair as hairdressings. May cause drying of the skin.

SULFUR. Brimstone.   A mild antiseptic in antidandruff shampoos, dusting powders, ointments, and permanent wave solutions. Occurs in the earth's crust in the free state and in combination. Used in hair tonic to stimulate the scalp and in acne creams and lotions. Also a stimulant to healing when used on skin rashes; derivatives are used in depilatories. May cause irritation of the skin. A case of death was reported following absorption of cold wave solution containing free sulfur through the scalp. Death was attributed to acute hydrogen sulfide poisoning.

SUNBURN LOTION. Includes Creams and Sprays. Serious sunburn requires medical attention and the use of oils, including butter, is not recommended. However, there are a number of soothing lotions, creams, and sprays for mild sunburn on the market. A common formula includes mineral oil, light, 10 percent; lanolin, 2.5 percent; propylene glycol, 2.5 percent; triethanolamine oleate, 5.0 percent (*see all*) ; and water, distilled, 80 percent.

SUNFLOWER SEED OIL. Oil obtained by milling the seeds of the large flower produced in the USSR, India, Egypt, and Argentina. A bland, pale yellow oil, it contains large amounts of Vitamin E (see Tocopherols) and forms a "skin" after drying. Used in food and salad oils, and in resin and soap manufacturing. No known toxicity.

SUNSCREEN PREPARATIONS. See Suntan Preparations.

SUNTAN PREPARATIONS. Preparations to prevent painful sunburn that encourage a change in pigmentation (a tan) have a large market. Suntan creams (emulsions) may contain para-aminobenzoic acid, mineral oil, sorbitan stearate, poloxamers (*see all*), and 62 percent water. A suntan ointment may contain petrolatum, stearyl alcohol, mineral oil, sesame oil, and calcium stearate (*see all*). A suntan lotion may contain methyl anthranilate, propylene glycol, ricinoleate, glycerin (*see all*), and about 65 percent alcohol and 10 percent water. A suntan oil may contain salicylates, about 40 percent sesame oil (*see both*), and 55 percent mineral oil. Suntan preparations may also contain alcohol, p-aminobenzoic acid and derivatives, benzy salicylate, cinnamic acid derivatives, and coumarin (*see all*). A common suntan oil formula includes 2-ethyl hexyl salicylate, 5 percent; sesame oil, 40 percent; mineral oil, about 55 percent; perfume; color; and an antioxidant. Complaints to the FDA concerning sunscreen preparations include rash, blisters, burns, yellowed skin, and even death.

SURFACE-ACTIVE AGENT. A surfactant, a compound that makes it easier to effect contact between two surfaces: in cosmetics usually between the skin and a cream or lotion. A surfactant reduces surface tension, for example, such as lecithin (*see*) does.

SURFACTANT. See Surface-Active Agent.

SWEET ALMOND OIL. Used in perfumes and in the manufacture of fine soaps and emollients. Expressed from the seeds of a plant.

Colorless or pale yellow, oily liquid, almost odorless, with a bland taste. Insoluble in water. No known skin toxicity. See Bitter Almond Oil.

SWEET BAY OIL. Used in perfumes. It is the yellow green volatile oil from the leaves of the laurel. No known toxicity.

SWEET BIRCH. See Methyl Salicylate.

SWEET MARJORAM OIL. Marjoram Pot. Used in perfumery and hair preparations. The natural extract of the flowers and leaves of two varieties of the fragrant marjoram. Also a food flavoring. No known toxicity.

SYLVIC ACID. See Abietic Acid.

SYNTHETIC SPERMACETI. See Spermaceti.

T

TALC. French Chalk. Used in baby powders, dusting powders, face powders, eye shadows, liquid powders, protective creams, dry rouges, face masks, foundation cake makeups, skin fresheners, foot powders, and face creams. Gives a slippery sensation to powders and creams. Talc is finely powdered native magnesium silicate, a mineral. It usually has small amounts of other powders such as boric acid or zinc oxide added as a mild antiseptic. White to grayish white and insoluble in water. Also used as a coloring agent. Prolonged inhalation can cause lung problems because it is similar in chemical composition to asbestos, a known lung irritant and cancer-causing agent.

TALL OIL. Liquid Rosin. A by-product of the pine wood pulp industry and used to scent shampoos, soaps, varnishes, and fruit sprays. "Tall" is Swedish for "pine." Dark brown liquid; acrid odor. A fungicide and cutting oil. It may be a mild irritant and sensitizer.

TALLOW. The fat from the fatty tissue of bovine cattle and sheep in North America. Used in shaving creams, lipsticks, shampoos, and soaps. White, almost tasteless when pure, and generally harder than grease. May cause eczema and blackheads.

TALLOW ACID. See Tallow.

TALLOW AMIDE. See Tallow.

TALLOW AMINE. See Tallow.

TALLOW AMINE OXIDE. See Tallow.

TALLOW TRIMONIUM CHLORIDE. Tallow Trimethyl Ammonium Chloride. See Quaternary Ammonium Compounds.

TALLOWETH-6. See Tallow.

TANGERINE OIL.   Derived from any of various citrus fruits that have deep orange to almost scarlet rinds. Used in perfumes and flavor-ings. Yellow to yellowish green. Can cause allergic reactions.

TANNIC ACID.   Used in sunscreen preparations, eye lotions, and antiperspirants. It occurs in the bark and fruit of many plants, notably in the bark of the oak and sumac, and in cherry, coffee, and tea. Used medicinally as a mild astringent, and when applied it may turn the skin brown. Also used in food flavorings. Tea (*see*) contains tannic acid, and this explains its folk use as an eye lotion. Excessive use in creams or lotions in hypersensitive persons may lead to irrita-tion, blistering, and increased pigmentation.

TARRAGON.   Used in perfumery to improve the note (*see*) of chypre-type perfumes (*see*). Derived from the dried leaves of a small European perennial wormwood herb. Pale yellow oil grown for its aromatic, pungent foliage. Also used in making pickles and vinegar. No known toxicity.

TARS.   An antiseptic, deodorant, and bug killer. Any of the various dark brown or black bituminous, usually odorous, viscous liquids or semiliquids obtained by the destructive distillation of wood, coal, peat, shale, and other organic materials. Used in hair tonics and sham-poos. Can be irritating to the skin and may cause allergic reactions.

TARTARIC ACID.   Effervescent acid used in bath salts, denture powders, nail bleaches, hair-grooming aids, hair rinses, depilatories, and hair coloring. Widely distributed in nature in many fruits but usually obtained as a by-product of winemaking. Consists of colorless or translucent crystals or a white fine-to-granular crystalline powder, which is odorless and has an acid taste. In strong solutions it may be mildly irritating to the skin.

TBS.   See Tribromsalan.

TCC.   See Triclocarban.

TEA.   The leaves, leaf buds, and internodes of plants having leaves and fragrant white flowers, prepared and cured to make an aromatic beverage. Cultivated principally in China, Japan, Ceylon, and other Asian countries. Tea is a mild stimulant and its tonic properties are due to the alkaloid caffeine; tannic acid (*see*) makes it astringent. Used by natural cosmeticians to reduce the puffiness around the eyes. A cotton or gauze pad is dampened with a weak solution of tea and placed on the eyelids. One then lies down for five to ten minutes. No known toxicity.

TEA-COCO HYDROLYZED PROTEIN.   See Proteins.

TEA-COCOATE.   The triethanolamine (*see*) soap derived from coconut fatty acids (*see*). No known toxicity.

TEA-COCYL GLUTAMATE.   A softener. See Glutamate.
TEA-DODECYLBENZENESULFONATE.   See Triethanolamine.
TEA-HYDROGENATED TALLOW GLUTAMATE.   A softener. See Glutamate.
TEA-LAURAMINOPROPIONATE.   See Lauryl Alcohol.
TEA-LAUROYL GLUTAMATE.   A softener. See Glutamate.
TEA-LAURYL BENZENE SULFONATE. Triethanolamine Lauryl Benzene Sulfonate.   See Sodium Lauryl Sulfate.
TEA-LAURYL SULFATE.   See Sodium Lauryl Sulfate.
TEA-MONOOLEAMIDOSULFOSUCCINATE.   See Succinic Acid.
TEA-OLEATE. Triethanolamine Oleate.   See Ethanolamines.
TEA-PCA.   See Ethanolamines.
TEA-TREE OIL.   The essential oil obtained from the leaves of an Australian tree. Light yellow. Used as a germicide in cosmetics. Eleven to 13 times as powerful as carbolic acid. Penetrates the skin quickly and accelerates the healing of skin disorders. No known toxicity.
TEA-TRIDECYLBENZENESULFONATE. Triethanolamine Tridecylbenzene Sulfonate.   See Ethanolamines.
TERPENES.   A class of unsaturated hydrocarbons (*see*). Its removal from products improves their flavor and gives them a more stable stronger odor. However, some perfumers feel that the removal of terpenes destroys some of the original odor. Has been used as an antiseptic. No known toxicity.
TERPINEOL.   Viscous, colorless liquid with sweet lilac odor. Found in many essential oils. Used in fragrances, as a clarifying agent, and in shampoos. It is also a denaturing agent for fats for soap manufacture and has been used as an antiseptic. In concentration of 2 percent may cause a burn, but less than 1 percent in cosmetics is apparently harmless. Can be a sensitizer.
TESTOSTERONE PROPIONATE.   Isolated from bull testes. It is the propionic ester of the male hormone. Used in creams and lotions. White crystals, freely soluble in alcohol and ether. Soluble in vegetable oils. See Hormone Creams and Lotions.
TETRABROMOFLUORESCEIN. Eosine Yellowish.   A red color with a yellowish or brownish tinge prepared by adding bromine fluorescein (*see*). Used to make lipstick indelible and to color nail polish. It may be a photosensitizer (*see*), causing inflammed lips and respiratory and gastrointestinal symptoms. Tetrabromofluorescein is also used to dye wool, silk, and paper.
TETRACHLOROROETHYLENE. Perchloroethylene.   A colorless,

nonflammable liquid, with a pleasant odor, made from acetylene and chlorine. Used as a solvent in cosmetics. Used medicinally against hookworms. Narcotic in high doses. Has a drying action on the skin and can lead to adverse skin reactions.

TETRAHYDROFURFURYL ACETATE.   See Furfural.

TETRAHYDROFURFURYL ALCOHOL.   A liquid that absorbs water and is flammable in air. A solvent for cosmetic fats, waxes, and resins. Mixes with water, ether, and acetone. Mildly irritating to the skin and mucous membranes. See Furfural.

TETRAHYDROGERANYL HYDROXY STEARATE.   See Stearic Acid.

TETRAHYDROGERANYL MYRISTATE PALMITATE.   See Myristic Acid.

TETRAHYDROXYPROPYL ETHYLENEDIAMINE.   Clear, colorless, thick liquid, a component of the bacteria-killing substance in sugar cane. It is strongly alkaline and is used as a solvent and preservative. It may be irritating to the skin and mucous membranes and may cause skin sensitization.

TETRAMETHYLAMMONIUM   CHLORIDE.   See   Quaternary Ammonium Compounds.

TETRAMETHYLTHIURAM DISULFIDE. Thiram.   An agriculture chemical found to be a degerming agent when incorporated in soap. A disinfectant, insecticide, fungicide, and bacteria killer. May cause irritation of nose, throat, and skin. Also, it may be harmful if swallowed or inhaled. One should not breathe the spray or mist and should avoid contact with eyes, skin, or clothing. Causes allergic skin reactions.

TETRASODIUM EDTA. Sodium Edetate.   Powdered sodium salt that reacts with metals. A sequestering agent and chelating agent (*see both*) used in cosmetic solutions. Can deplete the body of calcium if taken internally. See Ethylenediamine Tetraacetic Acid. No known toxicity on the skin.

TETRASODIUM PYROPHOSPHATE. TSPP.   A sequestering agent, clarifying agent, and buffering agent for shampoos. Produced by molecular dehydration of dibasic sodium phosphate. Insoluble in alcohol. A water softener in bath preparations. No known toxicity.

TEXTURIZER.   A chemical used to improve the texture of various cosmetics. For instance, in creams that tend to become lumpy, calcium chloride (*see*) is added to keep them smooth.

TFC. Tricloflucarban.   A disinfectant used in cosmetics. No known toxicity.

THEOPHYLLINE. A white powder, soluble in water. Occurs in tea. Its current use in cosmetics has not been revealed. However, it is a smooth muscle relaxant, heart stimulant, and ·diuretic (reduces body water). It can cause nausea and vomiting if ingested. The toxic dose in man is only 2.9 milligrams per kilogram of body weight.

THIAMINE HCL. Vitamin B₁. A white crystalline powder used in emollients and as a dietary supplement in prepared breakfast foods, peanut butter, milk, and noodle products. Acts as a helper in important energy-yielding reactions in the body. Practically all commercial Vitamin B₁ is synthetic. The vitamin is destroyed by alkalies and alkaline drugs. No known toxicity.

THICKENING AGENTS. Substances to add body to lotions and creams. Those usually employed include such natural gums as sodium alginate and pectins.

THIODIGLYCOL. See Thioglycolic Acid Compounds.

THIODIPROPIONIC ACID. An acid freely soluble in hot water, alcohol, and acetone. Used as an antioxidant for soap products and polymers (*see*) of ethylene. No known toxicity.

THIOGLYCEROL. Used in soothing skin lotions. Prepared by heating glycerin (*see*) and alcohol. Yellowish, very viscous liquid, with a slight sulfur odor. Used to promote wound healing. No known toxicity.

THIOGLYCOLIC ACID COMPOUNDS. Prepared by the action of sodium sulfhydrate on sodium chloroacetate. A liquid with a strong unpleasant odor; mixes with water and alcohol. The ammonium and sodium salts are used in permanent wave solutions and as a hair straightener. The calcium salts are used in depilatories, hair-waving solutions, and lotions. Thioglycolates can cause hair breakage, skin irritations, severe allergic reactions, and pustular reactions.

THIOINDIGOID DYE. See Vat Dyes and Indigo.

THIOKOL. One of the first synthetic elastomers (*see*), it is used in face masks and nail enamels and in the manufacture of rubbers and resins. No known toxicity.

THIOLACTIC ACID. Used in depilatories and hair-waving preparations. See Thioglycolic Acid.

THIOSALICYLIC ACID. Sulfur yellow flakes, slightly soluble in hot water. Used in the manufacture of cosmetic dyes. No known toxicity.

THIOUREA. It forms compounds with metallic salts. Used in the manufacture of cosmetic resins and as an accelerator in hair dyes.

Formerly used as an antithyroid agent. As little as 1 milligram per kilogram of body weight has produced death in rats. Continued use can affect the blood. Single dose not found very toxic. No known toxicity on the skin.

THREONINE.   An essential amino acid (*see*); the last to be discovered (1935). Prevents the buildup of fat on the liver. Occurs in whole eggs, skim milk, casein, and gelatin.

THUJA OIL.   See White Cedar Leaf Oil.

THYME.   Used to flavor toothpaste, mouthwashes, and to scent perfumes, after-shave lotions, and soap. It is a seasoning from the dried leaves and flowering tops of the wild creeping thyme grown in Eurasia and throughout the United States. Used as a flavoring in cough medicines. Once used as a muscle relaxant. May cause skin irritation.

THYMOL.   Used in mouthwashes, toothpastes, shampoos, and hair tonics. Obtained from the essential oil of lavender, origanum oil, and other volatile oils. It destroys mold, preserves anatomical specimens, and is a topical antifungal agent with a pleasant aromatic odor. Ingestion can cause vomiting, diarrhea, dizziness, and heart slowdown. It is omitted from hypoallergenic cosmetics because it can cause allergic reactions.

TIN OXIDE.   A coloring agent used in cosmetics. A brownish black powder insoluble in water. No known toxicity.

TINCTURE OF BENZOIN.   See Benzoin.

TIPA-STEARATE.   See Stearic Acid.

TITANIUM DIOXIDE.   The greatest covering and tinting power of any white pigment used in bath powders, nail whites, depilatories, eyeliners, white eye shadows, antiperspirants, face powders, protective creams, liquid powders, lipsticks, hand lotions, and nail polish. Occurs naturally in three different crystal forms. Used chiefly as a white pigment and as an opacifier; also a white pigment for candy, gum, and marking ink. No known toxicity when used externally. In high concentrations the dust may cause lung damage.

TOCOPHEROLS. Vitamin E.   An antioxidant in baby preparations, deodorants, and hair-grooming aids. Obtained by the vacuum distillation of edible vegetable oils. Used as a dietary supplement and as an antioxidant for essential oils, rendered animal fats, or a combination of such fats with vegetable oils. Helps form normal red blood cells, muscle, and other tissues. Protects fat in the body's tissues from abnormal breakdown. Experimental evidence shows Vitamin E may protect the heart and blood vessels and retard aging.

TOILET SOAP. A mild, mostly pure soap made from fatty materials of high quality, usually by milling and molding to form cakes. Usually contains an emollient (*see*), perfume, color, and a stabilizer with preservatives. More pleasant to use and less drying to the skin.

TOILET WATER. The scent is similar to that of perfume, but it does not last as long and is not as strong or as expensive. Usually made by adding a large amount of alcohol to the perfume formula. In Europe it is called lotion—8 ounces of perfume oil per gallon as compared to 20 to 24 ounces per gallon for perfumes. Considered moderately toxic if swallowed. Skin reaction depends upon ingredients.

TOLUENE. Used in nail polish. Obtained from petroleum or by distilling balsam Tolu. Used chiefly as a solvent. Resembles benzene but less volatile, flammable, or toxic. May cause mild anemia if ingested, and it is narcotic in high concentrations. Being tested at the U.S. Frederick Cancer Research Center for possible cancer-causing effects.

TOLUENE-2,5-DIAMINE. See Toluene.

o-TOLYL BIGUANIDE. See Toluene.

TONER. In cosmetics, an organic pigment that is used in full strength. For example, D & C Red No. 7 (*see*).

TOOTHPASTE. See Dentifrices.

TOPCOAT. Same ingredients as in base coat (*see*) so as to give the nail enamel a greater gloss and to help prevent chipping.

TOP-NOTE. The first impression of a fragrance upon the sense of smell. The most volatile part of the perfume. It is one of the most important factors in the success of the perfume, but does not persist after the first sniff.

TRAGACANTH. See Gum Tragacanth.

TRANSLUCENT POWDER. Because it contains more titanium dioxide (*see*) than other face powders, translucent makeups are actually more opaque. But other than that, they contain the same ingredients.

TRIACETIN. Glyceryl Triacetate. Primarily a solvent for hair dyes. Also a fixative in perfume and used in toothpaste. A colorless, somewhat oily liquid with a slight fatty odor and a bitter taste. Obtained from adding acetate to glycerin (*see both*). Soluble in water and miscible with alcohol. No known toxicity in above use. Large subcutaneous injections are lethal to rats.

TRIBROMSALAN. TBS. 3,4',5-Tribromosalicylanilide. Used in medicated cosmetics; an antiseptic and fungicide. Irritating to the skin and may cause allergic reaction when skin is exposed to the sun.

Salicylanilide is an antifungal compound used to treat ringworm. TBS is in the most popular soaps to kill skin bacteria. Used as a germicide frequently replacing hexachlorophene (*see*).

TRICALCIUM PHOSPHATE.   The calcium salt of phosphate (*see*). A polishing agent in dentifrices; also an anticaking agent in table salt and vanilla powder, and a dietary supplement. No known toxicity. See Calcium Phosphate.

TRICHLOROETHANE.   Used in cosmetics as a solvent and degreasing agent. Nonflammable liquid. Insoluble in and absorbs some water. Less toxic than carbon tetrachloride, which is used in fire extinguishers. Trichloroethane solutions are irritating to the eyes and mucous membranes, and in high concentrations can be narcotic. Can be absorbed through the skin. Inhalation and ingestion produce serious symptoms ranging from vomiting to death.

TRICLOCARBAN. TCC.   A bacteria killer and antiseptic in soaps, medicated cosmetics, and cleansing creams. Prepared from aniline (*see*). No known toxicity.

TRICLOSAN.   A broad spectrum antibacterial agent that is active primarily against some types of bacteria. It is used in deodorant soaps and other cosmetic products as well as in drugs and household products. Its deodorant properties are due to the inhibition of bacterial growth. No known toxicity.

TRICRESYL PHOSPHATE. TCP.   A plasticizer in nail polishes and a strengthener in lubricants. Colorless or pale yellow liquid. Can cause paralysis many days after exposure. For instance, in 1960, approximately 10,000 Moroccans became ill after ingesting cooking oil adulterated with turbojet engine oil containing 3 percent TCP. Can be absorbed through the skin and mucous membranes, causing poisoning. Persons sensitive to the plasticizer in eyeglass frames may develop a skin rash from tricresyl. Toxic dose in man is only 6 milligrams per kilogram of body weight.

TRIDECETH-3 (PEG-3 Tridecyl Ether).   See Polyethylene Glycols.

TRIDECYL ALCOHOL.   Derived from tridecane, a paraffin hydrocarbon obtained from petroleum. Used as an emulsifier in cosmetic creams, lotions, and lipsticks. No known toxicity.

TRIDECYLBENZENE SULFONIC ACID.   See Sulfonamide Formaldehyde.

TRIDETH-3.   See Tridecyl Alcohol.
TRIDETH-6.   See Tridecyl Alcohol.

TRIDETH-10.   See Tridecyl Alcohol.
TRIDETH-12.   See Tridecyl Alcohol.
TRIETHANOLAMINE DODECYLBENZENE SULFONATE. Linear.
Made from ethylene oxide and used in bubble baths and soapless
shampoos. May be mildly irritating to the skin. See Ethanolamines.
*TRIETHANOLAMINE - d - 1 - 2 - PYRROLIDONE - 5 - CARBOXY-
METHYLATE. Triethanolamines.* A colorless liquid, soluble in
water, and used as a soap base and oil emulsifier. See Ethanolamines.
TRIETHANOLAMINE STEARATE.   Made from ethylene oxide.
Used in brilliantines, cleansing creams, foundation creams, hair lacquers, liquid makeups, fragrances, liquid powders, mascara, protective
creams, baby preparations, shaving creams and lathers, and preshave
lotions. A moisture absorber, viscous, used in making emulsions.
Cream colored, turns brown on exposure to air. May be irritating to
the skin and mucous membranes, but less so than many other amines
(*see*).
TRIETHANOLAMINE TRISODIUM PHOSPHATE.   Made from
ethylene oxide and used in cuticle softeners. May be mildly irritating
to the skin. See Ethanolamines.
TRIETHYL CITRATE. Citric Acid. Ethyl Citrate.   A plasticizer in
nail polish. Odorless, practically colorless, bitter; also used in dried
egg as a sequestering agent (*see*), and to prevent rancidity. Citrates
may interfere with laboratory tests for blood, liver, and pancreatic
function, but no known skin toxicity.
TRIETHYLENE GLYCOL.   Used in stick perfume. Prepared from
ethylene oxide and ethylene glycol. Used as a solvent. See Polyethylene Glycol for toxicity.
TRIIODOTHYRONINE.   Possesses 5 times the activity of the thyroid drug L-thyroxine used in thyroid replacement therapy. Its cur-
rent use in cosmetics has not been revealed.
TRIISOPROPANOLAMINE.   See Propyl Alcohol.
TRILANETH-4 PHOSPHATE.   See Lanolin Alcohols.
TRILAURIN.   See Lauric Acid.
TRILAURYLAMINE.   See Lauryl Alcohol.
TRIMAGNESIUM PHOSPHATE. Magnesium Phosphate, Tribasic.
Occurs in nature as the mineral bobierrite. A white crystalline
powder, it absorbs water and is used in cosmetics as an alkali. No
known toxicity.
TRIMETHYLHEXANOL.   See Hexanol.
TRIMETHYLOLPROPANE TRIOCTANOATE.   See Caprylic Acid.
TRIMYRISTIN. Glyceryl Trimyristate.   Solid triglyceride of myris-

tic acid that occurs in many vegetable fats and oils, particularly in coconut oil and nutmeg butter. White to yellowish gray, it is used as an emollient in cold creams and for shampoos. No known toxicity.
TRIOLEIN. Glyceryl Trioleate. From the Palestine olive and one of the chief constituents of nondrying oils and fats used in cosmetics. Colorless to yellowish, tasteless, odorless. Used in cosmetic creams and oils. No known toxicity.
TRIOLETH-8 PHOSPHATE. Derived from phosphoric acid and oleyl alcohol (*see both*).
TRIOLEYL PHOSPHATE. Used as an emulsifier. No known toxicity. See Oleyl Alcohol.
TRIPALMITIN. Occurs in fats and is prepared from glycerol and palmitic acid (*see both*). Insoluble in water. See Palmitic Acid for toxicity.
TRIPHENYL PHOSPHATE. A noncombustible substitute for camphor in celluloid. Colorless; insoluble in water. Stable, fireproof, and used as a plasticizer in nail polish. Causes paralysis if ingested and skin rash in hypersensitive people. Inhalation of only 3.5 milligrams per kilogram of body weight is toxic to man.
TRIPHENYLMETHANE GROUP. Tritan. Certified dyes made from the reduction (*see*) of carbon tetrachloride and benzene with aluminum chloride. Very soluble in water; affected by light and alkalies. Among the triphenylmethane group are FD & C Blue No. 1 and FD & C Green Nos. 1, 2, and 3. See Colors for toxicity.
TRIPOLYPHOSPHATE. A buffering agent in shampoos. A phosphorus salt. Used to soften water, as an emulsifier, and a dispersing agent. Can be irritating because of its alkalinity. May cause esophageal stricture if swallowed. Moderately irritating to the skin and mucous membranes. Ingestion can cause violent vomiting.
TRIS (HYDROXYMETHYL) NITROMETHANE. Crystals from ethyl acetate and benzene (*see both*). Soluble in alcohol. Inhibits bacterial growth in water systems, cutting oils, nonprotein glues, and sizings. Irritating to the skin and mucous membranes.
TRISODIUM EDTA. See Tetrasodium EDTA.
TRISODIUM HYDROXY EDTA. See Tetrasodium EDTA.
TRISODIUM HYDROXYETHYL ETHYLENEDIAMINETRIACETATE. See Tetrasodium EDTA.
TRISODIUM PHOSPHATE. Obtained from phosphate rock. Highly alkaline. Used in shampoos, cuticle softeners, bubble baths, and bath salts for its water-softening and cleansing actions. Phosphorus was formerly used to treat rickets and degenerative disorders and is

now used as a mineral supplement for foods; also in incendiary bombs and tracer bullets. Can cause skin irritation from alkalinity.

TROMETHAMINE. Made by the reduction (*see*) of nitro compounds, it is a crystalline mass used in the manufacture of surface-active agents (*see*). Used as an emulsifying agent for cosmetic creams and lotions, mineral oil, and paraffin wax emulsions. Used medicinally to correct an overabundance of acid in the body. No known toxicity.

TRUE FIXATIVE. This holds back the evaporation of the other materials. Benzoin is an example. See Fixatives.

TUBEROSE OIL. Derived from a Mexican bulbous herb commonly cultivated for its spike of fragrant white single or double flowers that resemble small lilies. Tuberose oil is used in perfumes as an absolute (*see*). Red liquid with fragrant lasting odor. Can cause allergic reaction.

TURKEY-RED OIL. One of the first surface-active agents (*see*). Used in shampoos. Contains sulfated castor oil. It has been used to obtain bright clear colors in dyeing fabrics. See Sulfonated Oils.

TURPENTINE GUM. A solvent in hair lotions, waxes, perfume soaps, and to soothe skin. It is the oleoresin (*see*) from a species of pines. Also a food flavoring. Readily absorbed through the skin. Irritating to the skin and mucous membranes. In addition to being a local skin irritant, it is a central nervous system depressant. Death from ingestion is usually due to respiratory failure. It can also cause allergic reactions.

TURTLE OIL. Extracted from the muscles and genitals of giant sea turtles. Promoted as a sensational ingredient in cosmetics, but there is no scientific proof that turtle oil is any more effective at keeping the skin supple and beautiful than any other oil. Also used in emollients and nail creams. No known toxicity.

U

ULTRAMARINE BLUE. Blue lumps or powder occurring naturally in the mineral lapis lazuli. It was originally obtained naturally from ground lapis lazuli but is now produced synthetically. Used in eye shadows, mascaras, and face powders. Also used for bluing in laundry products and for coloring tiles. Workmen packaging the powdered product suffer from nose and lung symptoms including ulceration and perforation of the wall separating the nostrils. No known toxicity in cosmetics. See Colors.

ULTRAMARINE GREEN. A synthetic pigment that is actually the intermediate (*see*) in the synthesis of ultramarine blue (*see*). See Colors.

ULTRAMARINE PINK.   A synthetic pigment. The manufacturing process is unreported but it is believed to be made by replacing sulfur with selenium or tellurium in ultramarine blue (*see*). See Colors.

ULTRAMARINE RED.   A pigment obtained by treating ultramarine violet (*see*) with hydrochloric or nitric acid. It is the acid of which ultramarine violet is the sodium salt. See Colors.

ULTRAMARINE VIOLET.   The pigment obtained by heating ultramarine blue (*see*) with ammonium chloride (*see*) or chlorine and hydrochloric acid followed by washing and drying. It is the sodium salt of ultramarine red (*see*). See Colors.

UMBELLIFERONE. 7-Hydroxycoumarin.   The umbelliferae is a family of plants to which parsley, carrots, and parsnips belong. They bear white or yellow umbrella-shaped flowers. The crystalline substance obtained from the resins of the umbelliferae is used in sunscreen preparations. No known toxicity.

UMBER.   A brown earth that is a variety of iron ore and used to color face powders. Darker than ocher and sienna because of its manganese oxides. No known toxicity.

UNDECYCLICACID. Undecanoic Acid.   See Undecylenic Acid.

UNDECYLENAMIDE DEA.   See Undecylenic Acid.

UNDECYLENAMIDE MEA. Undecylenoyl Monethanolamide.   A fungicide. See Undecylenic Acid.

UNDECYLENIC ACID.   Occurs in sweat. Obtained from ricinoleic acid (*see*). A liquid or crystalline powder, with an odor suggestive of perspiration. Used as a fungicide in cosmetics. Has been given orally but it causes dizziness, headaches, and stomach upset. No known skin toxicity.

UREA. Carbamide.   An antiseptic and deodorizer used in liquid antiperspirants, ammoniated dentifrices, roll-on deodorants, mouthwashes, hair colorings, hand creams, lotions, and shampoos. A product of protein metabolism and excreted from human urine. It is used to "brown" baked goods such as pretzels, and consists of colorless or white odorless crystals that have a cool salty taste. Medicinally, urea is used as a topical antiseptic and as a diuretic to reduce body water. Its largest use, however, is a fertilizer, and only a small part of its production goes into the manufacture of other urea products. No known toxicity.

UREA PEROXIDE.   White crystals or powder derived from urea. They absorb water from the air and are soluble in water. An antibacterial agent used as a mouth and throat disinfectant. See Urea.

UREA-FORMALDEHYDE RESIN.   Urea (*see*) is condensed with formaldehyde (*see*) to give a clear resin, which is then compounded with a filler to modify its physical properties. It is primarily used to strengthen the mechanical properties of resins (*see*), which are used in cosmetics. See Formaldehyde for toxicity.

UREASE.   An enzyme that hydrolyzes urea (*see*) to ammonium carbonate (*see*).

URIC ACID.   Prepared from urea and present in the urine of all carnivorous animals. White, odorless, tasteless crystals. Used as a sunburn preventative in lotions and creams. See Urea.

UV ABSORBER-4.   5(3,3-Dimethyl-2-Norborynliden-3 Penten-2-one).   See Absorption Bases.

UV ABSORBER-5.   See Absorption Bases.

V

VAGINAL DEODORANTS. Feminine Hygiene Sprays.   Introduced in 1966, vaginal deodorant sprays have grown very popular. Marketed as mists or powders in aerosol sprays and widely advertised as products to keep women feeling "feminine," they are designed to prevent "feminine odor" and to give that "clean feeling." Classified as cosmetics, these deodorants did not need clearance for the ingredients. Reports to the FDA of irritations and other problems from the sprays within the last two years include bladder infections, burning, itching, swelling, rash, boils in the vaginal area, and blood in the urine. Physicians recommend soap and water as more beneficial than the sprays, and that concentrating chemicals, including perfumes, in one area is not wise because of the possibility of allergic reactions and irritations. Most of the products also used hexachlorophene (*see*). Alberto Culver, the largest maker of feminine sprays (FDS), said that two laboratory studies were performed, one by Hilltop Research, with 75 women in the FDS test group, and 26 women in the soap-and-water control group. Over a five-week period 29 percent of the women using soap and water showed redness in the vaginal area but only 12 percent of the FDS users did. In the second study performed by 252 women volunteers over a period of one month of multiple FDS daily use, there was no increased hexachlorophene in the FDS users' blood. Again, in a control group using soap and water only, the irritation of the vaginal-anal area was 8 percent, whereas the incidence in FDS users was 3 percent. The FDA has recommended that a warning be placed on containers that the product not be used more than once a day

VALERIAN. See Valeric Acid.

VALERIC ACID. Used in the manufacture of perfumes. Occurs naturally in apples, cocoa, coffee, oil of lavender, peaches, and strawberries. Colorless, with an unpleasant odor. Usually distilled from valerian root. It is used also as a synthetic flavoring, and some of its salts are used in medicine. No known toxicity.

VANCIDE FP. See Captan.

VANILLA EXTRACT. Used in perfumes and flavorings. Extracted from the full-grown unripe fruit of the vanilla plant of Mexico and the West Indies. Also a food flavoring. It can cause a sensitivity to light in some persons whose skin breaks out and swells when exposed to light.

VANILLIN. Used in perfumes. Occurs naturally in vanilla and potato parings but is an artificial flavoring and scent made synthetically from eugenol (*see*) ; also from the waste of the wood pulp industry. One part vanillin equals 400 parts vanilla pods. The lethal dose in mice is 3 grams (30 grams to the ounce) per kilogram of body weight. A skin irritant that produces a burning sensation and eczema. May also cause pigmentation of the skin.

VANISHING CREAM. An emollient cream that creates the feeling of vanishing when rubbed on the skin. See Emollients.

VAT DYES. Water-soluble aromatic organic compounds. They dissolve in water when vatted with an alkaline solution of the reducing (*see*) agent sodium hydrosulfite. Good fastness. Considered low in toxicity.

VEGETABLE GUMS. Includes derivatives from quince seed, karaya, acacia, tragacanth, Irish moss, guar, sodium alginate, potassium alginate, ammonium alginate, propylene glycol alginate. All are subject to deterioration and always need a preservative. The gums function as liquid emulsions, that is, they thicken cosmetic products and make them cream. No known toxicity other than allergic reactions in hypersensitive persons.

VEGETABLE OILS. Peanut, sesame, olive, and cottonseed oil obtained from plants and used in baby preparations, cleansing creams, emollient creams, face powders, hair-grooming aids, hypoallergenic cosmetics, lipsticks, nail creams, shampoos, shaving creams, and wave sets. No known toxicity.

VETIVER OIL. Vetiverol. Stable, brown to reddish brown oil from the roots of a fragrant grass. Used in soaps and perfumes, it has an aromatic to harsh woodsy odor. No known toxicity.

VIBURNUM EXTRACT. Haw Bark. Black Extract. Extract of the fruit of a hawthorn shrub or tree. Used in fragrances and in butter, caramel, cola, maple, and walnut flavorings for beverages. Has been used as a uterine antispasmodic. No known toxicity.

VINEGAR.   Used for hundreds of years to remove lime soap after shampooing. It is a solvent for cosmetic oils and resins. Vinegar is about 4 to 6 percent acetic acid. Acetic acid occurs naturally in apples, cheese, grapes, milk, and other foods. No known toxicity.

VINYL ACETATE.   See Vinyl Polymers.

VINYL CHLORIDE.   See Vinyl Polymers.

VINYL POLYMERS.   Includes resins used in false nails and nail lacquer preparations. A major class of polymer (*see*) material widely used in plastics, synthetic fibers, and surface coatings. Such materials are derived from the polymerization of vinyl groups, which include vinyl acetate and vinyl chloride. Vinyls are made from the reaction between acetylene and certain compounds such as alcohol, phenol, and amines. Inhalation of 300 parts per million is toxic in man.

VINYL PYRROLIDONE.   See Polyvinylpyrrolidone.

VIOLET EXTRACT. Flowers and Leaves.   Green liquid with the typical odor of violet. It is taken from the plant widely grown in the United States. Used in perfumes, face powders, and for coloring inorganic pigments. May produce skin rash in the allergic.

VITAMIN A. Acetate and Palmitate.   A yellow viscous liquid insoluble in water. Used in lubricating creams and oils for its alleged skin-healing properties. Can be absorbed through the skin. Its absence from the diet leads to a loss in weight, retarded growth, and eye diseases. Its benefits on the skin are controversial. No known toxicity.

VITAMIN C.   See Ascorbic Acid.

VITAMIN D$_2$. Calciferol.   A pale yellow oily liquid, odorless, tasteless, insoluble in water. Used for its alleged skin-healing properties in lubricating creams and lotions. The absence of Vitamin D in the food of young animals leads to the development of rickets unless the animal is exposed to sunlight. It is soluble in fats and fat solvents and is present in animal fats. Absorbed through the skin. Its value in cosmetics is not proven. No known toxicity on the skin.

VITAMIN E.   See Tocopherols.

VITAMIN E ACETATE.   See Tocopherols.

VITAMIN E SUCCINATE.   See Tocopherols.

W

WATER.   The major constituent of all living matter and the ingredient used most in the cosmetic industry. Because of this fact, the industry fought labeling that required listing ingredients in descending order because water would be first most of the time. However, listing in descending order is now required. It is important that the water used in cosmetics be sterile to avoid contamination of the product. Manufacturers may also have to soften water in some areas because of the high mineral content that may affect the texture and appearance of the finished product.

WAVE SET.   See Setting Lotions.

WAXES.   Obtained from insects, animals, and plants. Waxes have a wide application in the manufacture of cosmetics. Beeswax, for instance, is a substance secreted by the bee's special glands on the underside of its abdomen. The wax is glossy and hard but plastic when warm. Insoluble in water but partially soluble in boiling alcohol. Used in hair-grooming preparations, hair straighteners, as an epilatory (hair pull) to remove unwanted hair, and as the traditional stiffening agent (*see*) in lipsticks. Wax esters such as lanolin or spermaceti (*see both*) differ from fats in being less greasy, harder, and more brittle. Waxes are generally nontoxic to the skin but may cause allergic reactions in the hypersensitive depending upon the source of the wax.

WETTING AGENT.   Any of numerous water-soluble agents that promote spreading of a liquid on a surface or penetration into a material such as skin. It lowers surface tension for better contact and absorption.

WHEAT GERM.   The golden germ of the wheat is high in Vitamin E. See Tocopherols. It is used by organic cosmetics enthusiasts to make a face mask to counteract dry skin. Here is the formula: Crush ¼ cup wheat germ plus 1 tablespoon sesame seeds with a mortar and pestle or with the back of a spoon. Add 2 tablespoons of fresh olive oil and mix well. Spread on face and neck. Leave on for 10 minutes. Remove with lukewarm water. Then rinse with cold water. Apply a rinse of chilled witch hazel (*see*).

WHEAT GERM OIL.   See Tocopherols.

WHEAT GLUTEN.   Used in powders and creams as a base. A mixture of proteins present in wheat flour and obtained as an extremely sticky yellowish gray mass by making a dough and then washing out the starch. It consists almost entirely of two proteins, gliadin and glutenin. It contributes to the porous and spongy structure of bread. No known toxicity.

WHEAT STARCH.   A product of cereal grain. It swells when water is added. Used as a demulcent, emollient, and in dusting and face powders. May cause allergic reactions such as red eyes and stuffy nose.

WHITE. Inorganic pigments are widely used to "color" cosmetics white. The most widely used are zinc oxide and titanium dioxide to whiten face powders. Also used are gloss white (aluminum hydrate), barium sulfate (blanc fixe), and alumina (*see all*).

WHITE CEDAR LEAF OIL. Oil of Arborvitae. Stable, pale yellow volatile oil obtained by steam distillation from the fresh leaves and branch ends of the eastern arborvitae. Has a strong camphoraceous and sagelike scent. Used as a perfume and scent for soaps and room sprays. Also used as a flavoring agent. Soluble in most fixed oils. See Cedar for toxicity.

WILD CHERRY. Wild Black Cherry Bark. The dried stem bark collected in autumn in North America. Used in lipsticks and cherry flavorings for food and medicines. Also used as a sedative and expectorant medicinally. No known toxicity.

WILD INDIGO ROOT. Baptisia. Bastard Indigo. A wild uncultivated plant of North America with showy yellow or blue flowers. Used as a coloring. Has been used internally and externally for various infections. No known toxicity.

WILD THYME EXTRACT. The flowering tops of a plant grown in Eurasia and throughout the United States. The dried leaves are used in emollients and fragrances and as a seasoning in foods. Has also been used as a muscle relaxant. No known toxicity.

WINTERGREEN OIL. Methyl Salicylate. Used in toothpaste, tooth powder, and perfumes. Obtained naturally from betula, sweet birch, or teaberry oil. Present in certain leaves and bark but usually prepared by treating salicylic acid with methanol (*see both*). Also used as a food and beverage flavoring. Wintergreen is a strong irritant. Ingestion of relatively small amounts may cause severe poisoning and death. Average lethal dose in children is 10 milliliters and in adults 30 milliliters. It is very irritating to the mucous membranes and skin and can be absorbed rapidly through the skin.

WISTERIA. Used in perfumes. The extract from the Asiatic, mostly woody vines of the family that produces showy blue, white, purple, or rose flowers. No known toxicity.

WITCH HAZEL. A skin freshener, local anesthetic, and astringent made from the leaves and/or twigs of *Hamamelis virginiana*. Collected in the autumn. Witch hazel has an ethanol content of 70 to 80 percent and a tannin content of 2 to 9 percent. Witch hazel water, which is what you buy at the store, contains 15 percent ethanol. See Ethanol for toxicity.

WOOD TAR. Tricosolfan and Sulfur. Tar obtained by distillation of wood and used as a preservative. See Sulfur.

WOODRUFF. Master of the Woods. Used in perfumes and sachets. Made of the leaves of an herb grown in Europe, Siberia, North Africa, and Australia. It is a symbol of spring, and has a clean fresh smell. No known toxicity.

WOOL FAT. Crude lanolin (*see*).

WRINKLE REMOVERS. Periodically, the cosmetic industry comes up with a magic ingredient that will prevent or cure wrinkles. Among such ingredients in recent years was serum albumin (from bulls) and estrogen. Another wrinkle remover contained some unidentified ingredient that irritated the skin so that it "puffed up" and the wrinkles "filled out." Turtle oil, natural proteins, and polyunsaturates, among many others, were supposed to feed aging skin but there is no apparent biochemical or physiological activity in any of them. It is difficult for the Federal Trade Commission to get after promoters of wrinkle creams. By the time the agency gets the manufacturers to court, it has taken several years and a great deal of money and manpower. Then all the manufacturer has to do is open up under a different name and start selling wrinkle creams all over again. Unfortunately, there is nothing that can treat wrinkles other than surgical procedures.

X

XANTHAN GUM. See Xanthene Group.

XANTHENE GROUP. Xanthene is a coal tar derivative. A group of brillant fluorescent yellow to pink to bluish red dyes characterized by the presence of the xanthene nucleus, which produces the iridescent effect. Widely used in bright lipstick-staining colors. Phthalein and rhodamine dyes are examples. See D & C Red No. 10, for instance. Each batch of xanthene colors must be certified by the federal government as safe for use. See Coal Tar for toxicity.

XYLENE. A colorless, refractive liquid obtained from coal tar and coal gas with a characteristic odor, and which burns with a smoky flame. A solvent used in the manufacture of synthetic resins and of lacquers and dyes used in cosmetics; also a degreaser in cosmetics. Solvents and degreasers dissolve skin fat, leading to dry skin. Xylene is a skin irritant and can cause allergic reactions.

XYLOCAINE®. Lidocaine. Used in after-shave lotions. A local anesthetic that interferes with the transmission of nerve impulses, thereby effecting local anesthetic action. Recommended by manufacturer for topical use on mucous membranes only. Can cause allergic reactions. Not permitted in cosmetics in Switzerland.

Y

YARROW.   A strong scented, spicy, wild herb used in astringents and shampoos. Its astringent qualities have caused it to be recommended by herbalists for greasy skins. According to old herbal recipes, it prevents baldness when the hair is washed regularly with it. Used medicinally as an astringent, tonic, and stimulant. May cause a sensitivity to sunlight and artificial light, in which the skin breaks out and swells.

YLANG-YLANG OIL.   A light yellow very fragrant liquid obtained in the Philippine Islands from flowers. Used for perfumes and as a food and beverage flavoring. May cause allergic reactions.

YUCCA EXTRACT. Mohave Extract. Joshua Tree. Adam's Needle. Derived from a Southwestern United States plant and used as a base for organic cosmetics and as a root beer flavoring for beverages and ice creams. No known toxicity.

Z

ZEIN.   Used in face masks, nail polishes, and as a plasticizer. It is the principal protein in corn. Obtained as a yellowish powder by extracting corn gluten with an alcohol; also used to make textile fibers, plastics, printing inks, varnishes, and other coatings and adhesives. No known toxicity.

ZINC.   A white brittle metal insoluble in water and soluble in acids or hot solutions of alkalies. Widely used as an astringent for mouthwashes and as a reducing agent (*see*) and reagent (*see*).

ZINC CARBONATE.   A cosmetic coloring agent, it is a crystalline salt of zinc occurring in nature as smithsonite. See Zinc for toxicity.

ZINC CHLORIDE. Butter of Zinc.   A zinc salt used as an antiseptic and astringent in shaving creams, dentifrices, and mouthwashes. Odorless and water absorbing; also a deodorant and disinfectant. Can cause contact dermatitis and is mildly irritating to the skin. Can be absorbed through the skin.

ZINC HYDROLYZED ANIMAL PROTEIN. See Hydrolyzed and Protein.

ZINC OLEATE-STEARATE. A white, dry, greasy powder, insoluble in water, soluble in alcohol. An antiseptic and astringent in cosmetic creams. Used medicinally to treat eczema and other skin rashes. No known toxicity.

ZINC OXIDE. Flowers of Zinc. Used to impart opacity to face powders, foundation creams, and dusting powders. A creamy white ointment used medicinally as an astringent, antiseptic, and protective in skin diseases. Zinc is believed to encourage healing of skin disorders. It is insoluble in water. In cosmetics it is also used in baby powder, bleach and freckle creams, depilatories, face packs, antiperspirants, foundation cake makeup, nail whiteners, protective creams, rouge, shaving creams, and white eye shadow. Workers suffer skin eruptions called zinc pox under the arm and in the groin when working with zinc. Zinc pox is believed to be caused by the blocking of the hair openings. Because of its astringent qualities, zinc oxide may be unsuitable for dry skins. Generally harmless, however, when used in cosmetics.

ZINC PEROXIDE. Zinc Superoxide. Disinfectant, antiseptic, deodorant, and astringent applied as a dusting powder alone or with talc or starch. White to yellowish white powder. Liberates hydrogen peroxide, a bleach. It is used in bleach and freckle creams and medicinally as a deodorant for festering wounds and skin diseases. No known toxicity.

ZINC PYRITHIONE. See Zinc.

ZINC SALICYLATE. A zinc salt used as an antiseptic and astringent in dusting powders and antiperspirants. White odorless needles or crystalline powder. It is omitted from hypoallergenic cosmetics. Causes both skin irritations and allergic reactions.

ZINC STEARATE. Zinc Soap. A mixture of the zinc salts of stearic and palmitic acids (*see both*). Widely used in cosmetic preparations because it contributes to adhesive properties. Also used as a coloring agent. Baby powders of 3 to 5 percent zinc are water repellent and prevent urine scale. Zinc soap is also used in bath preparations, deodorants, face powders, hair-grooming preparations, hand creams, lotions, and ointments. It is used in tablet manufacture and in pharmaceutical powders and ointments. Inhalation of powder may cause lung problems and produce death in infants from pneumonitis with lesions resembling those caused by talc, but more severe. No known toxicity on the skin.

ZINC SULFATE. White Vitriol. The reaction of sulfuric acid with zinc. Mild crystalline zinc salt used in shaving cream, eye lotion, astringents, styptic, as a gargle spray, skin tonic, and after-shave lotion. Used medicinally as an emetic. Irritating to the skin and mucous membranes. May cause an allergic reaction. Injection under the skin of 2.5 milligrams per kilogram of body weight caused tumors in rabbits.

ZINC SULFOCARBOLATE. See Zinc Sulfate.

ZINC UNDECYLENATE. A zinc salt. Occurs in sweat. Used to combat fungus in cosmetics and on the skin. Made by dissolving zinc oxide (*see*) in diluted undecylenic acid (*see*). Has an odor suggestive of perspiration. No known toxicity.

ZIRCONIUM. Discovered in 1789. Bluish black powder or grayish white flakes used as a bo: ling agent and abrasive; also in the preparation of dyes. High quality zirconium is used as a pigment toner and solvent. Mildly acidic, it has been used in body deodorants and antiperspirants. Zirconium hydroxide is used in nail whiteners. Low systemic toxicity, but a disease of the skin has been reported in users of a deodorant containing sodium zirconium lactate. Manufacturers voluntarily removed zirconium from spray antiperspirants in 1976 because the element was found harmful to monkey lungs. The FDA has said that zirconium is safe in formulations other than sprays.

ZIRCONIUM SILICATE. See Zirconium.

ZIRCONYL CHLORIDE. Zirconium Oxychloride. Used to make other zirconium compounds and to precipitate acid dyes. Acts as a solvent. Mildly acidic. It has been used in deodorants and antiperspirants but because of skin bumps, particularly under the arm, it has been discontinued.

ZIRCONYL HYDROXYCHLORIDE. Colorless powder that absorbs moisture. See Zirconium.

NOTES

The notes in this dictionary refer to *The Merck Index* (listed in the Notes as *Merck*), 8th ed., Rahway, N.J.: Merck, Sharp and Dohme Research Laboratories, 1968; *Clinical Toxicology of Commercial Products* (listed in the Notes by the author "Gleason") by Marion N. Gleason, et al., Baltimore: The Williams & Wilkins Co., 1969; *Hazards of Medication* (listed under its full title) by Eric W. Martin, et al., Philadelphia: J. B. Lippincott Co., 1971); *The Handbook of Cosmetic Materials* (listed as *Cosmetic Materials*) by Leon A. Greenberg and David Lester, New York: Interscience Publishers, 1954; *Toxic Substances* (listed under its full title), U.S. Department of Health, Education and Welfare, June 1971; "Cutaneous Reactions to Cosmetics" (listed by the author "March") by Cyril March, M.D., and Alexander Fisher, M.D., Chicago: American Medical Association publication, Chicago, 1965; "Toxic Reactions to Common Household Products" (listed by the author "Done") by Alan K. Done, San Francisco: Read in the Symposium on Adverse Reactions sponsored by the Drug Utilization Committee, Council on Drugs, at the 117th annual meeting of the AMA, June 19, 1968; "Hypo-Allergenic Cosmetics" (listed by the author "Kahn") by Julius Kahn, *NARD Journal*, February 20, 1967; *The Look You Like* (listed under its full title) by Linda Allen, Chicago: Committee on Cutaneous Health and Cosmetics, American Medical Association, 1971; *Physicians' Desk Reference* (listed under its full title), Oradell N.J.: Medical Economics, 1973; and FDA personal correspondence with author (listed as FDA), September 1972. All other references in the Notes are listed in full.

The first note refers to page 15 of the dictionary, the seventh line down, and the original source for the material can be found on page 7 in "Gleason."

p. 15, line 7—Gleason, p. 7; p. 15, line 27—Gleason, p. 7; p. 15, line 39—*Merck*, p. 4; p. 16, line 8—*Merck*, p. 4; p. 16, line 13—*Merck*, p. 4; p. 16, line 21—*Merck*, p. 5; *AMA Drug Evaluations*, American Medical Association, Chicago, 1971, p. 181; p. 16, line 30—Gleason, p. 7; p. 16, line 32—*Cosmetic Materials*, p. 21; p. 16, line 39—*Merck*, p. 7; p. 17, line 2—March; p. 17, line 6—*Merck*, p. 1027; p. 20, line 2—*Merck*, p. 17; p. 20, line 9—*Merck*, p. 17; p. 20, line 9—*Toxic Substances*, p. 21; p. 20, line 16—*Toxic Substances*, p. 23; p. 20, line 17—*Merck*, p. 21; p. 20, line 26—Gleason, p. 71; p. 20, line 28—*Journal of the American Medical Association*, October 5, 1970, vols. 2, 14, no. 1; p. 20, line 41—*Aerosols*, Donald Davis, Drug and Cosmetic Industry, March 1973, p. 68; p. 21, line 32—*Cosmetic Materials*, p. 25; p. 22, line 14—Gleason, p. 38; p. 22, line 18—Gleason, p. 13; p. 23, line 6—Gleason, p. 10; p. 23, line 27—Gleason, p. 11; p. 23, line 30—Gleason, p. 10; p. 24, line 2—Gleason, p. 11; p. 25, line 12—Gleason, p. 13; p. 25, line 13—Kahn; p. 25, line 19—Merck, p. 46; p. 25, line 27—Kahn; p. 25, line 28—*Merck*, p. 47; p. 25, line 29—Gleason, p. 27; p. 25, line 35—Gleason, p. 13; p. 25, line 40—Gleason, p. 13; p. 25, line 41—*Toxic Substances*, p. 28; p. 26, line 2—March; p. 26, line 3—Gleason, p. 13; p. 27, line 22—March; p. 27, line 23—*Toxic Substances*, p. 29; p. 28, line 12—Andrej Lazner, M.D., and Albert Kligman, M.D., "Aminobenzoic Acid Type Sunscreen Makes for Tanning Without Burning," *Archives of Dermatology*, September 1972; *Merck*, p. 55; *Hazards of Medication*, p. 350; p. 28, line 25—*Merck*, p. 779; p. 28, line 26—Gleason, p. 14; p. 28, line 33—Gleason, p. 15; p. 28, line 37—*Merck*, p. 60; p. 29, line 7—*Merck*, p. 64; p. 29, line 8—March; p. 29, line 12—*Merck*, p. 64; p. 29, line 13—Gleason, p. 18, Section II; p. 29, line 17—March; p. 29, line 20—Gleason, p. 15; p. 29, line 21—*Merck*, p. 659; p. 29, line 41—*Cosmetic Materials*, p. 48; p. 30, line 7—*Merck*, p. 66; p. 30, line 8—*Toxic Substances*, p. 40; p. 30, line 9—Gleason, p. 18; p. 30, line 16—*Merck*, p. 64; p. 30, line 17—March; p. 30, line 35—*Merck*, p. 70; p. 30, line 36—*Toxic Substances*, p. 45; p. 31, line 7— *Toxic Substances*, p. 45; p. 31, line 12—*Merck*, p. 72; p. 31, line 12—*Cosmetic Materials*, p. 50; p. 31, line 20—*Merck*, p. 1042; p. 31, line 21—*Toxic Substances*, p. 45; p. 31, line 26—*Merck*, p. 1122; p. 32, line 12—Gleason, p. 80; p. 32, line 17— *Toxic Substances*, p. 394; p. 33, line 3—Gleason, p. 16; p. 33, line 10—*Hazards of Medication*, p. 33, line 22—*Toxic Substances*, p. 49; p. 33, line 26—Arthur Lippman, "Drug and Chemical Induced Photosensitivity," *Modern Medicine*, March 1, 1976, p. 81; p. 34, line 2—*Merck*, p. 86; p. 34, line 18—*Hazards of Medication*, p. 350; p. 34, line 22—*Merck*, p. 89; p. 34, line 29—*Merck*, p. 92; p. 34, line 30— Kahn; p. 34, line 40—*Toxic Substances*, p. 55; p. 35, line 32—Gleason, p. 18; p. 35, line 33—*Cosmetic Materials*, p. 56; p. 36, line 3—Kahn; p. 36, line 8—*Merck*, p. 101; p. 36, line 9—Kahn; p. 36, line 10—*Hazards of Medication*, p. 350; p. 36, line 25—FDA; p. 37, line 8—*The Look You Like*, p. 50; p. 37, line 20—March; p. 37, line 29—*Merck*, p. 116; p. 38, line 7—FDA; p. 38, line 37—Gleason, p. 30; p. 38, line 38—Kahn; p. 39, line 13—Kahn; p. 39, line 16—*Cosmetic Materials*, p. 61; p. 40, line 35—FDA; p. 41, line 11—FDA; p. 41, line 17—*Merck*, p. 956; p. 41, line 24—Done; p. 41, line 30—*Cosmetic Materials*, p. 202; p. 42, line 2—*Cosmetic Materials*, p. 62; p. 42, line 34—*Toxic Substances*, p. 68; p. 42, line 39—Kahn; p. 42, line 40— *Toxic Substances*, p. 68; p. 43, line 4—A. A. Fisher and M. A. Stillman, *Archives of Dermatology*, 106: pp. 169–71, August 1972; p. 43, line 5—*Toxic Substances*, p. 68; p. 43, line 8—*Merck*, p. 128; p. 43, line 11—*Hazards of Medication*, p. 350; p. 43, line 21—Gleason, p. 66; p. 43, line 22—*Hazards of Medication*, p. 352; p. 43, line 27—*Merck*, p. 133; p. 43, line 34—Kahn; p. 43, line 40—*Toxic Substances*, p. 81; p. 44, line 1—Gleason, p. 80; p. 44, line 6—*Merck*, p. 137; p. 44, line 11— Gleason, p 23; p. 44, line 22—*Merck*, p. 139; p. 44, line 26—*Hazards of Medication*, p. 350; p. 44, line 34—Gleason, p. 23; p. 45, line 1—*Hazards of Medication*, p. 350; p. 45, line 19—*Merck*, p. 715; Gleason, p. 100; p. 45, line 20—Kahn; p. 46, line 25—Gleason, p. 24, Kahn; p. 46, line 36—*The Look You Like*, AMA Committee on Cutaneous Health, 1971; p. 47, line 2—March; p. 47, line 13—Kahn; p. 47, line 16—*Cosmetic Materials*, p. 205; p. 48, line 20—Gleason, p. 46, Section II; p. 48, line 33—Gleason, p. 46, Section II; p. 48, line 37—*Merck*, p. 160; p. 49, line 18— Gleason, p. 46; p. 49, line 26—*Merck*, p. 741; p. 50, line 16—Done: p. 50, line 19— FDA; p. 51, line 15—*Merck, p.* 177, Gleason, p. 28; p. 51, line 16—*Toxic Substances*, p. 107; p. 51, line 21—*Toxic Substances*, p. 107; p. 51, line 38—Gleason, p. 28; p. 53, line 2—Gleason, p. 29; p. 53, line 24—Gleason, p. 29; p. 53, line 30—*Toxic Substances*, p. 114; p. 54, line 12—Gleason, p. 146, Section II; p. 54, line 20— *Merck*, p. 194; p. 55, line 3—*Merck*, p. 195; p. 55, line 22—Kahn; p. 55. line 26— Gleason, p. 141; p. 56, line 7—*Merck*, p. 199; p. 56, line 8—*Cosmetic Materials*, p. 79; p. 56, line 20—*Merck*, p. 201; p. 56, line 40—*Cosmetic Materials*, p. 81; p. 57, line 1—Gleason, p. 30; p. 47, line 13—*Cosmetic Materials*, p. 207; p. 57, line 18— *Merck*, p. 206; p. 57, line 33—*Cosmetic Materials*, p. 83; p. 57, line 38—*Merck*, p. 208; p. 58, line 22—*Cosmetic Materials*, p. 84; p. 58, line 35—*Merck*, p. 212; p. 59, line 30—Kahn; p. 60, line 7—Gleason, p. 32, *Merck*, p. 218; p. 60, line 14— *Cosmetic Materials*, p. 87; p. 60, line 17—*Hazards of Medication*, p. 350; p. 61, line 10—*Cosmetic Materials*, p. 89; p. 62, line 12—Gleason, p. 198; p. 62, line 25— Gleason, p. 32; p. 63, line 30—*Merck, p.* 228; p. 64, line 19—*Merck*, p. 232; p. 64, line 26—*Cosmetic Materials*, p. 91; p. 64, line 34—*Merck*, p. 239, Gleason, p. 34; p. 65, line 3—*FDA Papers*, April 1972, p. 5; p. 65, line 6—*Merck*, p. 243; p. 65, line 20—*Hazards of Medication*, p. 350; p. 65, line 31—Gleason, pp. 37, 190; p. 65, line 36—Gleason, p. 37; p. 66, line 9—Kahn; p. 66, line 20—Gleason, p. 38; p. 66, line 23—Gleason, p. 38; p. 66, line 28—Gleason, p. 38; p. 66, line 34—Kahn; p. 67, line 18—Gleason, p. 105; p. 67, line 19—Ar-Ex; p. 67, line 22—*Merck*, p. 916; p. 68, line 40—*Merck*, p. 758; p. 69, line 1—*Cosmetic Materials*, p. 213; p. 69, line 11—*Merck*, p. 363; p. 69, line 34—Kahn; p. 70, line 4—*Cosmetic Materials*, p. 213; p. 70, line 32—Dr. Naomi Kanof, Chairman of the AMA's Committee on Cutaneous Health and Cosmetics, *AMA News Feature*, September 17, 1973; p. 70, line 38—*Cosmetic Materials*, p. 79; p. 71, line 3—Gleason, p. 39; p. 71, line 12—Gleason, p. 86, Section VI; p. 73, line 24—*Cosmetic Materials*, p. 100; p. 73, line 40—*Merck*, p. 946; p. 74, line 4—*Cosmetic Materials*, p. 214; p. 74, line 16—Kahn; p. 74, line 30—Kahn; p. 74, line 40—Kahn; p. 75, line 5—Gleason, p. 41; p. 75, line 26—*Merck*, p. 292; p. 76, line 1—*Merck*, p. 300; p. 76, line 7—*Merck*, p. 302; p. 76, line 19—FDA; p. 76, line 40—Gleason, p. 227; p. 77, line 13—Charles Cameron, M.D., former medical director, American Cancer Society, *The Truth About Cancer*, Collier Books, N.Y., 1968, p. 65; p. 77, line 30—*Merck*, p. 913; p. 77, line 40—*Merck*, p. 88; p. 82, line 22—*Federal Register*, May 8, 1969; p. 84, line 2—FDA; p. 84, line 4—Irwin Lubowe, M.D., "Antiseborrheic Preparations," *Handbook of Non-prescription Drugs*, American Pharmaceutical Association, Washington, D.C., 1971, pp. 150–52; p. 84, line 22—*Merck*, p. 324; p. 84, line 37—Gleason, p. 46; p. 86, line 3—FDA; p. 86, line 35—Done; p. 86, line 36—*Hazards of Medication*, p. 350; p. 86, line 37—FDA; p. 87, line 1—G. W. Ward, Jr. et al., "Lung Changes Secondary to Inhalation of Underarm Aerosol Deodorants," presented at the American Thoracic Society Annual Meeting, Los Angeles, California, May 16–19, 1971; p. 87, line 8—*Cosmetic Materials*, p. 106; p. 87, line 29—FDA; p. 88, line 6—W. C. Heuper and W. D. Conway, *Chemical Carcinogenesis and Cancers*, Springfield, Illinois: Charles C. Thomas, 1964, p. 22; p. 88, line 10—*Cosmetic Materials*, p. 106; p. 88, line 16—*Merck*, p. 336, *Toxic Substances*, p. 168; p. 88, line 24—*Toxic Substances*, p. 169; p. 88, line 40—*Merck*, p. 556; p. 88, line 41—*Cosmetic Materials*, p. 154; p. 89, line 7—March; p. 89, line 12—Gleason, p. 145; p. 89, line 17—*Toxic Substances*, p. 347; p. 89, line 22—Gleason, p. 28; p. 89, line 23—*Cosmetic Materials*, p. 107; p. 89, line 40—*Merck*, p. 356; p. 90, line 5—Gleason, p. 69; p. 90, line 10—*Merck*, p. 374; p. 90, line 19—*Merck*, p. 434; p. 90, line 21—*Cosmetic Materials*, p. 109; p. 90, line 26—*Merck*, p. 361; p. 90, line 34—Rudolph Baer, M.D., and Leonard D. Harber, M.D., "Photosensitivity Induced by Drugs," *Journal of the American Medical Association*, June 14, 1965, vol. 192, pp. 989–90; p. 91, line 10—*Toxic Substances*, p. 193; p. 91, line 23—*Merck*, p. 370; p. 91, line 34—*Merck*, p. 372; p. 91, line 40—*Merck*, p. 373; p. 92, line 18—*Merck*, p. 378; p. 92, line 28—*Merck*, p. 374; p. 92, line 30—*Merck*, p. 374; p. 93, line 8—Gleason, p. 114; p. 93, line 16—*Merck*, p. 383; p. 93, line 34—Gleason, p. 111; p. 93, line 40—*Physicians' Desk Reference*, p. 1200; p. 95, line 24—*Merck*, p. 964; p. 96, line 27—*Merck*, p. 958; p. 98, line 20—Robert L. Day, "Dry Skin and Chapping Aids," *Handbook of Non-prescription Drugs*, American Pharmaceutical Association, Washington, D.C., 1971, pp. 167–70; p. 99, line 1—H. Blank, Ph.D., "Mechanism of Action of Emollient Creams," prepared at the request of the AMA Committee on Cutaneous Cosmetics; p. 99, line 22—FDA; p. 100, line 17—*Merck*, p. 410; p. 101, line 4—*Merck*, p. 737; p. 101, line 15—*Merck*, p. 580; p. 101, line 31—*Merck*, p. 424; p. 101, line 39—*Merck*, p. 29; p. 102, line 1—*Merck*, p. 610; p. 102, line 13—*Toxic Substances*, p. 34; p. 102, line 14—Gleason, p. 98; p. 102, line 20—Gleason, p. 66; p. 102, line 25—Gleason, p. 31; p. 102, line 30—Gleason, p. 31; p. 102, line 35—Gleason, p. 65; p. 102, line 40—Gleason, p. 65; p. 103, line 6—*Merck*, p. 430; p. 103, line 7—*Cosmetic Materials*, p. 121; p. 104, line 5—*Hazards of Medication*, p. 419; p. 104, line 20—*Merck*, p. 435; p. 104, line 27—*Merck*, p. 640; p. 104, line

37—*Merck*, p. 434; p. 105, line 4—Gleason, p. 70; p. 105, line 13—Kahn; p. 105, line 13—Gleason, p. 70; p. 105, line 19—Gleason, p. 70; p. 106, line 28—FDA; p. 106, line 34—FDA; p. 107, line 4—FDA; p. 107, line 15—*The Look You Like*, p. 22; p. 107, line 32—FDA; p. 108, line 25—FDA; p. 109, line 14—FDA; p. 109, line 20—FDA; p. 110, line 11—Charles Cameron, M.D., former medical director, American Cancer Society, *The Truth About Cancer*, N.Y.: Collier Books, 1968, p. 65; p. 110, line 31—*The Truth About Cancer*, p. 65; p. 112, line 31—*Cosmetic Materials*, p. 218; p. 114, line 12—*Merck*, p. 469; p. 114, line 15—Gleason, p. 71; p. 114, line 18—American Medical Association, personal communications, September 1971; p. 114, line 24—Gleason, p. 71; p. 115, line 18—FDA; p. 116, line 1—*Merck*, p. 476, Gleason, p. 72; p. 116, line 33—Kahn; p. 116, line 38—Gleason, p. 65; p. 117, line 6—Gleason, p. 11; p. 117, line 11—*Cosmetic Materials*, p. 138; p. 118, line 19—Gleason, p. 73; p. 118, line 34—*Toxic Substances*, p. 266; p. 119, line 10—*Merck*, p. 501; p. 119, line 23—*Cosmetic Materials*, p. 142; p. 119, line 41—*Merck*, p. 503; p. 120, line 2—*Merck*, p. 503; p. 120, line 13—*Merck*, p. 507; p. 120, line 31—*Cosmetic Materials*, p. 143; p. 120, line 37—*Toxic Substances*, p. 269; p. 121, line 2—*Toxic Substances*, p. 269; p. 121, line 12—Kahn; p. 121, line 35—Kahn; p. 122, line 3—*Cosmetic Materials*, p. 145; p. 122, line 31—FDA; p. 123, line 2—FDA; p. 123, line 39—*Cosmetic Science and Technology*, edited by Edward Sagarin, Harold Goulden, Emil Klarmann, and Donald Powers, Interscience, June 1957, p. 503; p. 124, line 12—*Cosmetic Science and Technology*, p. 516; p. 124, line 24—FDA; p. 125, line 9—*The Look You Like*; p. 125, line 36—FDA; p. 126, line 21—Done; p. 126, line 39—FDA; p. 127, line 27—FDA; p. 127, line 38—*Cosmetic Science and Technology*, p. 171; p. 128, line 9—FDA; p. 129, line 10—*Merck*, p. 518; p. 129, line 16—Kahn; p. 129, line 17—*Cosmetic Materials*, p. 145; p. 129, line 24—*The Look You Like*, p. 26, *Merck*, p. 522; p. 129, line 29—*Federal Register*, April 26, 1969; p. 129, line 41—*Merck*, p. 524; p. 130, line 11—*Toxic Substances*, p. 1416; p. 131, line 34—Gleason, p. 78; p. 131, line 40—*Cosmetic Materials*, p. 220; p. 132, line 18—*The Look You Like*; p. 132, line 24—John S. Strauss, M.D., Department of Dermatology, Boston University, "Hormones in Cosmetics," *Journal of The American Medical Association*, March 1966; p. 133, line 14—*Cosmetic Materials*, p. 221; p. 133, line 34—*Merck*, p. 541; p. 134, line 2—*Merck*, p. 545; p. 135, line 32—*Merck*, p. 547; p. 135, line 34—*Merck*, p. 547; p. 135, line 35—*Merck*, p. 547; p. 135, line 36—March; p. 136, line 2—Kahn; p. 136, line 15—*Toxic Substances*, p. 289; p. 136, line 25—*Merck*, p. 558; p. 137, line 6—Gleason, p. 81; p. 137, line 16—*Cosmetic Materials*, p. 153; p. 137, line 35—*Merck*, p. 570; p. 137, line 39—*Merck*, p. 577; p. 138, line 2—Gleason, pp. 128–39, Section III; p. 138, line 31—*Merck*, p. 589; p. 139 line 14—*Cosmetic Materials*, p. 270; p. 139, line 21—*Merck*, p. 794; p. 139, line 32—*Merck*, p. 590; p. 140, line 8—*Merck*, p. 591; p. 140, line 13—*Toxic Substances*, p. 304; p. 140, line 18—*Merck*, p. 590; p. 140, line 42—*Merck*, p. 833; p. 141, line 4—*Merck*, p. 594; p. 141, line 10—*Cosmetic Materials*, p. 161; p. 141, line 13—*Cosmetic Materials*, p. 221; p. 141, line 17—*Cosmetic Materials*, p. 221; p. 141, line 21—*Merck*, p. 596; p. 141, line 22—*Toxic Substances*, p. 307; p. 141, line 28—Gleason, p. 84; p. 141, line 35—*Merck*, p. 551; p. 141, line 37—Gleason, p. 80; p. 141, line 39—Gleason, p. 84; p. 142, line 12—*Toxic Substances*, p. 308; p. 142, line 17—Weisburger, "Colon Carcinogens," *Cancer*, July 1971, vol. 28, no. 1; p. 142, line 33—Gleason, p. 85; p. 142, line 39—*Merck*, p. 606; p. 143, line 33—H. Blank, Ph.D., "Mechanism of Action of Emollient Creams," prepared at the request of the AMA Committee on Cutaneous Cosmetics; p. 144, line 33—*Webster's Third International Dictionary*, p. 1276; p. 144, line 34—*Cosmetic Materials*, p. 166; p. 145, line 18—*Merck*, p. 610; p. 145, line 34—Gleason, p. 86; p. 146, line 10—

Kahn; *Hazards of Medication*, p. 146, line 15—*Merck*, p. 612; p. 146, line 17—
Cosmetic Materials, p. 169; p. 146, line 39—Linda Allen, *Today's Health*, December
1971; p. 147, line 11—W. C. Heuper and W. D. Conway, *Chemical Carcinogenesis
and Cancers*, Springfield, Illinois: Charles C Thomas, 1964, p. 67; p. 147, line 17—
Gleason, p. 106; p. 147, line 27—*Physicians' Desk Reference*, p. 316; p. 148, line
1—*Hazards of Medication*, p. 350; p. 148, line 3—*Merck*, p. 619; p. 148, line 15—
Merck, p. 619; p. 148, line 24—Kahn; p. 149, line 1—*Cosmetic Materials*, p. 171;
p. 149, line 5—*Cosmetic Materials*, p. 171; p. 149, line 11—*Cosmetic Materials*,
p. 227; p. 150, line 16—FDA; p. 150, line 30—Gleason, p. 87; p. 150, line 30—
Merck, p. 623, Gleason, p. 87; p. 151, line 16—*Cosmetic Materials*, p. 146; p. 151,
line 32—*Merck*, p. 630; p. 152, line 14—*Cosmetic Materials*, p. 174; p. 152, line
22—*Merck*, p. 638; p. 152, line 23—*Cosmetic Materials*, p. 174, p. 153, line 18—
Merck, p. 640; p. 153, line 19—*Cosmetic Materials*, p. 176; p. 153, line 25—*Cosmetic
Materials*, p. 176; p. 153, line 32—*Toxic Substances*, p. 641; p. 154, line 2—*Toxic
Substances*, p. 320; p. 154, line 6—*Toxic Substances*, p. 463; p. 154, line 17—
Cosmetic Materials, p. 247; p. 154, line 33—Linda Schoen, *Today's Health*, July
1973, p. 15; p. 155, line 19—*The Look You Like*; p. 155, line 27—*Toxic Substances*,
p. 105; p. 155, line 34—*Merck*, p. 649; p. 156, line 10—*Merck*, p. 653; p. 156,
line 11—*Cosmetic Materials*, p. 177; p. 156, line 17—March; p. 156, line 26—
Gleason, p. 91; p. 157, line 8—*Cosmetic Materials*, p. 179; p. 157, line 25—*Cosmetic
Materials*, p. 180; p. 157, line 35—*Cosmetic Materials*, p. 181; p. 158, line 10—
Cosmetic Materials, p. 184; p. 158, line 28—*Merck*, p. 691, Gleason, p. 96; p. 158,
line 37—*Merck*, p. 680, Gleason, p. 15; p. 159, line 12—*Toxic Substances*, p. 339;
p. 159, line 13—*Cosmetic Materials*, p. 182; p. 159, line 18—Gleason, p. 94; p. 159,
line 20—*American Medical News*, Feb. 2, 1976; p. 159, line 27—*Merck*, p. 689;
p. 160, line 4—*Cosmetic Materials*, p. 189; p. 160, line 10—*Cosmetic Materials*,
p. 228; p. 161, line 2—*Merck*, p. 986; p. 161, line 15—*Merck*, p. 700; p. 161, line
25—*Merck*, p. 700; p. 161, line 36—*Merck*, p. 703; p. 161, line 37—Gleason, p. 99;
p. 162, line 10—*Today's Health Guide*, p. 578; p. 162, line 27—*Cosmetic Materials*,
p. 192; p. 162, line 31—L. Mackenzie Miall and D. W. A. Sharp, *A Dictionary of
Chemistry*, New York: John Wiley & Sons, Inc., 1968, p. 23; p. 164, line 12—*The
Look You Like*, p. 10; p. 164, line 4—FDA; p. 164, line 15—FDA; p. 164, line 21—
Gleason, p. 86, Section VI; p. 164, line 23—FDA; p. 164, line 34—Gleason, p. 99;
p. 165, line 13—*Cosmetic Materials*, p. 229; p. 165, line 27—*Cosmetic Materials*,
p. 195; p. 166, line 8—Gleason, p. 101, *Merck*, p. 727; p. 166, line 9—Gleason,
p. 101, *Merck*, p. 727; p. 166, line 17—*Merck*, p. 735; p. 166, line 22—*Merck*,
p. 736; p. 166, line 31—*Toxic Substances*, p. 370; p. 166, line 38—*Merck*, p. 744;
p. 169, line 7—*Cosmetic Materials*, p. 199; p. 169, line 40—*Merck*, p. 763; p. 170,
line 35—*Cosmetic Materials*, p. 230; p. 171, line 5—*Cosmetic Materials*, p. 231;
p. 171, line 24—Kahn; p. 172, line 2—*Merck*, p. 772; p. 172, line 6—*Cosmetic
Materials*, p. 251; p. 172, line 17—*Toxic Substance List*, HEW, 1974 edition, p. 691;
p. 173, line 15—*Cosmetic Materials*, p. 252; p. 173, line 25—*Merck*, p. 781; p. 173,
line 34—*Toxic Substances*, p. 388; p. 173, line 36—*Cosmetic Materials*, p. 252; p. 173,
line 40—*Hazards of Medication*, p. 350; p. 173, line 41—*Cosmetic Materials*, p. 233;
p. 174, line 6—*Cosmetic Materials*, p. 233; p. 174, line 22—*Cosmetic Materials*,
p. 233; p. 174, line 27—*Toxic Substances*, p. 269; p. 176, line 28—Kahn; p. 178,
line 15—*Merck*, p. 794; p. 178, line 25—*Merck*, p. 968; p. 178, line 38—*Cosmetic
Materials*, p. 235; p. 178, line 39—T. H. Eickhold, et al., "Toxicities of Peppermint," *Journal of Pharmacological Sciences*, vol. 54, pp. 1071-72, 1965; p. 179,
line 32—FDA; p. 180, line 11—*Merck*, p. 1042; p. 180, line 14—FDA; p. 180, line
17—March; p. 180, line 29—*Cosmetic Materials*, p. 235; p. 181, line 3—*Cosmetic

Materials, p. 255; p. 181, line 4—*Physicians' Desk Reference*, p. 924; p. 181, line 24—*Merck*, p. 807; p. 181, line 24—William Schorr, *Cosmetic Allergy*, *Cosmetics and Perfumery*, vol. 89, no. 7, July 1974; p. 181, line 28—*Merck*, p. 810, Gleason, p. 189; p. 181, line 38—*Cosmetic Materials*, p. 256; p. 182, line 14—*Cosmetic Materials*, p. 257; p. 182, line 33—*Merck*, p. 817; p. 182, line 34—March; p. 182, line 35—*Hazards of Medication*, p. 350; p. 183, line 6—*Physicians' Desk Reference*, p. 1542; p. 183, line 10—*Cosmetic Materials*; p. 183, line 14—*Merck*, p. 818; p. 183, line 22—*Cosmetic Materials*, p. 44; p. 183, line 28—*Cosmetic Materials*, p. 44; p. 184, line 7—*Merck*, p. 829; p. 184, line 16—*Merck*, p. 827; p. 184, line 20—*Merck*, p. 827; p. 184, line 23—*Merck*, p. 381; p. 184, line 37—*Cosmetic Materials*, p. 264; p. 185, line 2—*Cosmetic Materials*, p. 236; p. 185, line 9—*Merck*, p. 835; p. 185, line 12—*Merck*, p. 835; p. 185, line 25—*Merck*, p. 839; p. 185, line 26—*Cosmetic Materials*, p. 145; p. 186, line 33—*Merck*, p. 17; p. 186, line 36—*Merck*, p. 176; p. 187, line 1—*Toxic Substances*, p. 429; p. 187, line 3—*Cosmetic Materials*, p. 83; p. 187, line 39—*Cosmetic Materials*, p. 324; p. 188, line 27—*Merck*, p. 990; p. 189, line 6—Gleason, p. 117; p. 189, line 7—*Toxic Substances*, p. 429; p. 189, line 22—*Merck*, p. 852; p. 189, line 31—*Cosmetic Materials*, p. 267; p. 189, line 38—*Cosmetic Materials*, p. 267; p. 190. line 5—*Merck*, p. 852; p. 190, line 7—*Cosmetic Materials*, p. 267; p. 190, line 31—*Toxic Substances*, p. 430; p. 190, line 33—*Cosmetic Materials*, p. 268; p. 190, line 37—*Toxic Substances*, p. 430; p. 190, line 38—*Cosmetic Materials*, p. 268; p. 191, line 7—Gleason, p. 118; p. 191, line 20—*Federal Register*, April 26, 1969; p. 191, line 23—*Merck*, p. 857; p. 192, line 11—*Cosmetic Materials*, p. 304; p. 194, line 16—"Microbiological Control of Cosmetic Products," Arthur Dunnigan, Ph.D., Food and Drug Administration, Joint Conference on Cosmetic Sciences, April 23, 1968, Washington, D.C.; p. 194, line 28—Allan L. Lorincz, M.D., Associate Professor of Dermatology, University of Chicago, *Drug and Cosmetic Industry*, 88:442, April 1961 and 1966; p. 194, line 32—*Merck*, p. 871; p. 194, line 35—*Merck*, p. 1069; p. 195, line 15—*Toxic Substances*, p. 442; p. 195, line 22—*Merck*, p. 875; p. 195, line 29—*Cosmetic Materials*, p. 30; p. 195, line 37—*Merck*, p. 875; p. 196, line 8—Gleason, p. 121; p. 196, line 6—*Toxic Substances*, p. 434; p. 196, line 26—*Cosmetic Materials*, p. 271; p. 197, line 23—Dr. Naomi M. Kanof, Chairman of the AMA's Committee on Cutaneous Health and Cosmetics, *AMA News Feature*, September 17, 1973; p. 197, line 33—*Hazards of Medication*, p. 350; p. 198, line 1—*Cosmetic Materials*, p. 272; p. 198, line 11—*Toxic Substances*, p. 486; p. 198, line 16—*Merck*, p. 890; p. 198, line 23—*Toxic Substances*, p. 459; p. 198, line 35—*Merck*, p. 892; p. 198, line 41—*Merck*, p. 894; p. 199, line 7—*Merck*, p. 895; p. 199, line 10—Kahn; p. 199, line 18—*Merck*, p. 824; p. 199, line 41—Gleason, pp. 197–99, Section III; p. 201, line 4—*Cosmetic Materials*, p. 274; p. 201, line 15—Kahn; p. 201, line 21—*Merck*, p. 905; p. 201, line 41—*Cosmetic Materials*, p. 236; p. 202, line 20—*Cosmetic Materials*, p. 81; p. 202, line 40—*Merck*, p. 913; p. 202, line 41—*Cosmetic Materials*, p. 276; p. 204, line 5—Howard Rapaport, M.D., and Shirley Motter Linde, M.S., *The Complete Allergy Guide*, N.Y.: Simon and Schuster, 1970, p. 383; p. 204, line 10—*The Complete Allergy Guide*, p. 383; p. 204, line 23—*The Complete Allergy Guide*, p. 383; p. 204, line 33—Gleason, p. 65; p. 204, line 39—*Cosmetic Materials*, p. 278; p. 205, line 25—FDA; p. 206, line 13—*The Complete Allergy Guide*, p. 383; p. 207, line 22—Gleason, p. 125, *Merck*, p. 930; p. 207, line 23—Samuel Solomon, M.D., and Samuel Bluefar, M.D., "Photoallergic Contact Dermatitis Due to Halogenated Salicylanilides," *Industrial Medicine*, 38: pp. 54–57, 1969; p. 207, line 23—*Merck*, p. 930; p. 207, line 38—*Cosmetic Materials*, p. 280; p. 208, line 7—*Cosmetic Materials*, p. 239; p. 208, line 39—*Cosmetic Materials*, p. 239; p. 209, line 9—*Merck*, p. 940·

p. 209, line 21—*Merck*, p. 913; p. 209, line 41—FDA; p. 210, line 30—Done; p. 210, line 32—FDA; p. 211, line 7—*The Look You Like*, p. 80; p. 212, line 7—FDA; p. 212, line 13—*Cosmetic Materials*, p. 283; p. 213, line 8—*Cosmetic Materials*, p. 284; p. 213, line 13—*Merck*, p. 947; p. 213, line 21—*Merck*, p. 948; p. 213, line 37—Merck, p. 951; p. 214, line 8—*The Look You Like*, p. 85, and personal communication with author, AMA Science News Department; p. 214, line 16—FDA; p. 215, line 4—FDA; p. 215, line 29—FDA; p. 216, line 22—*Cosmetic Materials*, p. 288; p. 216, line 27—*Merck*, p. 955; p. 216, line 35—*Cosmetic Materials*, p. 289; p. 217, line 8—*Merck*, p. 956; p. 217, line 29—*Cosmetic Materials*, p. 291; p. 218, line 2—*Merck*, p. 958; p. 218, line 8—Gleason, p. 46; p. 218, line 15—*Merck*, p. 958; p. 218, line 21—*Merck*, p. 959; p. 219, line 4—*Toxic Substances*, p. 483; p. 219, line 5—*Merck*, p. 968; p. 219, line 28—*Cosmetic Materials*, p. 294; p. 219, line 39—FDA; p. 220, line 22—*Merck*, p. 772; p. 220, line 32—*Cosmetic Materials*, p. 295; p. 220, line 36—*Cosmetic Materials*, p. 296; p. 220, line 37—*Merck*, p. 963; p. 221, line 1—*Cosmetic Materials*, p. 116; p. 221, line 9—*Merck*, p. 964; p. 221, line 18—*Merck*, p. 965; p. 221, line 36—*Cosmetic Materials*, p. 297; p. 221, line 39—*Merck*, p. 965; p. 221, line 40—*Cosmetic Materials*, p. 298; p. 222, line 5—*Merck*, p. 965; p. 222, line 25—*Cosmetic Materials*, p. 299; p. 223, line 4—*Merck*, p. 968; p. 223, line 36—*Toxic Substances*, p. 520; p. 224, line 8—*Merck*, p. 971; p. 225, line 5—Theresa Mondeika, AMA Department of Food, *Journal of the American Medical Association*, September 20, 1971, vol. 217, no. 12; p. 225, line 20—*Cosmetic Materials*, p. 241; p. 225, line 27—*Cosmetic Materials*, p. 241; p. 225, line 37—*Cosmetic Materials*, p. 303; p. 226, line 23—*Merck*, p. 978; p. 226, line 27—*Merck*, p. 979; p. 227, line 3—*Cosmetic Materials*, p. 304; p. 227, line 35—*Cosmetic Materials*, p. 305; p. 228, line 34—*Cosmetic Materials*, p. 306; p. 229, line 10—*Cosmetic Materials*, p. 306; p. 229, line 15—*Cosmetic Materials*, p. 306; p. 229, line 24—*Merck*, p. 990; p. 229, line 35—*Toxic Substances*, p. 490; p. 230, line 3—*Cosmetic Materials*, p. 307; p. 230, line 13—*Merck*, p. 997; p. 230, line 19—March; p. 230, line 22—March; p. 230, line 29—*Toxic Substances*, p. 493; p. 230, line 37—*Cosmetic Materials*, p. 191; p. 231, line 2—*Merck*, p. 1004; p. 231, line 3—*Cosmetic Materials*, p. 309; p. 231, line 34—FDA; p. 232, line 27—*Medical World News*, p. 76A, October 8, 1971; Key Nam, M.D., and Douglas Gracey, "Pulmonary Talcosis from Cosmetic Talcum Powder," *Journal of the American Medical Association*, July 31, 1971, vol. 221, no. 5, pp. 492-93; p. 232, line 35—*Cosmetic Materials*, p. 311; p. 233, line 3—*Cosmetic Materials*, p. 227; p. 233, line 11—*Cosmetic Materials*, p. 311; p. 233, line 21—*Cosmetic Materials*, p. 243; p. 233, line 28—*Merck*, p. 1014; p. 234, line 24—*Cosmetic Materials*, p. 244; p. 234, line 29—*Cosmetic Materials*, p. 313; p. 234, line 30—William Schorr, *Cosmetic Allergy, Cosmetics and Perfumery*, vol. 89, no. 7, July 1974; p. 234, line 39—March; p. 235, line 4—*Merck*, p. 1023; p. 235, line 9—*Merck*, p. 1027; p. 235, line 17—*Merck*, p. 500; p. 235, line 26—*Merck*, p. 1047; p. 235, line 31—*Merck*, p. 958; p. 236, line 4—*Merck*, p. 1034; p. 236, line 5—*Toxic Substances*, p. 505; p. 236, line 28—*Merck*, p. 1042; p. 236, line 29—*Cosmetic Materials*, p. 315; p. 237, line 4—*Merck*, p. 1047, Gleason, p. 143; p. 237, line 13—*Cosmetic Materials*, p. 244; p. 237, line 20—*Cosmetic Materials*, p. 315; p. 237, line 33—*Merck*, p. 1055; p. 238, line 13—Gleason, p. 87, Section VI; p. 238, line 15—*Merck*, p. 1058; p. 238, line 38—*Toxic Substances*, p. 519; p. 239, line 14—*Merck*, p. 1068, Gleason, p. 147; p. 239, line 27—Gleason, p. 147; p. 239, line 30—*Cosmetic Materials*, p. 320; p. 239, line 31—*Toxic Substances*, p. 524; p. 240, line 5—*Merck*, p. 1072; p. 240, line 15—*Merck*, p. 1072; p. 240, line 19—*Merck*, p. 1072; p. 241, line 18—Gleason, p. 148; p. 241, line 19—*Hackh's Chemical Dictionary*, 4th ed., Julius Grant, McGraw-Hill Book Co., 1969, p. 693; p. 241, line 20—*Toxic Substances,* p. 529; p. 241, line 29—Gleason, p. 148; p. 241, line 30—*Merck,* p. 968; p. 241, line 34—*Merck,* p. 1082; p. 242, line 2—*Cosmetic Materials,* p. 297; p. 242, line 13—*Cosmetic Materials,* p. 224; p. 242, line 22—*Merck,* p. 1089, Gleason, p. 223; p. 242, line 24—Kahn; p. 242, line 39—*Cosmetic Materials,* p. 325; p. 243, line 28—Gleason, p. 150; p. 244, line 32—Press Release, December 16, 1971, Alberto Culver, 2525 West Armitage Avenue, Melrose Park, Illinois 60160; p. 245, line 11—*Hazards of Medication,* p. 353; p. 245, line 17—*Cosmetic Materials,* p. 328; p. 246, line 13—*Toxic Substances,* p. 136; p. 246, line 19—*Cosmetic Materials,* p. 245; p. 247, line 41—*Cosmetic Materials,* p. 304; p. 248, line 28—*Merck,* p. 691, Gleason, p. 152; p. 249, line 40—*Cosmetic Materials,* p. 333; p. 250, line 4—*Physicians' Desk Reference,* p. 562; p. 250, line 13—*Hazards of Medication,* p. 353; p. 250, line 17—Kahn; p. 250, line 18—*Merck,* p. 1128; p. 250, line 39—*Cosmetic Materials,* p. 334; p. 251, line 18—*Cosmetic Materials,* p. 336; p. 251, line 30—*Cosmetic Materials,* p. 337; p. 252, line 1—*Merck,* p. 1130, Gleason, p. 154; p. 252, line 7—*Merck,* p. 1130; p. 252, line 9—*Toxic Substances,* p. 547; p. 252, line 20—*Merck,* p. 1132; p. 252, line 29—*Merck,* p. 1132.